Telecourse Student Guide

to accompany

Child Development
Stepping Stones

Richard O. Straub

Coast
LEARNING SYSTEMS

D1299426

Coast Community College District

William M. Vega, Chancellor, Coast Community College District
Ding-Jo H. Currie, President, Coastline Community College
Dan C. Jones, Administrative Dean, Instructional Systems Development
Laurie R. Melby, Director of Production
Lynn M. Dahnke, Marketing Director
Judy Garvey, Publications Supervisor
Robert D. Nash, Instructional Designer
Wendy Sacket, Senior Publications Assistant
Thien Vu, Publications Assistant

The Telecourse Child Development: Stepping Stones is produced by the Coast Community College District in cooperation with Worth Publishers and KOCE-TV, Channel 50.

ISBN: 0-7167-5553-X (EAN: 9780716755531)

Third printing

Worth Publishers
41 Madison Avenue
New York, NY 10010

www.worthpublishers.com

Contents

Introduction

To the Student

Welcome to *Child Development: Stepping Stones*. This course has been designed to cover the concepts, vocabulary, and subjects that are typical of an on-campus, college-level child development course. This course presents the development process in three distinct categories or domains—biosocial, cognitive, and psychosocial.

While most children achieve developmental milestones, each child will take his or her own unique path. The twenty-six half-hour video lessons feature an assortment of real-life examples, historical footage, and an array of subject-matter experts. Throughout this course we will emphasize how the development principles you will be learning can be used to improve the quality of your everyday life, as well as those around you.

As with any college-level course, this course has a textbook, a student guide, assignments, and tests. In lieu of classroom lectures, however, you will be watching half-hour video programs. The designers, academic advisors, and producers of this telecourse have produced an engaging and comprehensive course that will entertain you as you learn about the fascinating field of child development.

Telecourse Components

Student Guide

The telecourse student guide is an integral part of this course. Think of this guide as your "road map." It gives you a starting point for each lesson, as well as directions and exercises that will help you successfully navigate your way through the telecourse. Reading this guide will provide you with the information that you normally would receive in the classroom if you were taking this course on campus. Each lesson in this telecourse student guide includes the following components:

- **Preview:** An overview of the lesson that informs you of the importance of the subject you are about to study and gives you a brief snapshot of the upcoming video lesson.

- **Prior Telecourse Knowledge:** A list of concepts, theories, terms, and other knowledge presented in previous lessons that you should recall in order to prepare for the current lesson.

- **Learning Objectives:** Your instructional goals for the lesson, which will guide your reading, viewing, thinking, and studying. Upon completing each lesson, you should be able to satisfy each of the learning objectives. (Hint: Instructors often develop test questions directly from learning objectives.)

- **Reading Assignment:** Description of page numbers and sections in the textbook that should be read for each lesson.

- **Summary:** A summary of the lesson—to be read after reading the textbook and viewing the video lesson—that clarifies key points.

- **Viewing Assignment:** Instructions on which video lesson to view, as well as mention of each segment within the video lesson.

- **Key Terms:** Much of education is learning the meaning of new terms, and concepts. It is important to be able to define each of the key terms and concepts for each lesson.

- **Practice Questions:** These self-test questions (multiple-choice and true/false questions) help you review and master basic facts and definitions presented in each lesson.

- **Applying Your Knowledge:** These self-test questions (multiple-choice) help you evaluate your understanding of the lesson's broader and conceptual material and its application to real-world situations.

- **Answer Key:** Answers to the key terms and self-test items are conveniently located at the end of each lesson so that you can get immediate feedback. The answers reference pages in the textbook and segments in the video lesson where the information is presented, as well as the learning objective the question covers. After completing the Key Terms section and other self-tests, be sure to check the Answer Key to make sure you correctly understand the material.

- **Lesson Review:** This chart has been designed to act as a study tool to help you achieve each learning objective. It lists pages in the textbook, segments in the video lesson, and sections in the telecourse student guide where you can find more information on each objective. Use this tool to master concepts and skills that you feel are your weak points.

Textbook

The recommended textbook for this course is *The Developing Person Through Childhood and Adolescence*, sixth edition, by Kathleen Stassen Berger (Worth Publishers, 2003). In much the same way as the telecourse lessons, the textbook is complete with real-life stories—some funny, some dramatic, others quite personal. This textbook allows you to learn about child development by observing and hearing about the lives of real, ordinary people. You will repeatedly discover how the field of child development can enrich the lives of anyone who takes the time to study human change and behavior.

Video Programs

Each of the video lessons features a real-life situation—a story line that will help you recognize and appreciate how development affects the lives of ordinary people. The award-winning producers and directors at Coast Learning Systems have brought together top professionals from various fields of psychology to help explain different aspects of child development.

How to Take a Telecourse

If this is your first experience with a college telecourse, welcome. Telecourses are designed for busy people whose schedules do not permit them to take a traditional on-campus college course.

This guide is designed to help you study effectively and learn the material presented in both the textbook and the video lessons. To complete a telecourse successfully, you will need schedule sufficient time to watch each lesson, read the textbook, and study the materials outlined in this guide. In conjunction with your instructor, this guide will provide you with:

- directions on how to take this course.

- study recommendations.

- a preview for each lesson.

- a set of learning objectives for each lesson.

- a list of key terms and concepts for each lesson.

- several different types of study activities and self-tests for each lesson.

The telecourse student guide is a complement to the textbook and the video lessons. It is not a substitute. You will not be able to complete this course successfully unless you purchase and read the textbook, watch the video program—and study. By following the instructions in this guide, you should be able to easily master the learning objectives for each lesson.

To complete this course successfully, you will need to:

- contact your instructor to find about any course requirements, time lines, meetings, and scheduled exams.

- purchase a copy of the course textbook.

- read and study the textbook.

- view each video lesson in its entirety.

- understand the key terms and concepts presented in this guide.

- be able to satisfy the learning objectives for each lesson.

- complete the self-tests.

- complete any additional assignments your instructor may require.

Even though you do not have a scheduled class to attend each week, please keep in mind that this is a college-level course. You will not be able to "look at some of the videos" or "just scan the text" and pass this course. It is important that you schedule sufficient time to watch, read, study, and reflect. While taking a telecourse provides you the convenience of not having to meet at a prearranged time, do not make the mistake of not scheduling enough time to complete the work and study. All learning demands a good measure of self-discipline. Unless you put in the effort, take the time to study, and think about what you are learning, you will not learn.

Try your best to keep up with your work. It is very difficult to catch up if you allow yourself to get a few weeks behind schedule. We strongly recommend that you set aside specific times each week for viewing, reading, and studying. You will do better and will be more likely to succeed if you make a study schedule and stick to that schedule. When you watch the video lessons, try to do so without any interruptions. Each video lesson is approximately thirty minutes long. If you are interrupted during your viewing time, you may miss an important point. If possible, take some time immediately after watching the video program to reflect on what you have just viewed. This is an excellent time to discuss the video lesson with a friend or family member. Remember that your active involvement promotes your success.

It is our goal to give you a good, basic understanding of the field of child development. This course will provide you with all the basic information required for a college-level introductory class in child development.

Minds are like parachutes; they only function when open.
—Thomas R. Dewar

And, don't forget to always check with your instructor. He or she will explain the specific course requirements for your assigned class. We sincerely hope you enjoy your introduction to the discipline of child development.

Study Recommendations

Everyone has his or her own unique learning style. Some people learn best by reading alone the first thing each morning, others by discussing ideas with a group of friends, still others by listening to experts and taking notes. While there is no "best" way to learn, psychologists and educators have identified several things you can do that will help you study and learn more effectively.

One of the advantages of distance learning is that you have many choices in how you learn and study. You can tailor this course to fit your "best" way to learn. Below are several study tips. These are proven methods that will help you learn and retain what you are studying. Please take the time to read through this list. You will discover that by using one or more of these techniques you can significantly improve your ability to learn and remember new information.

Open your mind: One of the major obstacles to learning new information is that new information often differs from what we already "know." For example, if you believe that obesity is caused by depression, it will be difficult for you to learn about new information that reveals that there is no cause-and-effect relationship between obesity and depression. To learn, you need to have an open mind. We are not suggesting you simply believe everything you are told. We want you to think critically about what you are told. However, be cautious and guard against letting old beliefs or opinions stop you from learning anything new.

Reduce interference: One of the major reasons for forgetting information is that new information interferes with other information. When you are studying more than one subject at a time, you are increasing the likelihood of interference occurring. If possible, try to study one thing at a time. If you must take multiple subjects, try to take courses with very different subjects, such as art and psychology or math and history. For example, it would not be a good idea to take Child Development and Introduction to Psychology during the same semester. Of course, visiting with friends, watching television, listening to the radio, or any distraction while you are studying will also interfere with your ability to learn new information. When you engage in these types of activities during or just after studying, you risk letting the information you have just learned interfere with other information. Give yourself time to absorb new information.

Don't cram: You probably already know that staying up all night cramming for an exam the following morning is not a good way to study. The opposite of cramming is, in fact, one of the best ways to study. Spacing out your studying into smaller and more frequent study periods will improve retention. Instead of studying for six hours in one evening, you will learn more and retain more if you study one hour per night for six nights.

Reduce stress: In addition to being bad for your health, stress is bad for learning. Stress and anxiety interfere with learning. You will learn more and enjoy it more if you are relaxed when you study. One of the most effective ways of relaxing that does not interfere with learning is exercise. A good brisk walk or run before you settle in to study is a good prescription for success. Ideally, you would study some, take a break, then get some exercise while you think about what you have just learned. And later, when you are relaxed, return and study some more.

Be a Smart Student: Most top students have one thing in common. They all have excellent study habits. Students who excel have learned, or were fortunate enough to have someone teach them, how to study effectively. There is no magic formula for successful studying. However, there are a few universal guidelines.

Do make a commitment to yourself to learn.

Don't let other people interrupt you when you are studying.

Do make a study schedule and stick to it.

Don't study when you are doing something else, like watching television.

Do create a specific place to study.

Don't study if you are tired, upset, or overly stressed.

Do exercise and relax before you study.

Don't study for extended periods of time without taking a break.

Do give yourself ample time to study.

Don't complain that you have to go study.

Do take a positive approach to learning.

Make the most of your assignments: You will master this material more effectively if you make a commitment to completing all your assignments. The lessons will make more sense to you, and you will learn more, if you follow these instructions:

- Set aside a specific time to view, read, and study each lesson.

- Before you view each video lesson, read the Preview and Learning Objectives outlined in this guide.

- Read the assigned textbook pages for the lesson you are studying.

- View the video lesson.

- Review the Key Terms. Check your understanding of all unfamiliar terms in the glossary notes in the textbook.

- Complete the Practice Questions for each lesson.

Think about what you have learned: You are much more likely to remember new information if you use it. Remember that learning is not a passive activity. Learning is active. As soon as you learn something, try to repeat it to someone or discuss it with a friend. If you will think about what you just learned, you will be much more likely to retain that information. The reason we remember certain information has to do mostly with (1) how important that information is to us, and (2) whether or not we actively use the information. For example, if you suffer from headaches and the textbook or video is discussing various headache remedies, this information will be valuable to you. Because of your personal interest in this subject, you will have little difficulty remembering this information. What do you do, however, when you need to learn some information that is not personally valuable or interesting to you? The best way to remember this type of information is to reinforce it—and the best reinforcer is actively using the information.

Get feedback on what you are studying: Study alone, learn with others. You need feedback to help reinforce learning. Also, feedback helps make sure you correctly understand the information. The study activities and self-tests in this guide are specifically designed to give you feedback and reinforce what you are learning. The more time and practice you devote to learning, the better you will be at remembering that information. When you take a self-test, make sure you immediately check your answers with the answer key. Don't wait and check your answers later. If you miss a question, review that section of the textbook to reinforce the correct understanding of the material.

A good gauge of how well you understand some information is your ability to explain that information to another person. If you are unable to explain some term or concept to a friend, you probably will need to review and study that term or concept further.

Contact your instructor: If you are having an especially difficult time with learning some information, contact your instructor. Your instructor is there to help you. Often a personal explanation will do wonders in helping you clear up a misunderstanding. Your instructor wants to hear from you and wants you to succeed. Don't hesitate to call, write, e-mail, or visit your instructor.

Some students do better with study groups; others do better studying alone. If study groups are helpful to you, let your instructor know of your preference. However, be aware that study groups are not a substitute for studying alone. Study groups often turn into friendly chats and not much actually gets learned. So, remember that study groups are not a substitute for individual effort.

Learn it well: Retention is the key to long-term knowledge. One of the best methods to increase your retention is to overlearn material. It is a common mistake to think that just because you can answer a question or give a brief definition of a term or concept, you really know and will remember that term or concept. Think back about how many things you have already "learned." How much do you really remember? Much of what we learn is quickly forgotten. If you want to really learn some information, learn it in a way that you will not forget it—overlearn it.

Overlearning is simple. After you have learned a fact or new word, spend an additional ten or fifteen minutes actively reviewing that fact or word. You will be amazed how much this will increase your long-term retention.

Enjoy learning: You do not need to suffer to learn. In fact, the opposite is true. You will learn more if you enjoy learning. If you have the attitude that "I hate to study" or "schoolwork is boring," you are doing yourself a real disservice.

You will to progress better and learn more if you adopt a positive attitude about learning and studying. Since you are choosing to learn, you will be well served by also choosing to enjoy the adventure.

We are sure you will enjoy *Child Development: Stepping Stones*

Acknowledgments

Several of the individuals responsible for the creation of this telecourse are listed on the copyright page of this book. In addition, appreciation is expressed for these contributions:

Members of the Telecourse Advisory Committee

The following gifted scholars, professionals, and teachers helped focus the approach and content of the video lessons, faculty manual, and telecourse student guide to ensure accuracy, academic validity, accessibility, significance, and instructional integrity.

Pauline Abbott, Ed.D., California State University, Fullerton
Mary Belcher, M.A., Orange Coast College
Joyce Bishop, Ph.D., Golden West College
Fredda Blanchard-Fields, Ph.D., Georgia Institute of Technology
Michael Catchpole, Ph.D., R. Psych., North Island College, British Columbia, Canada
Chuansheng Chen, Ph.D., University of California, Irvine
Donald Cusumano, Ph.D., St. Louis Community College
Linda Flickinger, M.A., St. Clair County Community College
Andrea R. Fox, M.D., M.P.H., University of Pittsburgh and VA Pittsburgh Healthcare System
Ellen Greenberger, Ph D., University of California, Irvine
Jutta Heckhausen, Ph.D., University of California, Irvine
Sally Hill, M.A., Bakersfield College
Sandra J. McDonald, M.S., Sierra College
Mary K. Rothbart, Ph.D., University of Oregon
Susan Siaw, Ph.D., California State Polytechnic University, Pomona
Barbara W. K. Yee, Ph.D., University of South Florida
Judy Yip, Ph.D., University of Southern California
Elizabeth Zelinski, Ph.D., University of Southern California

Lead Academic Advisors

Amy Himsel, M.A., University of California, Irvine
Doug Hughey, M.A., Mt. San Antonio College
Jeanne Ivy, M.S., L.P.A., Tyler Community College
Phyllis Lembke, M.A., Coastline Community College
Robert D. Nash, M.S., Ed., Coast Learning Systems

Telecourse Production Team

Vanessa Chambers, Jason Daley, Sharon Dymmel, Liz Ervin, Jim Jackson, Becky Koppenhaver, Alejandro Lopez, Dorothy McCollom, Laurie R. Melby, Salma Montez, Evelyn Moore, Harry Ratner, Greg Rogers, Mike Rust, Wendy Moulton-Tate, Charlie Powell, and the many other talented people who helped make the programs.

The Developing Person

Lesson 1

Introduction:
Theories of Development

Preview

The first lesson of this telecourse introduces the **scientific study of human development**, beginning with a description of the domains into which development is often divided, a description of the scope of the field, and an overview of the major **developmental theories** that have guided research over the past century. A philosopher once said that "nothing is more practical than a good theory," and such has proven to be the case in developmental psychology. Theories help psychologists organize large amounts of information, and focus their research on specific, testable ideas about development.

Several major themes are introduced in this lesson that will be woven throughout the telecourse, including the idea that development is influenced as much by external factors as by internal factors. This theme, framed initially by philosophers many years ago, continues to drive the field today as researchers weigh the relative contributions of biological factors (such as heredity) and environmental factors (such as learning) in development.

The impact of external factors on development is revealed in the many contexts in which development occurs, especially the context of social relationships. And therein lies a second theme: Each of us as individuals is affected by other individuals (such as family members and friends); groups of individuals (such as the neighbors and fellow community members); and larger systems in the environment (such as ethnicity and culture.) In turn, we affect other people and our environment by our own decisions and actions.

A third theme of the lesson and telecourse is that development is a lifelong process. Although some early theorists believed that our personalities and fates are fully shaped by the end of childhood, developmental psychologists today recognize that people continue to grow and change until the day they die.

As you complete this lesson (and all the lessons in this telecourse), consider your own development. What factors have combined to create the person you are today? Study your immediate family members and note any genetic similarities. Think about your physical growth as a child and recall anything that might have affected that development. Recall your intellectual growth and school experiences. Consider your upbringing at home, your circle of friends, and romantic relationships. How have they influenced you? As you learn more in this lesson about the theories which developmentalists use, consider how these theories might help explain the changes you've experienced over time.

Learning Objectives

Use this information to guide your reading, viewing, thinking, and studying. After successfully completing this lesson, you should be able to:

1. Define the study of human development and discuss some of its major themes.
2. Describe the three major domains of human development and discuss how they interrelate.
3. Describe the many contexts and systems that can affect a person's development, and discuss how they are interrelated.
4. Identify the characteristics of development described by the life-span perspective.
5. Define developmental theory, and describe how theories help explain human behavior and guide researchers who study development.
6. Discuss the major focus of psychoanalytic theory, contrasting the psychosexual development proposed by Freud with the psychosocial development described by Erikson.
7. Discuss the major focus of behaviorism (learning theory), and explain the basic principles of classical and operant conditioning as well as social learning theory.
8. Discuss the major focus of cognitive theory, and summarize Piaget's stages of cognitive development.
9. Discuss the basic ideas of Vygotsky and the sociocultural theory of development.
10. Discuss the basic ideas of epigenetic systems theory.
11. Summarize the contributions and criticisms of the major developmental theories, and compare the position of the theories regarding three controversies of development.

📖 **Read Chapter 1, "Introduction," pages 1–19; and Chapter 2, "Theories of Development," pages 35–41 and 43–63.**

 View the video for Lesson 1, "The Developing Person."

Segment 1: *Contexts and Systems*

Segment 2: *Theories of Development*

Segment 3: *The Life-Span Perspective*

Summary

The **scientific study of human development** is the science that seeks to understand how and why people change with increasing age, and how and why they remain the same.

According to Urie Bronfenbrenner's **ecological model**, human development is supported by systems at four nested levels: the *microsystem* (immediate social setting), the *mesosystem* (connections among various microsystems), the *exosystem* (the community structures and local educational, medical, employment, and communications systems), and the *macrosystem* (cultural values, political philosophies, economic patterns, and social conditions).

The **life-span perspective** underscores the fact that development is lifelong, *multidirectional*, *multicontextual*, *multicultural*, *multidisciplinary*, and *plastic*. Human development is also *multidimensional* in that it includes many dimensions of many domains. The three major domains of development include the **biosocial domain** (brain and body as well as changes in them and the social influences that guide them), the **cognitive domain** (thought processes, perceptual abilities, and language mastery, as well as the educational institutions that encourage them), and the **psychosocial domain** (emotions, personality, and interpersonal relationships with family, friends, and the wider community).

Developmental theories fall into different categories, but they all provide scientists with formal principles with which to study and explain human development. Theories guide researchers in their work and provide us all with a means of explaining and even predicting human behavior.

Psychoanalytic theory interprets human development in terms of intrinsic drives and motives, many of which are irrational and unconscious. According to Sigmund Freud, development progresses through psychosexual stages; at each stage, sexual interest and pleasure is focused on a particular part of the body.

In his psychosocial theory of human development, Erik Erikson proposed eight developmental stages throughout the life span, each of which is characterized by a particular challenge, or developmental crisis. Erikson emphasized each person's relationship to the social environment and the importance of family and cultural influences in determining how well prepared individuals are to meet these crises.

Proponents of **behaviorism** (learning theory) formulated laws of behavior that operate at every age. As demonstrated by Ivan Pavlov, **classical conditioning** involves learning by association: the subject comes to associate a neutral **stimulus** with a meaningful one. In **operant conditioning**, proposed by B. F. Skinner, the individual learns that a particular behavior produces a particular consequence. **Social learning theory** emphasizes the ways in which people learn new behaviors by observing and imitating, or **modeling**, the behavior of other people they consider admirable, powerful, or similar.

Cognitive theory focuses on the structure and development of the individual's thought processes and their effect on his or her understanding of the world. Jean Piaget viewed cognitive development as a process that follows a universal sequence of age-related periods. According to Piaget, each person strives for **cognitive equilibrium**—that is, a state of mental balance achieved through the development of mental concepts that explain his or her experiences.

Sociocultural theory seeks to explain individual knowledge, development, and competencies in terms of the guidance, support, and structure provided by the broader cultural context. Lev Vygotsky believed that the development of cognitive competencies results from social interaction between children and more mature members of the society in what has been called an "**apprenticeship in thinking**." The basis of this apprenticeship is **guided participation**, in which a skilled tutor engages the learner in joint activities.

Epigenetic systems theory emphasizes the interaction between genes and the environment. "Epi-" refers to the various environmental factors that affect the expression of each person's genetic instructions. These include facilitating factors, such as nourishing food and freedom to play, as well as potentially disruptive factors such as injury, temperature, or crowding. "Genetic" refers both to the genes that make each person unique and to the genes humans share with all other humans. The "systems" aspect of the theory points out that changes in one part of the individual's system may cause corresponding adjustments and changes in every other part.

These five theories complement one another, as each emphasizes a somewhat different aspect of development and, in itself, is too restricted to account for the diversity of human behavior. **Psychoanalytic theory** calls attention to the importance of early childhood experiences and "hidden dramas" that influence daily life. **Learning theory** (**behaviorism**) highlights the effect of the immediate environment on behavior. **Cognitive theory** promotes a greater understanding of how intellectual processes and thinking affect our behavior. **Sociocultural theory** reminds us that development is embedded in a rich and multifaceted cultural context. **Epigenetic systems theory** emphasizes the inherited forces that affect each person—and all humankind—within particular contexts.

Developmentalists agree that, at every point, the interaction between nature and nurture is the crucial influence on any particular aspect of development. Today, most developmentalists have an **eclectic perspective**. Instead of limiting themselves to only one school of thought, they apply insights drawn from various theoretical views.

📖 **Review all reading assignments for this lesson.**

💻 **As assigned by your instructor, complete the optional online component for this lesson.**

Key Terms

Using your own words, write a brief definition or explanation of each of the following terms on a separate piece of paper.

1. scientific study of human development
2. linear change
3. dynamic systems
4. butterfly effect
5. life-span perspective
6. biosocial domain
7. cognitive domain
8. psychosocial domain
9. cohort
10. social construction
11. culture
12. socioeconomic status (SES)
13. poverty line
14. ethnic group
15. race
16. developmental theory
17. psychoanalytic theory
18. learning theory (behaviorism)
19. classical conditioning
20. operant conditioning
21. reinforcement
22. social learning theory
23. modeling
24. self-efficacy
25. cognitive theory
26. cognitive equilibrium
27. sociocultural theory
28. apprenticeship in thinking
29. guided participation
30. zone of proximal development
31. epigenetic systems theory
32. selective adaptation
33. ethology
34. nature
35. nurture
36. eclectic perspective
37. ecological model
38. stimulus
39. response

Practice Questions I

Multiple-Choice Questions

1. The scientific study of human development is defined as the study of
   a. how and why people change or remain the same over time.
   b. psychosocial influences on aging.
   c. individual differences in learning over the life span.
   d. all of the above.

2. The cognitive domain of development includes
   a. perception.
   b. thinking.
   c. language.
   d. all of the above.

3. Changes in height, weight, and bone thickness are part of the
   _____ domain.
   a. cognitive
   b. biosocial
   c. psychosocial
   d. physical

4. Psychosocial development focuses primarily on personality, emotions, and
   a. intellectual development.
   b. sexual maturation.
   c. relationships with others.
   d. perception.

5. The ecological model of developmental psychology focuses on the
   a. biochemistry of the body systems.
   b. cognitive domain only.
   c. internal thinking processes.
   d. overall environment of development.

6. Researchers who take a life-span perspective on development focus on
   a. the sources of continuity from the beginning of life to the end.
   b. the sources of discontinuity throughout life.
   c. the "nonlinear" character of human development.
   d. all of the above.

7. That fluctuations in body weight are affected by genes, appetite, caregiving, culture, and food supply indicates that body weight
   a. is characterized by linear change.
   b. is a dynamic system.
   c. often has a butterfly effect.
   d. is characterized by all of the above.

8. A developmentalist who is interested in studying the influences of a person's immediate environment on his or her behavior is focusing on which system?

    a. mesosystem

    b. macrosystem

    c. microsystem

    d. exosystem

9. Socioeconomic status (SES) is determined by a combination of variables, including

    a. age, education, and income.

    b. income, ethnicity, and occupation.

    c. income, education, and occupation.

    d. age, ethnicity, and occupation.

10. The purpose of a developmental theory is to

    a. provide a broad and coherent view of the complex influences on human development.

    b. offer guidance for practical issues encountered by parents, teachers, and therapists.

    c. generate testable hypotheses about development.

    d. do all of the above.

11. Which developmental theory emphasizes the influence of unconscious drives and motives on behavior?

    a. psychoanalytic

    b. learning

    c. cognitive

    d. sociocultural

12. Which of the following is the correct order of the psychosexual stages proposed by Freud?

    a. oral stage; anal stage; phallic stage; latency; genital stage

    b. anal stage; oral stage; phallic stage; latency; genital stage

    c. oral stage; anal stage; genital stage; latency; phallic stage

    d. anal stage; oral stage; genital stage; latency; phallic stage

13. Erikson's psychosocial theory of human development describes

    a. eight crises all people are thought to face.

    b. four psychosocial stages and a latency period.

    c. the same number of stages as Freud's, but with different names.

    d. a stage theory that is not psychoanalytic.

14. An American psychologist who explained complex human behaviors in terms of operant conditioning was

    a. Lev Vygotsky.

    b. Ivan Pavlov.

    c. B. F. Skinner.

    d. Jean Piaget.

15. Pavlov's dogs learned to salivate at the sound of a bell because they associated the bell with food. Pavlov's experiment with dogs was an early demonstration of
    a. classical conditioning.
    b. operant conditioning.
    c. positive reinforcement.
    d. social learning.

16. The nature-nurture controversy considers the degree to which traits, characteristics, and behaviors are the result of
    a. early or lifelong learning.
    b. genes or heredity.
    c. heredity or experience.
    d. different historical concepts of childhood.

17. Modeling, an integral part of social learning theory, is so called because it
    a. follows the scientific model of learning.
    b. molds character.
    c. follows the immediate reinforcement model developed by Albert Bandura.
    d. involves people's patterning their behavior after that of others.

18. Which developmental theory suggests that each person is born with genetic possibilities that must be nurtured in order to grow?
    a. sociocultural
    b. cognitive
    c. learning
    d. epigenetic systems

19. Vygotsky's theory has been criticized for neglecting
    a. the role of genes in guiding development.
    b. developmental processes that are not primarily biological.
    c. the importance of language in development.
    d. social factors in development.

20. Which is the correct sequence of stages in Piaget's theory of cognitive development?
    a. sensorimotor, preoperational, concrete operational, formal operational
    b. sensorimotor, preoperational, formal operational, concrete operational
    c. preoperational, sensorimotor, concrete operational, formal operational
    d. preoperational, sensorimotor, formal operational, concrete operational

21. When an individual's existing understanding no longer fits his or her present experiences, the result is called
    a. a psychosocial crisis.
    b. equilibrium.
    c. disequilibrium.
    d. negative reinforcement.

22. In explaining the origins of homosexuality, the major theories of development have traditionally emphasized

    a. nature over nurture.

    b. nurture over nature.

    c. a warped mother-son or father-daughter relationship.

    d. the individual's voluntary choice.

23. The zone of proximal development refers to

    a. the control process by which information is transferred from the sensory register to working memory.

    b. the influence of a pleasurable stimulus on behavior.

    c. the range of skills a child can exercise with assistance but cannot perform independently

    d. the mutual interaction of a person's internal characteristics, the environment, and the person's behavior.

24. Nature is to nurture as

    a. tabula rasa is to blank slate.

    b. Jean Rousseau is to John Locke.

    c. B. F. Skinner is to Ivan Pavlov.

    d. Urie Bronfenbrenner is to Kurt Lewin.

Matching Items

Match each definition or description with its corresponding term.

Terms

25. _____ psychoanalytic theory

26. _____ nature

27. _____ learning theory

28. _____ social learning theory

29. _____ cognitive theory

30. _____ nurture

31. _____ sociocultural theory

32. _____ conditioning

33. _____ modeling

34. _____ epigenetic systems theory

Descriptions or Definitions

a. emphasizes the impact of the immediate environment on behavior

b. emphasizes that people learn by observing others

c. environmental influences that affect development

d. a process of learning, as described by Pavlov or Skinner

e. emphasizes the "hidden dramas" that influence behavior

f. emphasizes the cultural context in development

g. emphasizes how our thoughts shape our actions

h. the process whereby a person learns by imitating someone else's behavior

i. emphasizes the interaction of genes and environmental forces

j. traits that are inherited

Practice Questions II

Multiple-Choice Questions

1. An individual's context of development refers to his or her
   a. microsystem and mesosystem.
   b. exosystem.
   c. macrosystem.
   d. microsystem, mesosystem, exosystem, and macrosystem.

2. The three domains of developmental psychology are
   a. physical, cognitive, and psychosocial.
   b. physical, biosocial, and cognitive.
   c. biosocial, cognitive, and psychosocial.
   d. biosocial, cognitive, and emotional.

3. Which of the following is true of the three domains of development?
   a. They are important at every age.
   b. They interact in influencing development.
   c. They are more influential in some cultures than in others.
   d. Answers a and b are true.

4. According to the ecological model, the macrosystem would include
   a. the peer group.
   b. the community.
   c. cultural values.
   d. the family.

5. When developmentalists speak of the "power of continuity," they are referring to the insight that
   a. a change in one developmental system often affects many other things.
   b. a small change can become huge.
   c. a large change may have no perceptible effect.
   d. all of the above occur.

6. A cohort is defined as a group of people
   a. of similar national origin.
   b. who share a common language.
   c. born within a few years of each other.
   d. who share the same religion.

7. Which developmental theorist has been criticized for suggesting that every child, in every culture, in every nation, passes through certain fixed stages?
   a. Sigmund Freud
   b. Erik Erikson
   c. Jean Piaget
   d. all of the above

8. Of the following terms, the one that does **NOT** describe a stage of Freud's theory of childhood sexuality is
   a. phallic.
   b. oral.
   c. anal.
   d. sensorimotor.

9. We are more likely to imitate the behavior of others if we particularly admire and identify with them. This belief finds expression in
   a. stage theory.
   b. sociocultural theory.
   c. social learning theory.
   d. Pavlov's experiments.

10. According to Erikson, an adult who has difficulty establishing a secure, mutual relationship with a life partner might never have resolved the crisis of
    a. initiative versus guilt
    b. autonomy versus shame
    c. intimacy versus isolation
    d. trust versus mistrust

11. Who would be most likely to agree with the statement, "Anything can be learned"?
    a. Jean Piaget
    b. Lev Vygotsky
    c. John Watson
    d. Erik Erikson

12. Classical conditioning is to _____ as operant conditioning is to _____.
    a. Skinner; Pavlov
    b. Watson; Vygotsky
    c. Pavlov: Skinner
    d. Vygotsky; Watson

13. Learning theorists have found that they can often solve a person's seemingly complex psychological problem by
    a. analyzing the patient.
    b. admitting the existence of the unconscious.
    c. altering the environment.
    d. administering well-designed punishments.

14. According to Piaget, an infant first comes to know the world through
    a. sucking and grasping.
    b. naming and counting.
    c. preoperational thought.
    d. instruction from parents.

15. According to Piaget, the stage of cognitive development that generally characterizes preschool children (2 to 6 years old) is the

    a. preoperational stage.

    b. sensorimotor stage.

    c. oral stage.

    d. psychosocial stage.

16. In Piaget's theory, cognitive equilibrium refers to

    a. a state of mental balance.

    b. a kind of imbalance that leads to cognitive growth.

    c. the ultimate stage of cognitive development.

    d. the first stage in the processing of information.

17. You teach your dog to "speak" by giving her a treat each time she does so. This is an example of

    a. classical conditioning.

    b. respondent conditioning.

    c. reinforcement.

    d. modeling.

18. A child who must modify an old idea in order to incorporate a new experience is using the process of

    a. assimilation.

    b. accommodation.

    c. cognitive equilibrium.

    d. guided participation.

19. Which of the following is a common criticism of sociocultural theory?

    a. It places too great an emphasis on unconscious motives and childhood sexuality.

    b. Its mechanistic approach fails to explain many complex human behaviors.

    c. Development is more gradual than its stages imply.

    d. It neglects developmental processes that are not primarily social.

20. A major pioneer of the sociocultural perspective was

    a. Jean Piaget.

    b. Albert Bandura.

    c. Lev Vygotsky.

    d. Ivan Pavlov.

21. Stimulus is to response as

    a. action is to reaction.

    b. reaction is to action.

    c. nature is to nurture.

    d. nurture is to nature.

22. A pioneer of social learning theory, who studied modeling in children, was
    a. Kurt Lewin.
    b. Ivan Pavlov.
    c. Albert Bandura.
    d. Urie Bronfenbrenner.

True or False Items

Write T (for true) or F (for false) on the line in front of each statement.

23. _____ Behaviorists study what people actually do, not what they might be thinking.

24. _____ Erikson's eight developmental stages are centered not on a body part but on each person's relationship to the social environment.

25. _____ Most developmentalists agree that the nature-nurture controversy has been laid to rest.

26. _____ Few developmental theorists today believe that humans have instincts or abilities that arise from our species' biological heritage.

27. _____ Of the major developmental theories, cognitive theory gives the most emphasis to the interaction of genes and experience in shaping development.

28. _____ New research suggests that homosexuality is at least partly genetic.

29. _____ According to Piaget, a state of cognitive equilibrium must be attained before cognitive growth can occur.

30. _____ In part, cognitive theory examines how an individual's understandings and expectations affect his or her behavior.

31. _____ According to Piaget, children begin to think only when they reach preschool age.

32. _____ Most contemporary researchers have adopted an eclectic perspective on development.

Applying Your Knowledge

1. Dr. Ramirez conducts research on the psychosocial domain of development. She is most likely to be interested in a child's
   a. perceptual abilities.
   b. brain wave patterns.
   c. emotions.
   d. use of language.

2. Jahmal is writing a paper on the role of the social context in development. He would do well to consult the writings of
   a. Jean Piaget.
   b. Sigmund Freud.
   c. Urie Bronfenbrenner.
   d. B. F. Skinner.

3. Dr. Wong looks at human development in terms of the individual's supporting ecosystems. Evidently, Dr. Wong subscribes to the _____ model.

   a. psychosocial
   b. ecological
   c. biosocial
   d. cognitive

4. When we say that the idea of old age as we know it is a "social construction," we are saying that

   a. the idea is built on the shared perceptions of members of society.
   b. old age has only recently been regarded as a distinct period of life.
   c. old age cannot be defined.
   d. the idea is based on a well-tested hypothesis.

5. As compared with parents in developing countries, middle-class parents in the United States emphasize cognitive and social stimulation in their child-rearing efforts because

   a. they are more likely to regard children as an economic asset.
   b. their families are larger.
   c. they do not have to be as concerned about infant mortality.
   d. of all the above reasons.

6. Many songbirds inherit a genetically programmed species song that enhances their ability to mate and establish a territory. The evolution of such a trait is an example of

   a. selective adaptation.
   b. continuity vs. discontinuity.
   c. accommodation.
   d. assimilation.

7. When a pigeon is rewarded for producing a particular response, and so learns to produce that response to obtain rewards, psychologists describe this chain of events as

   a. operant conditioning.
   b. classical conditioning.
   c. modeling.
   d. reflexive actions.

8. Research studies have shown that human handling of rat pups makes them smarter as adults. This is because handling

   a. increases the mother's grooming of her pup.
   b. indirectly decreases the release of stress hormones.
   c. leads to less brain degeneration in the face of adult stresses.
   d. does all of the above.

9. Dr. Cleaver's research focuses on the biological forces that shape each child's characteristic way of reacting to environmental experiences. Evidently, Dr. Cleaver is working from a(n) _____ perspective.

   a. psychoanalytic
   b. cognitive
   c. sociocultural
   d. epigenetic systems

10. Which of the following is the best example of guided participation?

    a. After watching her mother change her baby sister's diaper, four-year-old Brandy changes her doll's diaper.
    b. To help her son learn to pour liquids, Linda engages him in a bathtub game involving pouring water from cups of different sizes.
    c. Seeing his father shaving, three-year-old Jack pretends to shave by rubbing whipped cream on his face.
    d. After reading a recipe in a magazine, Kyle gathers ingredients from the cupboard.

11. A child who calls all furry animals "doggie" will experience cognitive _____ when she encounters a hairless breed for the first time. This may cause her to revamp her concept of "dog" in order to _____ the new experience.

    a. disequilibrium; accommodate
    b. disequilibrium; assimilate
    c. equilibrium; accommodate
    d. equilibrium; assimilate

12. A confirmed neo-Freudian, Dr. Thomas strongly endorses the views of Erik Erikson. She would be most likely to disagree with Freud regarding the importance of

    a. unconscious forces in development.
    b. irrational forces in personality formation.
    c. early childhood experiences.
    d. sexual urges in development.

13. After watching several older children climbing around a new jungle gym, five-year-old Jennie decides to try it herself. Which of the following best accounts for her behavior?

    a. classical conditioning
    b. modeling
    c. guided participation
    d. reinforcement

14. I am 8 years old, and although I understand some logical principles, I have trouble thinking about hypothetical concepts. According to Piaget, I am in the _____ stage of development.

    a. sensorimotor
    b. preoperational
    c. concrete operational
    d. formal operational

15. Two-year-old Bjorn has a simple understanding for "dad," and so each time he encounters a man with a child, he calls him "dad." When he learns that these other men are not "dad," Bjorn experiences
    a. conservation.
    b. cognition.
    c. equilibrium.
    d. disequilibrium.

16. Most adults become physiologically aroused by the sound of an infant's cries, coos, and laughter. These interactive reactions, in which caregivers and babies elicit responses in each other
    a. help ensure the survival of the next generation.
    b. do not occur in all human cultures.
    c. are the result of conditioning very early in life.
    d. are more often found in females than in males.

17. The school psychologist believes that each child's developmental needs can be understood only by taking into consideration the child's broader social and cultural background. Evidently, the school psychologist is working within the _____ perspective.
    a. psychoanalytic
    b. epigenetic systems
    c. social learning
    d. sociocultural

18. Four-year-old Rashad takes great pride in successfully undertaking new activities. Erikson would probably say that Rashad is capably meeting the psychosocial challenge of
    a. trust vs. mistrust.
    b. initiative vs. guilt.
    c. industry vs. inferiority.
    d. identity vs. role confusion.

19. Dr. Bazzi's developmental research draws upon insights from several theoretical perspectives. Evidently, Dr. Bazzi is working from a(n) _____ perspective.
    a. cognitive
    b. learning
    c. eclectic
    d. sociocultural

20. Dr. Ivey believes that development is a lifelong process of gradual and continuous growth, and does not occur in age-related stages. Based on this information, with which of the following theories would Dr. Ivey most likely agree?
    a. Piaget's cognitive theory
    b. Erikson's psychosocial theory
    c. Freud's psychoanalytic theory
    d. learning theory

Answer Key

Key Terms

1. The scientific study of human development is the science that seeks to understand how and why people change, and how and why they remain the same, as they grow older. (p. 1; video lesson, introduction; objective 1)

2. Linear change describes a process in which change occurs in a gradual and predictable sequence. (p. 2; objective 1)

3. Dynamic systems describes a process in which changes within a person or group are systematically connected to each other. That means that each aspect of a person's development can potentially affect all other aspects. (p. 2; objectives 1 & 3)

4. The butterfly effect is the insight that even small events (such as the breeze created by the flap of a butterfly's wings) may set off series of changes that culminate in a major event. (p. 2; objectives 1 & 3)

5. The life-span perspective on human development recognizes that human growth is lifelong and characterized by both continuity (as in personality) and discontinuity (as in the number of brain cells). (p. 5; video lesson, segment 3; objective 4)

6. The biosocial domain is concerned with brain and body changes and the social influences that guide them. (p. 6; objective 2)

7. The cognitive domain is concerned with thought processes, perceptual abilities, and language mastery, and the educational institutions that encourage these aspects of development. (p. 6; objective 2)

8. The psychosocial domain is concerned with emotions, personality, interpersonal relationships with family, friends, and the wider community. (p. 6; objective 2)

9. A cohort is a group of people who, because they were born within a few years of each other, experience many of the same historical and social emotions. (p. 8; objective 3)

10. A social construction is an idea about the way things are, or should be, that is built more on the shared perceptions of members of a society than on objective reality. (p. 9; objective 3)

11. Culture refers to the set of shared values, assumptions, customs, and physical objects that a group of people have developed over the years as a design for living to structure their life together. (p. 10; objective 3)

12. An individual's socioeconomic status (SES) is determined by his or her income, education, place of residence, and occupation. (p. 14; objective 3)

13. Estimated by the federal government, the "poverty line" is the minimum annual income a family needs to pay for basic necessities. (p. 14; objective 3)

14. An ethnic group is a collection of people who share certain attributes, such as national origin, religion, ancestry, and/or language and who, as a result, tend to identify with each other and have similar daily encounters with the social world. (p. 16; objective 3)

15. Race is a social construction that was originally based on biological differences between people whose ancestors came from different regions of the world. (p. 16; objective 3)

16. A developmental theory is a systematic statement of principles and generalizations that explains behavior and development and provides a framework for future research. (p. 35; video lesson, segment 2; objective 5)

17. Psychoanalytic theory, a grand theory, interprets human development in terms of intrinsic drives and motives, many of which are irrational and unconscious. (p. 36; video lesson, segment 2; objective 6)

18. Learning theory, a grand theory based on behaviorism, emphasizes the sequences and processes of conditioning that underlie most of human and animal behavior. (p. 40; video lesson, segment 2; objective 7)

19. Classical conditioning is the learning process by which a neutral stimulus becomes associated with a meaningful stimulus. (p. 40; video lesson, segment 2; objective 7)

20. Operant conditioning is the process by which a response is gradually learned via reinforcement and/or punishment. (p. 41; video lesson, segment 2; objective 7)

21. Reinforcement is the process by which the consequences of a particular behavior strengthen the behavior, making it more likely that the behavior will be repeated. (p. 41; objective 7)

22. An extension of learning theory, social learning theory emphasizes that people often learn new behaviors through observation and imitation of other people. (p. 43; video lesson, segment 2; objective 7)

23. Modeling refers to the process by which we observe other people's behavior and then pattern our own after it. (p. 43; video lesson, segment 2; objective 7)

24. Self-efficacy is a person's belief that he or she is effective. According to social learning theory, it can motivate people to change. (p. 44; objective 7)

25. Cognitive theory emphasizes that the way people think and understand the world shapes their perceptions, attitudes, and actions. (p. 44; video lesson, segment 2; objective 8)

26. In Piaget's theory, cognitive equilibrium is a state of mental balance, in which a person's thoughts about the world seem not to clash with each other or with his or her experiences. (p. 45; objective 8)

27. Sociocultural theory seeks to explain development as the result of a dynamic interaction between developing persons and their surrounding culture. (p. 48; objective 9)

28. As described in sociocultural theory, an "apprenticeship in thinking" is the process by which a novice learns knowledge and skills through interaction with more competent members of society. (p. 49; objective 9)

29. Guided participation is a learning process in which the learner is tutored, or mentored, through social interaction with a skilled teacher. (p. 49; objective 9)

30. According to Vygotsky, developmental growth occurs when mentors draw children into the zone of proximal development, which is the range of skills the child can exercise with assistance but cannot perform independently. (p. 50; objective 9)

31. The epigenetic systems theory emphasizes the genetic origins of behavior but also stresses that genes, over time, are directly and systematically affected by environmental forces. (p. 51; objective 10)

32. Selective adaptation is the evolutionary process through which useful genes that enhance survival become more frequent within individuals. (p. 52; objective 10)

33. Ethology is the study of behavior as it relates to the evolution and survival of a species. (p. 54; objective 10)

34. Nature refers to all the traits, capacities, and limitations that a person inherits at the moment of conception. (p. 60; video lesson, introduction; objectives 1 & 11)

35. Nurture refers to all the environmental influences that affect a person's development following the moment of conception. (p. 60; video lesson, introduction; objectives 1 & 11)

36. Developmentalists who work from an eclectic perspective accept elements from several theories, instead of adhering to only a single perspective. (p. 62; video lesson, segment 3; objectives 1 & 11)

37. According to Urie Bronfenbrenner's ecological model, human development is supported by systems at four nested levels: the microsystem, the mesosystem, the exosystem, and the macrosystem. (p. 3; video lesson, segment 1; objective 3)

38. In learning theory, a stimulus is an event or action that triggers a reaction, or response in a person or animal. (video lesson, segment 2; objective 7)

39. In learning theory, a response is a behavior or reaction in a person or animal that has been elicited by a stimulus. (video lesson, segment 2; objective 7)

Practice Questions I

Multiple-Choice Questions

1. a. is the correct answer. (p. 1; video lesson, introduction; objective 1)

   b. & c. are incorrect. The study of development is concerned with a broader range of phenomena, including biosocial aspects of development, than these answers specify.

2. d. is the correct answer. (p. 6; objective 2)

3. b. is the correct answer. (p. 6; objective 2)

   a. is incorrect. This domain is concerned with thought processes.

   c. is incorrect. This domain is concerned with emotions, personality, and interpersonal relationships.

   d. is incorrect. This is not a domain of development.

4. c. is the correct answer. (p. 6; objective 2)

   a. is incorrect. This falls within the cognitive and biosocial domains.

   b. is incorrect. This falls within the biosocial domain.

   d. is incorrect. This falls within the cognitive domain.

5. d. is the correct answer. This approach sees development as occurring within four interacting levels, or environments. (p. 3; video lesson, segment 1; objective 3)

6. d. is the correct answer. (p. 5; video lesson, segment 3; objective 4)

7. b. is the correct answer. (p. 2; objective 4)

   a. is incorrect. Body weight does not always increase in a linear fashion.

   c. is incorrect. Although it is possible that a small change in a person's body weight could set off a series of changes that culminate in a major event, the question is concerned with the interconnectedness of body weight, nutrition, and other dynamic developmental systems.

8. c. is the correct answer. (p. 3; video lesson, segment 1; objective 3)

   a. is incorrect. This refers to systems that link one microsystem to another.

   b. is incorrect. This refers to cultural values, political philosophies, economic patterns, and social conditions.

   d. is incorrect. This includes the community structures that affect the functioning of smaller systems.

9. c. is the correct answer. (p. 14; objective 3)

10. d. is the correct answer (p. 35; video lesson, segment 2; objective 5)

11. a. is the correct answer. (p. 36; video lesson, segment 2; objective 6)

b. is incorrect. Learning theory emphasizes the influence of the immediate environment on behavior.

c. is incorrect. Cognitive theory emphasizes the impact of conscious thought processes on behavior.

d. is incorrect. Sociocultural theory emphasizes the influence on development of social interaction in a specific cultural context.

12. a. is the correct answer. (pp. 37, 39; objective 6)

13. a. is the correct answer. (pp. 38–39; video lesson, segment 2; objective 6)

b. & c. are incorrect. Whereas Freud identified four stages of psychosexual development, Erikson proposed eight psychosocial stages.

d. is incorrect. Although his theory places greater emphasis on social and cultural forces than Freud's did, Erikson's theory is nevertheless classified as a psychoanalytic theory.

14. c. is the correct answer. (p. 41; video lesson, segment 2; objective 7)

15. a. is the correct answer. In classical conditioning, a neutral stimulus—in this case, the bell—is associated with a meaningful stimulus—in this case, food. (p. 40; video lesson, segment 2; objective 7)

b. is incorrect. In operant conditioning, the consequences of a voluntary response determine the likelihood of its being repeated. Salivation is an involuntary response.

c. & d. are incorrect. Positive reinforcement and social learning pertain to voluntary, or operant, responses.

16. c. is the correct answer. (pp. 60–61; video lesson, introduction; objective 11)

a. is incorrect. These are both examples of nurture.

b. is incorrect. Both of these refer to nature.

d. is incorrect. The impact of changing historical concepts of childhood on development is an example of how environmental forces (nurture) shape development.

17. d. is the correct answer. (p. 43; video lesson, segment 2; objective 7)

a. & c. are incorrect. These can be true in all types of learning.

b. is incorrect. This was not discussed as an aspect of developmental theory.

18. d. is the correct answer. (p. 51; objective 10)

a. & c. are incorrect. Sociocultural and learning theories focus almost entirely on environmental factors (nurture) in development.

b. is incorrect. Cognitive theory emphasizes the developing person's own mental activity but ignores genetic differences in individuals.

19. a. is the correct answer. (p. 51; objective 9)

b. is incorrect. Vygotsky's theory does not emphasize biological processes.

c. & d. are incorrect. Vygotsky's theory places considerable emphasis on language and social factors.

20. a. is the correct answer. (p. 45; video lesson, segment 2; objective 8)

21. c. is the correct answer. (p. 45; objective 8)

a. is incorrect. This refers to the core of Erikson's psychosocial stages, which deals with people's interactions with the environment.

b. is incorrect. Equilibrium occurs when existing schemes do fit a person's current experiences.

d. is incorrect. Negative reinforcement is the removal of a stimulus as a consequence of a desired behavior.

22. b. is the correct answer. (pp. 60–61; objective 11)

    c. is incorrect. This is only true of psychoanalytic theory.

    d. is incorrect. Although the grand theories have emphasized nurture over nature in this matter, no theory suggests that sexual orientation is voluntarily chosen.

23. c. is the correct answer. (p. 50; objective 9)

    a. is incorrect. This describes attention.

    b. is incorrect. This describes positive reinforcement.

    d. is incorrect. This describes reciprocal determinism.

24. b. is the correct answer. Locke believed that the mind at birth is a *tabula rasa,* or "blank slate" onto which learning (nurture) leaves its mark. Rousseau emphasized the natural (biological) goodness of human beings. (video lesson, introduction; objectives 1 & 11)

Matching Items

25. e (p. 36; video lesson, segment 2; objective 6)

26. j (p. 60; video lesson, introduction; objective 11)

27. a (p. 40; video lesson, segment 2; objective 7)

28. b (p. 43; video lesson, segment 2; objective 7)

29. g (p. 44; video lesson, segment 2; objective 8)

30. c (p. 60; video lesson, introduction; objective 11)

31. f (p. 48; objective 9)

32. d (p. 40; video lesson, segment 2; objective 7)

33. h (p. 43; video lesson, segment 2; objective 7)

34. i (p. 51; objective 10)

Practice Questions II

Multiple-Choice Questions

1. d. is the correct answer. (p. 3; objective 3)

2. c. is the correct answer. (p. 6; objective 2)

3. d. is the correct answer. (pp. 6–7; objective 2)

   c. is incorrect. Research has not revealed cultural variations in the overall developmental influence of the three domains.

4. c. is the correct answer. (pp. 2–3; video lesson, segment 1; objective 3)

   a. & d. are incorrect. These are part of the microsystem.

   b. is incorrect. This is part of the exosystem.

5. c. is the correct answer. (p. 3; objective 1)

   a. is incorrect. This is the insight of interacting systems.

   b. is incorrect. This insight is the butterfly effect.

6. c. is the correct answer. (p. 8; objective 3)

   a., b., & d. are incorrect. These are attributes of an ethnic group.

7. d. is the correct answer. (p. 47; objective 11)

8. d. is the correct answer. This is one of Piaget's stages of cognitive development. (pp. 37–39; video lesson, segment 2; objective 6)

9. c. is the correct answer. (p. 43; video lesson, segment 2; objective 7)

10. d. is the correct answer. (p. 38; objective 6)

11. c. is the correct answer. (pp. 39–40; objective 7)

a. is incorrect. Piaget formulated a cognitive theory of development.

b. is incorrect. Vygotsky formulated a sociocultural theory of development.

d. is incorrect. Erikson formulated a psychoanalytic theory of development.

12. c. is the correct answer. (pp. 40–41; video lesson, segment 2; objective 7)

13. c. is the correct answer. (p. 41; objective 7)

a. & b. are incorrect. These are psychoanalytic approaches to treating psychological problems.

d. is incorrect. Learning theorists generally do not recommend the use of punishment.

14. a. is the correct answer. These behaviors are typical of infants in the sensorimotor stage. (p. 45; objective 8)

b., c., & d. are incorrect. These are typical of older children.

15. a. is the correct answer. (p. 45; video lesson, segment 2; objective 8)

b. is incorrect. The sensorimotor stage describes development from birth until age 2.

c. is incorrect. This is a psychoanalytic stage described by Freud.

d. is incorrect. This is not the name of a stage; "psychosocial" refers to Erikson's stage theory.

16. a. is the correct answer. (p. 45; objective 8)

b. is incorrect. This describes disequilibrium.

c. is incorrect. This is formal operational thinking.

d. is incorrect. Piaget's theory does not propose stages of information processing.

17. c. is the correct answer. (p. 41; video lesson, segment 2; objective 7)

a. & b. are incorrect. Teaching your dog in this way is an example of operant, rather than classical (respondent), conditioning.

d. is incorrect. Modeling involves learning by imitating others.

18. b. is the correct answer. (pp. 45–46; objective 8)

a. is incorrect. Assimilation occurs when new experiences do not clash with existing ideas.

c. is incorrect. Cognitive equilibrium is mental balance, which occurs when ideas and experiences do not clash.

d. is incorrect. This is Vygotsky's term for the process by which a mentor engages a child in shared learning activities.

19. d. is the correct answer. (p. 51; objectives 9 & 11)

a. is incorrect. This is a common criticism of psychoanalytic theory.

b. is incorrect. This is a common criticism of learning theory.

c. is incorrect. This is a common criticism of psychoanalytic and cognitive theories that describe development as occurring in a sequence of stages.

20. c. is the correct answer. (p. 49; objective 9)

21. a. is the correct answer. (video lesson, segment 2; objective 7)

b. is incorrect. This answer would have been correct had the question read "Response is to stimulus as…"

c & d. are incorrect. Nature and nurture refer to internal and external influences on development, respectively.

22. c. is the correct answer. (pp. 43–44; video lesson, segment 2; objective 7)

True or False Items

23. T (p. 39; video lesson, segment 2; objective 7)

24. T (pp. 38–39; video lesson, segment 2; objective 6)

25. F Although most developmentalists believe that nature and nurture interact in shaping development, the practical implications of whether nature or nurture plays a greater role in certain abilities keep the controversy alive. (pp. 59–60; video lesson, introduction; objective 11)

26. F This assumption lies at the heart of epigenetic systems theory. (pp. 51–52; objective 10)

27. F Epigenetic systems theory emphasizes the interaction of genes and experience. (p. 51; objective 10)

28. T (pp. 60–61; objective 11)

29. F On the contrary, disequilibrium often fosters greater growth. (p. 45; objective 8)

30. T (p. 44; video lesson, segment 2; objective 8)

31. F The hallmark of Piaget's theory is that, at every age, individuals think about the world in unique ways. (pp. 44–45; objective 8)

32. T (p. 62; video lesson, segment 3; objective 11)

Applying Your Knowledge

1. c. is the correct answer. (p. 6; objective 2)

   a. & d. are incorrect. These pertain to the cognitive domain.

   b. is incorrect. This pertains to the biosocial domain.

2. c. is the correct answer. (pp. 2–3; video lesson, segment 1; objective 3)

   a. is incorrect. Piaget is notable in the area of cognitive development.

   b. is incorrect. Freud was a pioneer of psychoanalysis.

   d. is incorrect. Skinner is notable in the history of learning theory.

3. b. is the correct answer. (pp. 2–3; video lesson, segment 1; objective 3)

   a., c., & d. are incorrect. These are the three domains of development.

4. a. is the correct answer. (p. 9; objective 3)

5. c. is the correct answer. (pp. 10–11; objective 3)

6. a. is the correct answer. (p. 52; objective 10)

   b. is incorrect. This term was not used to describe development.

   c. & d. are incorrect. These terms describe the processes by which cognitive concepts incorporate (assimilate) new experiences or are revamped (accommodated) by them.

7. a. is the correct answer. This is an example of operant conditioning because a response recurs due to its consequences. (p. 41; video lesson, segment 2; objective 7)

   b. & d. are incorrect. In classical conditioning, the individual learns to associate a neutral stimulus with a meaningful stimulus.

   c. is incorrect. In modeling, learning occurs through the observation of others, rather than through direct exposure to reinforcing consequences, as in this example.

8. d. is the correct answer. (p. 53; objective 10)

9. d. is the correct answer. (p. 51; objective 10)

   a. is incorrect. Psychoanalytic theorists focus on the role of unconscious forces in development.

   b. is incorrect. Cognitive theorists emphasize how the developing person actively seeks to understand experiences.

   c. is incorrect. Sociocultural theorists focus on the social context, as expressed through people, language, and customs.

10. b. is the correct answer. (p. 49; objective 9)

    a. & c. are incorrect. These are both examples of modeling.

    d. is incorrect. Guided participation involves the coaching of a mentor. In this example, Kyle is simply following written directions.

11. a. is the correct answer. (pp. 45–46; objective 8)

    b. is incorrect. Because the dog is not furry, the child's concept of dog cannot incorporate (assimilate) the discrepant experience without being revamped.

    c. & d. are incorrect. Equilibrium exists when ideas (such as what a dog is) and experiences (such as seeing a hairless dog) do not clash.

12. d. is the correct answer. (p. 38; objective 6)

13. b. is the correct answer. Evidently, Jennie has learned by observing the other children at play. (p. 43; video lesson, segment 2; objective 7)

    a. is incorrect. Classical conditioning is concerned with the association of stimuli, not with complex responses, as in this example.

    c. is incorrect. Guided participation involves the interaction of a mentor and a child.

    d. is incorrect. Reinforcement is a process for getting a response to recur.

14. c. is the correct answer. (p. 45; video lesson, segment 2; objective 8)

15. d. is the correct answer. When Bjorn experiences something that conflicts with his existing understanding, he experiences disequilibrium. (p. 45; objective 8)

    a. is incorrect. Conservation is the ability to recognize that objects do not change when their appearances change.

    b. is incorrect. Cognition refers to all mental activities associated with thinking.

    c. is incorrect. If Bjorn's thinking were in equilibrium, all men would be "dad"!

16. a. is the correct answer. (pp. 54–55; objective 10)

    b. & c. are incorrect. Infant social reflexes and adult caregiving impulses occur in all cultures (b), which indicates that they are the product of nature rather than nurture (c).

    d. is incorrect. The textbook does not address the issue of gender differences in infant reflexes or caregiving impulses.

17. d. is the correct answer. (p. 48; objective 9)

18. b. is the correct answer. (pp. 38–39; video lesson, segment 2; objective 6)

    a. is incorrect. According to Erikson, this crisis concerns younger children.

    c. & d. are incorrect. In Erikson's theory, these crises concern older children.

19. c. is the correct answer. (p. 62; video lesson, segment 3; objective 11)

    a., b., & d. are incorrect. These are three of the many theoretical perspectives upon which someone working from an eclectic perspective might draw.

20. d. is the correct answer. (p. 40; objective 7)

    a., b., & c. are incorrect. Each of these theories emphasizes that development is a discontinuous process that occurs in stages.

Lesson Review

Lesson 1

Introduction
The Development Person

Please Note: Use this matrix to guide your study and achieve the learning objectives of this lesson. It will also help you to view the video, which defines and demonstrates important concepts and skills as they relate to everyday life.

Learning Objective	Textbook	Telecourse Student Guide	Video Lesson
1. Define the study of human development and discuss some of its major themes.	pp. 1–3, 60–62	Key Terms: 1, 2, 3, 4, 34, 35, 36; Practice Questions I: 1, 7, 24; Practice Questions II: 5.	Introduction
2. Describe the three major domains of human development and discuss how they interrelate.	pp. 6–7	Key Terms: 6, 7, 8; Practice Questions I: 2, 3, 4; Practice Questions II: 2, 3; Applying Your Knowledge: 1.	
3. Describe the many contexts and systems that can affect a person's development, and discuss how they are interrelated.	pp. 2–3, 8–16	Key Terms: 3, 4, 9, 10, 11, 12, 13, 14, 15, 37; Practice Questions I: 5, 7, 8, 9; Practice Questions II: 1, 4, 6; Applying Your Knowledge: 2, 3, 4, 5.	Segment 1: *Contexts and System*
4. Identify the characteristics of development described by the life-span perspective.	p. 5	Key Terms: 5; Practice Questions I: 6.	Segment 3: *The Life-Span Perspective*
5. Define developmental theory, and describe how theories help explain human behavior and guide researchers who study development.	p. 35	Key Terms: 16; Practice Questions I: 10.	Segment 2: *Theories of Development*
6. Discuss the major focus of psychoanalytic theory, contrasting the psychosexual development proposed by Freud with the psychosocial development described by Erikson.	pp. 36–39	Key Terms: 17; Practice Questions I: 11, 12, 13, 25; Practice Questions II: 8, 10, 24; Applying Your Knowledge: 12, 18.	Segment 2: *Theories of Development*

Learning Objective	Textbook	Telecourse Student Guide	Video Lesson
7. Discuss the major focus of behaviorism (learning theory), and explain the basic principles of classical and operant conditioning as well as social learning theory.	pp. 39–45	Key Terms: 18, 19, 20, 21, 22, 23, 24, 38, 39; Practice Questions I: 14, 15, 17, 27, 28, 32, 33; Practice Questions II: 9, 11, 12, 13, 17, 21, 22, 23; Applying Your Knowledge: 7, 13, 14, 20.	Segment 2: *Theories of Development*
8. Discuss the major focus of cognitive theory, and summarize Piaget's stages of cognitive development.	pp. 44–46	Key Terms: 25, 26; Practice Questions I: 20, 21, 28; Practice Questions II: 14, 15, 16, 18, 29, 30, 31; Applying Your Knowledge: 11, 15.	Segment 2: *Theories of Development*
9. Discuss the basic ideas of Vygotsky and the sociocultural theory of development.	pp. 48–51	Key Terms: 27, 28, 29, 30; Practice Questions I: 19, 23, 31; Practice Questions II: 19, 20; Applying Your Knowledge: 10, 17.	
10. Discuss the basic ideas of epigenetic systems theory.	pp. 51–55	Key Terms: 31, 32, 33; Practice Questions I: 18, 34; Practice Questions II: 26, 27; Applying Your Knowledge: 6, 8, 9, 16.	
11. Summarize the contributions and criticisms of the major developmental theories, and compare the position of the theories regarding three controversies of development.	pp. 47, 51, 59–62	Key Terms: 34, 35, 36; Practice Questions I: 16, 22, 24, 26, 30; Practice Questions II: 7, 19, 25, 28, 32; Applying Your Knowledge: 19.	Introduction, Segment 2: *Theories of Development*

A Scientific Approach

Lesson 2

Developmental Study as a Science

Preview

Human development is a science that seeks to understand how and why people change over time, and how and why they remain the same. Central to this effort is the set of principles and procedures scientists use to conduct research and produce the most objective results possible. Lesson 2 discusses these principles and procedures, beginning with the **scientific method**. The lesson continues by introducing some of the different research methods and designs that scientists use to gather data and test ideas. As these methods are described, several classic studies in developmental psychology are summarized.

The final section of the lesson discusses the ethics of research with humans. To ensure confidentiality and safety, developmentalists who study children are especially concerned that the benefits of research outweigh the risks.

As you complete this lesson, recall a scientific study you've heard or read about. What was the purpose of the study? How was it conducted? Who conducted it? Who paid for the study? What methods or procedures did the researchers use to gather their data? What conclusions did the researchers come to? Does anyone dispute these findings? Are you confident in the results of the study? Why or why not?

Prior Telecourse Knowledge that Will Be Used in this Lesson

- This telecourse lesson focuses primarily on research methods, drawing on material from each of the three domains of development. Recall from Lesson (1) that the three domains of development include: (1) the *biosocial* domain, including changes in brain and body and the social influences that guide them, (2) the *cognitive* domain, which includes thought processes, perceptual abilities, and language mastery, as well as the educational institutions that encourage them, and (3) the *psychosocial* domain, including emotions, personality, and interpersonal relationships with family, friends, and the wider community. All three domains are important at every age, and each of the domains is affected by the other two.

- In its discussion of different research designs, this lesson will use the concept of a *cohort*. Recall that a cohort is a group of people who, because they were born within a few years of each other, experience many of the same historical and social conditions.

Learning Objectives

Use this information to guide your reading, viewing, thinking, and studying. After successfully completing this lesson, you should be able to:

1. List and describe the basic steps of the scientific method, and discuss the challenge researchers face in identifying variables for a particular study.
2. Describe scientific observation, surveys, and case studies as research methods, noting at least one advantage (or strength) and one disadvantage (or weakness) of each.
3. Define what correlation means in science and offer examples of its use in the study of human development.
4. Describe the components of an experiment, and discuss the main advantage and some limitations of this research method.
5. Describe three basic research designs used by developmental psychologists to study changes over time.
6. Discuss the code of ethics that should be followed by researchers in the field of developmental psychology.

📖 **Read Chapter 1, "Introduction," pages 19–31, and review Chapter 2, "Thinking Like a Scientist," pages 42–43.**

📼 **View the video for Lesson 2, "A Scientific Approach."**

Segment 1: *The Scientific Method*

Segment 2: *Research Methods*

Segment 3: *Studying Changes over Time*

Summary

The **scientific method** consists of five basic steps: (1) formulate a research question, (2) develop a **hypothesis**, (3) test the hypothesis, (4) draw conclusions, and (5) make the findings available. **Replication** of research findings strengthens confidence in the results and leads researchers to more definitive and extensive conclusions.

Scientists often discuss findings in terms of **variables**, those characteristics or actions that may differ between people, from situation to situation, or perhaps even within one person from one moment to the next. Because the variables in research are numerous, it is difficult to determine whether all the relevant ones have been identified in a particular investigation. Most research projects begin with a review of all relevant literature—journal articles that describe previous research on the topic—which can help scientists formulate a research question and identify the important variables to study.

There are many ways to test hypotheses. One method is **scientific observation** of people in their natural environment or in a laboratory setting. Naturalistic observation is limited in that it tells us only if two variables are correlated.

Correlation is a statistical technique used to determine whether two variables are related. In other words, correlation describes the extent to which changes in one variable are associated with changes in another variable. It does not prove what causes these changes. Only **experiments** can reveal cause-and-effect relationships by allowing researchers to observe whether a change in an **independent variable** produces a corresponding change in a **dependent variable**. Experiments are not, however, without their limitations. Because experiments are so carefully designed and controlled, the behavior demonstrated may not mirror behavior in the "real world."

The scientific **survey** asks individuals to report on their own attitudes, feelings, or behaviors by completing questionnaires or structured interviews. This method is especially vulnerable to bias: the phrasing of the questions may affect the responses obtained and people may give answers they think the researcher wants to hear. Although a **case study** can be useful in providing an in-depth analysis of one person's experience, it also is not without limitations. Data from this method can be misinterpreted because of the researcher's biases.

While these different research methods are often described separately, they are not mutually exclusive. For example, researchers often use scientific observation during experiments, such as those conducted by Harry Harlow and Mary Ainsworth that were discussed in the video.

To study changes over time, scientists can choose between different research designs. In **cross-sectional research**, groups of people who are different in age but similar in all other important ways are compared on the characteristic that is of interest to the researcher(s). One limitation of cross-sectional research is that it is always possible that some variable other than age differentiates the groups. In **longitudinal research**, the same group of people is studied over a period of time. Longitudinal research is particularly useful in studying developmental trends that occur over a long age span.

Both longitudinal and cross-sectional researchers must bear in mind that research on a single *cohort* may not be valid for people developing in an earlier or later cohort. A cohort is a group of people born within a few years of each other who are exposed to similar historical and societal experiences. In **cross-sequential research**, several groups of people at different ages (cross-sectional component) are followed over time (longitudinal component).

When studying people, scientists take special care to ensure that participation is voluntary, harmless, and that the study's benefits outweigh its costs. Sometimes scientists conduct a meta-analysis, or a compilation of data from studies previously published, so that no participants are directly involved.

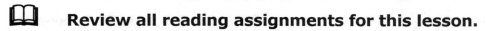 **Review all reading assignments for this lesson.**

As assigned by your instructor, complete the optional online component for this lesson.

Key Terms

Using your own words, write a brief definition or explanation of each of the following terms on a separate piece of paper.

1. scientific method
2. hypothesis
3. replication
4. variable
5. scientific observation
6. correlation
7. experiment
8. independent variable
9. dependent variable
10. experimental group
11. comparison group
12. survey
13. case study
14. cross-sectional research
15. longitudinal research
16. cross-sequential research
17. code of ethics
18. Strange Situation
19. random assignment

Practice Questions I

Multiple-Choice Questions

1. A hypothesis is a
   a. conclusion.
   b. prediction to be tested.
   c. statistical test.
   d. correlation.

2. One disadvantage of experiments is that
   a. people may behave differently in the artificial environment of the laboratory.
   b. comparison groups are too large to be accommodated in most laboratories.
   c. they are the method most vulnerable to bias on the part of the researcher.
   d. proponents of the ecological approach overuse them.

3. In an experiment testing the effects of group size on individual effort in a tug-of-war task, the number of people in each group is the
   a. hypothesis.
   b. independent variable
   c. dependent variable.
   d. level of significance.

4. Which research method would be most appropriate for investigating the relationship between parents' religious beliefs and their attitudes toward middle school sex education?
   a. experimentation
   b. longitudinal research
   c. naturalistic observation
   d. the survey

5. Developmentalists who carefully observe the behavior of schoolchildren during recess are using a research method known as

   a. the case study.

   b. cross-sectional research.

   c. naturalistic observation.

   d. cross-sequential research.

6. In an experiment to determine the effects of attention on memory, memory is the

   a. comparison condition.

   b. intervening variable.

   c. independent variable.

   d. dependent variable.

7. Harry Harlow found that when monkeys were reared in social isolation, they would seek

   a. contact comfort as much as nourishment.

   b. nourishment over contact comfort.

   c. the company of other monkeys that had been socially isolated.

   d. no food, water, or nourishment of any kind.

8. If shoe size and IQ are negatively correlated, which of the following is true?

   a. People with large feet tend to have high IQs.

   b. People with small feet tend to have high IQs.

   c. People with small feet tend to have low IQs.

   d. IQ is unpredictable based on a person's shoe size.

Matching Items

Match each definition or description with its corresponding term.

Terms

9. _____ code of ethics

10. _____ cross-sequential

11. _____ correlation

12. _____ scientific observation

13. _____ variable

14. _____ hypothesis

15. _____ scientific method

16. _____ cross-sectional

17. _____ longitudinal research

Definitions or Descriptions

a. a general procedural model that helps researchers remain objective

b. any quantity, characteristic, or action that can take on different values

c. a testable prediction

d. a statistical measure of relationship between two variables

e. a set of moral principles

f research study retesting one group of people at several different times

g. research study comparing people of different ages at the same time

h. research study that follows groups of people of different ages over time

i. unobtrusively watching and recording of the behavior of a group of research subjects

Multiple-Choice Questions

1. Professor Cohen predicts that because "baby boomers" grew up in an era that promoted independence and assertiveness, people in their 40s and 50s will respond differently to a political survey than will people in their 20s and 30s. The professor's prediction regarding political attitudes is an example of a(n)

    a. meta-analysis.

    b. hypothesis.

    c. independent variable.

    d. dependent variable.

2. A cohort is defined as a group of people

    a. of similar national origin.

    b. who share a common language.

    c. born within a few years of each other.

    d. who share the same religion.

3. In a test of the effects of noise, groups of students performed a proofreading task in a noisy or a quiet room. To what group were students in the noisy room assigned?

    a. experimental

    b. comparison

    c. randomly assigned

    d. dependent

4. If developmentalists discovered that poor people are happier than wealthy people are, this would indicate that wealth and happiness are

    a. unrelated.

    b. positively correlated.

    c. negatively correlated.

    d. causally related.

5. In an experiment testing the effects of noise level on mood, mood is the

    a. hypothesis.

    b. independent variable.

    c. dependent variable.

    d. scientific observation.

6. Which of the following research strategies would be best for determining whether alcohol causes impairments to memory?

    a. case study

    b. naturalistic observation

    c. survey

    d. experiment

7. Which of the following research methods does **NOT** belong with the others?

    a. case study

    b. survey

    c. naturalistic observation

    d. experiment

8. The procedure designed to ensure that the experimental and comparison groups do not differ in any way that might affect the experiment's results is called

    a. variable controlling.

    b. random assignment.

    c. representative sampling.

    d. stratification.

9. In a test of the effects of noise, groups of students performed a proofreading task in a noisy or a quiet room. To what condition were students in the quiet room exposed?

    a. experimental

    b. comparison

    c. randomly assigned

    d. dependent

Matching Items

Match each definition or description with its corresponding term.

Terms

10. _____ independent variable   14. _____ experimental group

11. _____ dependent variable   15. _____ comparison group

12. _____ experiment   16. _____ case study

13. _____ replicate   17. _____ survey

Definitions or Descriptions

    a. an in-depth observational study of one person

    b. the "treatment-absent" condition in an experiment

    c. the "treatment-present" condition in an experiment

    d. the research strategy in which a representative sample of individuals is questioned

    e. to repeat an experiment to check the reliability of its results

    f. the variable manipulated in an experiment

    g. the method that can establish cause-and-effect relationships

    h. the variable measured in an experiment

Applying Your Knowledge

1. In order to study the effects of temperature on mood, Dr. Sanchez had students fill out questionnaires in very warm or very cool rooms. In this study, the independent variable consisted of
   a. the number of subjects assigned to each group.
   b. the students' responses to the questionnaire.
   c. the room temperature.
   d. the subject matter of the questions.

2. Esteban believes that high doses of caffeine slow a person's reaction time. In order to test his belief, he has five friends each drink three 8-ounce cups of coffee and then measures their reaction time on a learning task. What is wrong with Esteban's research strategy?
   a. No independent variable is specified.
   b. No dependent variable is specified.
   c. There is no control condition.
   d. There is no provision for replication of the findings.

3. When researchers find that the results of a study are statistically significant, this means that
   a. they may have been caused purely by chance.
   b. it is unlikely they could be replicated.
   c. it is unlikely they could have occurred by chance.
   d. the sample population was representative of the general population.

4. If height and body weight are positively correlated, which of the following is true?
   a. There is a cause-and-effect relationship between height and weight.
   b. Knowing a person's height, one can predict his or her weight.
   c. As height increases, weight decreases.
   d. All of the above are true.

5. An example of longitudinal research would be when an investigator compares the performance of
   a. several different age groups on a memory test.
   b. the same group of people, at different ages, on a test of memory.
   c. an experimental group and a comparison group of subjects on a test of memory.
   d. several different age groups on a test of memory as each group is tested repeatedly over a period of years.

6. For her developmental psychology research project, Lakia decides she wants to focus primarily on qualitative data. You advise her to conduct
   a. a survey.
   b. an experiment.
   c. a cross-sectional study.
   d. a case study.

7. Which of the following is **NOT** a major controversy in the study of development?

   a. nature vs. nurture

   b. difference vs. deficit

   c. continuity vs. discontinuity

   d. individual vs. society

8. Dr. Weston is comparing research findings for a group of 30-year-olds with findings for the same individuals at age 20, as well as with findings for groups who were 30 in 1990. Which research method is she using?

   a. longitudinal research

   b. cross-sectional research

   c. case study

   d. cross-sequential research

9. Professor Albertini wants to determine whether adopted children have personalities that are more similar to their biological parents or to their adoptive parents. In this instance, the professor is primarily concerned with the issue of

   a. deficit/difference.

   b. continuity/discontinuity.

   c. nature/nurture.

   d. individual/society.

10. A psychologist studies the play behavior of third-grade children by watching groups during recess at school. Which research technique is being used?

    a. correlation

    b. case study

    c. experimentation

    d. naturalistic observation

Answer Key

Key Terms

1. The scientific method is a general procedural model that helps researchers remain objective as they study behavior. The five basic steps of the scientific method are (1) formulate a research question; (2) develop a hypothesis; (3) test the hypothesis; (4) draw conclusions; and (5) make the findings available. (p. 20; video lesson, segment 1; objective 1)

2. In the scientific method, a hypothesis is a specific, testable prediction regarding development. (p. 20; video lesson, segment 1; objective 1)

3. To replicate a test of a research hypothesis is to repeat it using a different but related set of subjects or procedures in order to verify or refute the original study's conclusions. (p. 20; objective 1)

4. A variable is any quantity, characteristic, or action that can take on different values within a group of individuals or a single individual. (p. 20; video lesson, segment 2; objective 1)

5. Scientific observation is the unobtrusive watching and recording of subjects' behavior in a situation that is being studied, either in the laboratory or in a natural setting. (p. 21; video lesson, segment 2; objective 2)

6. Correlation is a statistical term that merely indicates whether two variables are related to each other such that one is likely (or unlikely) to occur when the other occurs or one is likely to increase (or decrease) when the other increases (or decreases). (p. 22; video lesson, segment 2; objective 3)

7. The experiment is the research method in which an investigator tests a hypothesis in a controlled situation in which the relevant variables are limited and can be manipulated by the experimenter. (p. 23; video lesson, segment 2; objective 4)

8. The independent variable is the variable that is manipulated in an experiment. (p. 23; video lesson, segment 2; objective 4)

9. The dependent variable is the variable that is being studied in an experiment. (p. 23; video lesson, segment 2; objective 4)

    Example: In the study of the effects of a new drug on memory, the subjects' memory is the dependent variable.

10. The experimental group of an experiment is one in which subjects are exposed to the independent variable being studied. (p. 23; video lesson, segment 2; objective 4)

11. The comparison group of an experiment is one in which the treatment of interest, or independent variable, is withheld so that comparison to the experimental group can be made. (p. 23; video lesson, segment 2; objective 4)

12. The scientific survey is the research method in which information is collected from a large number of people, either through written questionnaires or through interviews. (p. 25; video lesson, segment 2; objective 2)

13. The case study is the research method involving the intensive study of one person. (p. 25; objective 2)

14. In cross-sectional research, groups of people who differ in age but share other important characteristics are compared with regard to the variable under investigation. (p. 26; video lesson, segment 3; objective 5)

15. In longitudinal research, the same group of individuals is studied over a period of time to measure both change and stability as they age. (p. 28; video lesson, segment 3; objective 5)

16. Cross-sequential research follows a group of people of different ages over time, thus combining the strengths of the cross-sectional and longitudinal methods. (p. 29; objective 5)

17. Developmental psychologists and other scientists work from a code of ethics, which is a set of moral principles that guides their research. (p. 29; video lesson, segment 3; objective 6)

18. The Strange Situation is a laboratory research procedure used to measure an infant's attachment to his or her caregiver. (video lesson, segment 2; objectives 2 & 4)

19. Random assignment is the procedure of assigning participants to the experimental and control conditions of an experiment by chance in order to minimize preexisting differences between the groups. (video lesson, segment 2; objective 4)

Practice Questions I

Multiple-Choice Questions

1. b. is the correct answer. (p. 20; video lesson, segment 1; objective 1)

2. a. is the correct answer. (p. 24; objective 4)

3. b. is the correct answer. (p. 23; video lesson, segment 2; objective 4)

    a. is incorrect. A possible hypothesis for this experiment would be that the larger the group, the less hard a given individual will pull.

c. is incorrect. The dependent variable is the measure of individual effort.

d. is incorrect. Significance level refers to the numerical value specifying the possibility that the results of an experiment could have occurred by chance.

4. d. is the correct answer. (p. 25; video lesson, segment 2; objective 2)

a. is incorrect. Experimentation is appropriate when one is seeking to uncover cause-and-effect relationships; in this example, the researcher is only interested in determining whether the parents' beliefs predict their attitudes.

b. is incorrect. Longitudinal research would be appropriate if the researcher sought to examine the development of these attitudes over a long period of time.

c. is incorrect. Mere observation would not allow the researcher to determine the attitudes of the subjects.

5. c. is the correct answer. (pp. 21–22; video lesson, segment 2; objective 2)

a. is incorrect. In this method, one subject is studied over a period of time.

b. & d. are incorrect. In these research methods, two or more groups of subjects are studied and compared.

6. d. is the correct answer. (p. 23; video lesson, segment 2; objective 4)

a. is incorrect. The control condition is the comparison group, in which the experimental treatment is absent.

b. is incorrect. Memory is the dependent variable in this experiment.

c. is incorrect. Attention is the independent variable, which is being manipulated.

7. a. is the correct answer. (pp. 42–43; video lesson, segment 1; objectives 1 & 4)

8. b. is the correct answer. (p. 23; video lesson, segment 2; objective 3)

a. & c. are incorrect. These answers would have been correct had the question stated that there is a *positive* correlation between shoe size and IQ. Actually, there is probably no correlation at all!

Matching Items

9. e (p. 29; objective 6)

10. h (p. 29; video lesson, segment 3; objective 5)

11. d (p. 22; video lesson, segment 2; objective 3)

12. i (p. 21; video lesson, segment 2; objective 2)

13. b (p. 20; video lesson, segment 2; objective 1)

14. c (p. 20; video lesson, segment 1; objective 1)

15. a (p. 20; video lesson, segment 1; objective 1)

16. g (p. 26; video lesson, segment 3; objective 5)

17. f (p. 28; video lesson, segment 3; objective 5)

Practice Questions II

Multiple-Choice Questions

1. b. is the correct answer. (p. 20; video lesson, segment 1; objective 1)

a. is incorrect. In a meta-analysis, the results of a number of separate research studies are combined.

c. & d. are incorrect. Variables are treatments (independent) or behaviors (dependent) in experiments, which this situation clearly is not.

2. c. is the correct answer. (p. 8; video lesson, segment 3; objective 5)

a., b., & d. are incorrect. These are attributes of an ethnic group.

3. a. is the correct answer. The experimental group is the one in which the variable or treatment—in this case, noise, is present. (p. 23; video lesson, segment 2; objective 4)

   b. is incorrect. Students in the quiet room would be in the comparison condition.

   c. is incorrect. Presumably, all students in both groups were randomly assigned to their groups.

   d. is incorrect. The word *dependent* refers to a kind of variable in experiments; groups are either experimental or comparison.

4. c. is the correct answer. (p. 22; video lesson, segment 2; objective 3)

   a. is incorrect. Wealth and happiness clearly are related.

   b. is incorrect. This answer would be correct if wealthy people were found to be happier than poor people.

   d. is incorrect. Correlation does not imply causation.

5. c. is the correct answer. (p. 23; video lesson, segment 2; objective 4)

   a. is incorrect. Hypotheses make specific, testable predictions.

   b. is incorrect. Noise level is the independent variable.

   d. is incorrect. Scientific observation is a research method in which subjects are watched, while their behavior is recorded unobtrusively.

6. d. is the correct answer. In an experiment, it would be possible to manipulate alcohol consumption and observe the effects, if any, on memory. (p. 23 ; video lesson, segment 2; objective 4)

   a., b., & c. are incorrect because only by directly controlling the variables of interest can a researcher uncover cause-and-effect relationships.

7. d. is the correct answer. Only experiments can reveal cause-and-effect relationships; the other methods can only describe relationships. (p. 23; video lesson, segment 2; objectives 2 & 4)

8. b. is the correct answer. If enough subjects are used in an experiment and they are randomly assigned to the two groups, any differences that emerge between the groups should stem from the experiment itself. (video lesson, segment 2; objective 4)

   a., c., & d. are incorrect. None of these terms describes precautions taken in setting up groups for experiments.

9. b. is the correct answer. The comparison or control condition is the one in which the treatment—in this case, noise—is absent. (p. 23; video lesson, segment 2; objective 4)

   a. is incorrect. Students in the noisy room would be in the experimental condition.

   c. is incorrect. Presumably, all students in both groups were randomly assigned. Random assignment is a method for establishing groups, rather than a condition.

   d. is incorrect. The word dependent refers to a kind of variable in experiments; conditions are either experimental or comparison.

Matching Items

10. f (p. 23; video lesson, segment 2; objective 4)

11. h (p. 23; video lesson, segment 2; objective 4)

12. g (p. 23; video lesson, segment 2; objective 4)

13. e (p. 20; objective 1)

14. c (p. 23; video lesson, segment 2; objective 4)

15. b (p. 23; video lesson, segment 2; objective 4)

16. a (p. 25; objective 2)

17. d (p. 25; video lesson, segment 2; objective 2)

Applying Your Knowledge

1. c. is the correct answer. (p. 23; video lesson, segment 2; objective 4)

2. c. is the correct answer. In order to determine the effects of caffeine on reaction time, Esteban needs to measure reaction time in a control, or comparison, group that does not receive caffeine. (p. 23; video lesson, segment 2; objective 4)

   a. is incorrect. Caffeine is the independent variable.

   b. is incorrect. Reaction time is the dependent variable.

   d. is incorrect. Whether or not Esteban's experiment can be replicated is determined by the precision with which he reports his procedures, which is not an aspect of research strategy.

3. c. is the correct answer. (p. 23; objective 4)

4. b. is the correct answer. (p. 23; video lesson, segment 2; objective 3)

   a. is incorrect. Correlation does not imply causation.

   c. is incorrect. If height and body weight are positively correlated, as one increases so does the other.

5. b. is the correct answer. (pp. 28–29; video lesson, segment 3; objective 5)

   a. is incorrect. This is an example of cross-sectional research.

   c. is incorrect. This is an example of an experiment.

   d. is incorrect. This type of study is not described in the text.

6. d. is the correct answer. (p. 25; objective 2)

   a., b., & c. are incorrect. These research methods generally yield quantitative, rather than qualitative, data.

7. d. is the correct answer. On this issue, developmentalists are in agreement: individuals are inextricably involved with their social groups. (p. 21; objective 1)

8. d. is the correct answer. (p. 29; objective 5)

   a. & c. are incorrect. In these research methods, only one group of subjects is studied.

   b. is incorrect. Dr. Weston's design includes comparison of groups of people of different ages over time.

9. c. is the correct answer. (p. 21; objective 1)

   a. is incorrect. This issue concerns whether individual differences are considered problems that need correcting, or causes for celebration.

   b. is incorrect. This issue concerns whether development builds gradually, or occurs through sudden transformations.

   d. is incorrect. This issue concerns whether individual people can be studied apart from the social groups to which they belong.

10. d. is the correct answer. (p. 22; video lesson, segment 2; objective 2)

Lesson Review

Lesson 2

Developmental Study as a Science

Please Note: Use this matrix to guide your study and achieve the learning objectives of this lesson. It will also help you to view the video, which defines and demonstrates important concepts and skills as they relate to everyday life.

Learning Objective	Textbook	Telecourse Student Guide	Video Lesson
1. List and describe the basic steps of the scientific method, and discuss the challenge researchers face in identifying variables for a particular study.	pp. 20–21, 42–43	Key Terms: 1, 2, 3, 4; Practice Questions I: 1, 7, 13, 14, 15; Practice Questions II: 1, 13; Applying Your Knowledge: 7, 9.	Segment 1: *The Scientific Method*
2. Describe scientific observation, surveys, and case studies as research methods, noting at least one advantage (or strength) and one disadvantage (or weakness) of each.	pp. 21–23, 25	Key Terms: 5, 12, 13, 18; Practice Questions I: 4, 5, 12; Practice Questions II: 7, 16, 17; Applying Your Knowledge: 6, 10.	Segment 2: *Research Methods*
3. Define what correlation means in science and offer examples of its use in the study of human development.	pp. 22–23	Key Terms: 6; Practice Questions I: 8, 11; Applying Your Knowledge: 4.	Segment 2: *Research Methods*
4. Describe the components of an experiment, and discuss the main advantage and some limitations of this research method.	pp. 23–24, 42–43	Key Terms: 7, 8, 9, 10, 11, 18, 19; Practice Questions I: 2, 3, 6, 7; Practice Questions II: 3, 4, 5, 6, 7, 8, 9, 10, 11, 12, 14, 15; Applying Your Knowledge: 1, 2, 3.	Segment 2: *Research Methods*
5. Describe three basic research designs used by developmental psychologists to study changes over time.	pp. 26–29	Key Terms: 14, 15, 16; Practice Questions I: 10, 16, 17; Practice Questions II: 2; Applying Your Knowledge: 5, 8.	Segment 3: *Studying Changes over Time*
6. Discuss the code of ethics that should be followed by researchers in the field of developmental psychology.	p. 29	Key Terms: 17; Practice Questions I: 9.	

Nature and Nurture: The Dance of Life

Lesson 3

The Beginnings:
Heredity and Environment

Preview

Much is determined at the moment of *conception*, when a sperm and ovum unite to initiate the developmental processes that will culminate in the birth of a new human being. The genetic legacies of the mother and father influence virtually everything about the developing person—including physical traits, such as gender and appearance, as well as intellectual and personality characteristics. And yet, each person is also shaped by powerful external factors, such as nutrition, parental guidance, health care, schooling, peer groups, and so on.

This lesson describes the fusion of the female's ovum and the male's sperm and the biological mechanisms by which chromosomes and genes are transmitted to the developing person. But, although development is strongly influenced by **heredity** (genes), its ultimate course depends on a person's **environment** (the outside factors that affect how those genes are expressed). In other words, we are all the product of an ongoing interaction between *nature* and *nurture*.

This lesson also discusses the benefits of **genetic counseling** for prospective parents who are at risk of giving birth to children with genetic disorders. Prenatal diagnosis of genetic disorders has been greatly facilitated by recent advances in medical technology, allowing prospective parents to make more informed decisions about the risks of childbearing.

As you complete this video, consider your own heredity and environment. (If possible, you may want to interview your immediate relatives to discuss your family's background.) For example, in what ways are you like your mother and father? In what ways are you different? How are you similar to your aunts, uncles, and grandparents? Now, recall the different environmental factors or contexts that may have influenced your development—your parents, your siblings, your school experiences, your religion, your neighborhood, your friends and peers, your socioeconomic status (SES), cultural values, etc. Consider how these external influences may have interacted with your basic genetic makeup to "mold" you into the person you are today.

Prior Telecourse Knowledge that Will Be Used in this Lesson

- This telecourse lesson focuses primarily on the *biosocial domain* of development (introduced in Lesson 1). The biosocial domain includes all the growth and change that occurs in a person's body as well as the genetic, nutritional, and health factors that affect that growth and change. But keep in mind, although the division of human development into three domains makes it easier to study, development is a holistic, interactive process—changes in one domain often produce changes in another. Development reflects an interaction between all three domains.

- This lesson will also return to *epigenetic systems* (introduced in Lesson 1). Recall that this perspective emphasizes the interaction between genes and the environment in directing and shaping a person's development. The *nature-nurture controversy* (pages 59–61) may lead us to debate how much any given trait is result of genes and how much is the result of experience. But, experts agree that every aspect of our development is a product of both nature and nurture, not one or the other.

Learning Objectives

Use this information to guide your reading, viewing, thinking, and studying. After successfully completing this lesson, you should be able to:

1. Define gamete, describe conception, and discuss early development of the zygote.

2. Define gene, chromosome, and allele, describe how genetic instructions are transmitted from parents to their children, and explain how sex is determined.

3. Discuss the reasons for both genetic continuity and diversity, and distinguish between monozygotic and dizygotic twins.

4. Define genetic code, describe the Human Genome Project, and discuss the ethical considerations and social consequences of using our growing knowledge of genetics.

5. Differentiate genotype from phenotype, and explain the polygenic and multifactorial nature of human traits.

6. Explain the additive and nonadditive patterns of gene interaction, including the dominant-recessive pattern, and give examples of some traits that result from each type of interaction.

7. Discuss X-linked genes in terms of genotype and phenotype, and explain the concept of genetic imprinting.

8. Explain how scientists attempt to distinguish the effects of genes (nature) and environment (nurture) on human development.

9. Identify some environmental variables that can affect a person's phenotype, and describe how a particular trait—such as shyness (inhibition) or alcoholism—might be affected.

10. Describe some of the most common chromosomal abnormalities and genetic disorders, and explain the prenatal tests available to detect them.

11. Define genetic counseling, identify the four types of individuals/couples for whom experts recommend such counseling, and discuss some of the dilemmas and ethical questions that can result.

📖 **Read Chapter 3, "Heredity and Environment," pages 65–101.**

📹 **View the video for Lesson 3, "Nature and Nurture: The Dance of Life."**

        Segment 1: *The Beginning of Development*

        Segment 2: *The Twin Perspective*

        Segment 3: *From Genotype to Phenotype*

        Segment 4: *Genetic and Chromosomal Abnormalities*

Summary

Conception occurs when the male **gamete** (or sperm) penetrates the membrane of the female gamete (the ovum); the sperm and egg then fuse, and their genetic material combines in the one-celled **zygote**. Within hours, the zygote initiates human development through the processes of duplication and division. Each body cell created from these processes carries an exact copy of the zygote's genetic instructions.

Genes, the basic units of heredity, are discrete segments of a **chromosome**, and each chromosome is one molecule of **DNA (deoxyribonucleic acid)**. Every human body cell, except the sperm and ovum, has 23 pairs of chromosomes (one chromosome in each pair from each parent). In contrast, the sperm and ovum contain only 23 single chromosomes each. The **twenty-third pair** of chromosomes, which determines sex, is designated **XY** in the male and **XX** in the female. The critical factor in the determination of the zygote's sex is which sperm reaches the ovum first, a Y sperm, creating a boy, or an X sperm, creating a girl.

Approximately once in every 270 pregnancies a single zygote splits into two separate identical cells that develop into genetically identical, or **monozygotic twins**, who have the potential for developing the same physical appearance and psychological characteristics, and the same vulnerability to specific diseases. Fraternal or **dizygotic twins** occur about once in every sixty births. Dizygotic twins begin life as two separate zygotes and share no more genes than any other siblings (about 50 percent). The number of multiple births has doubled in many nations because of the increased use of fertility drugs.

Most human traits are **polygenic**—that is, affected by many genes—and **multifactorial**—that is, influenced by many factors, including factors in the environment. **Genotype** refers to the sum total of all the genes a person inherits. **Phenotype** refers to the sum total of all the genes that are actually expressed. Thus, people may carry genes that are not expressed.

The various genes underlying height and skin color, for example, interact in an **additive** pattern: the phenotype in question reflects the sum of all the genes involved. Less commonly, genes interact in a nonadditive fashion. Genes that have a controlling influence over weaker, **recessive genes** are called **dominant genes**. Hundreds of physical characteristics follow this dominant-recessive pattern (a nonadditive pattern). Note that recessive genes are not always completely suppressed by their dominant gene counterparts, an outcome called incomplete dominance.

Behavioral genetics is the study of the genetic origins of psychological characteristics. Research in this field has revealed that most behavioral traits are affected by the interaction of large numbers of genes with environmental factors. When social scientists discuss the effects of the environment on the individual, they are referring to everything that can interact with the person's genetic inheritance at every point of life, from the first prenatal days to the last breath. Environment, broadly defined, affects every human characteristic.

Scientists use twin research to help distinguish between genetic and environmental influences. For example, for any given characteristic, if monozygotic twins are much more alike than dizygotic twins, it seems likely that genes play a significant role in the appearance of that trait. Another approach is to compare adopted children with both their biological and adoptive parents. Adopted children, however, are often placed in families that are similar to their birth families; thus, shared culture rather than shared genes may account for similarities. The best way to separate the effects of genes and environment is to study identical twins who have been separated at birth and raised in different families.

An estimated half of all zygotes have too few or too many chromosomes. Most are lost through miscarriage, also called **spontaneous abortion**. Once in every 200 births, however, a baby is born with a chromosomal abnormality that leads to a recognizable syndrome.

Although most known genetic disorders are dominant, recessive and multifactorial disorders claim many more victims. Among the more common recessive genetic disorders are cystic fibrosis, thalassemia, and sickle-cell anemia. For most of human history, couples at risk for having a child with a genetic problem did not know it. **Genetic counseling** and prenatal testing is a means by which couples can learn more about their genes and make informed decisions about childbearing.

Genetic counseling is strongly recommended for individuals who have a parent, sibling, or child with a genetic abnormality or disorder; couples who have a history of spontaneous abortion, stillbirth, or infertility; couples who are from the same ethnic subgroup, especially if this group is small or if they are relatives; and women over age 34. Couples who have a high probability of producing a baby with a serious genetic condition have several alternatives—from avoiding pregnancy to adoption to considering abortion. In cases where the consequences of a disease are variable, the decision making is often more difficult.

📖　　**Review all reading assignments for this lesson.**

💻　　**As assigned by your instructor, complete the optional online component for this lesson.**

Key Terms

Using your own words, write a brief definition or explanation of each of the following terms on a separate piece of paper.

1. gamete
2. zygote
3. gene
4. chromosome
5. genetic code
6. twenty-third pair
7. monozygotic twins (identical)
8. dizygotic twins (fraternal)
9. polygenic
10. multifactorial
11. genotype
12. phenotype
13. carrier
14. additive gene
15. X-linked
16. genetic imprinting
17. fragile-X syndrome
18. genetic counseling
19. heredity
20. environment
21. amniocentesis
22. gene therapy
23. deoxyribonucleic acid (DNA)
24. Human Genome Project
25. allele
26. XX
27. XY
28. dominant gene
29. recessive gene
30. behavioral genetics
31. molecular genetics
32. spontaneous abortion

Practice Questions I

Multiple-Choice Questions

1. When a sperm and an ovum merge, a one-celled _____ is formed.
   a. zygote
   b. reproductive cell
   c. gamete
   d. monozygote

2. Genes are discrete segments that provide the biochemical instructions that each cell needs to become
   a. a zygote.
   b. a chromosome.
   c. a specific part of a functioning human body.
   d. deoxyribonucleic acid.

3. In the male, the twenty-third pair of chromosomes is designated _____; in the female, this pair is designated _____.
   a. XX; XY
   b. XY; XX
   c. XO; XXY
   d. XXY; XO

4. Since the twenty-third pair of chromosomes in females is XX, each ovum carries an
   a. XX zygote.
   b. X zygote.
   c. XY zygote.
   d. X chromosome.

5. When a zygote splits, the two identical, independent clusters that develop become
   a. dizygotic twins.
   b. monozygotic twins.
   c. fraternal twins.
   d. trizygotic twins.

6. In scientific research, the best way to separate the effects of genes and the environment is to study
   a. dizygotic twins.
   b. adopted children and their biological parents.
   c. adopted children and their adoptive parents.
   d. monozygotic twins raised in different environments.

7. Most of the known genetic disorders are
   a. dominant.
   b. recessive.
   c. seriously disabling.
   d. sex-linked.

8. When we say that a characteristic is multifactorial, we mean that
   a. many genes are involved.
   b. many chromosomes are involved.
   c. many genetic and environmental factors are involved.
   d. the characteristic is polygenic.

9. Genes are segments of molecules of
   a. genotype.
   b. deoxyribonucleic acid (DNA).
   c. karyotype.
   d. phenotype.

10. The potential for genetic diversity in humans is so great because
    a. there are approximately 8 million possible combinations of chromosomes.
    b. when the sperm and ovum unite, genetic combinations not present in either parent can be formed.
    c. just before a chromosome pair divides during the formation of gametes, genes cross over, producing recombinations.
    d. of all the above reasons.

11. A chromosomal abnormality that affects males only involves a(n)
    a. XO chromosomal pattern.
    b. XXX chromosomal pattern.
    c. YY chromosomal pattern.
    d. XXY chromosomal pattern.

12. Polygenic complexity is most apparent in _____ characteristics.
    a. physical
    b. psychological
    c. recessive gene
    d. dominant gene

13. Babies born with trisomy-21 (Down syndrome) are often
    a. born to older parents.
    b. unusually aggressive.
    c. abnormally tall by adolescence.
    d. blind.

14. To say that a trait is polygenic means that
    a. many genes make it more likely that the individual will inherit the trait.
    b. several genes must be present in order for the individual to inherit the trait.
    c. the trait is multifactorial.
    d. most people carry genes for the trait.

15. Some genetic diseases are recessive, so the child cannot inherit the condition unless both parents

    a. have Kleinfelter syndrome.

    b. carry the same recessive gene.

    c. have XO chromosomes.

    d. have the disease.

Matching Items

Match each definition or description with its corresponding term.

Terms

16. _____ gametes	23. _____ fragile-X syndrome
17. _____ chromosome	24. _____ carrier
18. _____ genotype	25. _____ zygote
19. _____ phenotype	26. _____ allele
20. _____ monozygotic twins	27. _____ XX
21. _____ dizygotic twins	28. _____ XY
22. _____ additive gene	

Definitions or Descriptions

    a. chromosome pair inherited by genetic females

    b. identical twins

    c. sperm and ovum

    d. the first cell of the developing person

    e. a person who has a recessive gene in his or her genotype that is not expressed in the phenotype

    f. fraternal twins

    g. a pattern in which each gene in question makes an active contribution to the final outcome

    h. a DNA molecule

    i. the behavioral or physical expression of genetic potential

    j. a chromosomal abnormality

    k. alternate versions of a gene

    l. chromosome pair inherited by genetic males

    m. a person's entire genetic inheritance

Practice Questions II

Multiple-Choice Questions

1. Which of the following provides the best broad description of the relationship between heredity and environment in determining height?

    a. Heredity is the primary influence, with environment affecting development only in severe situations.

    b. Heredity and environment contribute equally to development.

    c. Environment is the major influence on physical characteristics.

    d. Heredity directs the individual's potential and environment determines whether and to what degree the individual reaches that potential.

2. Research studies of monozygotic twins who were raised apart suggest that

    a. virtually every human trait is affected by both genes and environment.

    b. only a few psychological traits, such as emotional reactivity, are affected by genes.

    c. most traits are determined by environmental influences.

    d. most traits are determined by genes.

3. Males with fragile-X syndrome are

    a. feminine in appearance.

    b. less severely affected than females.

    c. frequently retarded intellectually.

    d. unusually tall and aggressive.

4. Disorders that are _____ are most likely to pass undetected from generation to generation.

    a. dominant

    b. dominant and polygenic

    c. recessive

    d. recessive and multifactorial

5. The incidences of sickle-cell anemia, phenylketonuria, thalassemia, and Tay-Sachs disease indicate that

    a. these disorders are more common today than 50 years ago.

    b. these disorders are less common today than 50 years ago.

    c. certain genetic disorders are more common in certain ethnic groups.

    d. both a and c are true.

6. Dizygotic twins result when

    a. a single egg is fertilized by a sperm and then splits.

    b. a single egg is fertilized by two different sperm.

    c. two eggs are fertilized by two different sperm.

    d. either a single egg is fertilized by one sperm or two eggs are fertilized by two different sperm.

7. Molecules of DNA that in humans are organized into twenty-three complementary pairs are called

   a. zygotes.
   b. genes.
   c. chromosomes.
   d. ova.

8. Shortly after the zygote is formed, it begins the processes of duplication and division. Each resulting new cell has

   a. the same number of chromosomes as was contained in the zygote.
   b. half the number of chromosomes as was contained in the zygote.
   c. twice, then four times, then eight times the number of chromosomes as was contained in the zygote.
   d. half the number of chromosomes except those that determine sex.

9. If an ovum is fertilized by a sperm bearing a Y chromosome

   a. a female will develop.
   b. cell division will not result.
   c. a male will develop.
   d. spontaneous abortion will likely occur.

10. When the male cells in the testes and the female cells in the ovaries divide to produce gametes, the process differs from that in the production of all other cells. As a result of the different process, the gametes have

    a. one rather than both members of each chromosome pair.
    b. twenty-three chromosome pairs.
    c. X but not Y chromosomes.
    d. chromosomes from both parents.

11. Most human traits are

    a. polygenic.
    b. multifactorial.
    c. determined by dominant-recessive patterns.
    d. both a and b.

12. Genotype is to phenotype as _____ is to _____.

    a. genetic potential; physical expression
    b. physical expression; genetic potential
    c. sperm; ovum
    d. gamete; zygote

13. The genes that influence height and skin color interact according to the _____ pattern.

    a. dominant-recessive
    b. X-linked
    c. additive
    d. nonadditive

14. X-linked recessive genes explain why some traits seem to be passed from
    a. father to son.
    b. father to daughter.
    c. mother to daughter.
    d. mother to son.

15. According to the textbook, the effects of environment on phenotype include
    a. direct effects only, such as nutrition, climate, and medical care.
    b. indirect effects only, such as the individual's broad economic, political, and cultural context.
    c. irreversible effects, such as those resulting from brain injury.
    d. everything that can interact with the person's genetic inheritance at every point of life.

True or False Items
Write T (for true) or F (for false) on the line in front of each statement.

16. _____ Most human characteristics are multifactorial, caused by the interaction of genetic and environmental factors.

17. _____ Less than 10 percent of all zygotes have harmful genes or an abnormal chromosomal makeup.

18. _____ Research suggests that susceptibility to alcoholism is at least partly the result of genetic inheritance.

19. _____ The human reproductive cells (ova and sperm) are called gametes.

20. _____ Only a very few human traits are polygenic.

21. _____ The zygote contains all the biologically inherited information—the genes and chromosomes—that a person will have during his or her life.

22. _____ A couple should probably seek genetic counseling if several earlier pregnancies ended in spontaneous abortion.

23. _____ Many genetic conditions are recessive; thus, a child will have the condition even if only the mother carries the gene.

24. _____ Two people who have the same phenotype may have a different genotype for a trait such as eye color.

25. _____ When cells divide to produce reproductive cells (gametes), each sperm or ovum receives only twenty-three chromosomes, half as many as the original cell.

Applying Your Knowledge

1. The international effort to map the complete human genetic code is complicated by the fact that
   a. the total number of human genes is far greater than the 100,000 previously estimated.
   b. some genes appear in several different versions.
   c. genes are made up of thousands of DNA particles called alleles.
   d. all of the above have complicated the effort to map the genetic code.

Lesson 3/The Beginnings: Heredity and Environment   **49**

2. Before their first child was born, Jack and Diane decided that they should be karyotyped, which means that

    a. their chromosomes were photographed.

    b. a genetic counselor filled out a complete history of genetic diseases in their families.

    c. they each took a fertility test.

    d. they selected the sex of their child.

3. Which of the following is an inherited abnormality that quite possibly could develop into a recognizable syndrome?

    a. Just before dividing to form a sperm or ovum, corresponding gene segments of a chromosome pair break off and are exchanged.

    b. Just before conception, a chromosome pair splits imprecisely, resulting in a mosaic of cells.

    c. A person inherits an X chromosome in which part of the chromosome is attached to the rest of it by a very slim string of molecules.

    d. A person inherits a recessive gene on his Y chromosome.

4. Some men are color-blind because they inherit a particular recessive gene from their mother. That recessive gene is carried on the

    a. X chromosome.

    b. XX chromosome pair.

    c. Y chromosome.

    d. X or Y chromosome.

5. If your mother is much taller than your father, it is most likely that your height will be

    a. about the same as your mother's, because the X chromosome determines height.

    b. about the same as your father's, because the Y chromosome determines height.

    c. somewhere between your mother's and father's heights because of genetic imprinting.

    d. greater than both your mother's and father's because of your grandfather's dominant gene.

6. If a dizygotic twin develops schizophrenia, the likelihood of the other twin experiencing serious mental illness is much lower than is the case with monozygotic twins. This suggests that

    a. schizophrenia is caused by genes.

    b. schizophrenia is influenced by genes.

    c. environment is unimportant in the development of schizophrenia.

    d. monozygotic twins are especially vulnerable to schizophrenia.

7. A person's skin turns yellow-orange as a result of a carrot-juice diet regimen. This is an example of

    a. an environmental influence.

    b. an alteration in genotype.

    c. polygenic inheritance.

    d. incomplete dominance.

8. The personality trait of inhibition (shyness) seems to be partly genetic. A child who inherits the genes for shyness will be shy

   a. under most circumstances.

   b. only if shyness is the dominant gene.

   c. if the environment does not encourage greater sociability.

   d. if he or she is raised by biological rather than adoptive parents.

9. If a man carries the recessive gene for Tay-Sachs disease and his wife does not, the chances of their having a child with Tay-Sachs disease is

   a. one in four.

   b. fifty-fifty.

   c. zero.

   d. dependent upon the wife's ethnic background.

10. One of the best ways to distinguish the relative influence of genetic and environmental factors on behavior is to compare children who have

    a. the same genes and environments.

    b. different genes and environments.

    c. similar genes and environments.

    d. the same genes but different environments.

11. When identical twins have been reared apart, researchers have generally found

    a. strong behavioral and psychological similarities.

    b. strong behavioral, but not necessarily psychological, similarities.

    c. striking behavioral and psychological differences.

    d. that it is impossible to predict how such twins will develop.

12. Susan and Bryan, who both have a history of alcoholism in their families, are concerned that the child they hope to have will inherit a genetic predisposition to alcoholism. Based on information presented in the textbook, what advice should you offer them?

    a. "Stop worrying, alcoholism is only weakly genetic."

    b. "It is almost certain that your child will become alcoholic."

    c. "Social influences, such as the family and peer environment, play a critical role in determining whether alcoholism is expressed."

    d. "Wait to have children until you are both middle aged, in order to see if the two of you become alcoholic."

13. Sixteen-year-old Karson experiences some mental slowness and hearing and heart problems, yet he is able to care for himself and is unusually sweet-tempered. Karson probably

    a. is mentally retarded.

    b. has Alzheimer's disease.

    c. has Kleinfelter syndrome.

    d. has Down syndrome.

14. Genetically, Billy's potential height is 6' 0". Because he did not receive a balanced diet, however, he grew to only 5' 9". Billy's actual height is an example of a

   a. recessive gene.

   b. dominant gene.

   c. genotype.

   d. phenotype.

15. Ann inherited a gene from her mother that, regardless of her father's contribution to her genotype, will be expressed in her phenotype. Evidently, the gene Ann received from her mother is a(n) _____ gene.

   a. polygenic

   b. recessive

   c. dominant

   d. X-linked

Answer Key

Key Terms

1. Gametes are the human reproductive cells, sperm for males and ova for females. (p. 69; objective 1)

2. The zygote (a term derived from the Greek word for "joint") is the fertilized egg, that is, the one-celled organism formed during conception by the fusion of sperm and ovum. (p. 69; video program, segment 2; objective 1)

3. Genes are discrete segments of a chromosome that are the basic units of heredity. (p. 69; video lesson, segment 1; objective 2)

4. Chromosomes are molecules of DNA that contain the genes organized in precise sequences. (p. 69; video lesson, segment 1; objective 2)

5. The precise nature of a gene's instructions, called the genetic code, is determined by the overall sequence of the four chemical bases along a segment of DNA. (p. 70; objective 4)

6. The twenty-third pair of chromosomes determines the individual's sex, among other things. (p. 72; objective 2)

7. Monozygotic, or identical, twins develop from one zygote that splits in two, producing two genetically identical zygotes. (p. 75; video lesson, segment 2; objective 3)

   Memory aid: Mono means "one"; monozygotic twins develop from one fertilized ovum.

8. Dizygotic, or fraternal, twins develop from two separate ova fertilized by different sperm at roughly the same time, and therefore are no more genetically similar than ordinary siblings. (p. 76; video lesson, segment 2; objective 3)

   Memory aid: A fraternity is a group of two (di) or more nonidentical individuals.

9. Most human traits, especially psychological traits, are polygenic traits; that is, they are affected by many genes. (p. 78; objective 5)

10. Most human traits are also multifactorial traits—that is, influenced by many factors, including genetic and environmental factors. (p. 78; objective 5)

    Memory aid: The roots of the words polygenic and multifactorial give their meaning: poly means "many" and genic means "of the genes"; multi means "several" and factorial obviously refers to factors.

11. The sum total of all the genes a person inherits—his or her genetic potential—is called the genotype. (p. 78; video lesson, segment 3; objective 5)

12. The actual physical or behavioral expression of a genotype, the result of the interaction of the genes with each other and with the environment, is called the phenotype. (p. 78; video lesson, segment 3; objective 5)

13. A person who has a recessive gene in his or her genotype that is not expressed in his or her phenotype is called a carrier of that gene. (p. 78; objective 5)

14. In the additive pattern of genetic interaction, the phenotype reflects the contributions of all the genes involved. The genes affecting height, for example, interact in this fashion. (p. 79; objective 6)

15. X-linked genes are genes that are located only on the X chromosome. Since males have only one X chromosome, they are more likely than females to have the characteristics determined by these genes in their phenotype. (p. 79; objective 7)

16. Genetic imprinting is the tendency of certain genes to be expressed differently when they are inherited from the mother than when they are inherited from the father. (p. 80; objective 7)

17. The fragile-X syndrome is a single-gene disorder in which part of the X chromosome is attached by such a thin string of molecules that it seems about to break off. Although the characteristics associated with this syndrome are quite varied, some mental deficiency is relatively common. (p. 92; objective 10)

18. Genetic counseling involves a variety of tests through which couples can learn more about their genes, and can thus make informed decisions about their childbearing and child-rearing future. (p. 96; video program, segment 4; objective 11)

19. Heredity refers to the transmission of traits and predispositions from parent to child through the genes. (video lesson, introduction; objective 2)

20. When social scientists discuss the effects of the environment on genes, they are referring to everything—from the impact of the immediate cell environment on the genes to the multitude of factors in the outside world, such as nutrition, climate, family interactions, and the cultural context—that can interact with the person's genetic inheritance at every point of life. (p. 84; video lesson, segment 1; objective 9)

21. Amniocentesis is a prenatal diagnostic procedure in which a sample of amniotic fluid is withdrawn by syringe and tested to determine if the developing fetus is healthy. (video lesson, segment 4; objective 10)

22. Gene therapy involves the altering of an organism's genetic instructions through the insertion and addition of normal genes by way of a blood transfusion, bone marrow transplant, or direct insertion into a cluster of cells. (video lesson, segment 4; objective 10)

23. DNA (deoxyribonucleic acid) is a nucleic acid molecule that determines our inherited characteristics by encoding the information needed to synthesize proteins and regulate all aspects of cellular metabolism. (video lesson, segment 1; objective 2)

24. Human Genome Project is an international effort to map the complete genetic code. (p. 70; objective 4)

25. A normal alteration is called an allele, one of several possible letter sequences that some genes have. Note that everyone has one allele or another of those variable genes. (p. 71; objective 2)

26. XX is a twenty-third pair that consists of two X-shaped chromosomes, one from the mother and one from the father. (p. 72; objective 2)

27. XY is a twenty-third pair that consists of one X-shaped chromosome from the mother and one Y-shaped chromosome from the father. (p. 72; objective 2)

28. The dominant gene is the stronger of an interacting pair of genes. (p. 79; video lesson, segment 3; objective 6)

29. The recessive gene is the weaker of an interacting pair of genes. (p. 79; video lesson, segment 3; objective 6)

30. The study of genetic origins of psychological characteristics, such as personality patterns, psychological disorders, and intellectual abilities, is called behavioral genetics. (p. 81; objective 8)

31. The study of genetics at the molecular level, including the study of the chemical codes that constitute a particular molecule of DNA, is called molecular genetics. (p. 83; objective 8)

32. Spontaneous abortion (also called miscarriage) is the naturally occurring termination of a pregnancy before the fetus is fully developed. (p. 89; objective 10)

Practice Questions I

Multiple-Choice Questions

1. a. is the correct answer. (p. 69; video lesson, segment 2; objective 1)

   b. & c. are incorrect. The reproductive cells (sperm and ova), which are also called gametes, are individual entities.

   d. is incorrect. Monozygote refers to one member of a pair of identical twins.

2. c. is the correct answer. (pp. 69–70; video lesson, segment 1; objective 2)

   a. is incorrect. The zygote is the first cell of the developing person.

   b. is incorrect. Chromosomes are molecules of DNA that carry genes.

   d. is incorrect. DNA molecules contain genetic information.

3. b. is the correct answer. (p. 72; objective 2)

4. d. is the correct answer. When the gametes are formed, one member of each chromosome pair splits off; because in females both are X chromosomes, each ovum must carry an X chromosome. (p. 72; objective 2)

   a., b., & c. are incorrect. The zygote refers to the merged sperm and ovum that is the first new cell of the developing individual.

5. b. is the correct answer. Mono means "one." Thus, monozygotic twins develop from one zygote. (p. 75; video lesson, segment 2; objective 3)

   a. & c. are incorrect. Dizygotic, or fraternal, twins develop from two (di) zygotes.

   d. is incorrect. A trizygotic birth would result in triplets (tri), rather than twins.

6. d. is the correct answer. In this situation, one factor (genetic similarity) is held constant while the other factor (environment) is varied. Therefore, any similarity in traits is strong evidence of genetic inheritance. (p. 83; video lesson, segment 2; objective 8)

7. a. is the correct answer. (p. 93; objective 6)

   c. & d. are incorrect. Most dominant disorders are neither seriously disabling, nor sex-linked.

8. c. is the correct answer. (p. 78; objective 5)

   a., b., & d. are incorrect. Polygenic means "many genes"; multifactorial means "many factors," which are not limited to either genetic or environmental ones.

9. b. is the correct answer. (p. 69; video lesson, segment 1; objective 2)

a. is incorrect. Genotype is a person's genetic potential.

c. is incorrect. A karyotype is a picture of a person's chromosomes.

d. is incorrect. Phenotype is the actual expression of a genotype.

10. d. is the correct answer. (p. 75; video program, segment 1; objective 3)

11. d. is the correct answer. (p. 92; objective 10)

a. & b. are incorrect. These chromosomal abnormalities affect females.

c. is incorrect. There is no such abnormality.

12. b. is the correct answer. (p. 81; objective 5)

c. & d. are incorrect. The textbook does not equate polygenic complexity with either recessive or dominant genes.

13. a. is the correct answer. (p. 93; objective 10)

14. b. is the correct answer. (p. 78; objective 5)

15. b. is the correct answer. (pp. 93, 95; video lesson, segment 4; objectives 6 & 11)

a. & c. are incorrect. These abnormalities involve the sex chromosomes, not genes.

d. is incorrect. In order for an offspring to inherit a recessive condition, the parents need only be carriers of the recessive gene in their genotypes; they need not actually have the disease.

Matching Items

16. c (p. 69; objective 1)

17. h (p. 69; video lesson, segment 1; objective 2)

18. m (p. 78; video lesson, segment 3; objective 5)

19. i (p. 78; video lesson, segment 3; objective 5)

20. b (p. 75; video lesson, segment 2; objective 3)

21. f (p. 76; video lesson, segment 2; objective 3)

22. g (p. 79; objective 6)

23. j (p. 92; objective 10)

24. e (p. 78; objective 5)

25. d (p. 69; video lesson, segment 2; objective 1)

26. k (p. 71; objective 2)

27. a (p. 72; objective 2)

28. l (p. 72; objective 2)

Practice Questions II

Multiple-Choice Questions

1. d. is the correct answer. (p. 82; objective 8)

2. a. is the correct answer. (p. 82; video lesson, segment 2; objective 8)

3. c. is the correct answer. (p. 93; objective 10)

a. is incorrect. Physical appearance is usually normal in this syndrome.

b. is incorrect. Males are more frequently and more severely affected.

d. is incorrect. This is true of the XYY chromosomal abnormality, but not the fragile-X syndrome.

4. d. is the correct answer. (p. 93; objectives 6 & 10)

5. c. is the correct answer. Sickle-cell anemia is more common among African Americans; phenylketonuria, among those of Norwegian and Irish ancestry; thalassemia, among Americans of Greek, Italian, Thai, and East Indian ancestry; and Tay-Sachs, among Jews as well as certain French-Canadians. (pp. 94–95; objective 10)

a. & b. are incorrect. The textbook does not present evidence indicating that the incidence of these disorders has changed.

6. c. is the correct answer. (p. 76; video lesson, segment 2; objective 3)

a. is incorrect. This would result in monozygotic twins.

b. is incorrect. Only one sperm can fertilize an ovum.

d. is incorrect. A single egg fertilized by one sperm would produce a single offspring or monozygotic twins.

7. c. is the correct answer. (p. 69; video lesson, segment 1; objective 2)

a. is incorrect. Zygotes are fertilized ova.

b. is incorrect. Genes are the smaller units of heredity that are organized into sequences on chromosomes.

d. is incorrect. Ova are female reproductive cells.

8. a. is the correct answer. (p. 69; video lesson, segment 1; objective 1)

9. c. is the correct answer. The ovum will contain an X chromosome, and with the sperm's Y chromosome, will produce the male XY pattern. (p. 72; objective 2)

a. is incorrect. Only if the ovum is fertilized by an X chromosome from the sperm will a female develop.

b. is incorrect. Cell division will occur regardless of whether the sperm contributes an X or a Y chromosome.

d. Spontaneous abortions are likely to occur when there are chromosomal or genetic abnormalities; the situation described is perfectly normal.

10. a. is the correct answer. (p. 72; objectives 1 & 2)

b. & d. are incorrect. These are true of all body cells except the gametes.

c. is incorrect. Gametes have either X or Y chromosomes.

11. d. is the correct answer. (p. 78; objective 5)

12. a. is the correct answer. Genotype refers to the sum total of all the genes a person inherits; phenotype refers to the actual expression of the individual's characteristics. (p. 78; video lesson, segment 3; objective 5)

13. c. is the correct answer. (p. 79; objective 6)

14. d. is the correct answer. X-linked genes are located only on the X chromosome. Because males inherit only one X chromosome, they are more likely than females to have these characteristics in their phenotype. (pp. 79–80; objective 7)

15. d. is the correct answer. (pp. 82–88; objectives 8 & 9)

True or False Items

16. T (p. 78; objective 5)

17. F An estimated half of all zygotes have an odd number of chromosomes. (p. 89; objective 10)

18. T (p. 86; objective 9)

19. T (p. 69; objective 1)

20. F Most traits are polygenic. (p. 78; objective 5)

21. T (p. 69; objective 1)

22. T (p. 96; video lesson, segment 4; objective 11)

23. F   A trait from a recessive gene will be part of the phenotype only when the person has two recessive genes for that trait. (pp. 79, 98; video lesson, segment 3; objectives 6 & 10)

24. T   (pp. 78–79; video lesson, segment 3; objectives 5 & 6)

25. T   (p. 72; objective 1)

Applying Your Knowledge

1. b. is the correct answer. (p. 71; objective 4)

   a. is incorrect. In fact, the total number of human genes is probably less than 100,000.

   c. is incorrect. Alleles are alternate versions of a specific gene.

2. a. is the correct answer. (p. 72; objectives 3 & 11)

3. c. is the correct answer. This describes the fragile-X syndrome. (p. 92; objective 10)

   a. is incorrect. This phenomenon, which is called crossing over, merely contributes to genetic diversity.

   b. is incorrect. This is merely an example of a particular nonadditive gene interaction pattern.

4. a. is the correct answer. (pp. 79–80; objective 7)

   b. is incorrect. The male genotype is XY, not XX.

   c. & d. are incorrect. The mother contributes only an X chromosome.

5. c. is the correct answer. (p. 79; objective 6)

   a., c., & d. are incorrect. It is unlikely that these factors account for height differences from one generation to the next.

6. b. is the correct answer. Since monozygotic twins are genetically identical, while dizygotic twins share only 50 percent of their genes, greater similarity of traits between monozygotic twins suggests that genes are an important influence. (p. 86; video lesson, segment 2; objective 9)

   a. & c. are incorrect. Even though schizophrenia has a strong genetic component, it is not the case that if one twin has schizophrenia the other also automatically does. Therefore, the environment, too, is an important influence.

   d. is incorrect. This does not necessarily follow.

7. a. is the correct answer. (p. 82; objective 8)

   b. is incorrect. Genotype is a person's genetic potential, established at conception.

   c. is incorrect. Polygenic inheritance refers to the influence of many genes on a particular trait.

   d. is incorrect. Incomplete dominance refers to the phenotype being influenced primarily, but not exclusively, by the dominant gene.

8. c. is the correct answer. (pp. 84–85; objective 9)

   a. & b. are incorrect. Research on adopted children shows that shyness is affected by both genetic inheritance and the social environment. Therefore, if a child's environment promotes socializing outside the immediate family, a genetically shy child might grow up much less timid socially than he or she would have been with less outgoing parents.

   d. is incorrect. Either biological or adoptive parents are capable of nurturing, or not nurturing, shyness in their children.

9. c. is the correct answer. Tay-Sachs is a recessive gene disorder; therefore, in order for a child to inherit this disease, he or she must receive the recessive gene from both parents. (pp. 93, 95; objective 10)

10. d. is the correct answer. To separate the influences of genes and environment, one of the two must be held constant. (p. 83; video lesson, segment 2; objective 8)

    a., b., & c. are incorrect. These situations would not allow a researcher to separate the contributions of heredity and environment.

11. a. is the correct answer. (p. 83; objective 8)

12. c. is the correct answer. (pp. 86–87; objective 9)

    a. is incorrect. Some people's inherited biochemistry makes them highly susceptible to alcoholism.

    b. is incorrect. Despite a strong genetic influence, the environment plays a critical role in the expression of alcoholism.

    d. is incorrect. Not only is this advice unreasonable, but it might increase the likelihood of chromosomal abnormalities in the parents' sperm and ova.

13. d. is the correct answer. (pp. 91–92; objective 10)

14. d. is the correct answer. (p. 78; objective 5)

    a. & b. are incorrect. Genes are discrete segments of a chromosome.

    c. is incorrect. Genotype refers to genetic potential.

15. c. is the correct answer. (pp. 78–79; objective 6)

    a. is incorrect. There is no such thing as a "polygenic gene." Polygenic means "many genes."

    b. is incorrect. A recessive gene paired with a dominant gene will not be expressed in the phenotype.

    d. is incorrect. X-linked genes may be dominant or recessive.

Lesson Review

Lesson 3

The Beginnings
Heredity and Environment

Please Note: Use this matrix to guide your study and achieve the learning objectives of this lesson. It will also help you to view the video, which defines and demonstrates important concepts and skills as they relate to everyday life.

Learning Objective	Textbook	Telecourse Student Guide	Video Lesson
1. Define gamete, describe conception, and discuss early development of the zygote.	pp. 67–75	Key Terms: 1, 2; Practice Questions I: 1, 16, 25; Practice Questions II: 8, 10, 19, 21, 25.	Segment 1: *The Beginning of Development,* Segment 2: *The Twin Perspective*
2. Define gene and chromosome, describe how genetic instructions are transmitted from parents to their children, and explain how sex is determined."	pp. 67–75	Key Terms: 3, 4, 6, 19, 23, 25, 26, 27; Practice Questions I: 2, 3, 4, 9, 17, 26, 27, 28; Practice Questions II: 7, 9, 10.	Introduction, Segment 2: *The Twin Perspective*
3. Discuss the reasons for both genetic continuity and diversity, and distinguish between monozygotic and dizygotic twins.	pp. 67–75	Key Terms: 7, 8; Practice Questions I: 5, 10, 20, 21; Practice Questions II: 6; Applying Your Knowledge: 2.	Segment 2: *The Twin Perspective*
4. Define genetic code, describe the Human Genome Project, and discuss the ethical considerations and social consequences of using our growing knowledge of genetics.	pp. 75–85	Key Terms: 5, 24; Applying Your Knowledge: 1.	
5. Differentiate genotype from phenotype, and explain the polygenic and multifactorial nature of human traits.	pp. 75–85	Key Terms: 9, 10, 11, 12, 13; Practice Questions I: 8, 12, 14, 18, 19, 24; Practice Questions II: 11, 12, 16, 20, 24; Applying Your Knowledge: 14.	Segment 3: *From Genotype to Phenotype*

Learning Objective	Textbook	Telecourse Student Guide	Video Lesson
6. Explain the additive and nonadditive patterns of gene interaction, including the dominant-recessive pattern, and give examples of some traits that result from each type of interaction.	pp. 75–85	Key Terms: 14, 28, 29; Practice Questions I: 7, 15, 22; Practice Questions II: 4, 13, 23, 24; Applying Your Knowledge: 5, 15.	Segment 3: *From Genotype to Phenotype*
7. Discuss X-linked genes in terms of genotype and phenotype, explain the concept of genetic imprinting, and describe the studies of behavioral and molecular genetics.	pp. 116–122	Key Terms: 15, 16; Practice Questions II: 2, 14; Applying Your Knowledge: 4.	Segment 2: *The Twin Perspective*
8. Explain how scientists attempt to distinguish the effects of genes (nature) and environment (nurture) on human development.	pp. 116–122	Key Terms: 30, 31; Practice Questions I: 6; Practice Questions II: 1, 2, 15; Applying Your Knowledge: 7, 10, 11.	Segment 2: *The Twin Perspective*
9. Identify some environmental variables that can affect a person's phenotype, and describe how a particular trait—such as shyness (inhibition) or alcoholism—might be affected.	pp. 85–91	Key Terms: 20; Practice Questions II: 15, 18; Applying Your Knowledge: 6, 8, 12.	
10. Describe some of the most common chromosomal abnormalities and genetic disorders, and explain the prenatal tests available to detect them.	pp. 89, 92–95	Key Terms: 17, 21, 22, 32; Practice Questions I: 11, 13, 23; Practice Questions II: 3, 4, 5, 17, 23; Applying Your Knowledge: 3, 9, 13.	Segment 4: *Genetic and Chromosomal Abnormalities*
11. Define genetic counseling, identify the four types of individuals/couples for whom experts recommend such counseling, and discuss some of the dilemmas and ethical questions that can result.	pp. 89, 92–95	Key Terms: 18; Practice Questions I: 15; Practice Questions II: 22; Applying Your Knowledge: 2.	Segment 4: *Genetic and Chromosomal Abnormalities*

The Wondrous Journey

Lesson 4

The Beginnings:
Prenatal Development and Birth

Preview

Anticipating the birth of a child is one of life's most enriching experiences. As the video for this lesson begins, we meet Sandra and Darrin in the anxious moments just before Sandra gives birth. The personal experiences of this young family throughout Sandra's pregnancy and delivery form the backdrop for the lesson's exploration of prenatal development and birth.

The period of prenatal development is a time of incredibly rapid growth during which the emerging person develops from a single cell into a fully functioning individual. This lesson describes that development, along with some of the problems that can occur—including prenatal exposure to disease, drugs, and other hazards—and the factors that moderate the risks of that exposure.

A person's birth marks the most radical transition of the entire life span. No longer sheltered from the outside world, the newborn becomes a separate human being who begins life almost completely dependent upon its caregivers. This lesson also examines the process of birth, its possible variations and problems, and the **parent–newborn bonding** process.

As you complete this video, recall your experiences with pregnancy or those of someone you know. (You may want to interview that person during your study of this lesson.) What did the mother look and feel like during the early, middle and final stages of this pregnancy? What sort of prenatal care did she receive? What did she do to stay healthy? For example, what did she eat and how did she exercise? Did she smoke, drink alcohol, or take any medications during the pregnancy? Was the baby born close to the "due date"? What was the birthing experience like? Where did the mother have the baby, in what type of facility? Did she have any surgical procedures performed? If so, which ones? Were there any complications during birth? If so, what were they and how were the mother and baby treated? Did the mother and father both get to hold and bond with the baby in the first few hours after birth? Did the mother experience any depression in the days and weeks after birth? If so, how was she treated?

Prior Telecourse Knowledge that Will Be Used in this Lesson
- This lesson begins with the development of the zygote after conception. Remember from Lesson 3 that conception occurs when the male's sperm and female's ovum unite. The resulting cell, called a zygote, then develops through a process of duplication and division.

- This lesson will also return to the epigenetic systems theory introduced in Lesson 1. Recall the basic tenet of this theory is that our development is shaped not only by our genetics or by the environment in which we live, but rather by the interaction between the two. Nature *and* nurture make us who we are. This is just as true for prenatal development (before birth) as it is for postnatal development (after birth).

Learning Objectives

Use this information to guide your reading, viewing, thinking, and studying. After successfully completing this lesson, you should be able to:

1. Describe the significant developments of the germinal period.
2. Describe the significant developments of the embryonic period.
3. Describe the significant developments of the fetal period, noting the importance of the age of viability.
4. Describe the developing senses of the fetus and the various responses to its immediate environment (the womb).
5. Define teratogens, and describe the factors that determine whether a particular teratogen will be harmful.
6. Outline the effects of at least three specific teratogens on the developing embryo or fetus, and describe protective steps that can be taken to moderate the risk of exposure.
7. Distinguish among low-birthweight (LBW), pre-term birth, and small-for-gestational-age (SGA) infants, and identify the causes of low-birthweight, focusing on the relationship of poverty to low birthweight.
8. Describe the normal process of birth, specifying the events of each stage.
9. Describe the test used to assess the newborn's condition at birth.
10. Describe the options available for medical attention during the birthing process, and discuss the pros and cons of medical intervention.
11. Explain the causes of cerebral palsy, and discuss the special needs of high-risk infants.
12. Explain the concept of parent-newborn bonding and the current view of most developmentalists regarding early bonding in humans.

📖 **Read Chapter 4, "Prenatal Development and Birth," pages 103–131.**

📹 **View the video for Lesson 4, "The Wondrous Journey."**

Segment 1: *The First Trimester*

Segment 2: *Risk Reduction*

Segment 3: *The Second Trimester*

Segment 4: *The Third Trimester*

Summary

The first two weeks of prenatal development are called the **germinal period**. Within hours after conception, the one-celled zygote begins the process of cell division and growth as it travels down the fallopian tube. The **embryonic period** begins as the organism begins differentiating into three layers of tissue that will become the various body systems. At the end of the first month, the cardiovascular system is functioning;

the eyes, ears, nose, mouth, and arm and leg buds start to form; and the embryo is about one-fifth of an inch (just 6 millimeters) long. By the end of the second month, the developing organism weighs about 1 gram, is 1 inch long, and has all the basic organs (except the sex organs) and features of a human being. During the third month, the **fetal period** begins, and the sex organs begin to take shape.

The crucial factor in the fetus's attaining the **age of viability**, beginning at about 22 to 24 weeks, is neurological maturation, which is essential to the regulation of the basic body functions of breathing, sucking, and sleeping. By 28 weeks, the typical fetus weighs about 1,300 grams (3 pounds) and has a greater than 50 percent chance of survival outside the womb.

Teratology is a science of **risk analysis**, which attempts to evaluate what factors can make prenatal harm more (or less) likely to occur. Three crucial factors that determine whether a specific teratogen will cause harm, and of what nature, are the timing of exposure, the amount of exposure, and the developing organism's genetic vulnerability to damage from the substance. Although each body structure has its own **critical period** during which it is most susceptible to teratogenic damage, for **behavioral teratogens** that affect the brain and nervous system the entire prenatal period is critical. Teratogens can also include conditions, such as maternal malnutrition and extreme levels of stress. Some **teratogens** have a cumulative effect on the developing individual. For other teratogens, there is a **threshold effect**; that is, the substance is virtually harmless until exposure reaches a certain frequency or dosage. However, the **interaction effect** of teratogens taken together may make them more harmful at lower dosage levels than they would be individually.

A major, preventable health hazard for the fetus is **low birthweight**, defined as birthweight that is less than 2,500 grams (5.5 pounds). Babies that weigh less than 3 pounds (1,500 grams) are classified as **very low birthweight**, while those that weigh less than 2 pounds (1,000 grams) are classified as **extremely low birthweight**. Infants who are born more than three weeks early are called **preterm**. Others, born close to the due date but weighing less than most full-term neonates, are called **small for gestational age (SGA)**.

The normal birth begins at about the 266th day after conception, when the fetus's brain signals the release of hormones that trigger uterine contractions in the mother. Labor usually lasts eight to twelve hours in first births and four to seven hours in subsequent births, but this can vary greatly. The **Apgar scale** is used to assign a score between 0 and 2 to the neonate's heart rate, breathing, muscle tone, color, and reflexes at one minute after birth and again at five minutes. A score of 7 or better indicates the newborn is not in danger; below 7, that the infant needs help in establishing normal breathing; and below 4, that the baby is in critical condition and needs immediate medical attention. Very few newborns score an immediate perfect 10, but most readily adjust to life outside the womb.

The quality of the birth experience depends on many factors, including the mother's preparation for birth, the support provided by others, and the nature and degree of medical intervention. Birth complications are much more likely if a fetus is at risk because of low weight, preterm birth, genetic abnormality, teratogenic exposure, or because the mother is unusually young, old, small, or in poor health. **Cerebral palsy**, for example, which was once thought to be solely caused by birth procedures (such as excessive analgesia or misapplied forceps) is now known to result from a combination of factors, including genetic vulnerability, exposure to teratogens, and **anoxia** (lack of oxygen) during birth.

The popular term **parent-newborn bond** is used to emphasize the tangible as well as intangible attachment between parent and child in the early moments after birth. In many animals, early contact between mother and infant can be crucial to bonding. Most developmentalists now believe that the importance of early contact between a human mother and child has been overly popularized and that the events right after birth are just one episode in a long-term process of bonding and development.

📖 **Review all reading assignments for this lesson.**

💻 **As assigned by your instructor, complete the optional online component for this lesson.**

Key Terms

Using your own words, write a brief definition or explanation of each of the following terms on a separate piece of paper.

1. germinal period
2. embryonic period
3. fetal period
4. implantation
5. neural tube
6. placenta
7. age of viability
8. teratogens
9. behavioral teratogens
10. risk analysis
11. critical period
12. threshold effect
13. interaction effect

14. human immunodeficiency virus (HIV)
15. fetal alcohol syndrome (FAS)
16. low-birthweight (LBW) infant
17 preterm birth
18. small for gestational age (SGA)
19. Apgar scale
20. cesarean section
21. cerebral palsy
22. anoxia
23. parent-newborn bond
24. postpartum depression
25. amniotic fluid
26. spina bifida

Practice Questions I

Multiple-Choice Questions

1. The first two weeks after conception are called the
   a. embryonic period.
   b. placental period.
   c. fetal period.
   d. germinal period.

2. Implantation occurs during the
   a. embryonic period.
   b. germinal period.
   c. ovarian period.
   d. fetal period.

3. To say that a teratogen has a "threshold effect" means that it is
   a. virtually harmless until exposure reaches a certain level.
   b. harmful only to low-birthweight infants.
   c. harmful to certain developing organs during periods when these organs are developing most rapidly.
   d. harmful only if the pregnant woman's weight does not increase by a certain minimum amount during her pregnancy.

4. By the eighth week after conception, the embryo has almost all the basic organs EXCEPT the
   a. skeleton.
   b. elbows and knees.
   c. sex organs.
   d. fingers and toes.

5. The most critical factor in attaining the age of viability is development of the
   a. placenta.
   b. eyes.
   c. brain.
   d. skeleton.

6. Neural tube defects, such as spina bifida, have been linked to a deficiency of _____ in an expectant mother's diet.
   a. vitamin A
   b. zinc
   c. guanine
   d. folic acid

7. An embryo begins to develop male sex organs if _____, and female sex organs if _____.
   a. genes on the Y chromosome send a biochemical signal; no signal is sent from an X chromosome.
   b. genes on the Y chromosome send a biochemical signal; genes on the X chromosome send a signal.
   c. genes on the X chromosome send a biochemical signal; no signal is sent from an X chromosome.
   d. genes on the X chromosome send a biochemical signal; genes on the Y chromosome send a signal.

8. A teratogen
   a. cannot cross the placenta during the embryonic period.
   b. is usually inherited from the mother.
   c. can be counteracted by good nutrition most of the time.
   d. may be a virus, drug, chemical, radiation, or environmental pollutants.

9. Among the characteristics of babies born with fetal alcohol syndrome are
   a. slowed physical growth and behavior problems.
   b. addiction to alcohol and methadone.
   c. deformed arms and legs.
   d. blindness.

10. The birth process begins
    a. when the fetus moves into the right position.
    b. when the uterus begins to contract at regular intervals to push the fetus out.
    c. about eight hours (in the case of firstborns) after the uterus begins to contract at regular intervals.
    d. when the baby's head appears at the opening of the vagina.

11. The Apgar scale is administered
    a. only if the newborn is in obvious distress.
    b. once, just after birth.
    c. usually twice, 1 minute and 5 minutes after birth.
    d. every two minutes for several hours.

12. Most newborns weigh about
    a. 5 pounds.
    b. 6 pounds.
    c. 7.5 pounds.
    d. 8.5 pounds.

13. Low-birthweight babies born near the due date but weighing substantially less than they should
    a. are classified as preterm.
    b. are called small for gestational age.
    c. usually have no sex organs.
    d. show many signs of immaturity.

14. Approximately 1 out of every 4 low-birthweight births in the United States is caused by maternal use of
    a. alcohol.
    b. tobacco.
    c. crack cocaine.
    d. household chemicals.

15. The idea of a parent-newborn bond in humans arose from
    a. observations in the delivery room.
    b. data on adopted infants.
    c. animal studies.
    d. studies of disturbed mother-newborn pairs.

Matching Items

Match each definition or description with its corresponding term.

Terms

16. _____ embryonic period

17. _____ fetal period

18. _____ placenta

19. _____ preterm

20. _____ teratogens

21. _____ HIV

22. _____ critical period

23. _____ neural tube

24. _____ fetal alcohol syndrome

25. _____ germinal period

Definitions or Descriptions

a. term for the period during which a developing baby's body parts are most susceptible to damage

b. the scientific study of birth defects

c. the age when viability is attained

d. the precursor of the central nervous system

e. characterized by abnormal facial characteristics, slowed growth, behavior problems, and mental retardation

f. a virus that gradually overwhelms the body's immune responses

g. the life-giving organ that nourishes the embryo and fetus

h. when implantation occurs

i. the prenatal period when all major body structures begin to form

j. a baby born three or more weeks early

Practice Questions II

Multiple-Choice Questions

1. During which period does cocaine use affect the fetus and/or newborn?

   a. throughout pregnancy
   b. before birth
   c. after birth
   d. during all of the above periods

2. In order, the correct sequence of prenatal stages of development is

   a. embryonic; germinal; fetal.
   b. germinal; fetal; embryonic.
   c. germinal; embryonic; fetal.
   d. ovarian; fetal; embryonic.

3. Tetracycline, retinoic acid, and most hormones

   a. can be harmful to the human fetus.
   b. have been proven safe for pregnant women after the embryonic period.
   c. will prevent spontaneous abortions.
   d. are safe when used before the fetal period.

4. One of the first teratogens to be recognized, possibly causing deafness, blindness, and brain damage if the fetus is exposed early during the pregnancy, is
   a. rubella (German measles).
   b. anoxia.
   c. acquired immune deficiency syndrome (AIDS).
   d. neural-tube defect.

5. The most realistic way for pregnant women to reduce the risk of birth defects in their unborn children is to avoid unnecessary drugs and
   a. have a diagnostic X ray or sonogram.
   b. improve their genetic predispositions.
   c. seek early and regular prenatal care.
   d. take extra vitamin and mineral supplements.

6. Among the characteristics rated on the Apgar scale are
   a. shape of the newborn's head and nose.
   b. presence of body hair.
   c. interactive behaviors.
   d. muscle tone and color.

7. A newborn is classified as low birthweight if he or she weighs less than
   a. 7 pounds.
   b. 6 pounds.
   c. 5.5 pounds.
   d. 4 pounds.

8. The most critical problem for preterm babies is
   a. the immaturity of the sex organs—for example, undescended testicles.
   b. spitting up or hiccupping.
   c. infection from intravenous feeding.
   d. breathing difficulties.

9. The most remarkable examples of learning by the developing fetus involve the sense of
   a. touch.
   b. vision.
   c. hearing.
   d. smell.

10. Which Apgar score indicates that a newborn is in normal health?
    a. 4
    b. 5
    c. 6
    d. 7

11. Many of the factors that contribute to low birthweight are related to poverty; for example, women of lower socioeconomic status tend to

    a. be less well nourished.

    b. have less education.

    c. be subjected to stressful living conditions.

    d. be all of the above.

12. The critical period for preventing physical defects appears to be

    a. the period of the zygote.

    b. the embryonic period.

    c. only the third trimester.

    d. the entire pregnancy.

True or False Items

Write T (for true) or F (for false) on the line in front of each statement.

13. _____ Newborns can recognize some of what they heard while in the womb.

14. _____ Eight weeks after conception, the embryo has formed almost all the basic organs.

15. _____ In general, behavioral teratogens have the greatest effect during the embryonic period.

16. _____ The effects of cigarette smoking during pregnancy remain highly controversial.

17. _____ The Apgar scale is used to measure vital signs such as heart rate, breathing, and reflexes.

18. _____ Newborns usually cry on their own, moments after birth.

19. _____ Research shows that immediate mother-newborn contact at birth is necessary for the normal emotional development of the child.

20. _____ Low-birthweight babies are more likely than other children to experience developmental difficulties in early childhood.

21. _____ Cesarean sections are rarely performed in the United States today because of the resulting danger to the fetus.

Applying Your Knowledge

1. Babies born to mothers who are powerfully addicted to a psychoactive drug are most likely to suffer from
   a. structural problems.
   b. behavioral problems.
   c. both a and b.
   d. neither a nor b.

2. I am about 1 inch long and 1 gram in weight. I have all of the basic organs (except sex organs) and features of a human being. What am I?
   a. a zygote
   b. an embryo
   c. a fetus
   d. an indifferent gonad

3. Karen and Brad report to their neighbors that, 5 weeks after conception, a sonogram of their child-to-be revealed female sex organs. The neighbors are skeptical of their statement because
   a. sonograms are never administered before the ninth week.
   b. sonograms only reveal the presence or absence of male sex organs.
   c. the fetus does not begin to develop female sex organs until about the ninth week.
   d. it is impossible to determine that a woman is pregnant until six weeks after conception.

4. Five-year-old Benjamin can't sit quietly and concentrate on a task for more than a minute. Dr. Simmons, who is a teratologist, suspects that Benjamin may have been exposed to _____ during prenatal development.
   a. human immunodeficiency virus
   b. a behavioral teratogen
   c. rubella
   d. lead

5. Sylvia and Stan, who are of British descent, are hoping to have a child. Doctor Caruthers asks for a complete nutritional history and is particularly concerned when she discovers that Sylvia may have a deficiency of folic acid in her diet. Doctor Caruthers is probably worried about the risk of _____ in the couple's offspring.
   a. FAS
   b. brain damage
   c. neural-tube defects
   d. FAE

6. Three-year-old Kenny was born underweight and premature. Today, he is small for his age. His doctor suspects that
   a. Kenny is a victim of fetal alcohol syndrome.
   b. Kenny suffers from fetal alcohol effects.
   c. Kenny's mother smoked heavily during her pregnancy.
   d. Kenny's mother used cocaine during her pregnancy.

7. Which of these fetuses is most likely to experience serious prenatal damage?

   a. a male whose 15-year-old mother has an unusually stressful home life

   b. a female whose mother did not begin to receive prenatal care until the second month of her pregnancy

   c. a female whose 30-year-old mother is on welfare

   d. a male whose mother was somewhat undernourished early in the pregnancy

8. Fetal alcohol syndrome is common in newborns whose mothers were heavy drinkers during pregnancy, whereas newborns whose mothers were moderate drinkers may suffer fetal alcohol effects. This finding shows that to assess and understand risk we must know

   a. the kind of alcoholic beverage (for example, beer, wine, or whiskey).

   b. the level of exposure to the teratogen.

   c. whether the substance really is teratogenic.

   d. the timing of exposure to the teratogen.

9. Your sister and brother-in-law, who are about to adopt a one-year-old, are worried that the child will never bond with them. What advice should you offer?

   a. Tell them that, unfortunately, this is true; they would be better off waiting for a younger child who has not yet bonded.

   b. Tell them that, although the first year is a biologically determined critical period for attachment, there is a fifty-fifty chance that the child will bond with them.

   c. Tell them that bonding is a long-term process between parent and child that is determined by the nature of interaction throughout infancy, childhood, and beyond.

   d. Tell them that if the child is female, there is a good chance that she will bond with them, even at this late stage.

10. Which of the following newborns would be most likely to have problems in body structure and functioning?

    a. Anton, whose Apgar score is 6.

    b. Debora, whose Apgar score is 7.

    c. Sheila, whose Apgar score is 3.

    d. Simon, whose Apgar score is 5.

11. At birth, Clarence was classified as small for gestational age. It is likely that Clarence

    a. was born in a rural hospital.

    b. suffered several months of prenatal malnutrition.

    c. was born in a large city hospital.

    d. comes from a family with a history of such births.

12. Of the following, who is most likely to give birth to a low-birthweight child?

    a. twenty-one-year-old Janice, who lives in the North

    b. twenty-five-year-old May Ling, who lives in China

    c. sixteen-year-old Donna, who lives in a remote, rural part of the United States

    d. thirty-year-old Maria, who lives in southern California

13. An infant born 266 days after conception, weighing 4 pounds, would be designated as which of the following?

  a. a preterm infant

  b. a low-birthweight infant

  c. a small-for-gestational-age infant

  d. b and c

14. An infant who was born at 35 weeks, weighing 6 pounds, would be called a _____ infant.

  a. preterm

  b. low-birthweight

  c. small-for-gestational-age

  d. premature

15. The five characteristics evaluated by the Apgar scale are

  a. heart rate, length, weight, muscle tone, and color.

  b. orientation, muscle tone, reflexes, interaction, and responses to stress.

  c. reflexes, breathing, muscle tone, heart rate, and color.

  d. pupillary response, heart rate, reflex irritability, alertness, and breathing.

Answer Key

Key Terms

1. The first two weeks of development, characterized by rapid cell division and the beginning of cell differentiation, are called the germinal period. (p. 103; video lesson, segment 1; objective 1)

   Memory aid: A germ cell is one from which a new organism can develop. The germinal period is the first stage in the development of the new organism.

2. The embryonic period is the third through the eighth week of prenatal development, when the rudimentary forms of all anatomical structures develop. (p. 103; video lesson, segment 1; objective 2)

3. From the ninth week until birth is the fetal period, when the organs grow in size and complexity. (p. 103; video lesson, segment 1; objective 3)

4. Implantation is the process by which the outer cells of the organism burrow into the uterine lining and rupture its blood vessels to obtain nourishment and trigger the bodily changes that signify the beginning of pregnancy. (p. 104; video lesson, segment 1; objective 1)

5. The neural tube forms from a fold of outer embryonic cells during the embryonic period; it is the precursor of the central nervous system. (p. 105; objective 2)

   Memory aid: Neural means "of the nervous system." The neural tube is the precursor of the central nervous system.

6. The placenta is the organ that connects the mother's circulatory system with that of her growing embryo, providing nourishment to the developing organism and removing wastes. (p. 107; video lesson, segment 1; objectives 1, 2, & 3)

7. About twenty-two weeks after conception, the fetus attains the age of viability, at which point it has at least some slight chance of survival outside the uterus if specialized medical care is available. (p. 107; video lesson, segment 3; objective 3)

8. Teratogens are external agents and conditions, such as viruses, bacteria, drugs, chemicals, stressors, and malnutrition, that can cause damage to the developing organism. (p. 111; video lesson, segment 2; objective 5)

9. Behavioral teratogens tend to damage the brain and nervous system, impairing the future child's intellectual and emotional functioning. (p. 111; objective 5)

10. The science of teratology is a science of risk analysis, meaning that it attempts to evaluate what factors make prenatal harm more or less likely to occur. (p. 111; video lesson, segment 2; objective 5)

11. The first eight weeks, as well as the last months, of pregnancy are often called critical period, because teratogenic exposure during these time periods can produce malformations of basic body organs and structure. (p. 112; video lesson, segment 2; objective 5)

12. A threshold effect is the harmful effect of a substance that occurs when exposure to it reaches a certain level. (p. 113; video lesson, segment 2; objective 5)

13. An interaction effect occurs when one teratogen intensifies the harmful effects of another. (p. 113; video lesson, segment 2; objective 5)

14. Human immunodeficiency virus (HIV) is the most devastating viral teratogen. HIV gradually overwhelms the body's immune system, making the individual vulnerable to the host of diseases and infections that constitute AIDS. (p. 114; objective 6)

15. Prenatal alcohol exposure may cause fetal alcohol syndrome (FAS), which includes abnormal facial characteristics, slowed physical growth, behavior problems, and mental retardation. Likely victims are those who are genetically vulnerable and whose mothers drink three or more drinks daily during pregnancy. (p. 115; objective 6)

16. Newborns who weigh less than 2,500 grams (5.5 pounds) are called low-birthweight (LBW) infants. Such infants are at risk for many immediate and long-term problems. (p. 119; video lesson, segment 3; objective 7)

17. A preterm birth occurs when infants are born three or more weeks, meaning 35 weeks after conception (or earlier) rather than the normal term of 38 weeks. (p. 120; objective 7)

18. Infants who weigh substantially less than they should, given how much time has passed since conception, are called small for gestational age (SGA), or small-for-dates. (p. 121; objective 7)

19. Newborns are rated at one and then at five minutes after birth according to the Apgar scale. This scale assigns a score of 0, 1, or 2 to each of five characteristics: heart rate, breathing, muscle tone, color, and reflexes. A score of 7 or better indicates that all is well. (p. 123; video lesson, segment 4; objective 9)

20. In a cesarean section, the fetus is removed from the mother surgically. (p. 125; objective 10)

21. Cerebral palsy is a muscular control disorder caused by damage to the brain's motor centers during or before birth. (p. 126; objective 11)

22. Anoxia is a temporary lack of fetal oxygen during the birth process that, if prolonged, can cause brain damage or even death. (p. 126; video lesson, segment 4; objective 11)

23. The term parent-newborn bond describes the strong feelings of attachment between parents and their newborn infants. (p. 128; video lesson, segment 4; objective 12)

24. Postpartum depression is a profound feeling of sadness and inadequacy sometimes experienced by new mothers. (p. 128; objectives 1, 2, & 3)

25. Amniotic fluid is a clear, slightly yellowish liquid that surrounds the unborn child (fetus) during pregnancy, protecting and cushioning its development. (video lesson, segment 1; objectives 2 & 3)

26. Spina bifida (or cleft spine) is a birth defect that results from the failure of the spine to close properly during the first month of pregnancy. Research has shown that folic acid (a common B vitamin) is one factor that can reduce the risk of having a baby with neural tube defects such as spina bifida. (p. 113; video lesson, segment 2; objective 6)

Practice Questions I
Multiple-Choice Questions

1. d. is the correct answer. (p. 103; video lesson, segment 1; objective 1)

   a. is incorrect. The embryonic period from the third through the eighth week after conception.

   b. is incorrect. This term, which refers to the germinal period, is not used in the lesson.

   c. is incorrect. The fetal period is from the ninth week until birth.

2. b. is the correct answer. (p. 104; objective 1)

3. a. is the correct answer. (p. 113; objective 6)

   b., c., & d. are incorrect. Although low birthweight (b), critical periods of organ development (c), and maternal malnutrition (d) are all hazardous to the developing person during prenatal development, none is an example of a threshold effect.

4. c. is the correct answer. The sex organs do not begin to take shape until the fetal period. (p. 106; objective 2)

5. c. is the correct answer. (p. 107; video lesson, segment 3; objective 3)

6. d. is the correct answer. (p. 113; video lesson, segment 2; objectives 5 & 6)

7. a. is the correct answer. (p. 106; objective 2)

8. d. is the correct answer. (p. 111; video lesson, segment 2; objective 5)

   a. is incorrect. In general, teratogens can cross the placenta at any time.

   b. is incorrect. Teratogens are agents in the environment, not heritable genes (although susceptibility to individual teratogens has a genetic component).

   c. is incorrect. Although nutrition is an important factor in healthy prenatal development, the textbook does not suggest that nutrition alone can usually counteract the harmful effects of teratogens.

9. a. is the correct answer. (p. 115; objective 6)

10. b. is the correct answer. (pp. 122–123; video lesson, segment 4; objective 8)

11. c. is the correct answer. (pp. 123–124; video lesson, segment 4; objective 9)

12. c. is the correct answer. (pp. 108–109; objective 8)

13. b. is the correct answer. (p. 121; objective 7)

14. b. is the correct answer. (p. 121; objectives 6 & 7)

15. c. is the correct answer. (p. 128; objective 12)

Matching Items

16. i (p. 103; video lesson, segment 1; objective 2)

17. c (pp. 103, 106–108; video lesson, segment 1; objective 3)

18. g (p. 107; video lesson, segment 1; objectives 1, 2, & 3)

19. j (p. 120; objective 7)

20. b (p. 111; video lesson, segment 2; objective 6)

21. f (p. 114; objective 6)

22. a (p. 112; video lesson, segment 2; objective 5)

23. d (p. 105; objective 2)

24. e (pp. 115–117; objective 6)

25. h (p. 103; video lesson, segment 1; objective 1)

Practice Questions II

Multiple-Choice Questions

1. d. is the correct answer. (p. 116; objective 6)

2. c. is the correct answer. (p. 103; video lesson, segment 1; objectives 1, 2, & 3)

3. a. is the correct answer. (p. 115; objective 5)

4. a. is the correct answer. (p. 114; objective 5)

5. c. is the correct answer. (p. 115; objective 10)

6. d. is the correct answer. (pp. 123–124; video lesson, segment 4; objective 9)

7. c. is the correct answer. (p. 119; video lesson, segment 4; objective 7)

8. d. is the correct answer. (p. 108; objective 7)

9. c. is the correct answer. (p. 109; objective 7)

10. d. is the correct answer. (p. 124; video lesson, segment 4; objective 9)

11. d. is the correct answer. (p. 122; objective 7)

12. b. is the correct answer. (p. 112; objective 6)

True or False Items

13. T (p. 109; objective 4)

14. T (p. 106; video lesson, segment 1; objective 2)

15. F Behavioral teratogens can affect the fetus at any time during the prenatal period. (pp. 111–113; video lesson, segment 2; objective 5)

16. F There is no controversy about the damaging effects of smoking during pregnancy; tobacco is a dangerous teratogen. (p. 115; objective 5)

17. T (pp. 123–124; video lesson, segment 4; objective 9)

18. T (p. 123; objective 9)

19. F Though highly desirable, mother-newborn contact at birth is not necessary for the child's normal development or for a good parent-child relationship. Many opportunities for bonding occur throughout childhood. (pp. 128–129; objective 12)

20. T (pp. 121–122; objective 7)

21. F Nearly one in four births in the United States are now cesarean. (p. 125; objectives 10 & 11)

Applying Your Knowledge

1. c. is the correct answer. (pp. 115–116; objective 6)

2. b. is the correct answer. (pp. 105–106; video lesson, segment 1; objective 2)

   a. is incorrect. The zygote is the fertilized ovum.

   c. is incorrect. The developing organism is designated a fetus starting at the ninth week.

   d. is incorrect. The indifferent gonad is the mass of cells that will eventually develop into female or male sex organs.

3. c. is the correct answer. (p. 106; objective 3)

4. b. is the correct answer. (pp. 111, 116; objective 6)

a. is incorrect. This is the virus that causes AIDS.

c. is incorrect. Rubella may cause blindness, deafness, and brain damage.

d. is incorrect. The textbook does not discuss the effects of exposure to lead.

5. c. is the correct answer. (p. 113; video lesson, segment 2; objectives 5 & 6)

a. is incorrect. FAS is caused in infants by the mother-to-be drinking three or more drinks daily during pregnancy.

b. is incorrect. Brain damage is caused by the use of social drugs during pregnancy.

d. is incorrect. FAE is caused in infants by the mother-to-be drinking 1 ounce of alcohol per day.

6. c. is the correct answer. (p. 121; video lesson, segment 2; objectives 6 & 7)

7. a. is the correct answer. (p. 122; objectives 6 & 7)

8. b. is the correct answer. (pp. 115–116; objective 5)

9. c. is the correct answer. (p. 128; video lesson, segment 4; objective 12)

a. & b. are incorrect. Bonding in humans is not a biologically determined event limited to a critical period, as it is in many other animal species.

d. is a correct. There is no evidence of any gender differences in the formation of the parent-newborn bond.

10. c. is the correct answer. If a neonate's Apgar score is below 4, the infant is in critical condition and needs immediate medical attention. (p. 124; video lesson, segment 4; objective 9)

11. b. is the correct answer. (p. 121; objective 7)

a., c., & d. are incorrect. Prenatal malnutrition and maternal tobacco use are the most common causes of a small-for-dates neonate.

12. c. is the correct answer. (pp. 121–122; objective 7)

a., b., & d. are incorrect. The incidence of low birthweight is higher among teenaged mothers.

13. d. is the correct answer. (pp. 119, 121; objective 7)

a. & c. are incorrect. At 266 days, this infant is full term.

14. a. is the correct answer. (p. 120; objective 7)

b. is incorrect. Low birthweight is defined as weighing less than 5.5 pounds.

c. is incorrect. Although an infant can be both preterm and small for gestational age, this baby's weight is within the normal range of healthy babies.

d. is incorrect. This term is no longer used to describe early births.

15. c. is the correct answer. (pp. 123–124; video lesson, segment 4; objective 9)

Lesson Review

Lesson 4

The Beginnings
Prenatal Development and Birth

Please Note: Use this matrix to guide your study and achieve the learning objectives of this lesson. It will also help you to view the video, which defines and demonstrates important concepts and skills as they relate to everyday life.

Learning Objective	Textbook	Telecourse Student Guide	Video Lesson
1. Describe the significant developments of the germinal period.	pp. 103–110	Key Terms: 1, 4, 6, 24; Practice Questions I: 1, 2, 18, 25; Practice Questions II: 2.	Segment 1: *The First Trimester*
2. Describe the significant developments of the embryonic period.	pp. 103–110	Key Terms: 2, 5, 6, 24, 25; Practice Questions I: 4, 7, 16, 18, 23; Practice Questions II: 2, 14; Applying Your Knowledge: 2.	Segment 1: *The First Trimester*
3. Describe the significant developments of the fetal period, noting the importance of the age of viability.	pp. 103–110	Key Terms: 3, 6, 7, 24, 25; Practice Questions I: 5, 17, 18; Practice Questions II: 2; Applying Your Knowledge: 3.	Segment 1: *The First Trimester*; Segment 3: *The Second Trimester*
4. Describe developing senses of the fetus and the various responses to its immediate environment (the womb).	pp. 103–110	Practice Questions II: 13.	
5. Define teratogens, and describe the factors that determine whether a particular teratogen will be harmful.	pp. 111–118	Key Terms: 8, 9, 10, 11, 12, 13; Practice Questions I: 6, 8, 22; Practice Questions II: 3, 4, 15, 16; Applying Your Knowledge: 5, 8.	Segment 2: *Risk Reduction*

Learning Objective	Textbook	Telecourse Student Guide	Video Lesson
6. Outline the effects of at least three specific teratogens on the developing embryo or fetus, and describe protective steps that can be taken to moderate the risk of exposure.	pp. 111–118	Key Terms: 14, 15, 26; Practice Questions I: 3, 6, 9, 14, 20, 21, 24; Practice Questions II: 1, 12; Applying Your Knowledge: 1, 4, 5, 6, 7.	Segment 2: *Risk Reduction*
7. Distinguish among low-birthweight (LBW), preterm birth, and small-for-gestational-age (SGA) infants, and identify the causes of low birthweight, focusing on the relationship of poverty to low birthweight.	pp. 119–122	Key Terms: 16, 17, 18; Practice Questions I: 13, 14, 19; Practice Questions II: 7, 8, 9, 11, 20; Applying Your Knowledge: 6, 7, 11, 12, 13, 14.	Segment 3: *The Second Trimester*
8. Describe the normal process of birth, specifying the events of each stage.	pp. 122–128	Practice Questions I: 10, 12.	Segment 4: *The Third Trimester*
9. Describe the test used to assess the newborn's condition at birth.	pp. 122–128	Key Terms: 19; Practice Questions I: 11; Practice Questions II: 6, 10, 16, 18; Applying Your Knowledge: 10, 15.	Segment 4: *The Third Trimester*
10. Describe the options available for medical attention during the birthing process, and discuss the pros and cons of medical intervention.	pp. 124–129	Key Terms: 20; Practice Questions II: 5, 21.	
11. Explain the causes of cerebral palsy, and discuss the special needs of high-risk infants.	pp. 126–127	Key Terms: 21, 22; Practice Questions II: 21.	
12. Explain the concept of parent-newborn bonding and the current view of most developmentalists regarding early bonding in humans.	pp. 128–130	Key Terms: 23; Practice Questions I: 15; Practice Questions II: 7, 19; Applying Your Knowledge: 9.	Segment 4: *The Third Trimester*

A Delicate Grasp

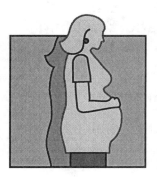

Lesson 5

The Beginnings:
Special Topic

Preview

Each of the major units in this course ("The Beginnings," "The First Two Years," "The Play Years," "The School Years," and "Adolescence") will end with a special topic and/or summary lesson. Lesson 5, the first of these special topic lessons, follows the stories of three couples who are struggling to have a child. Although each of their stories is unique, they share a common theme of hope—to be loving parents. Today, there are many options available for **infertile** couples, including alternate means of conception, alternative means of bringing the developing infant to term, and adoption.

Prior Telecourse Knowledge that Will Be Used in this Lesson
*   This lesson returns to the subject of infertility that was introduced in Lesson 3. Recall that a couple is considered "infertile" if they cannot conceive after a year of trying. Techniques for helping infertile couples will also be discussed, including **in vitro fertilization**.
*   This lesson will also discuss the conditions of preterm birth and low birthweight introduced in Lesson 4. Recall that an infant is preterm if it is born at least 3 weeks earlier than the normal full term of 38 weeks. These infants are often of low birthweight, which is defined as 5.5 pounds (2,500 grams) or less. The average normal birthweight is 7.5 pounds (3,400 grams).

Learning Objectives

Use this information to guide your reading, viewing, thinking, and studying. After successfully completing this lesson, you should be able to

1. List the odds of a zygote growing to become a living newborn baby and describe several reasons for this survival rate.
2. Define infertile and describe various options for infertile couples including artificial insemination, in vitro fertilization, and gestational surrogacy.
3. Discuss the potential problems of low-birthweight and preterm newborns.
4. Discuss several factors that determine whether a specific teratogen will be harmful and how a mother-to-be can avoid these harmful effects.
5. Explain several alternative methods of conception, and relate several personal and ethical questions raised by these methods.

📖 **Review pp. 76–78 ("Alternate Means of Conception;" "In Person: Whose Baby is It"); pp. 107–108 ("The Middle Three Months: Preparing to Survive"); p. 111 ("Risk Reduction"); and pp. 119–122 ("Low Birthweight"). (Note: Because of the overlapping content of Lessons 3, 4, and 5, the short reading assignment for this lesson is drawn from the two earlier lessons.)**

📟 **View the video for Lesson 5, "A Delicate Grasp."**

Segment 1: *Overcoming Infertility*

Segment 2: *The Ties That Bind*

Segment 3: *The Surrogate Mom*

Summary

Starting a family, for most couples, is a process that ends happily with the birth of a healthy child. Yet, for some couples who are infertile (unable to conceive despite a year of trying), the road is not so smooth. Infertility affects approximately 15 to 20 percent of the general population, with women and men contributing equally to the inability to conceive. One reason that infertility is more common in recent years is that many couples are waiting longer to have their first child.

The remedies for infertility include the use of medication to induce ovulation in women; **artificial insemination**, in which a sample of semen is collected from the male partner and inserted into the woman's uterus; and **in vitro fertilization (IVF)**, in which eggs are fertilized with sperm in the laboratory and the resulting zygote is inserted into the woman's uterus. For couples who are unable to conceive even with this **assisted reproductive technology (ART)**, surrogacy and adoption are often viable options.

Even after conception has occurred and prenatal development has begun, a healthy birth is not guaranteed. Miscarriages occur in about 15 percent of pregnancies (especially among older women), toxins called teratogens may interrupt or disrupt the development of the growing fetus, and the newborn may be born early and/or underweight.

The crucial factor in the fetus's attaining the age of viability, beginning from 22 to 24 weeks of pregnancy, is neurological maturation, which is essential to the regulation of the basic body functions of breathing, sucking, and sleeping. By 28 weeks, the typical fetus weighs about 1,300 grams (3 pounds) and has a greater than 50 percent chance of survival.

Teratology is a science of risk analysis, which attempts to evaluate what factors can make prenatal harm more, or less, likely to occur. Three crucial factors that determine whether a specific teratogen will cause harm, and of what nature, are the timing of exposure, the amount of exposure, and the developing organism's genetic vulnerability to damage from the substance.

A major, preventable health hazard for the fetus is low birthweight, defined as birthweight that is less than 2,500 grams (5.5 pounds). Babies that weigh less than 3 pounds (1,500 grams) are classified as very low birthweight, while those that weigh less than 2 pounds (1,000 grams) are classified as extremely low birthweight. Low-birthweight infants who are born more than three weeks early are called preterm. Others, born close to the due date but weighing less than most full-term neonates, are called small for gestational age (SGA).

📖   **Review all reading assignments for this lesson.**

💻   **As assigned by your instructor, complete the optional online component for this lesson.**

Key Terms

Using your own words, write a brief definition or explanation of each of the following terms on a separate piece of paper.

1. infertile
2. assisted reproductive technology (ART)
3. artificial insemination
4. in vitro fertilization (IVF)
5. low birthweight (LBW)
6. preterm birth
7. small for gestational age (SGA)
8. age of viability
9. teratogen
10. behavioral teratogen
11. gestational surrogacy

Practice Questions

Multiple-Choice Questions

1. To say that a teratogen has a "threshold effect" means that it is
   a. virtually harmless until exposure reaches a certain level.
   b. harmful only to low-birthweight infants.
   c. harmful to certain developing organs during periods when these organs are developing most rapidly.
   d. harmful only if the pregnant woman's weight does not increase by a certain minimum amount during her pregnancy.

2. The most critical factor in attaining the age of viability is development of the
   a. placenta.
   b. eyes.
   c. brain.
   d. skeleton.

3. A teratogen
   a. cannot cross the placenta during the embryonic period.
   b. is usually inherited from the mother.
   c. can be counteracted by good nutrition most of the time.
   d. may be a virus, a drug, a chemical, radiation, or environmental pollutants.

4. Low-birthweight babies born near the due date but weighing substantially less than they should
   a. are classified as preterm.
   b. are called small for gestational age.
   c. usually have no sex organs.
   d. show many signs of immaturity.

5. Approximately 1 out of every 4 low-birthweight births in the United States is caused by maternal use of

   a. alcohol.

   b. tobacco.

   c. crack cocaine.

   d. household chemicals.

6. One of the first teratogens to be recognized, possibly causing deafness, blindness, and brain damage if the fetus is exposed early during the pregnancy, is

   a. rubella (German measles).

   b. anoxia.

   c. acquired immune deficiency syndrome (AIDS).

   d. neural-tube defect.

7. The most critical problem for preterm babies is

   a. the immaturity of the sex organs—for example, undescended testicles.

   b. spitting up or hiccuping.

   c. infection from intravenous feeding.

   d. breathing difficulties.

8. Three-year-old Kenny was born underweight and premature. Today, he is small for his age. His doctor suspects that

   a. Kenny is a victim of fetal alcohol syndrome.

   b. Kenny suffers from fetal alcohol effects.

   c. Kenny's mother smoked heavily during her pregnancy.

   d. Kenny's mother used cocaine during her pregnancy.

9. Of the following, who is most likely to give birth to a low-birthweight child?

   a. 21-year-old Janice, who was herself a low-birthweight baby.

   b. 25-year-old May Ling, who gained 25 pounds during her pregnancy.

   c. 16-year-old Donna, who diets frequently despite being underweight and is under a lot of stress.

   d. 30-year-old Maria, who has already given birth to 4 children.

10. An infant born 266 days after conception and weighing 4 pounds would be designated as which of the following?

    a. preterm

    b. low birthweight

    c. small for gestational age

    d. b and c

11. An infant who was born at 35 weeks and weighing 6 pounds would be called a _____ infant.

    a. preterm

    b. low-birthweight

    c. small-for-gestational-age

    d. extremely low birthweight

12. The procedure in which an egg is fertilized by sperm in the laboratory is called
    a. artificial insemination.
    b. in vitro fertilization.
    c. gestational surrogacy.
    d. in vivo fertilization.

13. Approximately what percentage of all conceptions survive prenatal development to become newborn babies?
    a. 90 percent
    b. 75 percent
    c. 50 percent
    d. 31 percent

14. Infertility affects what percentage of the general population?
    a. less than 2 percent
    b. 15 to 20 percent
    c. 31 percent
    d. 40 percent

15. Most cases of infertility are caused by problems related to
    a. the male partner.
    b. the female partner.
    c. a ratio of 20/80 male to female factors.
    d. males and females contribute equally to infertility problems.

Matching Items
Match each definition or description with its corresponding term.

Terms
16. _____ in vitro fertilization
17. _____ age of viability
18. _____ artificial insemination
19. _____ preterm birth
20. _____ teratology
21. _____ low birthweight

22. _____ small for gestational age
23. _____ infertile
24. _____ assisted reproductive technology
25. _____ gestational surrogacy
26. _____ behavioral teratogen

Definitions or Descriptions
a. the scientific study of birth defects
b. when the fetus has a chance to survive outside the womb with medical help
c. a baby born 3 or more weeks early
d. egg and sperm are united in the laboratory
e. being unable to conceive after one year of trying
f. a woman carries another couple's embryo to term
g. a general term for the various techniques designed to help couples conceive
h. the preparation and placement of a semen sample inside a woman's uterus
i. a baby who weighs less than 5 pounds

j. a term applied to newborns who weigh substantially less than they should

k. a toxin that tends to harm the prenatal brain and affect intellectual functioning

Answer Key

Key Terms

1. A couple is said to be infertile when they have been unable to conceive after at least one year of trying. (p. 76; video lesson, segment 1; objective 2)

2. Assisted reproductive technology (ART) is a general term for the various techniques used to help couples conceive. (p. 76; objectives 2 & 5)

3. Artificial insemination is the preparation and placement of a semen sample inside a woman's uterus. (video lesson, segment 1; objectives 2 & 5)

4. In vitro fertilization (IVF) is a technique for helping infertile couples conceive in which ova are removed from a woman, mixed with sperm to form a viable zygote, and then inserted into the woman's uterus. (p. 76; video lesson, segment 1; objectives 2 & 5)

5. Newborns who weigh less than 2,500 grams (5.5 pounds) are called low-birthweight (LBW) infants. Such infants are at risk for many immediate and long-term problems. (p. 119; video lesson, segment 2; objective 3)

6. Infants who are born three or more weeks before the due date are called preterm. (p. 120; video lesson, segment 2; objective 3)

7. Infants who weigh substantially less than they should, given how much time has passed since conception, are called small for gestational age (SGA), or small-for-dates. (p. 121; objective 3)

8. Between 22 and 24 weeks after conception, the fetus attains the age of viability, at which point it has at least some slight chance of survival outside the uterus if specialized medical care is available. (p. 107; video lesson, segment 3; objective 1)

9. Teratogens are external agents and conditions, such as viruses, bacteria, drugs, chemicals, stressors, and malnutrition that can cause damage to the developing organism. (p. 111; video lesson, segment 3; objective 4)

10. Behavioral teratogens tend to damage the brain and nervous system, impairing the future child's intellectual and emotional functioning. (p. 111; objective 4)

11. Gestational surrogacy is an arrangement between the intended parents of the child and a woman who agrees to carry the embryo(s) made from the egg(s) and sperm of the intended parents. The child(ren) of gestational surrogacy is/are the genetic child(ren) of the intended parents, and the surrogate carries the embryo/fetus to term in the role of "host" uterus. In this form of surrogacy, the surrogate may also be called the "gestational mother." (video program, segment 3; objectives 2 & 5)

Practice Questions

Multiple-Choice Questions

1. a. is the correct answer. (p. 113; objective 4)

   b., c., & d. are incorrect. Although low birthweight (b), critical periods of organ development (c), and maternal malnutrition (d) are all hazardous to the developing person during prenatal development, none is an example of a threshold effect.

2. c. is the correct answer. (p. 107; objective 1)

3. d. is the correct answer. (p. 111; video lesson, segment 3; objective 4)

a. is incorrect. In general, teratogens can cross the placenta at any time.

b. is incorrect. Teratogens are agents in the environment, not heritable genes (although susceptibility to individual teratogens has a genetic component).

c. is incorrect. Although nutrition is an important factor in healthy prenatal development, the textbook does not suggest that nutrition alone can usually counteract the harmful effects of teratogens.

4. b. is the correct answer. (p. 121; objective 3)

5. b. is the correct answer. (p. 121; objectives 3 & 4)

6. a. is the correct answer. (p. 114; objective 4)

7. d. is the correct answer. (p. 108; objectives 1 & 3)

8. c. is the correct answer. (p. 121; objective 3)

9. c. is the correct answer. Donna has three risk factors that are related to having an LBW baby, including being a teenager, underweight, and stressed. (pp. 119–121; objective 3)

   a. & d. are incorrect. Neither of these has been linked to increased risk of having LBW babies.

   b. is incorrect. In fact, based only on her age and normal weight gain, May Ling's baby would not be expected to be LBW.

10. d. is the correct answer. (pp. 119, 121; video lesson, segment 2; objective 3)

    a. & c. are incorrect. At 266 days, this infant is full term.

11. a. is the correct answer. (p. 120; video lesson, segment 2; objective 3)

    b. is incorrect. Low birthweight is defined as weighing less than 5.5 pounds.

    c. is incorrect. Although an infant can be both preterm and small for gestational age, this baby's weight is within the normal range of healthy babies.

    d. is incorrect. This term is no longer used to describe early births.

12. b. is the correct answer. (p. 76; video lesson, segments 1 & 3; objective 2)

13. d. is the correct answer. (p. 105; objective 1)

14. b. is the correct answer. (pp. 76–78; video lesson, segment 1; objective 2)

15. d. is the correct answer. (pp. 75–78; video lesson, segment 1; objective 2)

Matching Items

16. d (p. 76; video lesson, segments 1 & 3; objective 2)

17. b (p.107; video lesson, segment 3; objective 1)

18. h (video lesson, segment 1; objective 2)

19. c (p. 120; video lesson, segment 3; objective 3)

20. a (p. 111; video lesson, segment 3; objective 4)

21. i (p. 119; video lesson, segment 3; objective 3)

22. j (p. 121; objective 3)

23. e (p. 76; video lesson, segment 1; objective 2)

24. g (p. 76; objective 2)

25. f (video lesson, segment 3; objective 2)

26. k (p. 111; objective 4)

Lesson Review

Lesson 5

A Delicate Grasp
Special Topic

Please Note: Use this matrix to guide your study and achieve the learning objectives of this lesson. It will also help you to view the video, which defines and demonstrates important concepts and skills as they relate to everyday life.

Learning Objective	Textbook	Telecourse Student Guide	Video Lesson
1. List the odds of a zygote growing to become a living newborn baby and describe several reasons for this survival rate.	pp. 76, 105–110	Key Terms: 8; Practice Questions: 2, 7, 13, 17.	Segment 3: *The Surrogate Mom*
2. Define infertile and describe various options for infertile couples including artificial insemination, in vitro fertilization, and gestational surrogacy.	pp. 75–78	Key Terms: 1, 2, 3, 4, 11; Practice Questions: 12, 14, 15, 16, 18, 23, 24, 25.	Segment 1: *Overcoming Infertility*
3. Discuss the potential problems of low-birthweight and preterm newborns.	pp. 108, 119–121	Key Terms: 5, 6, 7; Practice Questions: 4, 5, 7, 8, 9, 10, 11, 19, 21, 22.	Segment 2: *The Ties That Bind*
4. Discuss several factors that determine whether a specific teratogen will be harmful and how a mother-to-be can avoid these harmful effects.	pp. 111–114, 121	Key Terms: 9, 10; Practice Questions: 1, 3, 5, 6, 20, 26.	Segment 3: *The Surrogate Mom*
5. Explain several alternative methods of conception, and relate several personal and ethical questions raised by these methods.	pp. 76–78	Key Terms: 2, 3, 4, 11; Practice Questions: 12, 16, 18, 24, 25	Segment 1: *Overcoming Infertility*, Segment 3: *The Surrogate Mom*

Grow, Baby, Grow!

Lesson 6

The First Two Years:
Biosocial Development

Preview

This is the first of a five-lesson unit that describes the developing person from birth through age two in terms of biosocial, cognitive, and psychosocial development. This unit also includes *Summary* and *Special Topic* lessons. The biosocial domain is the part of human development that includes all the growth and changes that occur in a person's body. It also includes the social, cultural, and environmental factors that affect biological development, such as nutrition and health care.

The lesson begins with observations on the overall growth of infants, including their size and shape. A discussion of brain growth follows, including how a child's experiences can affect this development. At birth, the brain contains more than 100 billion nerve cells, or **neurons**, but the nerve fibers that interconnect them are incomplete. During the first few years of a child's life, extensive growth occurs in these neural pathways, enabling new capabilities in each domain of development.

The lesson then turns to the baby's developing senses, along with research on infant **sensation** and **perception**. This is followed by a look at how babies move and control their bodies and the ages at which the average infant advances in ability. Preventative medicine is discussed next, including the importance of **immunization**. The final section covers proper nutrition during the first two years and the consequences of severe **malnutrition**.

As you complete this lesson, consider a baby you know. What is the height and weight of this child and how does that compare to other babies of the same age? Note the child's ability to sense and perceive the world. Study reactions to outside stimuli and the way he or she moves arms, legs, fingers and toes. Talk to the baby's parents about the health care this child has received. Have they taken the baby to see a doctor? Which immunizations has the child received? Finally, discuss the mother and father's choices regarding nutrition. Did the mother breast-feed? If so, for how long? What is the child's diet now?

Prior Telecourse Knowledge that Will Be Used in this Lesson

- This is the first telecourse lesson to focus on a single "domain" of development (biosocial). Remember, although the division of human development into three domains makes it easier to study, development occurs holistically not in separate pieces. Virtually all aspects of human development reflect all three domains.

- This lesson will also return to the concept of *epigenetic systems* from Lesson 1. Recall that all development stems from the interaction between our genes and the influences of our environment.

Learning Objectives

Use this information to guide your reading, viewing, thinking, and studying. After successfully completing this lesson, you should be able to:

1. Describe the size and proportions of an infant's body, and discuss how babies change during the first two years and how their bodies compare with those of adults.
2. Describe the sleep patterns of children during the first two years, and discuss the influence of parental caregiving on these patterns.
3. Describe a typical brain cell and discuss ways in which the brain changes or matures during infancy.
4. Discuss the influence of experience on brain development.
5. Distinguish between sensation and perception, and describe the extent and development of an infant's perceptual abilities using hearing or vision as an example.
6. Describe the basic reflexes of the newborn and distinguish between gross motor skills and fine motor skills.
7. Describe the basic pattern of motor-skill development during the first two years and discuss variations in the timing of motor-skill acquisition.
8. Discuss the roles that preventative medicine and immunization have played in improving the survival of young children.
9. Identify risk factors and possible explanations for sudden infant death syndrome (SIDS), and list the methods that experts recommend for prevention.
10. Describe the nutritional needs of infants and toddlers, noting the benefits of mother's milk.
11. Distinguish between protein-calorie malnutrition and undernutrition, identify the causes and effects of these conditions, and discuss methods of prevention.

📖 **Read Chapter 5, "The First Two Years: Biosocial Development," pages 133–165.**

🔲 **View the video for Lesson 6, "Grow, Baby, Grow!"**
Segment 1: *Physical Growth and Health*
Segment 2: *Brain Growth and Development*
Segment 3: *Basic Reflexes and Motor Skills*
Segment 4: *Infant Nutrition*

Summary

Biosocial development during the first two years is so rapid that infants often seem to change before their parents' very eyes. The newborn seems top-heavy in body proportions, with its head being one-fourth of total body length (in comparison to one-eighth of body length as an adult). By age two, the average toddler's body weight is about one-fifth adult weight and body length has increased to about one-half adult height.

Brain development is also rapid during infancy. By age two, the brain has attained about 75 percent of its adult weight, and there has been a fivefold increase in the density of **dendrite** networks in the **cortex**.

The newborn's motor ability is limited to **reflexes**, including those that maintain adequate oxygen, body temperature, and nourishment. By 6 months, most babies can reach, grab, and hold onto dangling objects. The average child can walk with assistance at 9 months, stand momentarily at 10 months, and take steps unassisted at 12 months. Although all healthy infants develop the same **motor skills** in the same sequence, the age at which these skills are acquired varies greatly from infant to infant. Variations in the acquisition of motor skills can be attributed in part to inherited factors, such as activity level, rate of physical maturation, and body type. Environmental factors, such as medical care, nutrition, and patterns of infant care, are also influential. Note that the video for this lesson draws a distinction between reflexes, which are involuntary responses to stimuli, and motor skills, which require voluntary participation.

At birth, both **sensation** and **perception** are apparent. Vision is the least well developed of the senses. Newborns can focus better on objects that are between 4 and 30 inches away. By 6 months, visual acuity approaches 20/20, and infants can use both eyes to track moving objects well. In contrast, hearing is comparatively acute in the newborn. Newborns can differentiate their mother's voice from those of other women; by 1 month, they can perceive differences between very similar sounds.

For its nutritional benefits, breast milk is the ideal food for most babies. It is always sterile and at body temperature, contains more essential vitamins and iron than cow's milk, is more digestible, and provides the infant with the mother's immunity to disease. The primary cause of **protein-calorie malnutrition** in developing countries is early cessation of breast-feeding. Severe deficiency can cause **marasmus** in infants and **kwashiorkor** in toddlers. In developed countries, severe infant malnutrition is unusual; more prevalent is **undernutrition**, which is inadequate nutrition that causes no visible problems but makes a person shorter than average. Social and/or family problems are often responsible for undernutrition in developed countries.

📖 **Review all reading assignments for this lesson.**

💻 **As assigned by your instructor, complete the optional online component for this lesson.**

Key Terms

Using your own words, write a brief definition or explanation of each of the following terms on a separate piece of paper.

1. norm
2. head-sparing
3. percentile
4. wasting
5. stunting
6. REM sleep
7. neuron
8. cortex
9. axon
10. dendrite
11. synapse
12. transient exuberance
13. experience-expectant
14. experience-dependent
15. sensation
16. perception
17. binocular vision
18. reflexes
19. breathing reflex
20. sucking reflex
21. rooting reflex
22. gross motor skills
23. fine motor skills
24. immunization
25. sudden infant death syndrome (SIDS)
26. protein-calorie malnutrition
27. marasmus
28. kwashiorkor
29. undernutrition
30. failure-to-thrive
31. metabolism
32. enriched environment
33. motor skills
34. pincer grasp

Practice Questions I

Multiple-Choice Questions

1. The average North American newborn
   a. weighs approximately 6 pounds.
   b. weighs approximately 7 pounds.
   c. is "overweight" because of the diet of the mother.
   d. weighs 10 percent less than what is desirable.

2. Compared to the first year, growth during the second year
   a. proceeds at a slower rate.
   b. continues at about the same rate.
   c. includes more insulating fat.
   d. includes more bone and muscle.

3. The major motor skill most likely to be mastered by an infant before the age of 6 months is
   a. rolling over.
   b. sitting without support.
   c. turning the head in search of a nipple.
   d. grabbing an object with thumb and forefinger.

4. Norms among nations suggest that the earliest walkers in the world are infants from
   a. Western Europe.
   b. the United States.
   c. Uganda.
   d. Eastern Europe.

5. Head-sparing is the phenomenon in which
   a. the brain continues to grow even though the body stops growing as a result of malnutrition.
   b. The proportions of the infant's body often seem "top heavy."
   c. Axons develop more rapidly than dendrites.
   d. Dendrites develop more rapidly than axons.

6. Dreaming is characteristic of
   a. slow-wave sleep.
   b. transitional sleep.
   c. REM sleep.
   d. quiet sleep.

7. Proportionally, the head of the infant is about _____ of total body length; the head of an adult is about _____ of total body length.
   a. one-fourth; one-third
   b. one-eighth; one-fourth
   c. one-fourth; one-eighth
   d. one-third; one-fourth

8. Brain functions that require basic common experiences—such as babies' having things to see and people to feed them—are called
   a. experience-dependent.
   b. experience-expectant.
   c. pruning functions.
   d. transient exuberance.

9. Compared with formula-fed infants, breast-fed infants tend to have
   a. greater weight gain.
   b. fewer allergies and digestive upsets.
   c. less frequent feedings during the first few months.
   d. more social approval.

10. Marasmus and kwashiorkor are caused by
    a. bloating.
    b. protein-calorie deficiency.
    c. living in a developing country.
    d. poor family food habits.

11. The infant's first body movements are
    a. fine motor skills.
    b. gross motor skills.
    c. reflexes.
    d. pincer skills.

12. Which of the following is said to have had the greatest impact on human mortality reduction and population growth?
    a. improvements in infant nutrition
    b. oral rehydration therapy
    c. medical advances in newborn care
    d. childhood immunization

13. Babies are referred to as toddlers when
    a. their newborn reflexes have disappeared.
    b. they can walk well unassisted.
    c. they begin to creep or crawl.
    d. they speak their first word.

14. Which of the following is true of motor-skill development in healthy infants?
    a. It follows the same basic sequence the world over.
    b. It occurs at different rates from individual to individual.
    c. It follows norms that vary from one ethnic group to another.
    d. All of the above are true.

15. Most of the nerve cells that a human brain will ever possess are present
    a. at conception.
    b. about 1 month following conception.
    c. at birth.
    d. at age 5 or 6.

Matching Items

Match each definition or description with its corresponding term.

Terms

16. _____ neurons
17. _____ dendrites
18. _____ kwashiorkor
19. _____ marasmus
20. _____ gross motor skill
21. _____ fine motor skill
22. _____ reflex

23. _____ sucking reflex
24. _____ protein-calorie malnutrition
25. _____ transient exuberance
26. _____ wasting
27. _____ metabolism
28. _____ stunting

Definitions or Descriptions

a. a condition resulting from chronic malnutrition

b. protein deficiency during the first year in which growth stops and body tissues waste away

c. picking up an object

d. the most common serious nutrition problem of infancy

e. protein deficiency during toddlerhood

f. newborns suck anything that touches their lips

g. nerve fibers that allow communication among neurons

h. declining physiological response to a familiar stimulus

i. running or jumping

j. the process in which axons are coated with an insulating sheath

k. an involuntary response

l. the phenomenal increase in neural connections over the first 2 years

m. nerve cells

n. a condition resulting from acute malnutrition

o. the physical and chemical processes that sustain life

Practice Questions II

Multiple-Choice Questions

1. Dendrite is to axon as neural _____ is to neural _____.
   a. input; output
   b. output; input
   c. myelin; synapse
   d. synapse; myelin

2. A reflex is best defined as a(n)
   a. fine motor skill.
   b. motor ability mastered at a specific age.
   c. involuntary physical response to a given stimulus.
   d. gross motor skill.

3. A norm is
   a. a standard, or average, that is derived for a specific group or population.
   b. a point on a ranking scale of 1 to 99.
   c. a milestone of development that all children reach at the same age.
   d. all of the above.

4. Most babies can reach for, grasp, and hold onto an object by about the _____ month.
   a. second
   b. sixth
   c. ninth
   d. fourteenth

5. During the first weeks of life, babies seem to focus reasonably well on
   a. little in their environment.
   b. objects at a distance of 4 to 30 inches.
   c. objects at a distance of 1 to 3 inches.
   d. objects several feet away.

6. Which sleep stage increases markedly at about 3 or 4 months?
   a. REM
   b. Transitional
   c. Fast-wave
   d. Slow-wave

7. An advantage of breast milk over formula is that it
   a. is always sterile and at body temperature.
   b. contains traces of medications ingested by the mother.
   c. can be given without involving the father.
   d. contains more protein and vitamin D than does formula.

8. The primary cause of malnutrition in developing countries is

 a. formula feeding.

 b. inadequate food supply.

 c. disease.

 d. early cessation of breast-feeding.

9. Transient exuberance and pruning demonstrate that

 a. the pace of acquisition of motor skills varies markedly from child to child.

 b. newborns sleep more than older children because their immature nervous systems cannot handle the higher, waking level of sensory stimulation.

 c. the specifics of brain structure and growth depend partly on the infant's experience.

 d. good nutrition is essential to healthy biosocial development.

10. Climbing is to using a crayon as _____ is to _____.

 a. fine motor skill; gross motor skill

 b. gross motor skill; fine motor skill

 c. reflex; fine motor skill

 d. reflex; gross motor skill

11. Some infant reflexes

 a. are essential to life.

 b. disappear in the months after birth.

 c. provide the foundation for later motor skills.

 d. do all of the above.

12. A common cause of undernutrition in young children is

 a. ignorance of the infant's nutritional needs.

 b. the absence of socioeconomic policies that reflect the importance of infant nutrition.

 c. problems in the family, such as maternal depression.

 d. all of the above.

13. Neurotransmitters are chemical messengers that diffuse across the

 a. axon.

 b. myelin sheath.

 c. dendrite.

 d. synaptic gap.

14. Reflexes are _____ responses, whereas gross motor skills and fine motor skills _____.

 a. involuntary; require active participation

 b. voluntary; are involuntary

 c. slow-to-develop; require extensive practice

 d. permanent; are temporary

True or False Items

Write T (for true) or F (for false) on the line in front of each statement.

15. _____ By age 2, boys are slightly taller than girls, but girls are slightly heavier.

16. _____ Reflexive hiccups, sneezes, and thrashing are signs that the infant's reflexes are not functioning properly.

17. _____ Infants of all ethnic backgrounds develop the same motor skills at approximately the same age.

18. _____ The typical two-year-old is almost one-fifth its adult weight and one-half its adult height.

19. _____ Vision is better developed than hearing in most newborns.

20. _____ Today, most infants in the United States are breast-fed.

21. _____ Certain basic sensory experiences seem necessary to ensure full brain development in the human infant.

22. _____ Severe malnutrition is not widespread among young children in the United States.

23. _____ The only motor skills apparent at birth are reflexes.

24. _____ Infants typically grow about one inch per month during the first year.

25. _____ Over the first two years, the infant's metabolic activity decreases steadily.

Applying Your Knowledge

1. Newborns cry, shiver, and tuck their legs close to their bodies. This set of reflexes helps them
   a. ensure proper muscle tone.
   b. learn how to signal distress.
   c. maintain constant body temperature.
   d. communicate serious hunger pangs.

2. Research studies of the more than 100,000 Romanian children orphaned and severely deprived in infancy reported all **EXCEPT** which of the following?
   a. All of the children were wasted and stunted.
   b. The children had smaller heads.
   c. During early childhood many still showed signs of emotional damage.
   d. Most of the children placed in healthyadoptive homes eventually recovered.

3. Mrs. Bartholomew opens the door to her infant's room to be sure everything is all right. She notices that her son's eyes are flickering behind closed lids. The infant is in which stage of sleep?
   a. quiet sleep
   b. REM sleep
   c. transitional sleep
   d. one somewhere between b and c

4. Regarding body size, a child generally is said to be normal if he or she is
   a. between the 25th and 75th percentiles.
   b. at the 50th percentile or greater.
   c. between the 40th and 60th percentiles.
   d. between the 45th and 55th percentiles.

5. Which of the following has been offered as an explanation of why REM sleep decreases as a person ages?
   a. Less slow-wave sleep is needed to stimulate the older child's developing brain.
   b. Dreaming allows reorganization and interpretation of daily events, which become more complex as we grow older.
   c. Fast-wave sleep is entirely a product of brain maturation.
   d. All of the above have been offered as explanations.

6. Michael has 20/400 vision and is able to discriminate subtle sound differences. Michael most likely
   a. is a preterm infant.
   b. has brain damage in the visual processing areas of the cortex.
   c. is a newborn.
   d. is slow-to-mature.

7. A baby turns her head and starts to suck when her receiving blanket is brushed against her cheek. The baby is displaying the
   a. sucking reflex.
   b. rooting reflex.
   c. Babinski reflex.
   d. Moro reflex.

8. Sensation is to perception as _____ is to _____.
   a. hearing; seeing
   b. detecting a stimulus; making sense of a stimulus
   c. making sense of a stimulus; detecting a stimulus
   d. tasting; smelling

9. Adults often speak to infants in a high-pitched voice. This behavior occurs because they discover from experience that
   a. low-pitched sounds are more frightening to infants.
   b. infants are more sensitive to high-pitched sounds.
   c. high-pitched sounds are more soothing to infants.
   d. all of the above are true.

10. To say that most developmentalists are multidisciplinary and believe in plasticity means that they believe personality, intellect, and emotions
    a. change throughout life as a result of biological maturation.
    b. change throughout life for a combination of reasons.
    c. remain very stable throughout life.
    d. more strongly reveal the impact of genes as people get older.

11. Like all newborns, Serena is able to

    a. differentiate the sound of one consonant from another.

    b. see objects more than 30 inches from her face quite clearly.

    c. use her mouth to recognize objects by taste and touch.

    d. do all of the above.

12. Three-week-old Nathan should have the least difficulty focusing on the sight of

    a. stuffed animals on a bookshelf across the room from his crib.

    b. his mother's face as she holds him in her arms.

    c. the checkerboard pattern in the wallpaper covering the ceiling of his room.

    d. the family dog as it dashes into the nursery.

13. Geneva has been undernourished throughout childhood. It is likely that she will be

    a. smaller and shorter than her genetic potential would dictate.

    b. slow in intellectual development.

    c. less resistant to disease.

    d. all of the above.

14. Which of the following infants is likely to have the lowest risk of sudden infant death syndrome (SIDS)?

    a. a first-born, Asian female who sleeps on her back

    b. a later-born male of African descent who sleeps on his stomach

    c. a later-born female of European descent who sleeps on her stomach

    d. a first-born Asian male who sleeps on his stomach

Answer Key

Key Terms

1. A norm is an average age for the acquisition of a particular behavior, developed for a specific group population. (p. 135; objective 1)

2. Head-sparing is the phenomenon by which the brain continues to grow even though the body stops growing in a malnourished child. (p. 136; objective 1)

3. A percentile is any point on a ranking scale of 1 to 99; percentiles are often used to compare a child's development to group norms. (p. 136; objective 1)

4. Wasting is a condition in which a person's body weight is at the bottom 3 percent of the norm as a result of acute malnutrition. (p. 139; objective 1)

5. Stunting is a condition in which a person's height is at the bottom 3 percent of the norm as a result of chronic malnutrition. (p. 139; objective 1)

6. REM sleep, or rapid eye movement sleep, is a stage of sleep characterized by flickering eyes behind closed eyelids, dreaming, and rapid brain waves. (p. 139; objective 2)

7. A neuron, or nerve cell, is the main component of the central nervous system. (p. 141; video lesson, segment 2; objective 3)

8. The cortex is the thin outer layer of the brain that is involved in the voluntary, cognitive aspects of the mind. (p. 141; objective 3)

Memory aid: Cortex in Latin means "bark." As bark covers a tree, the cortex is the "bark of the brain."

9. An axon is the nerve fiber extension that sends impulses from one neuron to the dendrites of other neurons. (p. 141; video lesson, segment 2; objective 3)

10. Dendrites are nerve fiber extensions that receive the impulses transmitted from other neurons via their axons. (p. 141; video lesson, segment 2; objective 3)

11. A synapse is the point at which the axon of a sending neuron meets the dendrites of a receiving neuron. (p. 142; objective 3)

12. Transient exuberance is the dramatic increase in neural connections that occurs in an infant's brain over the first 2 years of life. (p. 142; video lesson, segment 2; objective 3)

13. Experience-expectant brain functions are those that require basic common experiences (such as having things to see and hear) in order to grow. (p. 143; objective 4)

14. Experience-dependent brain functions are those that depend on particular, and variable, experiences (such as experiencing language) in order to grow. (p. 143; objective 4)

15. Sensation is the process by which a sensory system detects a particular stimulus. (p. 146; objective 5)

16. Perception is the process by which the brain tries to make sense of a stimulus such that the individual becomes aware of it. (p. 146; objective 5)

17. Binocular vision is the ability to use both eyes together to focus on a single object. (p. 148; objective 5)

    Memory aid: Bi- indicates "two"; ocular means something pertaining to the eye. Binocular vision is vision for "two eyes."

18. Reflexes are involuntary physical responses to physical stimuli. (video lesson, segment 3; objective 6)

19. The breathing reflex is an involuntary physical response that ensures that the infant has an adequate supply of oxygen and discharges carbon dioxide. (p. 149; video lesson, segment 3; objective 6)

20. The sucking reflex is the involuntary tendency of newborns to suck anything that touches their lips. This reflex fosters feeding. (p. 150; video lesson, segment 3; objective 6)

21. The rooting reflex, which helps babies find a nipple, causes them to turn their heads and start to suck when something brushes against their cheek. (p. 150; video lesson, segment 3; objective 6)

22. Gross motor skills are physical abilities that demand large body movements, such as climbing, jumping, or running. (p. 150; video lesson, segment 3; objective 6)

23. Fine motor skills are physical abilities that require precise, small movements, such as picking up a coin. (p. 151; video lesson, segment 3; objective 6)

24. Immunization is the process through which the body's immune system is stimulated (as by a vaccine) to defend against attack by a particular contagious disease. (p. 155; objective 8)

25. Sudden infant death syndrome (SIDS) is a set of circumstances in which a seemingly healthy infant dies unexpectedly in sleep. (p. 156; objective 9)

26. Protein-calorie malnutrition results when a person does not consume enough nourishment to thrive. (p. 160; objective 11)

27. Marasmus is a disease caused by severe protein-calorie deficiency during the first year of life. Growth stops, body tissues waste away, and the infant dies. (p. 161; objective 11)

28. Kwashiorkor is a disease caused by protein-calorie deficiency during toddlerhood. The child's face, legs, and abdomen swell with water, sometimes making the child appear well fed. Other body parts are degraded, including the hair, which becomes thin, brittle, and colorless. (p. 161; objective 11)

29. Undernutrition is a nutritional problem in which a child is noticeably underweight or short in stature compared to the norms. (p. 162; video lesson, segment 4; objective 11)

30. Failure to thrive is undernutrition that involves a child who lives in an adequately nourished community but is not exhibiting normal childhood weight gain. (p. 167; video lesson, segment 4; objective 11)

31. Metabolism refers to the physical and chemical processes in the body that promote growth and sustain life. (video lesson, segment 2; objective 3)

32. An enriched environment is one that provides the developing child with a highly nurturing and stimulating atmosphere in which to grow and learn. (video lesson, segment 2; objective 4)

33. Motor skills are physical skills that involve large body movements, such as waving the arms, walking, and jumping (gross motor skills), and small body movements, such as picking up a coin or drawing (fine motor skills). (video lesson, segment 3; objective 6)

34. The pincer grasp is when the thumb and forefinger are used together to hold an object. (video lesson, segment 3; objective 6)

Practice Questions I

Multiple-Choice Questions

1. b. is the correct answer. (p. 136; objective 1)

2. a. is the correct answer. (p. 136; objective 1)

3. a. is the correct answer. (p. 152; objective 7)

   b. is incorrect. The age norm for this skill is 7.8 months.

   c. is incorrect. This is a reflex, rather than an acquired motor skill.

   d. is incorrect. This skill is acquired between 9 and 14 months.

4. c. is the correct answer. (p. 152; objective 7)

5. a. is the correct answer. (p. 136; objectives 1 & 11)

6. c. is the correct answer. (p. 139; objective 2)

7. c. is the correct answer. (p. 141; video lesson, segment 1; objective 1)

8. b. is the correct answer. (p. 143; objective 4)

   a. is incorrect. Experience-dependent functions depend on particular, and variable experiences in order to grow.

   c. is incorrect. Pruning refers to the process by which some neurons wither because experience does not activate them.

   d. is incorrect. This refers to the great increase in the number of neurons, dendrites, and synapses that occurs in an infant's brain over the first 2 years of life.

9. b. is the correct answer. Breast milk is more digestible than cow's milk or formula. (p. 159; video lesson, segment 4; objective 10)

a., c., & d. are incorrect. Breast- and bottle-fed babies do not differ in these attributes.

10. b. is the correct answer. (p. 161; objective 11)

11. c. is the correct answer. (p. 149; video lesson, segment 3; objective 6)

a., b., & d. are incorrect. These motor skills do not emerge until somewhat later; reflexes are present at birth.

12. d. is the correct answer. (pp. 154–155; objective 8)

13. b. is the correct answer. (p. 150; objective 7)

14. d. is the correct answer. (p. 152; objective 7)

15. c. is the correct answer. (p. 142; objective 3)

Matching Items

16. m (p. 141; video lesson, segment 2; objective 3)

17. g (p. 141; video lesson, segment 2; objective 3)

18. e (p. 161; objective 11)

19. b (p. 161; objective 11)

20. i (p. 150; video lesson, segment 3; objective 6)

21. c (p. 151; video lesson, segment 3; objective 6)

22. k (pp. 149–150; video lesson, segment 3; objective 6)

23. f (p. 150; video lesson, segment 3; objective 6)

24. d (p. 160; objective 11)

25. l (p. 142; video lesson, segment 2; objective 3)

26. n (pp. 138–139; objectives 1 & 11)

27. o (video lesson, segment 2; objective 3)

28. a (p. 138; objective 10)

Practice Questions II

Multiple-Choice Questions

1. a. is the correct answer. (pp. 141–142; video lesson, segment 2; objective 3)

2. c. is the correct answer. (p. 149; video lesson, segment 3; objective 6)

a., b., & d. are incorrect. Each of these refers to voluntary responses that are acquired only after a certain amount of practice; reflexes are involuntary responses that are present at birth and require no practice.

3. a. is the correct answer. (p. 136; objective 1)

4. b. is the correct answer. (p. 151; objective 7)

5. b. is the correct answer. (p. 148; objective 5)

a. is incorrect. Although focusing ability seems to be limited to a certain range, babies do focus on many objects in this range.

c. is incorrect. This is not within the range at which babies can focus.

d. is incorrect. Babies have very poor distance vision.

6. d. is the correct answer. (p. 139; objective 2)

7. a. is the correct answer. (p. 159; video lesson, segment 4; objective 10)

b. is incorrect. If anything, this is a potential disadvantage of breast milk over formula.

c. is incorrect. So can formula.

d. is incorrect. Breast milk contains more iron, vitamin C, and vitamin A than cow's milk; it does not contain more protein and vitamin D, however.

8. b. is the correct answer. (p. 160; objective 11)

9. c. is the correct answer. (pp. 142–143; objective 4)

10. b. is the correct answer. (pp. 150–151; video lesson, segment 3; objective 6)

c. & d. are incorrect. Reflexes are involuntary responses; climbing and using a crayon are both voluntary responses.

11. d. is the correct answer. (pp. 150–151; video lesson, segment 3; objective 6)

12. d. is the correct answer. (p. 162; objective 11)

13. d. is the correct answer. (pp. 141–142; objective 3)

14. a. is the correct answer. (video lesson, segment 3; objective 6)

b. & c. are incorrect. Reflexes are involuntary responses (therefore not b) that are present at birth (therefore not c).

d. Some reflexes disappear with age.

True or False Items

15. F   Boys are both slightly heavier and taller than girls at 2 years. (p. 136; objective 1)

16. F   Hiccups, sneezes, and thrashing are common during the first few days, and they are entirely normal reflexes. (p. 149; objective 6)

17. F   Although all healthy infants develop the same motor skills in the same sequence, the age at which these skills are acquired can vary greatly from infant to infant. (p. 152; objective 7)

18. T   (p. 136; objective 1)

19. F   Vision is relatively poorly developed at birth, whereas hearing is well developed. (pp. 147–148; objective 5)

20. F   Three out of every four infants under 6 months of age are formula fed. (p. 163; objective 10)

21. T   (p. 143; video lesson, segment 2; objective 4)

22. T   (p. 160; objective 11)

23. T   (p. 149; objective 6)

24. T   (p. 136; video lesson, segment 1; objective 1)

25. F   Metabolic activity increases, partly as a result of the dramatic growth occurring in the brain. (video lesson, segment 2; objective 3)

Applying Your Knowledge

1. c. is the correct answer. (p. 149; objective 6)

2. d. is the correct answer. Although all of the children improved, persistent deficits remained in many of them. (p. 145; objective 4)

d. is incorrect. This experiment was not concerned with sound localization.

3. b. is the correct answer. (p. 139; objective 2)

   a. is incorrect. Relatively slow and regular breathing and relaxed muscles characterize this state.

   c. is incorrect. This state is characterized by being half awake while dozing.

4. a. is the correct answer. (p. 136; objective 1)

5. b. is the correct answer. (p. 140; objective 2)

6. c. is the correct answer. (pp. 147–148; objective 5)

7. b. is the correct answer. (p. 150; video lesson, segment 3; objective 6)

   a. is incorrect. This is the reflexive sucking of newborns in response to anything that touches their lips.

   c. is incorrect. This is the response that infants make when their feet are stroked.

   d. is incorrect. In this response to startling noises, newborns fling their arms outward and then bring them together on their chests as if to hold on to something.

8. b. is the correct answer. (p. 146; objective 5)

   a. & d. are incorrect. Sensation and perception operate in all of these sensory modalities.

9. b. is the correct answer. (p. 147; objective 5)

   a. & c. The textbook does not suggest that its pitch determines whether a sound is soothing or frightening.

10. b. is the correct answer. (p. 144; objective 4)

11. a. is the correct answer. (p. 147; objective 5)

    b. is incorrect. Objects at this distance are out of focus for newborns.

    c. is incorrect. This ability does not emerge until about one month of age.

12. b. is the correct answer. This is true because, at birth, focusing is best for objects between 4 and 30 inches away. (p. 148; objective 5)

    a., c., & d. are incorrect. Newborns have very poor distance vision; each of these situations involves a distance greater than the optimal focus range.

13. d. is the correct answer. (p. 162; video lesson, segment 4; objective 11)

14. a. is the correct answer. (pp. 156–158; objective 9)

Lesson Review

Lesson 6

The First Two Years
Biosocial Development

Please Note: Use this matrix to guide your study and achieve the learning objectives of this lesson. It will also help you to view the video, which defines and demonstrates important concepts and skills as they relate to everyday life.

Learning Objective	Textbook	Telecourse Student Guide	Video Lesson
1. Describe the size and proportions of an infant's body, and discuss how babies change during the first two years and how their bodies compare with those of adults.	pp. 137–138	Key Terms: 1, 2, 3, 4, 5; Practice Questions I: 1, 2, 5, 7, 26; Practice Questions II: 3, 15, 18, 24; Applying Your Knowledge: 4.	Segment 1: *Physical Growth and Health*; Segment 2: *Brain Growth and Development*
2. Describe the sleep patterns of children during the first two years, and discuss the influence of parental caregiving on these patterns.	pp. 140–143	Key Terms: 6; Practice Questions I: 6; Practice Questions II: 6; Applying Your Knowledge: 3, 5.	
3. Describe a typical brain cell and discuss ways in which the brain changes or matures during infancy.	pp. 143–145	Key Terms: 7, 8, 9, 10, 11, 12, 31; Practice Questions I: 15, 16, 17, 25, 27; Practice Questions II: 1, 13, 25.	Segment 2: *Brain Growth and Development*
4. Discuss the influence of experience on brain development.	pp. 145–146	Key Terms: 13, 14, 32; Practice Questions I: 8; Practice Questions II: 9, 21; Applying Your Knowledge: 2, 10.	Segment 2: *Brain Growth and Development*; Segment 3: *Basic Reflexes and Motor Skills*
5. Distinguish between sensation and perception, and describe the extent and development of an infant's perceptual abilities using hearing or vision as an example.	pp. 147–148	Key Terms: 15, 16, 17; Practice Questions II: 5, 19; Applying Your Knowledge: 6, 8, 9, 11, 12.	

Learning Objective	Textbook	Telecourse Student Guide	Video Lesson
6. Describe the basic reflexes of the newborn and distinguish between gross motor skills and fine motor skills.	pp. 148–153	Key Terms: 18, 19, 20, 21, 22, 23, 33, 34; Practice Questions I: 11, 20, 21, 22, 23; Practice Questions II: 2, 10, 11, 14, 16, 23; Applying Your Knowledge: 1, 7.	Segment 3: *Basic Reflexes and Motor Skills*
7. Describe the basic pattern of motor-skill development during the first two years and discuss variations in the timing of motor-skill acquisition.	pp. 153–156	Practice Questions I: 3, 4, 13, 14; Practice Questions II: 4, 17.	
8. Discuss the roles that preventative medicine and immunization have played in improving the survival of young children.	pp. 156–159	Key Terms: 24; Practice Questions I: 12.	
9. Identify risk factors and possible explanations for sudden infant death syndrome (SIDS), and list the methods that experts recommend for prevention.	pp. 163–165	Key Terms: 25; Applying Your Knowledge: 14.	
10. Describe the nutritional needs of infants and toddlers, noting the benefits of mother's milk.	pp. 165–169	Practice Questions I: 9, 28; Practice Questions II: 7, 20.	Segment 4: *Infant Nutrition*
11. Distinguish between protein-calorie malnutrition and undernutrition, identify the causes and effects of these conditions, and discuss methods of prevention.		Key Terms: 26, 27, 28, 29, 30; Practice Questions I: 5, 10, 18, 19, 24, 26; Practice Questions II: 8, 12, 22; Applying Your Knowledge: 13.	Segment 4: *Infant Nutrition*

The Little Scientist

Lesson 7
The First Two Years:
Cognitive Development

Preview

Lesson 7 is the first of the telecourse lessons to focus on the domain of *cognition,* by which we mean the mental processes involved in thinking. The lesson focuses on the various ways in which infant cognitive development is revealed: through perception (which, as you'll recall from Lesson 6, refers to the mental processing of sensory information), memory, intelligence, and language development.

The video for this lesson, "The Little Scientist," outlines Jean Piaget's theory of **sensorimotor intelligence**, which maintains that infants think exclusively with their senses and motor skills. Piaget's six stages of sensorimotor intelligence are examined.

The lesson also discusses the key cognitive elements needed by infants to structure their environment. Researchers have found that the speed with which infants recognize familiarity and seek something novel is related to later cognitive skill. It points out the importance of memory to cognitive development.

The lesson also gives a description of infant perception and the influential theory of **affordances**. Central to this theory is the idea that infants gain cognitive understanding of their world through affordances, that is, opportunities to perceive and interact with the objects and environments around them.

Finally, the lesson turns to the most remarkable cognitive achievement of the first two years, the acquisition of language. Beginning with a description of the infant's first attempts at language, the video and chapter follow the sequence of events that leads to the child's ability to utter two-word sentences. The lesson concludes with an examination of language learning as teamwork involving babies and adults, who, in a sense, teach each other the unique human process of verbal communication.

As you complete this lesson, think about a baby you know (and/or interview the child's parents, if time allows). Would you describe this child as a smart baby? How does this infant express his or her intelligence? Observe how this child reacts to new stimuli and assimilates new information. Study the child's usual environment. What objects, people and situations does the child typically encounter that could afford him or her the opportunity to learn? What kinds of things can this baby remember, and under what circumstances? How far has this child's language advanced relative to other babies of the same age? What were his or her first vocalizations and/or first words? Speculate on how one could encourage language development in this child.

Prior Telecourse Knowledge that Will Be Used in this Lesson

- The textbook and video will return to Piaget's theory of cognitive development (Lesson 1) with a discussion of sensorimotor intelligence. (Recall that Piaget's theory specifies four major periods):

   1. **Sensorimotor (birth to 2 years)** ← **The First Two Years**
   2. Preoperational (2 to 6 years)
   3. Concrete Operational (7 to 11 years)
   4. Formal Operational (12 years through adulthood)

- You may wish to review the theories of B. F. Skinner and Lev Vygotsky (Lesson 1). They will come up again as the textbook and video lesson discuss how babies acquire language and what caregivers can do to help.

- In the section on perception, the textbook will refer to the importance of brain growth and development (Lesson 6). You may wish to review terms such as cortex, axons, dendrites, and myelination.

Learning Objectives

Use this information to guide your reading, viewing, thinking, and studying. After successfully completing this lesson, you should be able to:

1. Identify and describe Piaget's stages of sensorimotor intelligence, and give examples of the behavior associated with each stage.
2. Explain what object permanence is, how it is tested in infancy, and what these tests reveal.
3. Explain what habituation research has revealed about cognitive development in infancy.
4. Describe the information processing model of cognition.
5. Explain the Gibsons' contextual view of perception, and relate it to the idea of affordances, giving examples of affordances perceived by infants.
6. Explain how the infant's focus on movement and change enhances sensory and perceptual skills and thus overall cognitive growth.
7. Discuss research findings on infant memory and infants' understanding of categories.
8. Describe language development during the first two years, and identify its major hallmarks.
9. Explain the importance of baby talk (motherese), and identify its main features.
10. Summarize the different theories that explain early language learning, and discuss how each theory might help caregivers encourage their child's language development.

📖 **Read Chapter 6, "The First Two Years: Cognitive Development," pages 167–199.**

📼 **View the video for Lesson 7, "The Little Scientist."**

Segment 1: *Sensorimotor Intelligence*

Segment 2: *Language Development*

Summary

During the first two years of life, cognitive development proceeds at a phenomenal pace as the infant is transformed from a baby who can know its world only through a limited set of basic reflexes into a toddler capable of imitating others, anticipating and remembering events, and pretending. According to Jean Piaget—often called the "father of cognitive development"—infants learn about their environment by using their senses and motor skills (**sensorimotor intelligence**). They begin by using and then adapting their reflexes (Stages 1 and 2); soon thereafter they become aware of their own and others' actions and reactions, and this awareness guides their thinking (Stage 3). By the end of the first year, they are able to set and achieve simple goals (Stage 4). During the second year, toddlers discover new ways to achieve their goals, first by actively experimenting with objects and actions (Stage 5) and then by manipulating mental images of objects and behaviors (Stage 6). Most significant among the advances of infancy is the development of language. By age 2, the average toddler has a relatively large vocabulary and is able to converse effectively with others.

Although standard Piagetian tasks suggest that infants do not search for hidden objects until about 8 months of age, studies using the **habituation** technique demonstrate that infants as young as 3.5–4.5 months have a basic understanding of **object permanence** long before they can demonstrate this on a hidden-object task. Infants as young as 3 months are capable of anticipating what will occur next in a sequence of events they have observed repeatedly. By 9 months, infants can show **deferred imitation** of a model whose actions they had observed a day earlier.

Infants are well equipped to learn language from birth, partly because of innate readiness and partly because of their auditory experiences during the final prenatal months. All children follow the same sequence of accomplishments in early language development, although their timing may vary considerably. At every stage of development—including the preverbal stage when infants use cries, cooing, **babbling**, and gestures to communicate—children understand much more than they are capable of expressing.

Toddlers differ in their vocabulary growth: some learn mainly naming words, while others learn a higher proportion of words that facilitate social interaction. Toddlers initially show **underextension** of word meanings: words are applied more narrowly than they should be. **Overextension**, or overgeneralization of a small set of words to inappropriate objects, indicates that language development is proceeding normally, with the child forming and testing linguistic hypotheses. The first words, used as one-word sentences, occur by about 1 year, the first two-word sentence at about 21 months.

📖   **Review all reading assignments for this lesson.**

💻   **As assigned by your instructor, complete the optional online component for this lesson.**

Key Terms

Using your own words, write a brief definition or explanation of each of the following terms on a separate piece of paper.

1.	sensorimotor intelligence	19.	dynamic perception
2.	primary circular reactions	20.	infantile amnesia
3.	adaptation	21.	reminder session
4.	assimilation	22.	implicit memory
5.	accommodation	23.	explicit memory
6.	secondary circular reactions	24.	baby talk
7.	goal-directed behavior	25.	babbling
8.	object permanence	26.	naming explosion
9.	tertiary circular reactions	27.	holophrase
10.	"little scientist"	28.	underextension
11.	mental combinations	29.	overextension
12.	deferred imitation	30.	grammar
13.	habituation	31.	language acquisition device (LAD)
14.	fMRI	32.	reduplicative babbling
15.	information-processing theory	33.	semantics
16.	affordance	34.	intonation
17.	graspability	35.	language function
18.	visual cliff	36.	language structure

Practice Questions I

Multiple-Choice Questions

1. In general terms, the Gibsons' concept of affordances emphasizes the idea that the individual perceives an object in terms of its

   a. economic importance.

   b. physical qualities.

   c. function or use to the individual.

   d. role in the larger culture or environment.

2. According to Piaget, when a baby repeats an action that has just triggered a pleasing response from his or her caregiver, a stage _____ behavior has occurred.

   a. one

   b. two

   c. three

   d. six

3. Sensorimotor intelligence begins with a baby's first

   a. attempt to crawl.

   b. reflex actions.

   c. auditory perception.

   d. adaptation of a reflex.

4. To study an infant's categorization ability, researchers show a baby different objects in a category until _____ occurs. If the baby then _____ when an object from a different category is presented, it suggests that the child has discriminated between the different categories.

   a. intermodal perception; habituates

   b. cross-modal perception; dishabituates

   c. habituation; dishabituates

   d. dynamic perception; habituates

5. Piaget and the Gibsons would most likely agree that

   a. perception is largely automatic.

   b. language development is biologically predisposed in children.

   c. learning and perception are active cognitive processes.

   d. it is unwise to "push" children too hard academically.

6. By the end of the first year, infants usually learn how to

   a. accomplish simple goals.

   b. manipulate various symbols.

   c. construct mental combinations.

   d. pretend.

7. When an infant begins to understand that objects exist even when they are out of sight, she or he has begun to understand the concept of object

   a. displacement.

   b. importance.

   c. permanence.

   d. location.

8. Today, most cognitive psychologists view language acquisition as

   a. primarily the result of imitation of adult speech.

   b. a behavior that is determined primarily by biological maturation.

   c. a behavior determined entirely by learning.

   d. determined by both biological maturation and learning.

9. Despite cultural differences, children all over the world attain very similar language skills

   a. according to ethnically specific timetables.

   b. at about the same age in the same sequence.

   c. according to culturally specific timetables.

   d. according to timetables that vary widely from child to child.

10. The average baby speaks a few words at about

    a. 6 months.

    b. 9 months.

    c. 12 months.

    d. 24 months.

11. A single word used by toddlers to express a complete thought is

    a. a holophrase.

    b. baby talk.

    c. an overextension.

    d. an underextension.

12. Compared with children's rate of speech development, their comprehension of language develops

    a. more slowly.

    b. at about the same pace.

    c. more rapidly.

    d. more rapidly in certain cultures than it does in other cultures.

13. A distinctive form of language, with a particular pitch, structure, and other elements, that adults use in talking to infants is called

    a. a holophrase.

    b. the LAD.

    c. baby talk.

    d. conversation.

14. Infants who are younger than 6 months can categorize objects on the basis of

    a. angularity.

    b. shape.

    c. density.

    d. all of the above.

15. The imaging technique that reveals brain activity by showing increases in oxygen supply to various parts of the brain is called

    a. a PET scan.

    b. EEG.

    c. fMRI.

    d. a CAT scan.

16. A toddler who taps on the computer's keyboard after observing her mother sending e-mail is demonstrating

    a. assimilation.

    b. accommodation.

    c. deferred imitation.

    d. dynamic perception.

Matching Items

Match each definition or description with its corresponding term.

Terms

17. _____ mental combinations
18. _____ affordances
19. _____ object permanence
20. _____ visual cliff
21. _____ adaptation
22. _____ implicit memory
23. _____ sensorimotor intelligence

24. _____ babbling
25. _____ holophrase
26. _____ overextension
27. _____ explicit memory
28. _____ dynamic perception
29. _____ reduplicative babbling

Definitions or Descriptions

a. overgeneralization of a word to inappropriate objects, etc.
b. repetitive utterance of certain syllables
c. perception that focuses on movement and change
d. memory for events that can be recognized but not necessarily recalled
e. the realization that something that is out of sight continues to exist
f. trying out actions mentally
g. opportunities for interaction that an object or place offers
h. a device for studying depth perception
i. a single word used to express a complete thought
j. cognitive process by which information is taken in and responded to
k. memory that is available for immediate recall
l. thinking using the senses and motor skills
m. a type of babbling in which a baby puts two syllables together and repeats them over and over

Practice Questions II

Multiple-Choice Questions

1. Stage five (12 to 18 months) of sensorimotor intelligence is best described as
   a. first acquired adaptations.
   b. the period of the "little scientist."
   c. procedures for making interesting sights last.
   d. new means through symbolization.

2. Which of the following is **NOT** evidence of dynamic perception during infancy?
   a. Babies prefer to look at things in motion.
   b. Babies form simple expectations of the path that a moving object will follow.
   c. Babies use movement cues to discern the boundaries of objects.
   d. Babies quickly grasp that even though objects look different when seen from different viewpoints, they are the same objects.

3. Recent research suggests that the concept of object permanence
   a. fades after a few months.
   b. is a skill some children never acquire.
   c. may occur earlier and more gradually than Piaget recognized.
   d. involves pretending as well as mental combinations.

4. According to the Gibsons, graspability is
   a. an opportunity perceived by a baby.
   b. a quality that resides in toys and other objects.
   c. an ability that emerges at about 6 months.
   d. evidence of manual dexterity in the infant.

5. For Noam Chomsky, the "language acquisition device" refers to
   a. the human predisposition to acquire language.
   b. the portion of the human brain that processes speech.
   c. the vocabulary of the language the child is exposed to.
   d. all of the above.

6. The first stage of sensorimotor intelligence lasts until
   a. infants can anticipate events that will fulfill their needs.
   b. infants begin to adapt their reflexes to the environment.
   c. object permanence has been achieved.
   d. infants are capable of thinking about past and future events.

7. As an advocate of the social-pragmatic theory, Professor Robinson believes that
   a. infants communicate in every way they can because they are social beings.
   b. biological maturation is a dominant force in language development.
   c. infants' language abilities mirror those of their primary caregivers.
   d. language develops in many ways for many reasons.

8. Piaget was incorrect in his belief that infants under 8 months do not have
   a. object permanence.
   b. intelligence.
   c. goal-directed behavior.
   d. all of the above.

9. The purposeful actions that begin to develop in sensorimotor stage four are called
   a. reflexes.
   b. affordances.
   c. goal-directed behaviors.
   d. mental combinations.

10. What is the correct sequence of language development in babies?
    a. crying, babbling, cooing, first word
    b. crying, cooing, babbling, first word
    c. crying, babbling, first word, cooing
    d. crying, cooing, first word, babbling

11. Compared with hearing babies, deaf babies

    a. are less likely to babble.

    b. are more likely to babble.

    c. begin to babble vocally at about the same age.

    d. begin to babble manually at about the same age as hearing babies begin to babble vocally.

12. According to Skinner, children acquire language

    a. as a result of an inborn ability to use the basic structure of language.

    b. through reinforcement and conditioning.

    c. mostly because of biological maturation.

    d. in a fixed sequence of predictable stages.

Matching Items

Match each definition or description with its corresponding term.

Terms

13. _____ goal-directed behavior
14. _____ deferred imitation
15. _____ infantile amnesia
16. _____ intonation
17. _____ assimilation
18. _____ little scientist
19. _____ naming explosion
20. _____ underextension
21. _____ habituation
22. _____ accommodation
23. _____ LAD
24. _____ semantics
25. _____ baby talk

Definitions or Descriptions

a. the ability to witness, remember, and later copy a behavior that has been witnessed.

b. incorporating new information into an existing mental categories

c. a dynamic increase in an infant's vocabulary that begins at about 18 months of age

d. the inability to access memories from the first years of life

e. the process of getting used to an object or event through repeated exposure

f. a word is used more narrowly than its true meaning allows

g. a hypothetical device that facilitates language development

h. also called "motherese"

i. Piaget's term for the stage-five toddler

j. purposeful actions

k. modifying an existing mental category to reflect new information

l. the cadence, tone, or emphasis of speech

m. the underlying meaning of words

Applying Your Knowledge

1. A nine-month-old repeatedly reaches for his sister's doll, even though he has been told "no" many times. This is an example of

   a. pretend play.

   b. an overextension.

   c. delayed imitation.

   d. goal-directed behavior.

2. Eighteen-month-old Troy puts a collar on his stuffed dog, then pretends to take it for a walk. Troy's behavior is an example of a

   a. primary circular reaction.

   b. secondary circular reaction.

   c. tertiary circular reaction.

   d. first acquired adaptation.

3. According to Skinner's theory, an infant who learns to delight his father by saying "da-da" is probably benefiting from

   a. social reinforcers, such as smiles and hugs.

   b. modeling.

   c. learning by imitation.

   d. an innate ability to use language.

4. The child's tendency to call every animal "doggie" is an example of

   a. using a holophrase.

   b. babbling.

   c. motherese.

   d. overextension.

5. About six months after speaking his or her first words, the typical child will

   a. have a vocabulary of between 250 and 350 words.

   b. begin to speak in holophrases.

   c. put words together to form rudimentary sentences.

   d. do all of the above.

6. A twenty-month-old girl who is able to try out various actions mentally without having to actually perform them is learning to solve simple problems by using

   a. dynamic perception.

   b. object permanence.

   c. intermodal perception.

   d. mental combinations.

7. A baby who repeats an action that has triggered a reaction in a parent is demonstrating an ability that typically occurs in which stage of sensorimotor development?

   a. Stage 1

   b. Stage 2

   c. Stage 3

   d. Stage 4

8. Sixteen-month-old Carrie reserves the word "cat" for her pet feline. Her failure to refer to other felines as cats is an example of

   a. a holophrase.

   b. an overextension.

   c. babbling.

   d. an underextension.

9. A baby who realizes that a rubber duck that has fallen out of the tub must be somewhere on the floor has achieved

   a. object permanence.

   b. intermodal perception.

   c. mental combinations.

   d. cross-modal perception.

10. As soon as her babysitter arrives, twenty-one-month-old Christine holds on to her mother's legs and, in a questioning manner, says "bye-bye." Because Christine clearly is "asking" her mother not to leave, her utterance can be classified as

    a. babbling.

    b. an overextension.

    c. a holophrase.

    d. subject-predicate order.

11. The six-month-old infant's continual repetition of sound combinations such as "ba-ba-ba" is called

    a. cooing.

    b. reduplicative babbling.

    c. a holophrase.

    d. an overextension.

12. Which of the following is an example of a linguistic overextension that a two-year-old might make?

    a. saying "bye-bye" to indicate that he or she wants to go out

    b. pointing to a cat and saying "doggie"

    c. repeating certain syllables, such as "ma-ma"

    d. reversing word order, such as "want it, paper"

13. Many researchers believe that the infant's ability to detect the similarities and differences between shapes and colors marks the beginning of

    a. mental combinations.

    b. the stage of the little scientist.

    c. category or concept formation.

    d. full object permanence.

14 Like most Korean toddlers, Ok Cha has acquired a greater number of _____ in her vocabulary than her North American counterparts, who tend to acquire more _____.

a. verbs; nouns
b. nouns; verbs
c. adjectives; verbs
d. adjectives; nouns

Answer Key

Key Terms

1. Piaget's stages of sensorimotor intelligence (from birth to about 2 years old) are based on his theory that infants think exclusively with their senses and motor skills. (p. 168; video lesson, segment 1; objective 1)

2. In Piaget's theory, primary circular reactions are a type of feedback loop involving the infant's own body, in which infants take in experiences (such as sucking and grasping) and try to make sense of them. (p. 168; objective 1)

3. A key element of Piaget's theory, adaptation is the cognitive process by which information is taken in and responded to. (p. 168; objective 1)

4. In Piaget's theory, assimilation is the adaptation process in which new information is taken into the mind by incorporating it into existing mental schemas. (p. 168; objective 1)

5. In Piaget's theory, accommodation is the adaptation process in which new information is brought into the mind in such a way as to refine or expand existing mental schemas. (p. 169; objective 1)

6. Secondary circular reactions are a type of feedback loop involving the infant's responses to objects and other people. (p. 170; objective 1)

7. Goal-directed behavior refers to purposeful actions initiated by infants in anticipation of events that will fulfill their needs and wishes. (p. 171; video lesson, segment 1; objective 1)

8. Object permanence is the understanding that objects continue to exist even when they cannot be seen, touched, or heard. (p. 171; video lesson, segment 1; objective 2)

9. In Piaget's theory, tertiary circular reactions are the most sophisticated type of infant feedback loop, involving active exploration and experimentation. (p. 174; objective 1)

10. "Little scientist" is Piaget's term for the stage-five toddler who learns about the properties of objects in his or her world through active experimentation. (p. 174; video lesson, segment 1; objective 1)

11. In Piaget's theory, mental combinations are sequences of actions that are carried out mentally. Mental combinations enable stage-six toddlers to begin to anticipate and solve problems without resorting to trial-and-error experiments. (p. 174; video lesson, segment 1; objective 1)

12. Deferred imitation is the ability to witness, remember, and later copy a behavior that has been witnessed. (p. 174; video lesson, segment 1; objective 4)

13. Habituation is the process of becoming so familiar with a stimulus that it no longer triggers the responses it did when it was originally experienced. (p. 176; objective 3)

14. Functional magnetic resonance imaging (fMRI) is a new imaging technique in which the brain's magnetic properties are measured to reveal changes in activity levels in various parts of the brain. (p. 176; objective 4)

15. Information-processing theory is a theory of human cognition that compares thinking to the ways in which a computer analyzes data, through the processes of input, programming, and output. (p. 176; objective 4)

16. Affordances are perceived opportunities for interacting with objects, places, and environments. Infants perceive sucking, grasping, noisemaking, and many other affordances of objects at an early age. (p. 177; objective 5)

17. Graspability is the perception of whether or not an object is of the proper size, shape, texture, and distance to afford grasping or grabbing. (p. 178; objective 5)

18. A visual cliff is an apparent (but not actual) drop between one surface and another. (p. 178; objective 5)

19. Dynamic perception is perception that is primed to focus on movement and change. (p. 179; objective 6)

20. Infantile amnesia is the inability, according to Freud, to remember events before age 2. (p. 182; objective 4)

21. A reminder session involves the experiencing of some aspect of an event that triggers the entire memory of the event. (p. 182; objective 4)

22. Implicit memory is memory of experiences that can be recognized but not necessarily recalled. (p. 184; objective 4)

23. Explicit memory is memory that can be recalled on demand and demonstrated. (p. 184; objective 4)

24. Baby talk, or motherese, is a form of speech used by adults when talking to infants. Its hallmark is exaggerated expressiveness; it employs more questions, commands, and repetitions and fewer past tenses, pronouns, and complex sentences; it uses simpler vocabulary and grammar; it has a higher pitch and more low-to-high fluctuations. (p. 185; video lesson, segment 2; objective 9)

25. Babbling, which begins at 6 or 7 months, is characterized by the extended repetition of certain syllables (such as "ma-ma"). (p. 187; video lesson, segment 2; objective 9)

26. The naming explosion refers to the dramatic increase in the infant's vocabulary that begins at about 18 months of age. (p. 187; objective 8)

27. Another characteristic of infant speech is the use of the holophrase, in which a single word is used to convey a complete thought. (p. 188; objective 8)

28. An underextension of word meaning occurs when a baby applies a word more narrowly than its full meaning allows. (p. 188; objective 8)

29. Overextension is a characteristic of infant speech in which the infant overgeneralizes a known word by applying it to a large variety of objects or contexts. (p. 189; objective 8)

    Memory aid: In this behavior, the infant extends a word or grammatical rule beyond, or over, its normal boundaries.

30. The grammar of a language includes rules of word order, verb forms, and all other methods used to communicate meaning apart from words themselves. (p. 189; objective 8)

31. According to Chomsky, children possess an innate language acquisition device (LAD) that enables them to acquire language, including the basic aspects of grammar. (p. 192; video lesson, segment 2; objective 10)

32. Reduplicative babbling is a form of speech in which babies, at about seven to nine months, string together two syllables and repeat them over and over. (video lesson, segment 2; objective 8)

33. Semantics refers to the set of rules by which we derive meaning from the spoken sounds in a given language; also, the study of the meaning of words. (video lesson, segment 2; objective 8)

34. Intonation refers to the cadence, tone, or emphasis of a given utterance. Babies learn a great deal about intonation, including how to adjust the intonation of their sounds to change the meaning of an utterance. (video lesson, segment 2; objective 8)

35. Early communication skills, like crying, laughing, body movements, gestures, and facial expressions, can all have specific meaning. These early communication skills serve the primary role of language function: that is, to understand and be understood by others. (video lesson, segment 1; objective 8)

36. One of the keys to effective communication that babies must learn is language structure—that is, the particular words and rules of the infant's native tongue. Within the first two years of life, language structure begins to take shape.(video lesson, segment 1; objective 8)

Practice Questions I

Multiple-Choice Questions

1. c. is the correct answer. (p. 177; objective 5)

2. c. is the correct answer. (p. 170; video lesson, segment 1; objective 1)

3. b. is the correct answer. This was Piaget's most basic contribution to the study of infant cognition—that intelligence is revealed in behavior at every age. (p. 168; video lesson, segment 1; objective 1)

4. c. is the correct answer. (p. 175; objective 3)

   a. is incorrect. Intermodal perception involves associating information from one sensory modality with information from another.

   b. is incorrect. In cross-modal perception information from one sensory modality is used to imagine something in another modality.

   d. is incorrect. Dynamic perception is perception that focuses on movement.

5. c. is the correct answer. (pp. 167, 177; objectives 1 & 5)

   b. is incorrect. This is Chomsky's position.

   d. is incorrect. This issue was not discussed in the textbook.

6. a. is the correct answer. (p. 171; video lesson, segment 1; objective 1)

   b. & c. are incorrect. These abilities are not acquired until children are much older.

   d. is incorrect. Pretending is associated with stage six (18 to 24 months).

7. c. is the correct answer. (p. 171; video lesson, segment 1; objective 2)

8. d. is the correct answer. This is a synthesis of the theories of Skinner and Chomsky. (p. 196; video lesson, segment 2; objective 10)

9. b. is the correct answer. (p. 185; video lesson, segment 2; objective 8)

   a., c., & d. are incorrect. Children the world over, and in every Piagetian stage, follow the same sequence and approximately the same timetable for early language development.

10. c. is the correct answer. (p. 187; video lesson, segment 2; objective 8)

11. a. is the correct answer. (p. 188; objective 8)

   b. is incorrect. Baby talk is the speech adults use with infants.

c. is incorrect. An overextension is a grammatical error in which a word is generalized to an inappropriate context.

d. is incorrect. An underextension is the use of a word to refer to a narrower category of objects or events than the term signifies.

12. c. is the correct answer. At every age, children understand more speech than they can produce. (pp. 185–186; objective 8)

13. c. is the correct answer. (p. 185; video lesson, segment 2; objective 9)

a. is incorrect. A holophrase is a single word uttered by a toddler to express a complete thought.

b. is incorrect. According to Noam Chomsky, the LAD, or language acquisition device, is an innate ability in humans to acquire language.

d. is incorrect. These characteristic differences in pitch and structure are precisely what distinguish baby talk from regular conversation.

14. d. is the correct answer. (p. 180; objective 3)

15. c. is the correct answer. (pp. 175–176; objective 4)

16. c. is the answer (pp. 174–175; video lesson, segment 1; objective 7)

a. & b. are incorrect. In Piaget's theory, these refer to processes by which mental concepts incorporate new experiences (assimilation) or are modified in response to new experiences (accommodation).

d. is incorrect. Dynamic perception is perception that is primed to focus on movement and change.

Matching Items
17. f (p. 174; video lesson, segment 1; objective 1)
18. g (p. 177; objective 5)
19. e (p. 171; video lesson, segment 1; objective 2)
20. h (p. 178; objective 6)
21. j (p. 168; objective 1)
22. d (p. 184; objective 7)
23. l (p. 168; video lesson, segment 1; objective 1)
24. b (p. 187; video lesson, segment 2; objective 8)
25. i (p. 188; objective 8)
26. a (p. 189; objective 8)
27. k (p. 184; objective 7)
28. c (p. 179; objective 5)
29. m (video lesson, segment 2; objective 8)

Practice Questions II
Multiple-Choice Questions
1. b. is the correct answer. (p. 174; video lesson, segment 1; objective 1)

a. & c. These are stages two and three.

d. is incorrect. This is not one of Piaget's stages of sensorimotor intelligence.

2. d. is the correct answer. This is an example of perceptual constancy. (p. 179; objective 6)

3. c. is the correct answer. (pp. 171–173; video lesson, segment 1; objective 2)

4. a. is the correct answer. (pp. 177–178; objective 5)

b. is incorrect. Affordances are perceived by children; they don't reside in objects.

c. & d. are incorrect. Infants perceive graspability at an earlier age and long before their manual dexterity enables them to actually grasp successfully.

5. a. is the correct answer. Chomsky believed this device is innate. (p. 192; video lesson, segment 2; objective 10)

6. b. is the correct answer. (pp. 168–169; video lesson, segment 1; objective 1)

a. & c. are incorrect. Both of these occur later than stage one.

d. is incorrect. This is a hallmark of stage six.

7. a. is the correct answer. (p. 194; objective 10)

8. a. is the correct answer. (p. 173; video lesson, segment 1; objective 2)

9. c. is the correct answer. (p. 171; video lesson, segment 1; objective 1)

a. is incorrect. Reflexes are involuntary (and therefore unintentional) responses.

b. is incorrect. Affordances are perceived opportunities for interaction with objects.

d. is incorrect. Mental combinations are actions that are carried out mentally, rather than behaviorally. Moreover, mental combinations do not develop until a later age, during sensorimotor stage six.

10. b. is the correct answer. (pp. 185–187; video lesson, segment 2; objective 8)

11. d. is the correct answer. (p. 187; objective 8)

a. & b. are incorrect. Hearing and deaf babies do not differ in the overall likelihood that they will babble.

c. is incorrect. Deaf babies begin to babble vocally several months later than hearing babies do.

12. b. is the correct answer. (p. 190; video lesson, segment 2; objective 10)

a., c., & d. are incorrect. These views on language acquisition describe the theory offered by Noam Chomsky.

Matching Items

13. j (p. 171; video lesson, segment 1; objective 1)

14. a (p. 174; video lesson, segment 1; objective 4)

15. d (p. 182; objective 7)

16. l (video lesson, segment 2; objective 8)

17. b (p. 168; objective 1)

18. i (p. 174; video lesson, segment 1; objective 1)

19. c (p. 187; objective 8)

20. f (p. 188; objective 8)

21. e (p. 176; objective 3)

22. k (p. 169; objective 1)

23. g (p. 192; video lesson, segment 2; objective 8)

24. m (video lesson, segment 2; objective 10)

25. h (p. 185; video lesson, segment 2; objective 9)

Applying Your Knowledge

1. d. is the correct answer. The baby is clearly behaving purposefully, the hallmark of goal-directed behavior. (p. 171; objective 1)

   a. is incorrect. There is nothing imaginary in the child's behavior.

   b. is incorrect. An overextension occurs when the infant over generalizes the use of a word to an inappropriate object or context.

   c. is incorrect. Delayed imitation is the ability to imitate actions seen in the past.

2. c. is the correct answer. (p. 174; objective 1)

3. a. is the correct answer. The father's expression of delight is clearly a reinforcer in that it has increased the likelihood of the infant's vocalization. (p. 190; video lesson, segment 2; objective 10)

   b. & c. are incorrect. Modeling, or learning by imitation, would be implicated if the father attempted to increase the infant's vocalizations by repeatedly saying "da-da" himself, in the infant's presence.

   d. is incorrect. This is Chomsky's viewpoint; Skinner maintained that language is acquired through learning.

4. d. is the correct answer. The child is clearly overgeneralizing the word "dog" by applying it to other animals. (p. 189; objective 8)

   a. is incorrect. The holophrase is a single word that is used to express a complete thought.

   b. is incorrect. Babbling is the repetitious uttering of certain syllables, such as "ma-ma," or "da-da."

   c. is incorrect. Motherese, or baby talk, is the characteristic manner in which adults change the structure and pitch of their speech when conversing with infants.

5. c. is the correct answer. (p. 189; video lesson, segment 2; objective 8)

   a. is incorrect. At 18 months of age, most children have much smaller vocabularies.

   b. is incorrect. Speaking in holophrases is typical of younger infants.

6. d. is the correct answer. (p. 174; video lesson, segment 2; objective 1)

   a. is incorrect. Dynamic perception is perception primed to focus on movement and change.

   b. is incorrect. Object permanence is the awareness that objects do not cease to exist when they are out of sight.

   c. is incorrect. Intermodal perception is the ability to associate information from one sensory modality with information from another.

7. c. is the correct answer. (p. 170; video lesson, segment 2; objective 1)

8. d. is the correct answer. (p. 188; objective 8)

9. a. is the correct answer. Before object permanence is attained, an object that disappears from sight ceases to exist for the infant. (p. 171; video lesson, segment 1; objective 2)

   b. is incorrect. Intermodal perception is the ability to associate information from one sensory modality with information from another.

   c. is incorrect. Mental combinations are actions that are carried out mentally.

   d. is incorrect. Cross-modal perception is the ability to use information from one sensory modality to imagine something in another.

10. c. is the correct answer. (p. 188; objective 8)

   a. is incorrect. Because Christine is expressing a complete thought, her speech is much more than babbling.

   b. is incorrect. An overextension is the application of a word the child knows to an inappropriate context, such as "doggie" to all animals the child sees.

   d. is incorrect. The ability to understand subject-predicate order emerges later, when children begin forming two-word sentences.

11. b. is the correct answer. (p. 187; video lesson, segment 2; objective 8)

   a. is incorrect. Cooing is the pleasant-sounding utterances of the infant at about 2 months.

   c. is incorrect. The holophrase occurs later and refers to the toddler's use of a single word to express a complete thought.

   d. is incorrect. An overextension, or overgeneralization, is the application of a word to an inappropriate context, such as "doed" for the past tense of "do."

12. b. is the correct answer. In this example, the two-year-old has overgeneralized the concept "doggie" to all four-legged animals. (p. 189; objective 8)

13. c. is the correct answer. (p. 180; objective 3)

   a. is incorrect. Mental combinations, or sequences of action that are carried out mentally, are a hallmark of Piaget's stage four infant.

   b. is incorrect. The stage of the little scientist is Piaget's way of describing the infant as he or she begins to experiment and be creative.

   d. is incorrect. Object permanence, or the awareness that objects do not cease to exist simply because they are not in view, is not based on perceiving similarities among objects.

14. a. is the correct answer. (p. 188; objective 8)

Lesson Review

Lesson 7

The First Two Years
Cognitive Development

Please Note: Use this matrix to guide your study and achieve the learning objectives of this lesson. It will also help you to view the video, which defines and demonstrates important concepts and skills as they relate to everyday life.

Learning Objective	Textbook	Telecourse Student Guide	Video Lesson
1. Identify and describe Piaget's stages of sensorimotor intelligence, and give examples of the behavior associated with each stage.	pp. 167–171, 174, 177	Key Terms: 1, 2, 3, 4, 5, 6, 7, 9, 10, 11, 35, 36; Practice Questions I: 2, 3, 5, 6, 17, 21, 23; Practice Questions II: 1, 6, 9, 13, 17, 18, 22; Applying Your Knowledge: 1, 2, 6, 7.	Segment 1: *Sensorimotor Intelligence*
2. Explain what *object permanence* is, how it is tested in infancy, and what these tests reveal.	pp. 171–173	Key Terms: 8; Practice Questions I: 7, 19; Practice Questions II: 3, 8; Applying Your Knowledge: 9.	Segment 1: *Sensorimotor Intelligence*
3. Explain what habituation research has revealed about cognitive development in infancy.	pp. 175–176, 180	Key Terms: 13, 14, 15; Practice Questions I: 4, 14; Practice Questions II: 21; Applying Your Knowledge: 13.	
4. Describe the information processing model of cognition.	pp. 174–176, 182–184	Key Terms: 12, 20, 21, 22, 23; Practice Questions I: 15; Practice Questions II: 14.	
5. Explain the Gibsons' contextual view of perception, and relate it to the idea of *affordances*, giving examples of affordances perceived by infants.	pp. 167, 178–188	Key Terms: 16, 17, 18; Practice Questions I: 1, 5, 18; Practice Questions II: 4.	

Learning Objective	Textbook	Telecourse Student Guide	Video Lesson
6. Explain how the infant's focus on movement and change enhances sensory and perceptual skills and thus overall cognitive growth.	pp. 174–175, 178–179	Key Terms: 19; Practice Questions I: 20, 28; Practice Questions II: 2.	
7. Discuss research findings on infant memory and infants' understanding of categories.	pp. 174–175, 182–184	Practice Questions I: 16, 22, 27; Practice Questions II: 15.	Segment 1: *Sensorimotor Intelligence*
8. Describe language development during the first two years, and identify its major hallmarks.	pp. 185–189, 192	Key Terms: 26, 27, 28, 29, 30, 32, 33, 34, 35, 36; Practice Questions I: 9, 10, 11, 12, 24, 25, 26, 29; Practice Questions II: 10, 11, 16, 19, 20, 23; Applying Your Knowledge: 4, 5, 8, 10, 11, 12, 14.	Segment 2: *Language Development*
9. Explain the importance of *baby talk* (motherese), and identify its main features.	pp. 190–196	Key Terms: 31; Practice Questions I: 8; Practice Questions II: 5, 7, 12, 24 Applying Your Knowledge: 4	Segment 2: *Language Development*
10. Summarize the different theories that explain early language learning, and discuss how each theory might help caregivers encourage their child's language development.	pp. 185–187	Key Terms: 24, 25; Practice Questions I: 13; Practice Questions II: 25.	Segment 2: *Language Development*

Getting to Know You

Lesson 8

The First Two Years:
Psychosocial Development

Preview

Lesson 8 explores the psychosocial life of the developing person during the first two years. It begins with a description of the infant's emerging emotions and how they reflect increasing cognitive abilities. Newborns are innately predisposed to sociability, and are capable of expressing distress, sadness, contentment, and many other emotions, as well as responding to the emotions of other people.

This lesson also explores the social context in which a baby's emotions develop. By referencing their caregivers' signals, infants learn when and how to express their emotions. As **self-awareness** develops, many new emotions emerge, including embarrassment, shame, guilt, and pride. Parents who communicate effectively with their children are more responsive and tend to have children who are more skilled in communicating with others.

This lesson also presents the theories of Sigmund Freud and Erik Erikson that help us understand how the infant's emotional and behavioral responses begin to take on the various patterns that form personality. Important research on the nature and origins of **temperament**, which informs virtually every characteristic of the individual's developing personality, is also considered. Babies are not born with fully developed personalities. Instead, they come equipped with a basic set of temperamental tendencies in emotional expressiveness, activity level, and attention that, through their interactions with caregivers and others, are molded to form personality.

The final section of the lesson examines emotions and relationships from the perspective of parent–infant interaction. Videotaped studies of parents and infants, combined with laboratory studies, have greatly expanded our understanding of psychosocial development. In the video lesson, experts explain how the intricate patterns of parent-child interaction help infants learn to express and read emotions and promotes **attachment** to caregivers. Developmental psychologist Mary Ainsworth describes an experimental procedure she developed to measure the quality of attachment. The lesson concludes with a discussion of the impact of early day care on psychosocial development.

As you complete this lesson, consider an infant or toddler you know (and interview the child's parents if time allows). How would you describe the emotional development of this baby relative to others of the same age? What emotions have you noticed and in what situations? Describe the temperament of this child? For example, is this baby generally adventurous or cautious, easy going or fussy, active or sedentary? Does the child seem more attached to mom or dad at this stage? Does this emotional bond seem healthy and secure? What behavior leads you to believe that? Does this child attend day care? If so, describe the facility and the type of care provided. Would you say this is a "high-quality" facility? Why or why not?

Prior Telecourse Knowledge that Will Be Used in this Lesson

- The developmental theories of Sigmund Freud and Erik Erikson (from Lesson 1) will be used to help explain psychosocial development during the school years.

- Recall (from Lesson 1) that Freud's theory specifies five major stages of *psychosexual development,* during which the sensual satisfaction associated with the mouth, anus, or genitals is linked to the major developmental needs and challenges that are associated with that stage. This lesson focuses on the first two stages:

  1. **Oral Stage (birth to 1 year)** ← **The First Two Years**
  2. **Anal Stage (1 to 3 years)** ← **The First Two Years**
  3. Phallic Stage (3 to 6 years)
  4. Latency Stage (7 to 11 years)
  5. Genital Stage (adolescence through adulthood)

- Recall (from Lesson 1) that Erik Erikson's theory specifies eight stages of *psychosocial development,* each of which is characterized by a particular challenge, or *developmental crisis,* that is central to that stage of life and must be resolved. This lesson focuses on the first two stages:

  1. **Trust versus Mistrust (birth to 1 year)** ← **The First Two Years**
  2. **Autonomy versus Shame and Doubt** ← **The First Two Years** **(1 to 3 years)**
  3. Initiative versus Guilt (3 to 6 years)
  4. Industry versus Inferiority (7 to 11 years)
  5. Identify versus Role Confusion (adolescence)
  6. Intimacy versus Isolation (adulthood)
  7. Generativity versus Stagnation (adulthood)
  8. Integrity versus Despair (adulthood)

Learning Objectives

Use this information to guide your reading, viewing, thinking, and studying. After successfully completing this lesson, you should be able to:

1. Describe the basic emotions expressed by infants during the first days and months.
2. Describe the main developments in the emotional life of the child between 6 months and 2 years.
3. Discuss the concept of social referencing, including its development and role in shaping later emotions.
4. Discuss contemporary views on the role of the father in infant psychosocial development.
5. Discuss the links between an infant's emerging self-awareness and his or her continuing emotional development.
6. Discuss how Freud's psychosexual stages can be used to explain psychosocial development during the first two years.
7. Discuss how Erikson's psychosocial stages can be used to explain psychosocial development during the first two years.

8. Define and describe the concept of temperament, discuss its development as an interaction of nature and nurture, and explain the significance of research on temperament for parents and caregivers.

9. Describe the synchrony of parent–infant interaction during the first year, and discuss its significance for the developing person.

10. Define attachment, explain how it is measured and how it is influenced by context, and discuss the long-term consequences of secure and insecure attachment.

11. Describe four categories of adult attachments and how each affects the child's attachment to the parent.

12. Discuss the potential effects of nonmaternal care on a baby's development, and identify the factors that define high-quality day care.

📖 **Read Chapter 7, "The First Two Years: Psychosocial Development," pages 201–232.**

📷 **View the video for Lesson 8, "Getting to Know You."**
Segment 1: *Development through Crises*
Segment 2: *Attachment*
Segment 3: *Attachment and Day Care*

Summary

Contemporary developmentalists have revised a number of the traditional views of psychosocial development. It was once believed, for example, that infants did not have any real emotions. Researchers now know, however, that in the very first days and weeks of life, infants express and sense many emotions, including fear, anger, happiness, and surprise. Over the first two years, emotions change from a basic set of reactions to complex, self-conscious responses as infants become increasingly independent.

In the traditional view of personality development, the infant was seen as a passive recipient of the personality created almost entirely by the actions of his or her primary caregivers. Yet it is now apparent that many aspects of **temperament** are present in infants at birth and that active caregiver-infant interaction within a secure and nurturing environment is a central factor in the child's psychosocial development. During infancy, increasing independence, which Sigmund Freud explains in terms of the **oral** and **anal stages**, marks this development. Erik Erikson explains it in terms of "**trust versus mistrust**" and "**autonomy versus shame and doubt.**"

A key factor in this psychosocial development is **attachment**—the affectional tie between infants and their primary caregivers. In infants the world over, attachment develops at about 7 months, when babies first become aware that other people stay in existence even when they're out of sight. **Secure attachment** helps ensure that the relatively helpless infant receives the adult care he or she needs in order to survive, and sets the stage for the child's increasingly independent exploration of the world. By age 2, the toddler has a distinct personality that is the product of the social context and the innate temperament of the young infant.

Special Note: We will cover the specific effects that fathers can have on their children (pp. 211–212) in telecourse Lesson 10, "Fatherhood."

📖 **Review all reading assignments for this lesson.**

🖥 **As assigned by your instructor, complete the optional online component for this lesson.**

Key Terms

Using your own words, write a brief definition or explanation of each of the following terms on a separate piece of paper.

1. stranger wariness
2. separation anxiety
3. temperament
4. Big Five
5. approach-withdrawal
6. goodness of fit
7. colic
8. synchrony
9. still face technique
10. social referencing
11. self-awareness
12. oral stage
13. anal stage
14. trust versus mistrust
15. autonomy versus shame and doubt
16. working model
17. attachment
18. proximity-seeking behaviors
19. contact-maintaining behaviors
20. secure attachment
21. secure base for exploration
22. insecure attachment
23. insecure-avoidant attachment
24. insecure-resistant/ambivalent attachment
25. Strange Situation
26. disorganized attachment
27. nonmaternal/nonparental child care

Practice Questions I

Multiple-Choice Questions

1. Newborns have two identifiable emotions:
   a. shame and distress.
   b. distress and contentment.
   c. anger and joy.
   d. pride and guilt

2. Which of the following is customarily used to assess synchrony?
   a. the Strange Situation
   b. the habituation technique
   c. the still face technique
   d. social referencing

3. An infant's fear of being left by the mother or other caregiver, called _____, peaks at about _____.
   a. separation anxiety; 14 months
   b. stranger wariness; 8 months
   c. separation anxiety; 8 months
   d. stranger wariness; 14 months

4. Social referencing refers to
   a. parenting skills that change over time.
   b. changes in community values regarding, for example, the acceptability of using physical punishment with small children.
   c. the support network for new parents provided by extended family members.
   d. the infant response of looking to trusted adults for emotional cues in uncertain situations.

5. The "big five" temperament dimensions are
   a. emotional stability, openness, introversion, sociability, and locus of control.
   b. neuroticism, extroversion, openness, emotional stability, and sensitivity.
   c. agreeableness, conscientiousness, neuroticism, openness, and extroversion.
   d. neuroticism, gregariousness, extroversion, impulsiveness, and sensitivity.

6. The concept of a working model is most consistent with
   a. psychoanalytic theory.
   b. behaviorism.
   c. cognitive theory.
   d. sociocultural theory.

7. Freud's oral stage corresponds to Erikson's crisis of
   a. orality versus anality.
   b. trust versus mistrust.
   c. autonomy versus shame and doubt.
   d. secure versus insecure attachment.

8. Erikson feels that the development of a sense of trust in early infancy depends on the quality of the
   a. infant's food.
   b. child's genetic inheritance.
   c. relationship with caregiver.
   d. introduction to toilet training.

9. The increased tendency of toddlers to express frustration and anger is most closely linked to new developments in their cognitive abilities, especially those related to
   a. goal-directed actions.
   b. social referencing.
   c. self-awareness.
   d. stranger wariness.

10. "Easy," "slow to warm up," and "difficult" are descriptions of different
    a. forms of attachment.
    b. types of temperament.
    c. types of parenting.
    d. toddler responses to the Strange Situation.

11. Research studies of infant caregiving have found all of the following statements to be true **EXCEPT**:

    a. When both parents work outside the home, child care tends to be shared equally by mothers and fathers.

    b. Fathers can provide the emotional and cognitive nurturing that children need.

    c. Divorced fathers spend less time caring for infants than married fathers do.

    d. Contemporary fathers are more actively engaged with their children than fathers were in 1970.

12. Synchrony is a term that describes

    a. the carefully coordinated interaction between parent and infant.

    b. a mismatch of the temperaments of parent and infant.

    c. a research technique involving videotapes.

    d. the concurrent evolution of different species.

13. The emotional tie that develops between an infant and his or her primary caregiver is called

    a. self-awareness.

    b. synchrony.

    c. affiliation.

    d. attachment.

14. An important effect of secure attachment is the promotion of

    a. self-awareness.

    b. curiosity and self-directed behavior.

    c. dependency.

    d. all of the above.

15. The sight of almost any human face is most likely to produce a smile in a _____-month-old.

    a. three

    b. six

    c. nine

    d. twelve

True or False Items

Write T (for true) or F (for false) on the line in front of each statement.

16. _____ Most developmentalists think that infants must learn to be sociable.

17. _____ The major difference between a six-month-old and a twelve-month-old is that emotions become less intense.

18. _____ A baby at 11 months is likely to display both stranger wariness and separation anxiety.

19. _____ Emotional development is affected by cognitive development.

20. _____ A securely attached toddler is most likely to stay close to his or her mother even in a familiar environment.

21. _____ Current research shows that the majority of infants in day care are insecurely attached.

22. _____ Women are biologically predisposed to be better parents than men are.

23. _____ Temperament is genetically determined and is unaffected by environmental factors.

24. _____ Self-awareness enables toddlers to be self-critical and to feel guilt.

25. _____ Adult attachment classifications parallel those of infancy.

26. _____ Insecurely attached children display at least three different patterns of attachment behavior.

27. _____ Developmental psychologists express the greatest concerns about the early mental health of children who display insecure-resistant attachment.

28. _____ Studies show that the influence of nonparental child care can be both positive and negative.

Practice Questions II

Multiple-Choice Questions

1. Infant-caregiver interactions that are marked by inconsistency are usually classified as
   a. disorganized.
   b. insecure-avoidant.
   c. insecure-resistant.
   d. none of the above.

2. Freud's anal stage corresponds to Erikson's crisis of
   a. autonomy versus shame and doubt.
   b. trust versus mistrust.
   c. orality versus anality.
   d. identity versus role confusion.

3. Not until the sense of self begins to emerge do babies realize that they are seeing their own faces in the mirror. This realization usually occurs
   a. shortly before 3 months.
   b. at about 6 months.
   c. between 15 and 24 months.
   d. after 24 months.

4. Lately, three-month-old Kevin sleeps less at night than other infants and engages in prolonged bouts of fussiness and crying. Kevin's worried mother tells her pediatrician that her son seems to be
   a. slow to warm up.
   b. a "difficult" baby.
   c. suffering from colic.
   d. low reactive.

5. Emotions such as shame, guilt, embarrassment, and pride emerge at the same time that

   a. the social smile appears.

   b. aspects of the infant's temperament can first be discerned.

   c. self-awareness begins to emerge.

   d. parents initiate toilet training.

6. According to the research, the NYLS temperamental characteristics that are not particularly stable are quality of mood and

   a. rhythmicity.

   b. activity level.

   c. self-awareness.

   d. sociability (or shyness).

7. In the second six months, stranger wariness is a

   a. result of insecure attachment.

   b. result of social isolation.

   c. normal emotional response.

   d. setback in emotional development.

8. The caregiving environment can affect a child's temperament through

   a. the child's temperamental pattern and the demands of the home environment.

   b. parental expectations.

   c. both a and b.

   d. neither a nor b.

9. Compared to children who are insecurely attached, those who are securely attached are

   a. more independent.

   b. more curious.

   c. more sociable.

   d. characterized by all of the above.

10. The later consequences of secure and insecure attachment for children are

    a. subject to change due to the child's current rearing circumstances.

    b. irreversible, regardless of the child's current rearing circumstances.

    c. more significant in girls than in boys.

    d. more significant in boys than in girls.

11. The attachment pattern marked by anxiety and uncertainty is

    a. insecure-avoidant.

    b. insecure-resistant/ambivalent.

    c. disorganized.

    d. Type B.

12. Compared with mothers, fathers are more likely to
    a. engage in noisier, more boisterous play.
    b. encourage intellectual development in their children.
    c. encourage social development in their children.
    d. read to their toddlers.

13. Which of the following most accurately summarizes the relationship between early attachment and later social relationships?
    a. Attachment in infancy determines whether a child will grow to be sociable.
    b. Attachment relationships are sometimes, though rarely, altered as children grow older.
    c. There is, at best, only a weak correlation between early attachment and later social relationships.
    d. Early attachment biases, but does not inevitably determine, later social relationships.

14. In her research, Mary Main has discovered that
    a. adult attachment classifications parallel those of infancy.
    b. autonomous mothers tend to have insecurely attached babies.
    c. preoccupied mothers tend to have avoidant babies.
    d. all of the above are true.

Matching Items
Match each theorist, term, or concept with its corresponding description or definition.

Theorists, Terms, or Concepts
15. _____ temperament
16. _____ Erik Erikson
17. _____ the Strange Situation
18. _____ synchrony
19. _____ trust versus mistrust
20. _____ Sigmund Freud
21. _____ social referencing
22. _____ autonomy versus shame and doubt
23. _____ self-awareness
24. _____ Mary Ainsworth
25. _____ proximity-seeking behaviors
26. _____ contact-maintaining behaviors

Descriptions or Definitions
a. looking to caregivers for emotional cues
b. the crisis of infancy
c. the crisis of toddlerhood
d. approaching, following, and climbing
e. theorist who described psychosexual stages of development
f. researcher who devised a laboratory procedure for studying attachment
g. laboratory procedure for studying attachment
h. the relatively consistent, basic dispositions inherent in a person
i. clinging and resisting being put down
j. coordinated interaction between parent and infant
k. theorist who described psychosocial stages of development
l. a person's sense of being distinct from others

Applying Your Knowledge

1. In laboratory tests of attachment, when the mother returns to the playroom after a short absence, a securely attached infant is most likely to

   a. cry and protest the mother's return.

   b. climb into the mother's lap, then leave to resume play.

   c. climb into the mother's lap and stay there.

   d. continue playing without acknowledging the mother.

2. After a scary fall, eighteen-month-old Jaime looks to his mother to see if he should cry or laugh. Jaime's behavior is an example of

   a. proximity-seeking behavior.

   b. social referencing.

   c. insecure attachment.

   d. the crisis of trust versus mistrust.

3. Which of the following is a clear sign of an infant's attachment to a particular person?

   a. The infant turns to that person when distressed.

   b. The infant protests when that person leaves a room.

   c. The infant may cry when strangers appear.

   d. All of the above are signs of infant attachment.

4. If you had to predict a newborn baby's temperament "type" solely on the basis of probability, which classification would be the most likely?

   a. easy

   b. slow to warm up

   c. difficult

   d. There is not enough information to make a prediction.

5. Kenny becomes very emotional when talking about his relationship with his parents; consequently, he is unable to discuss his early attachment experiences objectively. Kenny's attachment classification is probably

   a. autonomous.

   b. dismissing.

   c. preoccupied.

   d. unresolved.

6. Which of the following mothers is most likely to have an avoidant son or daughter?

   a. Kathy, who is still coping with the loss of her parents

   b. Miriam, who idealizes her parents, yet devalues the importance of her own relationships

   c. Pearl, who is able to discuss her own early attachment experiences quite objectively, despite their painful nature

   d. Carmen, who spends a lot of time thinking about her own relationship with her parents

7. One way in which infant psychosocial development has changed is that today
   a. many infants have their first encounters with other infants at a younger age.
   b. parental influence is less important than it was in the past.
   c. social norms are nearly the same for the sexes.
   d. infants tend to have fewer social encounters than in the past.

8. Josh, who is about to become a father and primary caregiver, is worried that he will never have the natural caregiving skills that the child's mother has. Studies on father–infant relationships show that
   a. infants nurtured by single fathers are more likely to be insecurely attached.
   b. fathers can provide the emotional and cognitive nurturing necessary for healthy infant development.
   c. women are biologically predisposed to be better parents than men are.
   d. social development is usually slightly delayed in children whose fathers are the primary caregiver.

9. Arshad's mother left him alone in the room for a few minutes. When she returned, Arshad seemed indifferent to her presence. According to Mary Ainsworth's research with children in the Strange Situation, Arshad is probably
   a. a normal, independent infant.
   b. an abused child.
   c. insecurely attached.
   d. securely attached.

10. Rachael and Lev, who are first-time parents, are concerned because their one-month-old baby is difficult to care for and hard to soothe. They are worried that they are doing something wrong. You inform them that their child is probably that way because
    a. they are reinforcing the child's tantrum behaviors.
    b. they are not meeting some biological need of the child's.
    c. of his or her inherited temperament.
    d. at one month of age all children are difficult to care for and hard to soothe.

11. Two-year-old Anita and her mother visit a day-care center. Seeing an interesting toy, Anita runs a few steps toward it, then stops and looks back to see if her mother is coming. Anita's behavior illustrates
    a. the crisis of autonomy versus shame and doubt.
    b. synchrony.
    c. dyssynchrony.
    d. social referencing.

12. Felix eats, chews, and talks excessively in quest of pleasures that were denied in infancy. Freud would probably say that Felix is
    a. anally expulsive.
    b. anally retentive.
    c. fixated in the oral stage.
    d. experiencing the crisis of trust versus mistrust.

13. A researcher at the child development center places a dot on an infant's nose and watches to see if the infant reacts to her image in a mirror by touching her nose. Evidently, the researcher is testing the child's

   a. attachment.

   b. temperament.

   c. self-awareness.

   d. social referencing.

14. Four-month-old Aaron and his thirteen-month-old sister Carla are left in the care of a babysitter. As their parents are leaving, it is to be expected that

   a. Aaron will become extremely upset, while Carla will calmly accept her parents' departure.

   b. Carla will become more upset over her parents' departure than will Aaron.

   c. Aaron and Carla will both become quite upset as their parents leave.

   d. Neither Aaron nor Carla will become very upset as their parents leave.

15. You have been asked to give a presentation on "Mother–Infant Attachment" to a group of expectant mothers. Basing your presentation on the research of Mary Ainsworth, you conclude your talk by stating that mother–infant attachment depends mostly on

   a. an infant's innate temperament.

   b. the amount of time mothers spend with their infants.

   c. sensitive and responsive caregiving in the early months.

   d. whether the mother herself was securely attached as an infant.

Answer Key

Key Terms

1. A common early fear, stranger wariness (also called fear of strangers) is first noticeable at about 6 months. (p. 203; objective 2)

2. Separation anxiety, which is the infant fear of being left by the mother or other caregiver, emerges at about 8 or 9 months, peaks at about 14 months, and then gradually subsides. (p. 203; objective 2)

3. Temperament refers to the set of innate tendencies, or dispositions, that underlie and affect each person's interactions with people, situations, and events. (p. 204; objective 8)

4. The "big five" are the five major clusters of personality found in adults, including extroversion, agreeableness, conscientiousness, neuroticism, and openness. (p. 205; objective 8)

5. Approach-withdrawal is a trait whose measurement helps classify children as fearful, outgoing, or low-reactive. (p. 206; objective 9)

6. Goodness of fit is the match between the child's temperamental pattern and the demands of the environment. (p. 206; objective 8)

7. Colic is a condition of infancy in which indigestion triggers prolonged bouts of crying and fussiness. (p. 208; objective 1)

8. Synchrony refers to the coordinated interaction between caregiver and infant that helps infants learn to express and read emotions. (p. 208; objective 9)

9. The still face technique is a method of studying synchrony that measures an infant's reaction when his or her caregiver merely stares at the baby for a minute or two. (p. 210; objective 10)

10. When infants engage in social referencing, they are looking to trusted adults for emotional cues on how to interpret uncertain situations. (p. 210; objective 3)

11. Self-awareness refers to a person's sense of himself or herself as being distinct from other people that makes possible many new self-conscious emotions, including shame, guilt, embarrassment, and pride. (p. 213; objective 5)

12. In Freud's first stage of psychosexual development, the oral stage, the mouth is the most important source of gratification for the infant. (p. 215; objective 6)

13. According to Freud, during the second year infants are in the anal stage of psychosexual development and derive sensual pleasure from the stimulation of the bowels and psychological pleasure from their control. (p. 215; objective 6)

14. In Erikson's theory, the crisis of infancy is one of trust versus mistrust, in which the infant learns whether the world is a secure place in which basic needs will be met. (p. 215; objective 7)

15. In Erikson's theory, the crisis of toddlerhood is one of autonomy versus shame and doubt, in which toddlers strive to rule their own actions and bodies. (p. 216; objective 7)

16. According to cognitive theory, infants use social relationships to develop a set of assumptions called a working model that organizes their perceptions and experiences. (p. 217; objective 6)

17. Attachment is the enduring emotional tie that a person or animal forms with another. (pp. 218–219; objective 10)

18. Following, approaching, and other proximity-seeking behaviors are intended to place an individual close to another person to whom he or she is attached. (p. 219; objective 10)

19. Clinging, resisting being put down, and other contact-maintaining behaviors are intended to keep a person near another person to whom he or she is attached. (p. 219; objective 10)

20. A secure attachment is one in which the infant derives comfort and confidence from the "secure base" provided by a caregiver. (p. 219; objective 10)

21. Responsive caregivers promote secure attachment by providing a secure base for exploration from which their children feel confident in venturing forth. (p. 219; objective 11)

22. Insecure attachment is characterized by the infant's fear, anger, or seeming indifference toward the caregiver. (p. 219; objective 10)

23. Insecure-avoidant attachment is a form of insecure attachment in which the child is likely to disregard or avoid a caregiver. (p. 219; video lesson, segment 2; objective 10)

24. Insecure-resistant/ambivalent attachment is a form of attachment in which children become very upset when they are separated from a caregiver, but also fail to find comfort when the primary caregiver returns. (p. 219; video lesson, segment 2; objective 10)

25. The Strange Situation is a laboratory procedure developed by Mary Ainsworth for assessing attachment. Infants are observed in a playroom, in several successive episodes, while the caregiver (usually the mother) and a stranger move in and out of the room. (p. 220; objective 10)

26. Disorganized attachment is a form of attachment in which infants display inconsistent attachment behaviors, acting both avoidantly and resistantly to their primary caregivers. (p. 221; video lesson, segment 2; objective 10)

27. Nonmaternal child care means care provided by anyone but the mother, which can include the father or other relatives. Nonparental child care means care provided by anyone except the mother or father. As the child's age increases, this care is more likely to take the form of an organized and structured program conducted outside the home. (p. 224; video lesson, segment 3; objective 12)

Practice Questions I

Multiple-Choice Questions

1. b. is the correct answer. (p. 202; objective 1)

    a., c., & d. are incorrect. These emotions emerge later in infancy, at about the same time as self-awareness emerges.

2. c. is the correct answer. (p. 210; objective 11)

    a. is incorrect. The Strange Situation is used to measure attachment.

    b. is incorrect. Habituation, which is not discussed in this chapter, is used to measure an infant's perceptual abilities.

    d. is incorrect. Social referencing is not a research technique; it is the phenomenon in which infants look to trusted caregivers for emotional cues in uncertain situations.

3. a. is the correct answer. (p. 203; objective 2)

    b. & d. are incorrect. This fear, which is also called fear of strangers, peaks by 10 to 14 months.

4. d. is the correct answer. (p. 210; video lesson, segment 2; objective 3)

5. c. is the correct answer. (p. 205; objective 8)

6. c. is the correct answer. (p. 217; objective 2)

    a. is incorrect. Reinforcement and punishment have no place in the psychoanalytic perspective.

    c. is incorrect. This is Erikson's theory, which sees development as occurring through a series of basic crises.

    d. is incorrect. This perspective analyzes how genes and environment contribute to development.

7. b. is the correct answer. (p. 215; objectives 6 & 7)

    a. is incorrect. Orality and anality refer to personality traits that result from fixation in the oral and anal stages, respectively.

    c. is incorrect. According to Erikson, this is the crisis of toddlerhood, which corresponds to Freud's anal stage.

    d. is incorrect. This is not a developmental crisis in Erikson's theory.

8. c. is the correct answer. (p. 215; video lesson, segment 1; objective 7)

9. a. is the correct answer. Anger increases with age because toddlers are able to anticipate events and realize that other people's actions sometimes block their own efforts. (p. 203; objective 2)

10. b. is the correct answer. (p. 205; video lesson, segment 1; objective 8)

    a. is incorrect. "Secure" and "insecure" are different forms of attachment.

    c. is incorrect. The lesson does not describe different types of parenting.

    d. is incorrect. The Strange Situation is a test of attachment, rather than of temperament.

11. a. is the correct answer. (pp. 211–212; objective 4)

12. a. is the correct answer. (pp. 208–209; video lesson, segment 2; objective 9)

13. d. is the correct answer. (p. 218; video lesson, segment 2; objective 10)

a. is incorrect. Self-awareness refers to the infant's developing sense of "me and mine."

b. is incorrect. Synchrony describes the coordinated interaction between infant and caregiver.

c. is incorrect. Affiliation describes the tendency of people at any age to seek the companionship of others.

14. b. is the correct answer. (p. 223; video lesson, segment 2; objective 10)

a. is incorrect. The textbook does not link self-awareness to secure attachment.

c. is incorrect. On the contrary, secure attachment promotes independence in infants and children.

15. a. is the correct answer. (p. 208; objective 1)

b., c., & d. are incorrect. As infants become older, they smile more selectively.

True or False Items

16. F   Most developmentalists believe that infants are born with a tendency toward sociability as a means of survival. (p. 207; objective 1)

17. F   Emotions become more intense and are manifested more quickly and more persistently. (p. 210; objective 2)

18. T   (p. 203; objective 2)

19. T   (p. 203; objective 2)

20. F   A securely attached toddler is most likely to explore the environment, the mother's presence being enough to give him or her the courage to do so. (p. 219; video lesson, segment 2; objective 10)

21. F   Many researchers believe that high-quality day care is not likely to harm the child. In fact, it is thought to be beneficial to the development of cognitive and social skills. (p. 225; video lesson, segment 3; objective 12)

22. F   (pp. 211–212; objective 4)

23. F   Temperament is a product of both nature and nurture. (p. 206; objective 8)

24. T   (p. 213; objective 5)

25. T   (pp. 228–229; objective 11)

26. T   (p. 220; video lesson, segment 2; objective 10)

27. F   Experts express the greatest concerns about children who display insecure-disorganized attachment. (video lesson, segment 2; objective 10)

28. T   (video lesson, segment 3; objective 12)

Practice Questions II

Multiple-Choice Questions

1. a. is the correct answer. (p. 221; objective 11)

2. a. is the correct answer. (pp. 215–216; objectives 6 & 7)

3. c. is the correct answer. (p. 213; objective 5)

4. c. is the correct answer. (p. 208; objective 1)

a., b., & d. are incorrect. These terms relate to temperament; Kevin's condition developed only recently.

5. c. is the correct answer. (p. 213; objective 5)

a. & b. are incorrect. The social smile, as well as temperamental characteristics, emerge well before the first signs of self-awareness.

d. is incorrect. Contemporary developmentalists link these emotions to self-consciousness, rather than any specific environmental event such as toilet training.

6. a. is the correct answer. (pp. 205–206; objective 8)

   b. & d. are incorrect. Activity level and sociability are much less variable than rhythmicity and quality of mood.

   c. is incorrect. Self-awareness is not a temperamental characteristic.

7. c. is the correct answer. (p. 203; objective 2)

8. c. is the correct answer. (pp. 206–207; objective 8)

9. d. is the correct answer. (pp. 222–223; video lesson, segment 2; objective 10)

10. a. is the correct answer. (p. 223; video lesson, segment 2; objective 10)

    c. & d. are incorrect. The textbook does not suggest that the consequences of secure and insecure attachment differ in boys and girls.

11. b. is the correct answer. (p. 219; objective 11)

    a. is incorrect. Insecure-avoidant attachment is marked by behaviors that indicate an infant is uninterested in a caregiver's presence or departure.

    c. is incorrect. Disorganized attachment is marked only by the inconsistency of infant-caregiver behaviors.

    d. is incorrect. Type B, or secure attachment, is marked by behaviors that indicate an infant is using a caregiver as a secure base from which to explore the environment.

12. a. is the correct answer. (p. 212; objective 4)

13. d. is the correct answer. (p. 223; video lesson, segment 2; objective 10)

14. a. is the correct answer. (pp. 227–228; objective 11)

    b. is incorrect. Autonomous mothers tend to have securely attached infants.

    c. is incorrect. Preoccupied mothers tend to have resistant infants.

Matching Items

15. h (p. 204; video lesson, segment 1; objective 8)

16. k (p. 215; video lesson, segment 1; objective 7)

17. g (p. 220; video lesson, segment 2; objective 10)

18. j (p. 208; video lesson, segment 2; objective 9)

19. b (p. 215; video lesson, segment 1; objective 7)

20. e (pp. 214–215; objective 6)

21. a (p. 210; video lesson, segment 2; objective 3)

22. c (p. 216; video lesson, segment 1; objective 7)

23. l (p. 213; objective 5)

24. f (p. 219; video lesson, segment 2; objective 10)

25. d (p. 219; video lesson, segment 2; objective 10)

26. i (p. 219; video lesson, segment 2; objective 10)

Applying Your Knowledge

1. b. is the correct answer. (p. 220; video lesson, segment 2; objective 10)

   a., c., & d. are incorrect. These responses are more typical of insecurely attached infants.

2. b. is the correct answer. (pp. 210–212; video lesson, segment 2; objective 10)

3. d. is the correct answer. (pp. 218–219; video lesson, segment 2; objective 10)

4. a. is the correct answer. About 40 percent of young infants can be described as "easy." (p. 205; objective 8)

    b. is incorrect. About 15 percent of infants are described as "slow to warm up."

    c. is incorrect. About 10 percent of infants are described as "difficult."

5. c. is the correct answer. (p. 228; objective 11)

    a. is incorrect. Autonomous adults are able to talk objectively about their own early attachments.

    b. is incorrect. Dismissing adults devalue the importance of attachment relationships.

    d. is incorrect. Unresolved adults have not yet reconciled their own early attachments.

6. b. is the correct answer. (pp. 227–228; objective 11)

    a. is incorrect. Kathy would be classified as "unresolved."

    c. is incorrect. Autonomous adults, such as Pearl, tend to have securely attached infants.

    d. is incorrect. Preoccupied adults, such as Carmen, tend to have resistant offspring.

7. a. is the correct answer. (p. 234; objective 12)

8. b. is the correct answer. (pp. 212–213; objective 4)

9. c. is the correct answer. (p. 219; video lesson, segment 2; objective 10)

    a. & d. are incorrect. When their mothers return following an absence, securely attached infants usually reestablish social contact (with a smile or by climbing into their laps) and then resume playing.

    b. is incorrect. There is no evidence in this example that Arshad is an abused child.

10. c. is the correct answer. (pp. 204–205; objective 8)

    a. & b. are incorrect. There is no evidence in the question that the parents are reinforcing tantrum behavior or failing to meet some biological need of the child's.

    d. is incorrect. On the contrary, about 40 percent of infants are "easy" in temperamental style.

11. d. is the correct answer. (p. 210; video lesson, segment 2; objective 3)

    a. is incorrect. According to Erikson, this is the crisis of toddlerhood.

    b. is incorrect. This describes a moment of coordinated and mutually responsive interaction between a parent and an infant.

    c. is incorrect. Dyssynchrony occurs when the coordinated pace and timing of a synchronous interaction are temporarily lost.

12. c. is the correct answer. (p. 215; objective 6)

    a. & b. are incorrect. In Freud's theory, a person who is fixated in the anal stage exhibits messiness and disorganization or compulsive neatness.

    d. is incorrect. Erikson, rather than Freud, proposed crises of development.

13. c. is the correct answer. (pp. 213–214; objective 5)

14. b. is the correct answer. The fear of being left by a caregiver (separation anxiety) emerges at about 8 or 9 months, and peaks at about 14 months. For this reason, four-month-old Aaron can be expected to become less upset than his older sister. (p. 203; objective 2)

15. c. is the correct answer. (pp. 221–222; video lesson, segment 2; objective 10)

Lesson Review

Lesson 8

The First Two Years
Psychosocial Development

Please Note: Use this matrix to guide your study and achieve the learning objectives of this lesson. It will also help you to view the video, which defines and demonstrates important concepts and skills as they relate to everyday life.

Learning Objective	Textbook	Telecourse Student Guide	Video Lesson
1. Describe the basic emotions expressed by infants during the first days and months.	pp. 207–208, 210–211	Key Terms: 7; Practice Questions I: 1, 15, 16; Practice Questions II: 4.	
2. Describe the main developments in the emotional life of the child between 6 months and 2 years.	pp. 208–210	Key Terms: 1, 2; Practice Questions I: 3, 6, 9, 17, 18, 19; Practice Questions II: 7; Applying Your Knowledge: 14.	
3. Discuss the concept of social referencing, including its development and role in shaping later emotions.	pp. 210–211, 213–214	Key Terms: 10; Practice Questions I: 4; Practice Questions II: 21; Applying Your Knowledge: 11.	Segment 2: *Attachment*
4. Discuss contemporary views on the role of the father in infant psychosocial development.	pp. 211–213	Practice Questions I: 11, 22; Practice Questions II: 12; Applying Your Knowledge: 8.	Segment 2: *Attachment*
5. Discuss the links between an infant's emerging self-awareness and his or her continuing emotional development.	pp. 214–216	Key Terms: 11; Practice Questions I: 24; Practice Questions II: 3, 5, 23; Applying Your Knowledge: 13.	

Learning Objective	Textbook	Telecourse Student Guide	Video Lesson
6. Discuss how Freud's psychosexual stages can be used to explain psychosocial development during the first two years.	pp. 217–218	Key Terms: 12, 13, 16; Practice Questions I: 7; Practice Questions II: 2, 20; Applying Your Knowledge: 12.	Segment 1: *Development through Crises*
7. Discuss how Erikson's psychosocial stages can be used to explain psychosocial development during the first two years.	pp. 218–219	Key Terms: 14, 15; Practice Questions I: 7, 8; Practice Questions II: 2, 16, 19, 22.	Segment 1: *Development through Crises*
8. Define and describe the concept of temperament, discuss its development as an interaction of nature and nurture, and explain the significance of research on temperament for parents and caregivers.	pp. 219–223	Key Terms: 3, 4, 6; Practice Questions I: 5, 10, 23; Practice Questions II: 6, 8, 15; Applying Your Knowledge: 4, 10.	Segment 1: *Development through Crises*
9. Describe the synchrony of parent–infant interaction during the first year, and discuss its significance for the developing person.	pp. 221–225	Key Terms: 5, 8; Practice Questions I: 12; Practice Questions II: 18.	Segment 2: *Attachment*
10. Define attachment, explain how it is measured and how it is influenced by context, and discuss the long-term consequences of secure and insecure attachment.	pp. 210–211, 221–222, 225–231	Key Terms: 9, 17, 18, 19, 20, 22, 23, 24, 25, 26; Practice Questions I: 13, 14, 20, 26, 27; Practice Questions II: 9, 10, 13, 17, 24, 25, 26; Applying Your Knowledge: 1, 2, 3, 9, 15.	Segment 2: *Attachment*
11. Describe four categories of adult attachments and how each affects the child's attachment to the parent.	pp. 232–233	Key Terms: 21; Practice Questions I: 2, 25; Practice Questions II: 1, 11, 14; Applying Your Knowledge: 5, 6.	Segment 2: *Attachment*
12. Discuss potential effects of nonmaternal care on a baby's development, and identify the factors that define high-quality day care.	pp. 234–236	Key Terms: 27; Practice Questions I: 21, 28; Applying Your Knowledge: 7.	Segment 3: *Attachment and Day Care*

Off to a Good Start

Lesson 9

The First Two Years:
Summary

Preview

Each of the major developmental units in this telecourse ("The First Two Years," "The Play Years," "The School Years," and "Adolescence") will end with a summary lesson describing "The Developing Person So Far." Lesson 9, which is the first of these summary lessons, summarizes biosocial, cognitive, and psychosocial development in the first two years.

During the first two years of life, children are on a journey from a state of dependence on their caregivers to a growing independence. This journey is reflected separately in each of the three domains of development, as well as in interactions among the domains. This lesson underscores the fact that every family provides a unique environment for the developing child—an environment shaped by family members' culture, affluence, size, and patterns of interaction. Parents can help ensure their children's healthy development by providing a stable routine, filled with stimulating learning opportunities and interactions that promote the formation of strong healthy bodies, cognitive growth, and trusting relationships.

Prior Telecourse Knowledge that Will Be Used in this Lesson

- Biosocial development during the first two years (Lesson 6) will be referred to as we discuss the development of motor skills.

- Cognitive development during the first two years (Lesson 7) will be referred to as we examine language development, including the benefits of growing up in a bilingual home.

- Psychosocial development during the first two years (Lesson 8) will be referred to as we cover the nature and influence of temperament and attachment bonds between children and their caregivers.

Learning Objectives

Use this information to guide your reading, viewing, thinking, and studying. After successfully completing this lesson, you should be able to:

1. Give examples of the basic pattern of motor-skill development, and discuss variations in biosocial development during the first two years.

2. Summarize key aspects of cognitive development during the first two years, especially language development during this time.

3. Discuss psychosocial development during the first two years, focusing on the concepts of temperament and attachment and their influence on the developing child.

4. Discuss Erik Erikson's first two stages of psychosocial development, and offer examples of how caregivers can encourage trust and autonomy in their children.

5. Offer examples of how a child's development in any one domain (biosocial, cognitive, or psychosocial) can affect development in a different domain.

📖 **Read Chapter 5, "Summary: The First Two Years: Biosocial Development," page 164; Chapter 6, "Summary: The First Two Years: Cognitive Development," page 198; and Chapter 7, "Summary: The First Two Years: Psychosocial Development," page 231, and "The Developing Person So Far: The First Two Years," page 233.**

Video Viewing Tips

This video lesson will feature three children—Ryan (16 months), Omari (18 months), and Luke (2.5 years). In their typical daily routines, you will see living examples of some concepts you've learned in the last three lessons. As you view the video, it will help you to watch for particular issues and situations.

For example, note differences between the families in this program (size, socioeconomic status, and so on), and consider how this might affect their developing children. You'll see how dependent these children are on their caregivers, but notice also how they are attempting to assert more independence in thinking and acting for themselves. Watch what their parents are doing to allow them room to grow and explore, while still providing guidance and safety.

Also consider where these children are in their gross and fine motor skill development and how that might affect development in the other domains (cognitive and psychosocial).

Pay close attention to any cultural differences and consider how these factors might affect these children. Also take note of the individual variations between the children themselves, for example, any differences in temperament and personality that might affect how they interact with their world.

Finally, pay particular attention to the parent child-interactions in this video lesson. Try to discern any signs of secure or insecure attachment. Note how involved the parents are in their children's lives, how they model behavior they would like to see in their children, and speculate on how all this might ultimately affect development. Before you watch this lesson, it may help you to review the vocabulary in the Key Terms section below.

 View the video for Lesson 9, "Off to a Good Start."

    Segment 1: *Ryan*

    Segment 2: *Omari*

    Segment 3: *Luke*

    Segment 4: *Ryan, Omari, and Luke*

Summary

The pace of growth in each of the three domains of development during the first two years is remarkable. During these years, children reach half their adult height, develop cognitive abilities that startle their caregivers (and developmentalists), learn to express almost every human emotion, demonstrate distinct personalities, and move from a state of almost complete dependence on others to one of growing independence.

In the biosocial domain, over the first two years body weight quadruples and the brain triples in weight. As new connections between neurons are formed, the growing maturity of the brain enables the development of gross and fine motor skills that give babies the mobility they need to explore their world, leading to a greater number of learning opportunities which may stimulate growth in the cognitive domain. As they explore their environments, infants' active curiosity and developing sensory and perceptual abilities enable them to progress from knowing the world only through their immediate experiences to being able to "experiment" through the use of mental images and other developing cognitive skills.

Language development is another remarkable cognitive achievement during the first two years, as babies progress from simple cries, cooing, and babbling to speaking in short sentences. Cultural factors influence language development extensively. Bilingual children may have a cognitive advantage because they are exposed to a variety of linguistic and multicultural experiences, which creates a richer, more stimulating environment.

Infants' developing abilities to communicate enable them to become increasingly active participants in their social interactions with caregivers. They also become more sophisticated in expressing emotions, which change from simple reactions to the more complex, self-conscious responses that are a healthy sign of their increasing independence. By age 2, toddlers have formed distinct personalities.

Temperament refers to relatively consistent inborn dispositions that underlie and affect a person's response to people, situations, and events. Temperament is epigenetic: It begins in the child's genetic inheritance and is affected by many prenatal experiences, especially those relating to the nutrition and health of the mother. Later, the social context and the individual's experiences have an effect on temperament. Most infants can be described as possessing one of three relatively stable temperaments: easy, slow to warm up, and difficult.

📖   **Review all reading assignments for this lesson.**

💻   **As assigned by your instructor, complete the optional online component for this lesson.**

Key Terms

Using your own words, write a brief definition or explanation of each of the following terms on a separate piece of paper.

1. guided participation
2. attachment
3. modeling
4. temperament
5. toddler
6. gross motor skills
7. fine motor skills
8. self-awareness
9. secure attachment
10. enriched environment
11. trust versus mistrust
12. autonomy versus shame and doubt
13. babbling
14. reflexes
15. sensorimotor intelligence
16. stranger wariness
17. separation anxiety
18. neuron
19. social referencing
20. language acquisition device (LAD)
21. personality
22. insecure attachment

Practice Questions

Multiple-Choice Questions

1. Compared to the first year, growth during the second year
   a. proceeds at a slower rate.
   b. continues at about the same rate.
   c. includes more insulating fat.
   d. includes more bone and muscle.

2. The infant's first body movements are
   a. fine motor skills.
   b. gross motor skills.
   c. reflexes.
   d. pincer skills.

3. Babies are referred to as toddlers when
   a. their newborn reflexes have disappeared.
   b. they can walk well unassisted.
   c. they begin to creep or crawl.
   d. they speak their first word.

4. Which of the following is true of motor-skill development in healthy infants?
   a. It follows the same basic sequence the world over.
   b. It occurs at different rates from individual to individual.
   c. It follows norms that vary from one ethnic group to another.
   d. All of the above are true.

5. Most of the nerve cells that a human brain will ever possess are present
   a. at conception.
   b. about 1 month following conception.
   c. at birth.
   d. at age 5 or 6.

6. Climbing is to using a crayon as _____ is to _____.
   a. fine motor skill; gross motor skill
   b. gross motor skill; fine motor skill
   c. reflex; fine motor skill
   d. reflex; gross motor skill

7. Today, most cognitive psychologists view language acquisition as
   a. primarily the result of imitation of adult speech.
   b. a behavior that is determined primarily by biological maturation.
   c. a behavior determined entirely by learning.
   d. determined by both biological maturation and learning.

8. Despite cultural differences, children all over the world attain very similar language skills
   a. according to ethnically specific timetables.
   b. at about the same age in the same sequence.
   c. according to culturally specific timetables.
   d. according to timetables that vary widely from child to child.

9. The average baby speaks a few words at about
   a. 6 months.
   b. 9 months.
   c. 12 months.
   d. 24 months.

10. What is the correct sequence of language development in babies?
   a. crying, babbling, cooing, first word
   b. crying, cooing, babbling, first word
   c. crying, babbling, first word, cooing
   d. crying, cooing, first word, babbling

11. Social referencing refers to
   a. parenting skills that change over time.
   b. changes in community values regarding, for example, the acceptability of using physical punishment with small children.
   c. the support network for new parents provided by extended family members.
   d. the infant response of looking to trusted adults for emotional cues in uncertain situations.

12. Erikson feels that the development of a sense of trust in early infancy depends on the quality of the

   a. infant's food.

   b. child's genetic inheritance.

   c. relationship with caregiver.

   d. introduction of toilet training.

13. The increased tendency of toddlers to express frustration and anger is most closely linked to new developments in their cognitive abilities, especially those related to

   a. goal-directed actions.

   b. social referencing.

   c. self-awareness.

   d. stranger wariness.

14. The emotional tie that develops between an infant and his or her primary caregiver is called

   a. self-awareness.

   b. synchrony.

   c. affiliation.

   d. attachment.

15. An important effect of secure attachment is the promotion of

   a. self-awareness.

   b. social skills and independence.

   c. dependency.

   d. all of the above.

16. Which of the following most accurately summarizes the relationship between early attachment and later social relationships?

   a. Attachment in infancy determines whether a child will grow to be sociable.

   b. Attachment relationships are sometimes, though rarely, altered as children grow older.

   c. There is, at best, only a weak correlation between early attachment and later social relationships.

   d. Early attachment biases, but does not inevitably determine, later social relationships.

17. Which of the following is a clear sign of an infant's attachment to a particular person?

   a. The infant turns to that person when distressed.

   b. The infant protests when that person leaves a room.

   c. The infant may cry when strangers appear.

   d. All of the above are signs of infant attachment.

18. Regarding the importance of a stable family environment, developmental psychologists have discovered that

    a. predictable daily routines help children feel secure.

    b. stability in the home environment is less important than the overall stimulating quality of the child's experiences.

    c. predictable routines are more important for insecurely attached children.

    d. predictable routines are more important for children who are temperamentally "slow-to-warm-up."

True or False Items

Write T (for true) or F (for false) on the line in front of each statement.

19. ____ Regarding parent-infant interaction during the first two years, most developmentalists believe that quality is more important than quantity.

20. ____ Through guided participation in activities such as feeding, parents help their children achieve independence.

21. ____ Although most babies eventually reach the same developmental milestones, they don't always do it in the same way or at the same time.

22. ____ Crying babies who soothe themselves are displaying a healthy step on the way to greater independence.

23. ____ Most developmentalists think that infants must learn to be sociable.

24. ____ The major difference between a six-month-old and a twelve-month-old is that emotions become less intense.

25. ____ Emotional development is affected by cognitive development.

26. ____ A securely attached toddler is most likely to stay close to his or her mother even in a familiar environment.

27. ____ Cognitive development in bilingual children tends to be somewhat slower than that in children who learn a single language.

Questions for Reflection

1. **Students who are not parents:** Of all the changes that occur between birth and age 2, which is the most remarkable to you? Why? Do you believe that someone's personality is well set by the time he or she goes to school?

   Students who are parents: Did any of the episodes in this program provide insight into the development of your own child or children? Explain.

2. If you were growing at the rate of an infant, how much would you weigh one year from today? What would your height be one year from today?

3. Below is a list of achievements in the life of a normal baby girl. However, these achievements are not presented in the correct order. To demonstrate your understanding of Piaget's stages of sensorimotor intelligence, number the events in the proper sequence from 1 to 6 using the blanks provided.

   ____ (a) The baby cries when she sees her mother putting on her coat.

   ____ (b) The baby laughs when she is tickled and shakes her arm with pleasure when a rattle is put into her hand.

___ (c) The baby sucks the nipple and anything else that comes near her mouth.

___ (d) The baby experiments with her spoon, banging first the dish, then the high chair, and finally throwing the spoon on the floor.

___ (e) The baby refuses the pacifier and shows her displeasure by crying.

___ (f) The baby imitates a temper tantrum she has observed in an older child.

Answer Key

Key Terms

1. A learning process in which an individual learns through social interaction with a "tutor" (a parent, teacher, or more skilled peer) who offers assistance, structures opportunities, models strategies, and provides explicit instruction as needed is guided participation. (p. 49; video lesson, segment 1; objectives 1 & 2)

2. Attachment is the enduring emotional tie that a person or animal forms with another. (pp. 218–219; video lesson, segments 1 & 3; objective 3)

3. Modeling, or learning by imitation, is the process whereby a person observes the behavior of someone else and then tries to imitate that behavior. (p. 43; objectives 2)

4. Temperament refers to the set of innate tendencies, or dispositions, that underlie and affect each person's interactions with people, situations, and events. (p. 204; objective 3)

5. When babies can walk well without assistance (usually at about 12 months), they are given the name toddler because of the characteristic way they move their bodies from side to side. (p. 151; video lesson, segment 2; objective 1)

6. Gross motor skills are physical abilities that demand large body movements, such as climbing, jumping, or running. (p. 150; video lesson, segment 2; objective 1)

7. Fine motor skills are physical abilities that require precise, small movements, such as picking up a coin. (p. 151; video lesson, segment 2; objective 1)

8. Self-awareness refers to a person's sense of himself or herself as being distinct from other people that makes possible many new self-conscious emotions, including shame, guilt, embarrassment, and pride. (p. 213; video lesson, segment 2; objective 3)

9. A secure attachment is one in which the infant derives comfort and confidence from the "secure base" provided by a caregiver. (p. 219; video lesson, segment 3; objective 3)

10. An enriched environment is one that provides the developing child with a highly nurturing and stimulating atmosphere in which to grow and learn. (video lesson, segment 4; objectives 2 & 3)

11. In Erikson's theory, the crisis of infancy is one of trust versus mistrust, in which the infant learns whether the world is a secure place in which basic needs will be met. (p. 215; objective 4)

12. In Erikson's theory, the crisis of toddlerhood is one of autonomy versus shame and doubt, in which toddlers strive to rule their own actions and bodies. (p. 216; objective 4)

13. Babbling, which begins at 6 or 7 months, is characterized by the extended repetition of certain syllables (such as "ma-ma"). (p. 187; objective 2)

14. Reflexes are involuntary physical responses to specific stimuli. (pp. 149–150; objective 1)

15. Sensorimotor intelligence is Piaget's term for the intelligence of infants during the first period of cognitive development, when babies think by using the senses and motor skills. (p. 168; objective 2)

16. A common early fear, stranger wariness (also called fear of strangers) is first noticeable at about 6 months. (p. 203; objective 3)

17. Separation anxiety, which is the infant fear of being left by the mother or other caregiver, emerges at about 8 or 9 months, peaks at about 14 months, and then gradually subsides. (p. 203; objective 3)

18. A neuron, or nerve cell, is the main component of the central nervous system. (p. 141; objective 1)

19. When infants engage in social referencing, they are looking to trusted adults for emotional cues on how to interpret uncertain situations. (pp. 210–211; objective 3)

20. According to Noam Chomsky, children possess an innate language acquisition device (LAD) that enables them to acquire language, including the basic aspects of grammar. (pp. 192–193; objective 2)

21. Personality refers to the emotions, behaviors, and attitudes that make an individual unique. (pp. 205–206; objective 3)

22. Insecure attachment is characterized by the infant's fear, anger, or seeming indifference toward the caregiver. (p. 219; objective 3)

Practice Questions

Multiple-Choice Questions

1. a. is the correct answer. (p. 136; objective 1)

2. c. is the correct answer. (pp. 149–150; objective 1)

   a. & b. are incorrect. These motor skills do not emerge until somewhat later; reflexes are present at birth.

   d. is incorrect. On the contrary, reflexes are quite predictable.

3. b. is the correct answer. (p. 151; objective 1)

4. d. is the correct answer. (p. 152; objective 1)

5. c. is the correct answer. (pp. 141–142; objective 1)

6. b. is the correct answer. (pp. 150–151; video lesson, segment 2; objective 1)

   c. & d. are incorrect. Reflexes are involuntary responses; climbing and using a crayon are both voluntary responses.

7. d. is the correct answer. This is a synthesis of the theories of Skinner and Chomsky. (p. 196; video lesson, segment 2; objective 2)

8. b. is the correct answer. (p. 185; video lesson, segment 2; objective 2)

   a., c., & d. are incorrect. Children the world over, and in every Piagetian stage, follow the same sequence and approximately the same timetable for early language development.

9. c. is the correct answer. (p. 187; objective 2)

10. b. is the correct answer. (pp. 185–187; objective 2)

11. d. is the correct answer. (p. 210; objective 3)

12. c. is the correct answer. (p. 215; video lesson, segments 1 & 3; objective 4)

13. a. is the correct answer. Anger increases with age because toddlers are able to anticipate events and realize that other people's actions sometimes block their own efforts. (p. 203; video lesson, segment 3; objective 3)

14. d. is the correct answer. (pp. 218–219; video lesson, segments 1 & 3; objective 3)

a. is incorrect. Self-awareness refers to the infant's developing sense of "me and mine."

b. is incorrect. Synchrony describes the coordinated interaction between infant and caregiver.

c. is incorrect. Affiliation describes the tendency of people at any age to seek the companionship of others.

15. b. is the correct answer. (p. 223; video lesson, segments 1 & 3; objective 3)

a. is incorrect. The textbook does not link self-awareness to secure attachment.

c. is incorrect. On the contrary, secure attachment promotes independence in infants and children.

16. d. is the correct answer. (pp. 218–221; video lesson, segments 1 & 3; objective 3)

17. d. is the correct answer. (pp. 218–219; video lesson, segments 1 & 3; objective 3)

18. a. is the correct answer (video lesson, segment 1; objective 3)

b. is incorrect. Both stability and stimulation are important features of a health environment for child development.

c. & d. are incorrect. The video lesson did not discuss the relationships among children's temperaments, attachments, and the importance of predictable environmental routines.

True or False Items

19. F   Quality and quantity are equally important. (video lesson, segment 3; objective 3)

20. T   (video lesson, segment 1; objectives 1 & 2)

21. T   (p. 136; video lesson, segment 1; objective 1)

22. T   (video lesson, segment 1; objective 3)

23. F   Most developmentalists believe that infants are born with a tendency toward sociability as a means of survival. (p. 208; objective 3)

24. F   Emotions become more intense and are manifested more quickly and more persistently. (p. 204; objective 3)

25. T   (p. 203; objectives 3 & 5)

26. F   A securely attached toddler is most likely to explore the environment, the mother's presence being enough to give him or her the courage to do so. (p. 219; video lesson, segments 1 & 3; objective 3)

27. F   Bilingual children often benefit from the multiple perspectives provided by their rich linguistic environments. (video lesson, segment 2; objective 2)

Questions for Reflection

1. There is no single correct answer to this question. This question is intended to help you make meaningful connections with your personal experiences.

2. There is no single correct answer to this question. This question is intended to help you make meaningful connections with your personal experiences.

3. The proper sequence is c, e, b, d, a, f. (pp. 168–175; objective 2)

Lesson Review

Lesson 9

The First Two Years
Summary

Please Note: Use this matrix to guide your study and achieve the learning objectives of this lesson. It will also help you to view the video, which defines and demonstrates important concepts and skills as they relate to everyday life.

Learning Objective	Textbook	Telecourse Student Guide	Video Lesson
1. Give examples of the basic pattern of motor-skill development, and discuss variations in biosocial development during the first two years.	pp. 51, 135–154	Key Terms: 1, 3, 5, 6, 7, 14, 18; Practice Questions: 1, 2, 3, 4, 5, 6, 20, 21;	all segments
2. Summarize key aspects of cognitive development during the first two years, especially language development during this time.	pp. 44–45, 167–198	Key Terms: 1, 3, 10, 13, 15, 20; Practice Questions: 7, 8, 9, 10, 20, 27.	all segments
3. Discuss psychosocial development during the first two years, focusing on the concepts of temperament and attachment and their influence on the developing child.	pp. 201–230	Key Terms: 2, 4, 8, 9, 12, 16, 17, 19, 21, 22; Practice Questions: 11, 13, 14, 15, 16, 17, 18, 19, 22, 23, 24, 25, 26.	all segments
4. Discuss Erik Erikson's first two stages of psychosocial development, and offer examples of how caregivers can encourage trust and autonomy in their children.	pp. 215–216	Key Terms: 11, 12; Practice Questions: 12.	all segments
5. Offer examples of how a child's development in any one domain (biosocial, cognitive, or psychosocial) can affect development in a different domain.		Practice Questions: 25.	all segments

Fatherhood

Lesson 10
The First Two Years:
Special Topic

Preview

Traditional views of child development focused almost entirely on mothers, in part because fathers were often removed from most caregiving activities. Today, however, with more and more mothers working outside the home, fathers are taking an increasingly active role in household chores and caregiving duties for their children. This trend, which is apparent throughout the world, is applauded by virtually all developmental psychologists and educators. These experts agree that fathers have a significant role in influencing their children's cognitive, social, and emotional development. This lesson touches on several aspects of this role, including the powerful influence fathers have as role models for their children.

The lesson also explores fatherhood and attachment. Although historically, we have often thought only of mothers when discussing bonding and attachment, fathers form secure attachments with their children that are comparable to the bond between children and their mothers. These attachments are vividly revealed during playtime, especially the rough-and-tumble play that fathers often engage in with their children. However, despite the fact that fathers can and increasingly do master caregiving, women around the world still spend far more time at child care than men do, especially in the child's first few months. The video lesson concludes by exploring how couples can work together to support each other in sharing parenting and other childcare responsiblilities.

As you study this lesson, think about your own upbringing. What unique roles did your mother and father play in your care and development? If you have children yourself, what role have you played in their care and development? If you anticipate having children someday, what hopes do you have for the roles that you and your spouse will play in their care and upbringing?

Prior Telecourse Knowledge that Will Be Used in this Lesson

*   Social learning theory, the idea that people can learn by observing and imitating others (from Lesson 1), will be referred to as we discuss the impact that fathers have as role models on their children.

*   Attachment, the emotional bond between children and their caregivers (from Lesson 8), will be referred to as the lesson looks at the nature and development of attachment bonds between children and their mothers as compared to that of their fathers. Recall that attachments can be classified as either "secure" or "insecure."

Learning Objectives

Use this information to guide your reading, viewing, thinking, and studying. After successfully completing this lesson, you should be able to:

1. Discuss social learning theory as an extension of learning theory, focusing specifically on fathers as role models for their children.

2. Summarize how culture influences a father's role in the family, and how this in turn can affect a child's development.

3. Discuss contemporary views on the role of the father in infant psychosocial development, focusing on the development of attachment.

4. Discuss how some mothers may interfere with the developing relationship between father and child, and list some things couples can do to effectively share parenting roles.

📖 **Read the following sections of chapters listed below:**

Chapter 2, "Theories," pages 43–44 (Social Learning); Chapter 7, "The First Two Years: Psychosocial Development," pages 211–212 (Referencing to Dad).

📺 **View the video for Lesson 10, "Fatherhood."**

Segment 1: *Fatherhood Across Cultures*

Segment 2: *Attachment and Dad*

Segment 3: *Bonding with Dad*

Segment 4: *And Baby Makes Three*

Summary

As noted throughout this series, the social context of development teaches infants and children when and how to express their emotions and has a powerful influence on cognitive development as well. Along with mothers and other primary caregivers in a child's social context, fathers play a key role in this social referencing. An important aspect of the social context is modeling, in which infants observe behavior and then pattern their own after it. The age-old hypothesis that mothers, and only mothers, can provide the optimal care and modeling in the first two years of life has been discounted by research on infant care. Children form multiple attachments and learn from many people, including their fathers.

Fathers can and do master caregiving and today, throughout the world, fathers are increasingly taking on a significant share of the caregiving and nurturing responsibilities for their children. When fathers are more involved with their kids, the children—and the entire family—benefit. Even so, women worldwide still spend far more time at child care than men do, especially during the earliest years. A key challenge for couples today is working together to support each other's role in caregiving.

Survey research indicates that children living with both biological parents tend to have fewer physical, emotional, or learning difficulties than do children in other family structures. As adolescents and adults, they continue to fare better. This family structure confers at least two important advantages for children: (a) two adults generally provide more complete caregiving than one, (b) two-parent homes usually have a financial advantage over other forms (especially the single-parent home) enabling better health care, housing, nutrition, and education for their children.

The apparent advantage of original two-parent homes may be overstated, however, since survey data are often confounded by the fact that a disproportionate number of one-parent families are also low-income families. Two other caveats apply: (a) not every biological father or mother is a fit parent, and (b) not every marriage creates a nurturant household. Children who live in intact families with persistently high levels of conflict are especially likely to suffer.

📖 **Review all reading assignments for this lesson.**

💻 **As assigned by your instructor, complete the optional online component for this lesson.**

Key Terms

Using your own words, write a brief definition or explanation of each of the following terms on a separate piece of paper.

1. social learning theory
2. modeling
3. attachment

Practice Questions

Multiple-Choice Questions

1. Social learning is sometimes called modeling because it
   a. follows the scientific model of learning.
   b. molds character.
   c. follows the immediate reinforcement model developed by Bandura.
   d. involves people's patterning their behavior after that of others.

2. Compared to *their* fathers, modern-day fathers
   a. are more actively involved in the care of their children.
   b. are less actively involved in the care of their children.
   c. have about the same level of involvement in the care of their children.
   d. are much less predictable in their level of involvement in child care.

3. Fathers have a significant influence on their child's
   a. cognitive development.
   b. social development.
   c. emotional development.
   d. development in every domain.

4. The stereotypical "Ozzie and Harriet family" in which fathers were the breadwinners and mothers were the caregivers
   a. has been an accurate depiction of the American family since the late 1900s.
   b. has been on the rise since the late 1990s.
   c. probably never existed.
   d. is more typical of certain ethnic groups than others.

5. According to experts in the video lesson, which of the following was the major factor in the shift in fathers' caregiving responsibility?
   a. The rising cost of child care.
   b. The steady increase in the number of women working outside the home.
   c. The economic recession of the 1960s and 1970s.
   d. The steadily increasing divorce rate.

6. The number of women working outside their homes began to sharply increase in the _____ with the advent of the _____.
   a. 1950s; Korean War
   b. 1960s; Civil Rights Act
   c. 1960s and 1970s; Women's movement
   d. 1980s; School Lunch Act

7. An important way that fathers interact with infants is
   a. through physical play.
   b. demonstrating work habits.
   c. handling the majority of their physical care.
   d. all of the above.

8. Developmental psychologists believe that as men become more actively involved in caring for their children,
   a. children—but not necessarily their fathers—benefit.
   b. fathers—but not necessarily their children—benefit.
   c. both children and fathers benefit.
   d. children, their fathers, and other family members benefit.

9. Regarding culture and caregiving, which of the following is true?
   a. Some cultures provide fathers greater opportunity to co-parent their children than other cultures.
   b. As a general rule, fathers in developing countries have greater opportunity to co-parent than fathers in developed countries.
   c. Fathers in developed countries generally have greater opportunity to co-parent than fathers in developing countries.
   d. Throughout most of history, women and men have shared caregiving duties equally.

10. To a large extent, parenting and fathering
   a. are biologically constructed processes.
   b. are culturally constructed processes.
   c. are roles entirely shaped by the individuals that occupy them.
   d. haven't changed significantly since the dawn of human existence.

11. Compared to mothers, the amount of time that the average father spends caring for his infant is
   a. about the same.
   b. far less but of better quality.
   c. so greatly varied that it is nearly impossible to come up with an "average" amount of time.
   d. none of the above.

12. Throughout the world, children form attachments to their caregivers between _____ of age.
   a. one and two weeks
   b. one and two months
   c. four and seven weeks
   d. four and seven months

13. Compared to the attachments mothers form with their children, fathers form attachment bonds that tend to be
   a. comparable in security.
   b. slightly less secure.
   c. less predictable.
   d. less emotional.

14. The emotional tie that develops between a child and his or her caregiver is called
   a. self-awareness.
   b. synchrony.
   c. affiliation.
   d. attachment.

15. Developmental psychologists believe that children who form multiple attachments are
   a. probably insecurely attached to each caregiver.
   b. at increased risk for a wide range of developmental problems.
   c. rare exceptions to the rule, "one child, one attachment."
   d. quite normal, and likely to benefit from having multiple attachments.

16. The most significant benefit of children and parents reading together is the
   a. cognitive development of the child.
   b. social development of the child.
   c. emotional development of the child.
   d. strengthening of the parent-child bond.

17. The typical father-child pattern of play probably helps children

   a. learn to control their states of arousal and emotional excitement.
   b. become self-aware.
   c. develop a healthy fear of strangers.
   d. develop stronger bodies.

18. Josh, who is about to become a father and primary caregiver, is worried that he will never have the natural caregiving skills that the child's mother has. Studies on father–infant relationships show that

   a. infants nurtured by single fathers are more likely to be insecurely attached.
   b. fathers can provide the emotional and cognitive nurturing necessary for healthy infant development.
   c. women are biologically predisposed to be better parents than men are.
   d. social development is usually slightly delayed in children whose fathers are the primary caregiver.

19. We are more likely to imitate the behavior of others if we particularly admire and identify with them. This belief finds expression in

   a. stage theory.
   b. sociocultural theory.
   c. social learning theory.
   d. Pavlov's experiments.

True or False Items

Write T (for true) or F (for false) on the line in front of each statement.

   20. _____ Children can only become attached to one caregiver.

   21. _____ Children tend to attach to whomever is providing their care.

   22. _____ Children attach more readily to their mothers than they do to their fathers.

   23. _____ Cross-culturally, there is relatively little variation in the roles fathers play in caring for their children.

   24. _____ Despite popular belief, young children rarely mimic their parents' behavior.

   25. _____ Women are biologically predisposed to be better parents than men are.

Answer Key

Key Terms

   1. Social learning theory emphasizes that people often learn new behaviors through observation and imitation of other people. (p. 43; objective 1)

   2. Modeling refers to the process by which we observe other people's behavior and then pattern our own after it. (p. 43; objective 1)

   3. Attachment refers to the affectional or emotional bond the child develops to one or more principle caregivers. (pp. 218–219; video lesson, segment 2; objective 3)

Practice Questions

Multiple-Choice Questions

1. d. is the correct answer. (p. 43; objective 1)

   a. & c. are incorrect. These can be true in all types of learning.

   b. is incorrect. This was not discussed as an aspect of developmental theory.

2. a. is the correct answer. (p. 211; video lesson, segment 1; objective 2)

   d. is incorrect. Throughout history, fathers' involvement in the care of their children has been predictable.

3. d. is the correct answer. (video lesson, segment 2 objective 3)

4. c. is the correct answer. (video lesson; objective 2)

   a. & b. are incorrect. To the extent that the "Ozzie and Harriet family" existed, it is associated with families in the 1950s.

   d. is incorrect. The lesson does not differentiate parental roles and family "styles" by ethnic group.

5. b. is the correct answer. (video lesson, segment 1; objective 2)

6. c. is the correct answer. (video lesson, segment 1; objective 2)

7. a. is the correct answer. (p. 212; video lesson, segment 1; objectives 2 & 3)

8. d. is the correct answer. (pp. 211–212; video lesson, segment 2; objective 3)

9. a. is the correct answer. (video lesson, segment 1; objective 2)

   b. & c. are incorrect. The lesson does not differentiate the caregiving opportunities for fathers in developing and developed countries.

   d. is incorrect. In fact, throughout history women have tended to perform more caregiving than men.

10. b. is the correct answer. (video lesson, segment 1; objective 2)

    c. is incorrect. Although individuals do help to shape the roles they occupy, cultural values and expectations also have a substantial impact.

11. c. is the correct answer. (p. 212; video lesson, segment 1; objectives 2 & 3)

12. d. is the correct answer. (video lesson, segment 2; objective 3)

13. a. is the correct answer. (video lesson, segment 2; objective 3)

    b., c., & d. are incorrect. Fathers' attachment bonds are no less predictable or emotional than those mothers form with their children.

14. d. is the correct answer. (pp. 218–219; video lesson, segment 2; objective 3)

    a. is incorrect. Self-awareness refers to the child's developing sense of identity apart from that of others.

    b. is incorrect. Synchrony refers to the coordinated interaction between caregiver and infant that helps infants learn to express and read emotions.

    c. is incorrect. Affiliation refers to a general need to associate with other people; not just primary caregivers.

15. d. is the correct answer. Children can and often do form multiple attachments to the many different people who love and care for them. (video lesson, segment 2; objective 3)

16. a. is the correct answer. (video lesson, segment 3; objective 1)

    b., c., & d. are incorrect. Although children's social and emotional development certainly are likely to benefit from the close interactions involved in reading with caregivers, the question specifies the "most significant" benefit of reading.

17. a. is the correct answer. (video lesson, segment 4; objective 4)

    b., c., & d. are incorrect. The lesson does not address these issues.

18. b. is the correct answer. (pp. 211–212; objectives 3 & 4)

19. c. is the correct answer. (p. 43; objective 1)

True or False Items

20. F   Children can and often do form multiple attachments. (video lesson, segment 2; objective 3)

21. T   (video lesson, segment 2; objective 3)

22. F   Throughout the world, fathers readily form secure attachments with their children that are comparable to the bonds that are shared between children and their mothers. (video lesson, segment 2; objectives 1 & 3)

23. F   Cultures differ significantly in the roles that fathers are encouraged to play in caring for their children. (p. 212; video lesson, segment 1; objective 2)

24. F   Young children model their parents' behaviors extensively. (p. 43; objective 1)

25. F   (pp. 211–212; video lesson, segment 2; objective 3)

Lesson Review

Lesson 10

The First Two Years
Special Topic

Please Note: Use this matrix to guide your study and achieve the learning objectives of this lesson. It will also help you to view the video, which defines and demonstrates important concepts and skills as they relate to everyday life.

Learning Objective	Textbook	Telecourse Student Guide	Video Lesson
1. Discuss social learning theory as an extension of learning theory, focusing specifically on fathers as role models for their children.	p. 43	Key Terms: 1, 2; Practice Questions: 1, 16, 19, 22, 24.	Segment 2: *Attachment and Dad* Segment 3: *Bonding with Dad*
2. Summarize how culture influences a father's role in the family, and how this in turn can affect a child's development.	pp. 211–212	Practice Questions: 2, 4, 5, 6, 7, 9, 10, 11, 23.	Segment 1: *Fatherhood Across Culture*
3. Discuss contemporary views on the role of the father in infant psychosocial development, focusing on the development of attachment.	pp. 211–212	Key Terms: 3; Practice Questions: 3, 7, 8, 11, 12, 13, 14, 15, 18, 21, 22, 25.	Segment 2: *Attachment and Dad*
4. Discuss how some mothers may interfere with the developing relationship between father and child, and list some things couples can do to effectively share parenting roles.		Practice Questions: 17, 18.	Segment 4: *And Baby Makes Three*

Playing and Growing

Lesson 11

The Play Years:
Biosocial Development

Preview

Lesson 11 is the first lesson of 5 lessons covering the period called the play years, ages 2 to 6. These lessons emphasize the central importance of play to the biosocial, cognitive, and psychosocial development of preschoolers.

This lesson on biosocial development outlines the changes in size and shape that occur during this period. This is followed by a look at brain growth and development and its role in the development of physical and cognitive abilities. A description of the acquisition of gross and fine motor skills follows, noting that mastery of such skills develops steadily during the play years along with intellectual growth. The lesson also addresses the important issues of **injury control** and accidents, the major cause of childhood death in all but the most disease-ridden or war-torn countries. The lesson concludes with an in-depth exploration of **child maltreatment**, including its prevalence, contributing factors, consequences for future development, treatment, and prevention.

As you move through this lesson, think of children you know in this age range. Consider their size and shape, their eating habits, and their motor-skill capabilities—what they can do with their bodies and hands. Also consider any child maltreatment cases you know of or have read about. What were the circumstances? What type of maltreatment occurred? What was the response?

Prior Telecourse Knowledge that Will Be Used in this Lesson

- In this lesson, physical growth and the development of gross and fine motor skills during "The Play Years" will be compared to earlier development during infancy and toddlerhood (Lesson 6).

- This lesson will return to the topic of brain growth and development, which was introduced in Lesson 6. In children from ages 2 to 6, the growth of dendrites and axons continues, along with myelination, the insulating process that speeds up the transmission of neural impulses. This brain maturation leads to many other advances, including development of the visual pathways and eye-hand coordination that will make reading and writing possible.

Learning Objectives

Use this information to guide your reading, viewing, thinking, and studying. After successfully completing this lesson, you should be able to:

1. Describe normal physical growth during the play years, and account for variations in height and weight.
2. Describe changes in eating habits and nutritional needs during the preschool years.
3. Discuss the brain processes of myelination and lateralization and their development during the play years.
4. Describe the prevalence of accidental injuries during early childhood, describe some measures that have significantly reduced accidental death rates for children, and identify several factors that contribute to this problem.
5. Explain how the maturation of visual pathways and cerebral hemispheres in the brain allow for formal education to begin at about age 6.
6. Distinguish between gross and fine motor skills, and discuss the development of each during the play years.
7. Discuss the significance of artistic expression during the play years.
8. Identify the various categories and consequences of child maltreatment.
9. Discuss several factors that contribute to maltreatment, and describe current treatment and prevention efforts.

 Read Chapter 8, "The Play Years: Biosocial Development," pages 235–261.

View the video for Lesson 11, "Playing and Growing."

Segment 1: *Body and Brain Growth*

Segment 2: *Motor Skills*

Segment 3: *Maltreatment*

Summary

Children grow steadily taller and slimmer during the preschool years, with their genetic background and nutrition being responsible for most of the variation seen in children from various parts of the world. The most significant aspect of growth is the continued maturation of the nervous system and the refinement of the visual, muscular, and cognitive skills that will be necessary for the child to function in school. The brain becomes more specialized as it matures, with the left half usually becoming the center for speech, and the right the center for visual, spatial, and artistic skills.

Gross motor skills, such as running, climbing, jumping, and throwing, improve dramatically between ages 2 and 6, making it essential that children have access to safe play space and guided practice to assist in this developmental process. Fine motor skills, such as pouring, holding a pencil, and using a knife and fork, are much harder for preschoolers to master. This difficulty is due to several factors, including incomplete myelination of the nervous system and incomplete muscular control. Of course, for young children especially, art is not limited to coloring or drawing and often includes using markers, paintbrushes, clay, and other vehicles. In fact, very young children (who lack the fine motor skills required to hold a crayon, brush, or pencil) are more likely to use large arm movements (such as those involved in finger painting) in their art. Doing so is a powerful stimulus to the development of the fine motor skills, as children are drawn to practice these skills in order to produce the artistic results they desire.

Throughout childhood, accidents are the leading cause of death. The accident risk for a particular child depends on several factors. Boys, as a group, and low-socioeconomic status (SES) children suffer more serious injuries and accidental deaths than girls, and high-SES children.

Child maltreatment takes many forms, including physical, emotional, or sexual **abuse**, and emotional or physical **neglect**. Although certain conditions are almost universally harmful, some practices that are considered neglectful or abusive in one culture are acceptable in others. Maltreatment is especially likely if the family context is either too rigid in its schedules and role demands that no one can measure up to them or so chaotic and disorganized that no one knows what is expected. Maltreatment is also especially likely to develop in isolated families in which the parents are unusually suspicious or distrustful of outsiders.

The consequences of maltreatment to children include impaired learning, self-esteem, social relationships, and emotional control. Many people erroneously believe that maltreated children automatically become adults who abuse or neglect their own children. The most effective prevention strategies for maltreatment are those that enhance community support and address the specific material and emotional needs of troubled families. Adoption is the final option when families are inadequate and children are young.

The phenomenon of maltreated children invariably growing up to become abusive or neglectful parents themselves is a widely held, and very destructive, misconception. Experts believe that between 30 and 40 percent of children who were abused actually become child abusers themselves. Still, this rate is much higher than that in the general population, so it is safest to conclude that it is a real, although often-exaggerated, problem.

Special Note: We will discuss the topic of child maltreatment (pp. 252–260) in more detail in telecourse Lesson 15, "Hazards Along the Way."

📖 **Review all reading assignments for this lesson.**

🖥 **As assigned by your instructor, complete the optional online component for this lesson.**

Key Terms

Using your own words, write a brief definition or explanation of each of the following terms on a separate piece of paper.

1. myelination
2. corpus callosum
3. lateralization
4. prefrontal cortex
5. perseveration
6. activity level
7. injury control /harm reduction
8. primary prevention
9. secondary prevention
10. tertiary prevention
11. child maltreatment
12. child abuse
13. child neglect
14. failure to thrive
15. reported maltreatment
16. substantiated maltreatment
17. differential response
18. shaken baby syndrome
19. post-traumatic stress disorder (PTSD)
20. permanency planning
21. foster care
22. kinship care
23. adoption

Practice Questions I

Multiple-Choice Questions

1. During the preschool years, the most common nutritional problem in developed countries is
   a. serious malnutrition.
   b. excessive intake of sweets.
   c. insufficient intake of iron, zinc, and calcium.
   d. excessive caloric intake.

2. The brain center for speech is usually located in the
   a. right brain.
   b. left brain.
   c. corpus callosum.
   d. space just below the right ear.

3. Gender differences in childhood size and shape
   a. are consistent throughout the world.
   b. vary from one culture to another.
   c. are more pronounced in Western cultures.
   d. are more pronounced today than in the past.

4. Which of the following is **NOT** true regarding injury control?
   a. Broad-based television announcements do not have a direct impact on children's risk taking.
   b. Unless parents become involved, classroom safety education has little effect on children's actual behavior.
   c. Safety laws that include penalties are more effective than educational measures.
   d. Accidental deaths of one- to five-year-olds have held steady in the United States over the past two decades.

5. Like most U.S. adults, children in the United States tend to have too much _____ in their diet.
   a. iron
   b. fat
   c. sugar
   d. b and c

6. Skills that involve large body movements, such as running and jumping, are called
   a. activity-level skills.
   b. fine motor skills.
   c. gross motor skills.
   d. left-brain skills.

7. The brain's ongoing myelination during childhood helps children
    a. control their actions more precisely.
    b. react more quickly to stimuli.
    c. focus more easily on printed letters.
    d. do all of the above.

8. The leading cause of death in childhood is
    a. accidents.
    b. untreated diabetes.
    c. malnutrition.
    d. iron deficiency anemia.

9. Regarding lateralization, which of the following is **NOT** true?
    a. Some cognitive skills require only one side of the brain.
    b. Brain centers for generalized emotional impulses can be found in the right hemisphere.
    c. The left hemisphere contains brain areas dedicated to logic.
    d. The right side of the brain controls the left side of the body.

10. Which of the following factors is most responsible for differences in height and weight between children in developed and developing countries?
    a. the child's genetic background
    b. health care
    c. nutrition
    d. age of weaning

11. The so-called "executive" area of the brain that directs and controls the other areas is the
    a. corpus callosum.
    b. myelin sheath.
    c. prefrontal cortex.
    d. temporal lobe.

12. The relationship between accident rate and socioeconomic status can be described as
    a. a positive correlation.
    b. a negative correlation.
    c. curvilinear.
    d. no correlation.

13. Which of the following is true of the corpus callosum?
    a. It enables short-term memory.
    b. It connects the two halves of the brain.
    c. It must be fully myelinated before gross motor skills can be acquired.
    d. All of the above are correct.

14. The improvements in eye-hand coordination that allow preschoolers to catch and then throw a ball occur, in part, because
    a. the brain areas associated with this ability become more fully myelinated.
    b. the corpus callosum begins to function.
    c. fine motor skills have matured by age 2.
    d. gross motor skills have matured by age 2.

15. During the school years, inadequate lateralization of the brain and immaturity of the prefrontal cortex may contribute to deficiencies in
    a. cognition.
    b. peer relationships
    c. emotional control
    d. all of the above.

True or False Items

Write T (for true) or F (for false) on the line in front of each statement.

16. _____ Growth between ages 2 and 6 is more rapid than at any other period in the life span.

17. _____ During childhood, the legs develop faster than any other part of the body.

18. _____ For most people, the brain center for speech is located in the left hemisphere.

19. _____ The health care, genetic background, and nutrition of the preschool child are major influences on growth.

20. _____ Brain growth during childhood proceeds in spurts and plateaus.

21. _____ Fine motor skills are usually easier for preschoolers to master than are gross motor skills.

22. _____ Most serious childhood injuries truly are "accidents."

23. _____ Children often fare as well in kinship care as they do in conventional foster care.

24. _____ Concern for and protection of the well-being of children varies markedly from culture to culture.

25. _____ Most child maltreatment does not involve serious physical abuse.

Practice Questions II

Multiple-Choice Questions

1. Each year from ages 2 to 6, the average child gains and grows, respectively
    a. 2 pounds and 1 inch.
    b. 3 pounds and 2 inches.
    c. 4.5 pounds and 3 inches.
    d. 6 pounds and 6 inches.

2. The center for perceiving various types of visual configurations is usually located in the brain's
   a. right hemisphere.
   b. left hemisphere.
   c. right or left hemisphere.
   d. corpus callosum.

3. Which of the following best describes brain growth during childhood?
   a. It proceeds at a slow, steady, linear rate.
   b. The left hemisphere develops more rapidly than the right.
   c. The right hemisphere develops more rapidly than the left.
   d. It involves a nonlinear series of spurts and plateaus.

4. The textbook notes that art provides an important opportunity for the child to develop the skill of
   a. realistic representation of objects.
   b. reading.
   c. perspective.
   d. self-correction.

5. Which of the following is an example of secondary prevention of child maltreatment?
   a. removing a child from an abusive home
   b. jailing a maltreating parent
   c. home visitation of families with infants by health professionals
   d. public-policy measures aimed at creating stable neighborhoods

6. When parents or caregivers do not provide adequate food, shelter, attention, or supervision, it is referred to as
   a. abuse.
   b. neglect.
   c. endangering.
   d. maltreatment.

7. Which of the following is true of a developed nation in which many ethnic groups live together?
   a. Ethnic variations in height and weight disappear.
   b. Ethnic variations in stature persist, but are substantially smaller.
   c. Children of African descent tend to be tallest, followed by Europeans, Asians, and Latinos.
   d. Cultural patterns exert a stronger-than-normal impact on growth patterns.

8. Which of the following is an example of a fine motor skill?
   a. kicking a ball
   b. running
   c. drawing with a pencil
   d. jumping

9. Most gross motor skills can be learned by healthy children by about age
    a. 2.
    b. 3.
    c. 5.
    d. 7.

10. Two of the most important factors that affect height during the play years are
    a. socioeconomic status and health care.
    b. gender and health care.
    c. heredity and nutrition.
    d. heredity and activity level.

11. Over the past two decades in the United States, the accidental death rate for children between the ages of 1 and 5 has
    a. decreased, largely as a result of new city, state, and federal safety laws.
    b. decreased, largely because parents are more knowledgeable about safety practices.
    c. increased.
    d. remained unchanged.

12. During the play years, because growth is slow, children's appetites seem _____ they were in the first two years of life.
    a. larger than
    b. smaller than
    c. about the same as
    d. erratic, sometimes smaller and sometimes larger than

Matching Items
Match each definition or description with its corresponding term.

Terms
13. _____ corpus callosum
14. _____ gross motor skills
15. _____ fine motor skills
16. _____ myelination
17. _____ lateralization
18. _____ injury control
19. _____ perseveration

20. _____ activity level
21. _____ child abuse
22. _____ child neglect
23. _____ primary prevention
24. _____ secondary prevention
25. _____ tertiary prevention

Definitions or Descriptions
    a. an insulating process that speeds up neural transmission
    b. the differentiation of the two sides of the brain
    c. the tendency to repeat thoughts or actions
    d. a general measure of how much children move around
    e. procedures to prevent child maltreatment from ever occurring

f. running and jumping

g. actions that are deliberately harmful to a child's well-being

h. procedures for spotting and treating the early warning signs of child maltreatment

i. painting a picture or tying shoelaces

j. failure to appropriately meet a child's basic needs

k. an approach emphasizing "accident" prevention

l. procedures to halt maltreatment that has already occurred

m. band of nerve fibers connecting the right and left hemispheres of the brain

Applying Your Knowledge

1. An editorial in the local paper claims that there is no reason children younger than age 6 cannot be taught basic literacy skills. You write to the editor, noting that

    a. she has an accurate grasp of developmental processes.

    b. before age 6, brain myelination and development are too immature to enable children to form links between spoken and written language.

    c. although the right hemisphere is relatively mature at age 6, the left is not.

    d. although this may be true for girls, boys (who are slower to mature neurologically) would struggle.

2. Two-year-old Carrie is hyperactive, often confused between fantasy and reality, and jumps at any sudden noise. Her pediatrician suspects that she is suffering from

    a. shaken baby syndrome.

    b. failure to thrive.

    c. post-traumatic stress disorder.

    d. child neglect.

3. Following an automobile accident, Amira developed severe problems with her speech. Her doctor believes that the accident injured the _____ of her brain.

    a. left side

    b. right side

    c. communication pathways

    d. corpus callosum

4. Two-year-old Ali is quite clumsy, falls down frequently, and often bumps into stationary objects. Ali most likely

    a. has a neuromuscular disorder.

    b. has an underdeveloped right hemisphere of the brain.

    c. is suffering from iron deficiency anemia.

    d. is a normal two-year-old whose gross motor skills will improve dramatically during the preschool years.

5. Climbing a fence is an example of a

    a. fine motor skill.

    b. gross motor skill.

    c. circular reaction.

    d. launching event.

6. To prevent accidental death in childhood, some experts urge forethought and planning for safety and measures to limit the damage of such accidents as do occur. This approach is called

   a. protective analysis.

   b. safety education.

   c. injury control.

   d. childproofing.

7. Which of the following activities would probably be the most difficult for a five-year-old child?

   a. climbing a ladder

   b. catching a ball

   c. throwing a ball

   d. pouring juice from a pitcher without spilling it

8. Most child maltreatment

   a. does not involve serious physical abuse.

   b. involves a rare outburst from the perpetrator.

   c. involves a mentally ill perpetrator.

   d. can be predicted from the victim's personality characteristics.

9. A mayoral candidate is calling for sweeping policy changes to help ensure the well-being of children by promoting home ownership, high-quality community centers, and more stable neighborhoods. If these measures are effective in reducing child maltreatment, they would be classified as

   a. primary prevention.

   b. secondary prevention.

   c. tertiary prevention.

   d. differential response.

10. A factor that would figure very little into the development of fine motor skills, such as drawing and writing, is

    a. strength.

    b. muscular control.

    c. judgment.

    d. short, fat fingers.

11. Parents who were abused as children

    a. almost always abuse their children.

    b. are more likely to neglect, but not necessarily abuse, their children.

    c. are no more likely than anyone else to mistreat their children.

    d. do none of the above.

12. Three-year-old Kyle's parents are concerned because Kyle, who generally seems healthy, doesn't seem to have the hefty appetite or rate of growth he had as an infant. Should they be worried?

   a. Yes, because both appetite and growth rate normally increase throughout the preschool years.

   b. Yes, because appetite (but not necessarily growth rate) normally increases during the preschool years.

   c. No, because growth rate (and hence caloric need) is less during the preschool years than during infancy.

   d. There is not enough information to determine whether Kyle is developing normally.

Answer Key

Key Terms

1. Myelination is the insulating process that speeds up the transmission of neural impulses. (p. 240; objective 3)

2. The corpus callosum is a band of nerve fibers that connects the right and left hemispheres of the brain. (p. 241; objective 3)

3. Lateralization refers to the differentiation of the two sides of the brain so that each serves specific, specialized functions. (p. 241; objective 3)

4. The so-called "executive" area of the brain, the prefrontal cortex specializes in planning, selecting, and coordinating thoughts. (p. 243; objective 5)

5. Perseveration is the tendency to repeat thoughts or actions, even after they have become unhelpful or inappropriate. In young children, perseveration is a normal product of immature brain functions. (p. 244; objective 5)

   Memory Aid: To persevere is to continue, or persist, at something.

6. A general measure of how much children move around, activity level is related to both brain maturation and practice. (p. 245; objectives 1 & 8)

7. Injury control (also called harm reduction) is the practice of limiting the extent of injuries by planning ahead, controlling the circumstances, preventing certain dangerous activities, and adding safety features to others. (p. 249; objective 8)

8. Primary prevention refers to public policy measures designed to prevent child maltreatment (or other harm) from ever occurring. (p. 249; objective 9)

9. Secondary prevention involves home visitation and other efforts to spot and treat the early warning signs of maltreatment before problems become severe. (p. 249; objective 9)

10. Tertiary prevention involves efforts to stop child maltreatment after it occurs and to treat the victim. Removing a child from an abusive home, jailing the perpetrator, and providing health care to the victim are examples of tertiary prevention. (p. 249; objective 9)

11. Child maltreatment is intentional harm to, or avoidable endangerment of, anyone under age 18. (p. 252; objective 8)

12. Child abuse refers to deliberate actions that are harmful to a child's well-being. (p. 252; objective 8)

13. Child neglect refers to failure to appropriately meet a child's basic needs. (p. 252; objective 8)

14. A sign of possible child neglect, failure to thrive occurs when an otherwise healthy child gains little or no weight. (p. 252; objective 8)

15. Child maltreatment that has been officially reported to the police, or other authority, is called reported maltreatment. (p. 253; objective 9)

16. Child maltreatment that has been officially reported to authorities, and verified, is called substantiated maltreatment. (p. 253; objective 9)

17. Differential response refers to separating child maltreatment reports into two categories: high-risk cases that require immediate investigation and possible removal of the child, and low-risk cases that require supportive measures to encourage better parental care. (p. 254; objective 9)

18. A serious condition caused by sharply shaking an infant to stop his or her crying, shaken baby syndrome is associated with severe brain damage that results from internal hemorrhaging. (p. 256; objective 9)

19. Post-traumatic stress disorder (PTSD) is a syndrome triggered by exposure to an extreme traumatic stressor. In maltreated children, symptoms of PTSD include hyperactivity and hypervigilance, sleeplessness, and confusion between fantasy and reality. (p. 257; objective 8)

20. Permanency planning is the process of finding a long-term solution to the care of a child who has been abused. (p. 258; objective 9)

21. Foster care is a legally sanctioned, publicly supported arrangement in which children are removed from their biological parents and temporarily given to another adult to nurture. (p. 258; objective 9)

22. Kinship care is a form of foster care in which a relative of a maltreated child becomes the child's legal caregiver. (p. 258; objective 9)

23. Adoption is the process whereby nonbiological parents are given legal custody of a child. (p. 259; objective 9)

Practice Questions I

Multiple-Choice Questions

1. c. is the correct answer. (p. 238; objective 2)

   a. is incorrect. Serious malnutrition is much more likely to occur in infancy or in adolescence than in early childhood.

   b. is incorrect. Although an important health problem, eating too much candy or other sweets is not as serious as iron deficiency anemia.

   d. is incorrect. Since growth is slower during the preschool years, children need fewer calories per pound during this period.

2. b. is the correct answer. (p. 242; objective 5)

   a. & d. are incorrect. The right brain is the location of areas associated with recognition of visual configurations.

   c. is incorrect. The corpus callosum helps integrate the functioning of the two halves of the brain; it does not contain areas specialized for particular skills.

3. b. is the correct answer. (p. 238; video lesson, segment 1; objective 1)

4. d. is the correct answer. Accident rates have decreased during this time period. (p. 251; objective 7)

5. d. is the correct answer. (p. 239; objective 2)

6. c. is the correct answer. (p. 245; video lesson, segment 2; objective 6)

7. d. is the correct answer. (pp. 240, 243; video lesson, segment 1; objective 3)

8. a. is the correct answer. (p. 248; objective 4)

9. a. is the correct answer. (p. 242; objective 3)

10. c. is the correct answer. (p. 238; video lesson, segment 1; objective 1)

11. c. is the correct answer. (p. 243; objective 5)

a. is incorrect. The corpus callosum is the band of fibers that link the two halves of the brain.

b. is incorrect. The myelin sheath is the fatty insulation that surrounds some neurons in the brain.

d. is incorrect. The temporal lobes of the brain contain the primary centers for hearing.

12. b. is the correct answer. Children with lower socioeconomic status have higher accident rates. (p. 250; objective 4)

13. b. is the correct answer. (p. 241; video lesson, segment 1; objective 3)

a. is incorrect. The corpus callosum is not directly involved in memory.

c. is incorrect. Myelination of the central nervous system is important to the mastery of fine motor skills.

14. a. is the correct answer. (p. 240; objective 5)

b. is incorrect. The corpus callosum begins to function long before the play years.

c. & d. are incorrect. Neither fine nor gross motor skills have fully matured by age 2.

15. d. is the correct answer. (p. 244; objective 3)

True or False Items

16. F   Growth actually slows down during the play years. (p. 237; video lesson, segment 1; objective 1)

17. F   During childhood, the brain develops faster than any other part of the body. (p. 240; video lesson, segment 1; objectives 1 & 3)

18. T   (p. 242; objective 5)

19. T   (p. 238; video lesson, segment 1; objective 1)

20. T   (p. 244; video lesson, segment 1; objective 3)

21. F   Fine motor skills are more difficult for preschoolers to master than are gross motor skills. (p. 246; video lesson, segment 2; objective 6)

22. F   Most serious accidents involve someone's lack of forethought. (p. 249; objective 4)

23. T   (p. 259; objective 9)

24. T   (p. 255; objective 9)

25. T   (p. 252; video lesson, segment 3; objective 8)

Practice Questions II

Multiple-Choice Questions

1. c. is the correct answer. (p. 237; video lesson, segment 1; objective 1)

2. a. is the correct answer. (p. 242; objective 5)

b. & c. are incorrect. The left hemisphere of the brain contains areas associated with language development.

d. is incorrect. The corpus callosum does not contain areas for specific behaviors.

3. d. is the correct answer. (p. 244; video lesson, segment 1; objective 3)

b. & c. are incorrect. The left and right hemispheres develop at similar rates.

4. d. is the correct answer. (p. 247; objective 7)

5. c. is the correct answer. (p. 249; objective 9)

 a. & b. are incorrect. These are examples of tertiary prevention.

 d. is incorrect. This is an example of primary prevention.

6. b. is the correct answer. (p. 252; video lesson, segment 3; objective 8)

 a. is incorrect. Abuse is deliberate, harsh injury to the body.

 c. is incorrect. Endangerment was not discussed.

 d. is incorrect. Maltreatment is too broad a term.

7. c. is the correct answer. (pp. 237–238; objective 1)

8. c. is the correct answer. (p. 246; video lesson, segment 2; objective 6)

 a., b., & d. are incorrect. These are gross motor skills.

9. c. is the correct answer. (p. 245; video lesson, segment 2; objective 6)

10. c. is the correct answer. (p. 238; objective 1)

11. a. is the correct answer. (p. 251; objective 4)

 b. is incorrect. Although safety education is important, the decrease in accident rate is largely the result of new safety laws.

12. b. is the correct answer. (p. 238; objective 2)

Matching Items

13. m (p. 241; video lesson, segment 1; objective 3)

14. f (p. 245; video lesson, segment 2; objective 6)

15. i (p. 246; video lesson, segment 2; objective 6)

16. a (p. 240; objective 3)

17. b (p. 241; objective 3)

18. k (p. 249; objective 4)

19. c (p. 244; objective 5)

20. d (p. 245; objective 1)

21. g (p. 252; video lesson, segment 3; objective 8)

22. j (p. 252; video lesson, segment 3; objective 8)

23. e (p. 249; objective 9)

24. h (p. 249; objective 9)

25. l (p. 249; objective 9)

Applying Your Knowledge

1. b. is the correct answer. (p. 244; objective 5)

2. c. is the correct answer. (p. 257; objective 9)

 a. is incorrect. Shaken baby syndrome is a consequence of maltreatment associated with memory impairment and delays in logical thinking.

 b. is incorrect. Failure to thrive is associated with little or no weight gain, despite apparent good health.

 d. is incorrect. Child neglect simply refers to failure to meet a child's basic needs. Carrie's specific symptoms may be caused by neglect or maltreatment, but they are most directly signs of PTSD.

3. a. is the correct answer. In most people, the left hemisphere of the brain contains centers for language, including speech. (p. 242; objective 5)

4. d. is the correct answer. (p. 245; objective 6)

5. b. is the correct answer. (p. 245; video lesson, segment 2; objective 6)

   a. is incorrect. Fine motor skills involve small body movements, such as the hand movements used in painting.

   c. & d. are incorrect. These events were not discussed in this chapter.

6. c. is the correct answer. (p. 249; objective 4)

7. d. is the correct answer. (p. 246; video lesson, segment 2; objective 6)

   a., b., & c. are incorrect. Preschoolers find these gross motor skills easier to perform than fine motor skills such as that described in d.

8. a. is the correct answer. (p. 252; video lesson, segment 3; objective 8)

9. a. is the correct answer. (p. 259; objective 9)

   b. is incorrect. Had the candidate called for measures to spot the early warning signs of maltreatment, this answer would be true.

   c. is incorrect. Had the candidate called for jailing those who maltreat children or providing greater counseling and health care for victims, this answer would be true.

   d. is incorrect. Differential response is not an approach to prevention of maltreatment; rather, it refers to separate reporting procedures for high- and low-risk families.

10. a. is the correct answer. Strength is a more important factor in the development of gross motor skills. (p. 246; video lesson, segment 2; objective 6)

11. d. is the correct answer. Approximately 30–40 percent of adults who were abused as children themselves become abusive parents. (p. 258; objective 8)

12. c. is the correct answer. (p. 238; objective 2)

Lesson Review

Lesson 11

The Play Years
Biosocial Development

Please Note: Use this matrix to guide your study and achieve the learning objectives of this lesson. It will also help you to view the video, which defines and demonstrates important concepts and skills as they relate to everyday life.

Learning Objective	Textbook	Telecourse Student Guide	Video Lesson
1. Describe normal physical growth during the play years, and account for variations in height and weight.	pp. 237–239	Key Terms: 6; Practice Questions I: 3, 10, 16, 17, 19; Practice Questions II: 1, 7, 10, 20.	Segment 1: *Body and Brain Growth*
2. Describe changes in eating habits and nutritional needs during the preschool years.	pp. 237–240	Practice Questions I: 1, 5; Practice Questions II: 12; Applying Your Knowledge: 12.	
3. Discuss the brain processes of myelination and lateralization and their development during the play years.	pp. 240–245	Key Terms: 1, 2, 3; Practice Questions I: 7, 11, 13, 15, 18; Practice Questions II: 3, 15, 18, 19.	Segment 1: *Body and Brain Growth*
4. Describe the prevalence of accidental injuries during early childhood, describe some measures that have significantly reduced accidental death rates for children, and identify several factors that contribute to this problem.	pp. 249–251	Practice Questions I: 8, 12, 22; Practice Questions II: 11, 18; Applying Your Knowledge: 6.	Segment 2: *Motor Skills*
5. Explain how the maturation of visual pathways and cerebral hemispheres in the brain allow for formal education to begin at about age 6.	pp. 241–242	Key Terms: 4, 5; Practice Questions I: 2, 11, 14, 18; Practice Questions II: 2, 18; Applying Your Knowledge: 1, 3.	

Learning Objective	Textbook	Telecourse Student Guide	Video Lesson
6. Distinguish between gross and fine motor skills, and discuss the development of each during the play years.	pp. 245–246	Practice Questions I: 6, 21; Practice Questions II: 8, 9, 14, 15; Applying Your Knowledge: 4, 5, 7, 10.	Segment 2: *Motor Skills*
7. Discuss the significance of artistic expression during the play years.	pp. 247–248	Practice Questions I: 4; Practice Questions II: 4.	
8. Identify the various categories and consequences of child maltreatment.	pp. 252–257	Key Terms: 6, 7, 11, 12, 13, 14, 19; Practice Questions I: 25; Practice Questions II: 6, 21, 22; Applying Your Knowledge: 8, 11.	
9. Discuss several factors that contribute to maltreatment, and describe current treatment and prevention efforts.	pp. 252–260	Key Terms: 8, 9, 10, 15, 16, 17, 18, 20, 21, 22, 23; Practice Questions I: 23, 24; Practice Questions II: 5, 23, 24, 25; Applying Your Knowledge: 2, 9.	Segment 3: *Maltreatment*

Playing and Learning

Lesson 12

The Play Years:
Cognitive Development

Preview

Young children reveal themselves to be remarkably thoughtful, insightful, and perceptive thinkers in countless everyday instances, as well as in findings of numerous reasearch studies. Their memory of the past and mastery of language are sometimes astonishing. Lesson 12 begins by comparing Jean Piaget's and Lev Vygotsky's views of cognitive development at this age. According to Piaget, young children's thought is prelogical: between the ages of 2 and 6, they are unable to use logical principles and are limited by irreversible and static thinking. Lev Vygotsky, a contemporary of Piaget, saw learning more as a product of social interaction than of individual discovery.

The lesson next focuses on what preschoolers can do, including their competence in understanding number concepts, storing and retrieving memories, and theorizing about the world. This leads into a description of language development during early childhood. Although young children demonstrate rapid improvement in vocabulary and grammar, they have difficulty with abstractions, metaphorical speech, and certain rules of grammar. The lesson concludes with a discussion of preschool education, including a description of "quality" preschool programs and an evaluation of their lifelong impact on children.

As you complete this lesson, consider the cognitive development of any children you know in this age group (2 to 6). Consider what these children understand already and what they have yet to learn. Observe how they think—how they look at the world, interpret events, draw conclusions, and make decisions. Note how these children discover knowledge on their own and how they learn new skills through the guidance of parents, caregivers, and other children. Also, consider the memory skills of these children. For instance, how well can they remember events of their day and how well can they describe them? Consider their language skills—the extent of their vocabulary and their use of grammar. Finally, do any of these children go to day care or preschool? If so, what type of care are they receiving? What sort of learning experiences are they exposed to and how might that exposure affect their development later in life?

Prior Telecourse Knowledge that Will Be Used in this Lesson

- This lesson will return to Piaget's theory of cognitive development (from Lesson 1) with a discussion of *preoperational thought*. Recall that Piaget's theory specifies four major periods of cognitive development:

   1. Sensorimotor (birth to 2 years)

   2. **Preoperational (2 to 6 years) ← The Play Years**

   3. Concrete Operational (7 to 11 years)

   4. Formal Operational (12 years through adulthood)

- This lesson will return to the sociocultural theories of Lev Vygotsky (from Lesson 1). Recall that Vygotsky emphasized the importance of **guided participation**, a process in which an individual learns through social interaction with a mentor who offers assistance, models strategies, and provides explicit instruction as needed.

Learning Objectives

Use this information to guide your reading, viewing, thinking, and studying. After successfully completing this lesson, you should be able to:

1. Describe the major characteristics of preoperational thought, according to Piaget.

2. Contrast Vygotsky's views on cognitive development with those of Piaget, focusing on the concept of guided participation.

3. Explain the significance of the zone of proximal development and scaffolding in promoting cognitive growth.

4. Describe Vygotsky's view of the role of language in cognitive growth.

5. Discuss more recent research on conservation, and explain why findings have led to qualification or revision of Piaget's description of cognition during the play years.

6. Discuss preschoolers' understanding of number concepts.

7. Discuss young children's memory abilities and limitations, noting the role of personal meaning in their ability to recall events.

8. Explain the typical young child's theory of mind, noting how it is affected by culture and context, and relate it to the child's developing ability to understand pretense.

9. Outline the sequence by which vocabulary and grammar develop during the play years, and discuss limitations in the young child's language abilities.

10. Explain the role of fast mapping in children's acquisition of language.

11. Identify the characteristics of a high-quality preschool program, and discuss the long-term benefits of preschool education for the child and his or her family.

 Read Chapter 9, "The Play Years: Cognitive Development," pages 263–293.

View the video for Lesson 12, "Playing and Learning."

   Segment 1: *How Preschoolers Think*

   Segment 2: *Words and Memories*

   Segment 3: *Early Childhood Education*

Summary

Symbolic thought, which enables children to form mental representations of things and events they are not immediately experiencing, develops rapidly throughout the preschool years. Both language and imagination become tools of thought, making the typical four-year-old much more verbal and creative than the one-year-old.

Although preschool children can think symbolically, they cannot perform what Jean Piaget called "logical operations." One characteristic of this **preoperational thought** is **irreversibility**: Preschoolers do not generally understand that reversing a process will restore the original conditions. **Egocentrism** also limits the preschooler's ideas about the world to his or her own point of view. Preoperational children also fail to answer correctly problems involving **conservation**, indicating that they do not yet understand the idea that the amount of a substance is unaffected by changes in its shape or placement.

Centration refers to the tendency of preschoolers to focus or center their analysis on one aspect of a problem, for instance, the appearance of liquid in a glass. In tests of conservation, Piaget believed, the problem is that preschoolers center on only the height of the liquid and fail to consider the shape and diameter of the glass it is in. Another example of centration is the preschooler's tendency toward egocentrism—to see the world only from his or her perspective.

Piaget focused on the individual child's innate curiosity. In general, he believed that children will find a way to learn when they are ready to do so. In contrast, Lev Vygotsky emphasized the impact of cultural and social factors in learning, including the effects of mentors and teachers. For instance, Vygotsky believed that—for each individual—there is a **zone of proximal development**, which represents the cognitive distance between the child's actual and potential levels of development. To encourage development, mentors can **scaffold** learning—in other words, provide structured assistance to help the child master new skills. Vygotsky also believed that language advances thinking in two ways: through **private speech** that an individual child uses to assist his or her thinking, and as **social mediation**, a tool of verbal interaction between mentor and apprentice. While these approaches are sometimes described as contradictory, a closer examination reveals that they may simply emphasize two different aspects of cognitive development.

Recent experiments have shown that preschoolers are not as illogical as Piaget believed. For example, under certain circumstances, young children can demonstrate the concept of conservation. On the other hand, young children cannot count large amounts, cannot easily add or subtract, and are not skilled at deliberately storing or retrieving memories. By about age 4, however, they do understand basic counting principles and can devise and use **scripts**, or outlines of familiar events. They also develop an elementary theory of mind about their own and others' mental processes.

During the play years, children are gaining a better understanding of their own thoughts and feelings. In addition, they are beginning to develop informal theories about why other people act the way they do. In time this develops into what psychologists call a **theory of mind**, an understanding of human mental processes. This understanding helps children explain basic everyday questions, such as how a person's knowledge and emotions affect his or her actions and how people can have such different perceptions, intentions, and desires.

Language development during the play years includes learning 10,000 words or more, in a predictable sequence according to parts of speech. Words are often learned after only one hearing, through the process called **fast mapping**. By age 3, children demonstrate extensive grammatical knowledge, although they often apply grammatical rules even when they should not (**overregularization**).

Changes in family composition and work patterns have resulted in great increases in early-childhood education programs. A high-quality preschool program is characterized by a low child-teacher ratio, a staff with training and credentials in early-childhood education, a curriculum geared toward cognitive development rather than behavioral control, and an organization of space that facilitates creative and constructive play.

While children in the play years are developing rapidly, it's important to focus their learning experiences on age-appropriate activities and not force them into tasks that are beyond their capability. For example, before a child's brain develops the ability to link spoken and written language (at about age 5), he or she is not ready to learn to read. That's why formal instruction in reading usually begins at about age 6. (Of course, *preparation* for literacy—such as reading picture books and writing one's name—should begin much earlier.)

📖 **Review all reading assignments for this lesson.**

💻 **As assigned by your instructor, complete the optional online component for this lesson.**

Key Terms

Using your own words, write a brief definition or explanation of each of the following terms on a separate piece of paper.

1. preoperational thought	13. private speech
2. centration	14. social mediation
3. egocentrism	15. source memory
4. focus on appearance	16. script
5. static reasoning	17. theory of mind
6. irreversibility	18. imaginary companion
7. conservation	19. sensitive period
8. theory-theory	20. critical period
9. apprentice in thinking	21. fast mapping
10. guided participation	22. overregularization
11. zone of proximal development	23. high risk
12. scaffold	

Practice Questions I

Multiple-Choice Questions

1. Piaget believed that children are in the preoperational stage from ages
   a. 6 months to 1 year.
   b. 1 to 3 years.
   c. 2 to 6 years.
   d. 5 to 11 years.

2. Which of the following is **NOT** a characteristic of preoperational thinking?
   a. focus on appearance
   b. static reasoning
   c. lack of imagination
   d. centration

3. Which of the following provides evidence that early childhood is a sensitive period, rather than a critical period, for language learning?

   a. People can and do master their native language after early childhood.

   b. Vocabulary, grammar, and pronunciation are acquired especially easily during early childhood.

   c. Neurological characteristics of the young child's developing brain facilitate language acquisition.

   d. a and b

   e. a, b, and c

4. Preschoolers' poor performance on memory tests is primarily the result of

   a. their tendency to rely too extensively on scripts.

   b. their lack of efficient storage and retrieval skills.

   c. the incomplete myelination of cortical neurons.

   d. their short attention span.

5. The vocabulary of preschool children consists primarily of

   a. metaphors.

   b. self-created words.

   c. abstract nouns.

   d. verbs and concrete nouns.

6. Preschoolers sometimes apply the rules of grammar even when they shouldn't. This tendency is called

   a. overregularization.

   b. literal language.

   c. practical usage.

   d. single-mindedness.

7. The Russian psychologist Lev Vygotsky emphasized that

   a. language helps children form ideas.

   b. children form concepts first, then find words to express them.

   c. language and other cognitive developments are unrelated at this stage.

   d. preschoolers learn language only for egocentric purposes.

8. Private speech can be described as

   a. a way of formulating ideas to oneself.

   b. fantasy.

   c. an early learning difficulty.

   d. the beginnings of deception.

9. The child who has not yet grasped the principle of conservation is likely to

   a. insist that a tall, narrow glass contains more liquid than a short, wide glass, even though both glasses actually contain the same amount.

   b. be incapable of egocentric thought.

   c. be unable to reverse an event.

   d. do all of the above.

10. In later life, Head Start graduates showed
    a. better report cards, but more behavioral problems.
    b. significantly higher IQ scores.
    c. higher scores on achievement tests.
    d. alienation from their original neighborhoods and families.

11. The best preschool programs are generally those that provide the greatest amount of
    a. behavioral control.
    b. adult-child conversation.
    c. instruction in conservation and other logical principles.
    d. demonstration of toys by professionals.

12. Compared with their rate of speech development, children's understanding of language develops
    a. more slowly.
    b. at about the same pace.
    c. more rapidly.
    d. more rapidly in some cultures than in others.

13. Relatively recent experiments have demonstrated that preschoolers can succeed at tests of conservation when
    a. they are allowed to work cooperatively with other children.
    b. the test is presented as a competition.
    c. the children are informed that their parents are observing them.
    d. the test is presented in a simple, gamelike way.

14. Through the process called fast mapping, children
    a. immediately assimilate new words by connecting them through their assumed meaning to categories of words they have already mastered.
    b. acquire the concept of conservation at an earlier age than Piaget believed.
    c. are able to move beyond egocentric thinking.
    d. become skilled in the practical use of language.

True or False Items
Write T (for true) or F (for false) on the line in front of each statement.

15. _____ Piaget's description of cognitive development in early childhood has been universally rejected by contemporary developmentalists.

16. _____ In conservation problems, many preschoolers are unable to understand the transformation because they focus exclusively on appearances.

17. _____ Preschoolers who use private speech have slower cognitive growth than those who do not.

18. _____ Whether or not a preschooler demonstrates conservation in an experiment depends in part on the conditions of the experiment.

19. _____ One reason Japanese children are superior to American children in math may be that the Japanese language is more logical in its labeling of numbers.

20. _____ Piaget believed that preschoolers' acquisition of language makes possible their cognitive development.

21. _____ With the beginning of preoperational thought, most preschoolers can understand abstract words.

22. _____ A preschooler who says "You comed up and hurted me" is demonstrating a lack of understanding of English grammar.

23. _____ Successful preschool programs generally have a low teacher-to-child ratio.

24. _____ Vygotsky believed that cognitive growth is largely a social activity.

Practice Questions II

Multiple-Choice Questions

1. Three-year-old Megan insists that her brother spilled a glass of milk, even though he was nowhere nearby. The fact that the milk *was* spilled indicates that Megan is
   a. constructing a theory-theory.
   b. having difficulty with her source memory of the event.
   c. demonstrating centration.
   d. demonstrating static reasoning.

2. Piaget believed that preoperational children fail conservation-of-liquid tests because of their tendency to
   a. focus on appearance.
   b. fast map.
   c. overregularize.
   d. do all of the above.

3. A preschooler who focuses his or her attention on only one feature of a situation is demonstrating a characteristic of preoperational thought called
   a. centration.
   b. overregularization.
   c. reversibility.
   d. egocentrism.

4. One characteristic of preoperational thought is
   a. the ability to categorize objects.
   b. the ability to count in multiples of 5.
   c. the inability to perform logical operations.
   d. difficulty adjusting to changes in routine.

5. The zone of proximal development represents the
   a. skills or knowledge that are within the potential of the learner but are not yet mastered.
   b. influence of a child's peers on cognitive development.
   c. explosive period of language development during the play years.
   d. normal variations in children's language proficiency.

6. According to Vygotsky, language advances thinking through private speech and by
    a. helping children to review privately what they know.
    b. helping children explain events to themselves.
    c. serving as a mediator of the social interaction that is a vital part of learning.
    d. facilitating the process of fast mapping.

7. Irreversibility refers to the
    a. inability to understand that other people view the world from a different perspective than one's own.
    b. inability to think about more than one idea at a time.
    c. failure to understand that changing the arrangement of a group of objects doesn't change their number.
    d. failure to understand that undoing a process will restore the original conditions.

8. According to Piaget
    a. it is impossible for preoperational children to grasp the concept of conservation, no matter how carefully it is explained.
    b. preschoolers fail to solve conservation problems because they center their attention on the transformation that has occurred and ignore the changed appearances of the objects.
    c. with special training, even preoperational children are able to grasp some aspects of conservation.
    d. preschoolers fail to solve conservation problems because they have no theory of mind.

9. In order to scaffold a child's cognitive skills, parents
    a. simplify tasks.
    b. interpret the activity.
    c. help children find answers, while anticipating mistakes.
    d. do all of the above.

10. Which theorist would be most likely to agree with the statement, "Learning is a social activity more than it is a matter of individual discovery"?
    a. Piaget
    b. Vygotsky
    c. both a and b
    d. neither a nor b

11. Children first demonstrate some understanding of grammar
    a. as soon as the first words are produced.
    b. once they begin to use language for practical purposes.
    c. through the process called fast mapping.
    d. in their earliest two-word sentences.

12. Preschoolers sometimes seem forgetful because they
    a. are unable to benefit from using mental scripts.
    b. often do not attend to event features that are pertinent to older people.
    c. are egocentric in their thinking.
    d. have all of the above limitations.

13. During the preschool years, vocabulary increases exponentially, from about 500 words

    a. at age 2 to about 7,000 at age 6.

    b. at age 2 to more than 10,000 at age 6.

    c. at age 3 to more than 20,000 at age 7.

    d. at age 3 to about 25,000 at age 7.

14. Overregularization indicates that a child

    a. is clearly applying rules of grammar.

    b. persists in egocentric thinking.

    c. has not yet mastered the principle of conservation.

    d. does not yet have a theory of mind.

15. Regarding the value of preschool education, most developmentalists believe that

    a. most disadvantaged children will not benefit from an early preschool education.

    b. most disadvantaged children will benefit from an early preschool education.

    c. because of sleeper effects, the early benefits of preschool education are likely to disappear by grade 3.

    d. the relatively small benefits of antipoverty measures such as Head Start do not justify their huge costs.

Matching Items

Match each definition or description with its corresponding term.

Terms

16. _____ script

17. _____ scaffold

18. _____ theory of mind

19. _____ zone of proximal development

20. _____ overregularization

21. _____ fast mapping

22. _____ irreversibility

23. _____ centration

24. _____ conservation

25. _____ private speech

26. _____ guided participation

Definitions or Descriptions

    a. the idea that amount is unaffected by changes in shape or placement

    b. memory-facilitating outline of past experiences

    c. the cognitive distance between a child's actual and potential levels of development

    d. the tendency to think about one aspect of a situation at a time

    e. the process whereby the child learns through social interaction with a "tutor"

    f. our understanding of mental processes in ourselves and others

    g. the process by which words are learned after only one hearing

    h. an inappropriate application of rules of grammar

    i. the internal use of language to form ideas

    j. the inability to understand that original conditions are restored by the undoing of some process

    k. to structure a child's participation in learning encounters

Applying Your Knowledge

1. An experimenter first shows a child two rows of checkers that each have the same number of checkers. Then, with the child watching, the experimenter elongates one row and asks the child if each of the two rows still has an equal number of checkers. This experiment tests the child's understanding of

   a. reversibility.
   b. conservation of matter.
   c. conservation of number.
   d. centration.

2. A preschooler believes that a "party" is the one and only attribute of a birthday. She says that Daddy doesn't have a birthday because he never has a party. This thinking demonstrates the tendency Piaget called

   a. egocentrism.
   b. centration.
   c. conservation of events.
   d. mental representation.

3. A child who understands that $3 + 4 = 7$ means that $7 - 4 = 3$ has had to master the concept of

   a. reversibility.
   b. number.
   c. conservation.
   d. egocentrism.

4. A four-year-old tells the teacher that a clown should not be allowed to visit the class because "Pat is 'fraid of clowns." The four-year-old thus shows that he can anticipate how another will feel. This is evidence of the beginnings of

   a. egocentrism.
   b. deception.
   c. a theory of mind.
   d. conservation.

5. A Chinese visitor to a preschool in the United States would probably be struck by its emphasis on fostering _____ in children.

   a. conformity
   b. concern for others
   c. cooperation
   d. self-reliance

6. A nursery school teacher is given the job of selecting holiday entertainment for a group of preschool children. If the teacher agrees with the ideas of Vygotsky, she is most likely to select

   a. a simple television show that every child can understand.

   b. a hands-on experience that requires little adult supervision.

   c. brief, action-oriented play activities that the children and teachers will perform together.

   d. holiday puzzles for children to work on individually.

7. When asked to describe her friend's birthday party, three-year-old Hilary gives a general description of events that form a composite of all the parties she has attended. Hilary evidently

   a. is very egocentric in her thinking.

   b. is retrieving from a "birthday party script."

   c. failed to store memories that are specific to this party.

   d. has acquired a sophisticated theory of mind.

8. That a child produces sentences that follow such rules of word order as "the initiator of an action precedes the verb, the receiver of an action follows it" demonstrates a knowledge of

   a. grammar.

   b. semantics.

   c. pragmatics.

   d. phrase structure.

9. The two-year-old child who says, "We goed to the store," is making a grammatical

   a. overextension.

   b. overregularization.

   c. underextension.

   d. script.

10. An experimenter who makes two balls of clay of equal amount, then rolls one into a long, skinny rope and asks the child if the amounts are still the same, is testing the child's understanding of

    a. conservation.

    b. egocentrism.

    c. perspective.

    d. centration.

11. Dr. Jones, who believes that children's language growth greatly contributes to their cognitive growth, evidently is a proponent of the ideas of

    a. Piaget.

    b. Chomsky.

    c. Flavell.

    d. Vygotsky.

12. Jack constantly "talks down" to his three-year-old son's speech level. Jack's speech is

    a. appropriate because three-year-olds have barely begun to comprehend grammatical rules.

    b. commendable, given the importance of scaffolding in promoting cognitive growth.

    c. unnecessary because preschoolers are able to comprehend more complex grammar and vocabulary than they can produce.

    d. clearly within his son's zone of proximal development.

13. In describing the limited logical reasoning of preschoolers, a contemporary developmentalist is least likely to emphasize

    a. irreversibility.

    b. centration.

    c. egocentrism.

    d. private speech.

14. A preschooler fails to put together a difficult puzzle on her own, so her mother encourages her to try again, this time guiding her by asking questions such as, "For this space do we need a big piece or a little piece?" With Mom's help, the child successfully completes the puzzle. Lev Vygotsky would attribute the child's success to

    a. additional practice with the puzzle pieces.

    b. imitation of her mother's behavior.

    c. the social interaction with her mother that restructured the task to make its solution more attainable.

    d. modeling and reinforcement.

15. Mark is answering an essay question that asks him to "discuss the positions of major developmental theorists regarding the relationship between language and cognitive development." To help organize his answer, Mark jots down a reminder that _____ contended that language is essential to the advancement of thinking, as private speech, and as a _____ of social interactions.

    a. Piaget; mediator

    b. Vygotsky; mediator

    c. Piaget; theory

    d. Vygotsky; theory

Answer Key

Key Terms

1. According to Piaget, thinking between ages 2 and 6 is characterized by preoperational thought, meaning that children cannot yet perform logical operations; that is, they cannot use logical principles. (p. 264; video lesson, segment 2; objective 1)

    Memory aid: Operations are mental transformations involving the manipulation of ideas and symbols. Preoperational children, who lack the ability to perform transformations, are "before" this developmental milestone.

2. Centration is the tendency of young children to focus only on a single aspect of a situation or object. (p. 264; video lesson, segment 1; objective 1)

3. Egocentrism refers to the tendency of young children to view the world exclusively from their own perspective. (p. 264; video lesson, segment 1; objective 1)

4. Focus on appearance refers to the preoperational child's tendency to focus only on physical attributes and ignore all others. (p. 264; objective 1)

5. Preoperational thinking is characterized by static reasoning, by which is meant that the young child sees the world as unchanging. (p. 265; objective 1)

6. Irreversibility is the characteristic of preoperational thought in which young children fail to recognize that a process can be reversed to restore the original conditions of a situation. (p. 265; video lesson, segment 1; objective 1)

7. Conservation is the understanding that the amount or quantity of a substance or object is unaffected by changes in its shape or configuration. (p. 265; video lesson, segment 1; objective 1)

8. Theory-theory refers to the tendency of young children to attempt to construct theories to explain everything they experience. (p. 266; objective 8)

9. According to Vygotsky, a young child is an apprentice in thinking, whose intellectual growth is stimulated by more skilled members of society. (p. 267; video lesson, segment 1; objective 1)

10. According to Vygotsky, intellectual growth in young children is stimulated and directed by their guided participation in learning experiences. As guides, parents, teachers, and older children offer assistance with challenging tasks, model problem-solving approaches, provide explicit instructions as needed, and support the child's interest and motivation. (p. 267; video lesson, segment 1; objective 2)

11. According to Vygotsky, for each individual there is a zone of proximal development, which represents the skills that are within the potential of the learner but cannot be performed independently. (p. 268; video lesson, segment 1; objective 3)

12. Tutors who scaffold structure children's learning experiences by simplifying tasks, maintaining children's interest, and solving problems, anticipating mistakes, among other things. (p. 268; video lesson, segment 1; objective 3)

13. Private speech is the internal dialogue in which a person talks to himself or herself. Preschoolers' private speech, which often is uttered aloud, helps them think, review what they know, and decide what to do. (p. 268; objective 4)

14. In Vygotsky's theory, social mediation refers to the use of speech as a tool to bridge the gap in understanding or knowledge between a child and a tutor. (p. 269; objective 4)

15. Source memory, or the ability to remember who said or did something or the place where an event occurred, is particularly difficult for young children. (p. 272; objective 7)

16. Scripts are mental outlines of familiar, recurrent past experiences used to facilitate the storage and retrieval of memories. (p. 274; objective 7)

17. A theory of mind is an understanding of mental processes, that is, of one's own or another's emotions, perceptions, intentions, and thoughts. (p. 276; video lesson, segment 2; objective 8)

18. Many young children construct a make-believe person, animal, or other imaginary companion to talk to and play with. (p. 278; objective 8)

19. A sensitive period is a time when a certain type of development, such as language acquisition, occurs most rapidly. (p. 279; objectives 9 & 10)

20. A critical period is a time when a certain type of development must occur or it will never happen. (p. 279; objectives 9 & 10)

Lesson 12/The Play Years: Cognitive Development　　　　**193**

21. Fast mapping is the process by which children rapidly learn new words by quickly connecting them to words and categories that are already understood. (p. 280; video lesson, segment 2; objective 10)

22. Overregularization occurs when children apply rules of grammar when they should not. It is seen in English, for example, when children add "s" to form the plural even in irregular cases that form the plural in a different way. (p. 282; video lesson, segment 2; objective 9)

23. In the context of early-childhood education, high-risk children are those whose chances of poor achievement are much higher than average. (p. 289; objective 11)

Practice Questions I

Multiple-Choice Questions

1. c. is the correct answer. (p. 264; video lesson, segment 1; objective 1)

2. c. is the correct answer. In fact, preoperational children have excellent imaginations, as revealed by the creation of imaginary companions and other forms of symbolic play. (pp. 264–265, 278; objective 1)

3. e. is correct the answer. (p. 279; objectives 10 & 11)

4. b. is the correct answer. (p. 272; objective 7)

   a. is incorrect. Scripts tend to improve preschoolers' memory.

   c. & d. are incorrect. Although true, neither of these is the primary reason for preschoolers' poor memory.

5. d. is the correct answer. (pp. 281–282; objective 9)

   a. & c. are incorrect. Preschoolers generally have great difficulty understanding, and therefore using, metaphors and abstract nouns.

   b. is incorrect. Other than the grammatical errors of overregularization, the textbook does not indicate that preschoolers use a significant number of self-created words.

6. a. is the correct answer. (p. 282; video lesson, segment 2; objective 9)

   b. & d. are incorrect. These terms are not identified in the text and do not apply to the use of grammar.

   c. is incorrect. Practical usage, which also is not discussed in the textbook, refers to communication between one person and another in terms of the overall context in which language is used.

7. a. is the correct answer. (p. 268; objective 4)

   b. is incorrect. This expresses the views of Piaget.

   c. is incorrect. Because he believed that language facilitates thinking, Vygotsky obviously felt that language and other cognitive developments are intimately related.

   d. is incorrect. Vygotsky did not hold this view.

8. a. is the correct answer. (p. 268; objective 4)

9. a. is the correct answer. (pp. 265–266; video lesson, segment 1; objective 1)

   b., c., & d. are incorrect. Failure to conserve is the result of thinking that is centered on appearances. Egocentrism and irreversibility are also examples of centered thinking.

10. c. is the correct answer. (p. 289; objective 11)

    b. is incorrect. This is not discussed in the textbook. However, although there was a slight early IQ advantage in Head Start graduates, the difference disappeared by grade 3.

a. & d. are incorrect. There was no indication of greater behavioral problems or alienation in Head Start graduates.

11. b. is the correct answer. (p. 291; video lesson, segment 3; objective 11)

12. c. is the correct answer. (p. 283; video lesson, segment 2; objective 9)

13. d. is the correct answer. (p. 266; video lesson, segment 1; objective 5)

14. a. is the correct answer. (p. 280; video lesson, segment 2; objective 10)

True or False Items

15. F More recent research has found that children may understand conservation earlier than Piaget thought, given a more gamelike presentation. His theory has not been rejected overall, however. (pp. 265–266; video lesson, segment 1; objective 5)

16. T (pp. 265–266; video lesson, segment 1; objective 1)

17. F In fact, just the opposite is true. Children who have learning difficulties tend to be slower to develop private speech. (p. 269; objective 4)

18. T (p. 266; video lesson, segment 1; objective 5)

19. T (p. 271; objective 6)

20. F Piaget believed that language ability builds on the sensorimotor and conceptual accomplishments of infancy and toddlerhood. (p. 272; objective 1)

21. F Preschoolers have difficulty understanding abstract words; their vocabulary consists mainly of concrete nouns and verbs. (p. 281; video lesson, segment 2; objective 9)

22. F In adding "ed" to form a past tense, the child has indicated an understanding of the grammatical rule for making past tenses in English, even though the construction in these two cases is incorrect. (pp. 282–283; video lesson, segment 2; objective 9)

23. T (p. 291; video lesson, segment 3; objective 11)

24. T (p. 267; video lesson, segment 1; objective 2)

Practice Questions II

Multiple-Choice Questions

1. b. is the correct answer. (pp. 272–273; objective 7)

   a., c., & d. are incorrect. Although these *are* characteristics of preoperational thinking, they have nothing to do with a distorted memory of an actual event.

2. a. is the correct answer. (p. 266; objective 1)

   b. & c. are incorrect. Fast mapping and overregularization are characteristics of language development during the play years; they have nothing to do with reasoning about volume.

3. a. is the correct answer. (p. 264; video lesson, segment 1; objective 1)

   b. is incorrect. Overregularization is the child's tendency to apply grammatical rules even when he or she shouldn't.

   c. is incorrect. Reversibility is the concept that reversing an operation, such as addition, will restore the original conditions.

   d. is incorrect. This term is used to refer to the young child's belief that people think as he or she does.

4. c. is the correct answer. This is why the stage is called preoperational. (p. 264; video lesson, segment 1; objective 1)

5. a. is the correct answer. (p. 268; video lesson, segment 1; objective 3)

6. c. is the correct answer. (p. 269; objective 4)

a. & b. are incorrect. These are both advantages of private speech.

d. is incorrect. Fast mapping is the process by which new words are acquired, often after only one hearing.

7. d. is the correct answer. (p. 265; video lesson, segment 1; objective 1)

a. is incorrect. This describes egocentrism.

b. is incorrect. This is the opposite of centration.

c. is incorrect. This defines conservation of number.

8. a. is the correct answer. (pp. 265–266; objective 5)

b. is incorrect. According to Piaget, preschoolers fail to solve conservation problems because they focus on the appearance of objects and ignore the transformation that has occurred.

d. is incorrect. Piaget did not relate conservation to a theory of mind.

9. d. is the correct answer. (p. 268; video lesson, segment 1; objective 3)

10. b. is the correct answer. (p. 267; video lesson, segment 1; objective 2)

a. is incorrect. Piaget believed that learning is a matter of individual discovery.

11. d. is the correct answer. Preschoolers almost always put subject before verb in their two-word sentences. (p. 282; video lesson, segment 2; objective 9)

12. b. is the correct answer. (pp. 274–275; video lesson, segment 2; objective 7)

a. is incorrect. Preschoolers do tend to use mental scripts.

c. is incorrect. Although this type of thinking is somewhat characteristic of preschoolers, it has no impact on memory per se.

13. b. is the correct answer. (p. 279; objective 9)

14. a. is the correct answer. (pp. 282–283; video lesson, segment 2; objective 9)

b., c., & d. are incorrect. Overregularization is a linguistic phenomenon rather than a characteristic type of thinking (b & d), or a logical principle (c).

15. b. is the correct answer. (p. 290; objective 11)

Matching Items

16. b (p. 274; objective 7)

17. k (p. 268; video lesson, segment 1; objective 3)

18. f (p. 276; video lesson, segment 2; objective 8)

19. c (p. 268; video lesson, segment 1; objective 3)

20. h (p. 282; video lesson, segment 2; objective 9)

21. g (p. 280; video lesson, segment 2; objective 10)

22. j (p. 265; video lesson, segment 1; objective 1)

23. d (p. 264; video lesson, segment 1; objective 1)

24. a (p. 265; video lesson, segment 1; objective 1)

25. i (p. 268; objective 4)

26. e (p. 267; video lesson, segment 1; objective 2)

Applying Your Knowledge

1. c. is the correct answer. (pp. 265–266; video lesson, segment 1; objective 1)

a. is incorrect. A test of reversibility would ask a child to perform an operation, such as adding 4 to 3, and then reverse the process (subtract 3 from 7) to determine whether the child understood that the original condition (the number 4) was restored.

b. is incorrect. A test of conservation of matter would transform the appearance of an object, such as a ball of clay, to determine whether the child understood that the object remained the same.

d. is incorrect. A test of centration would involve the child's ability to see various aspects of a situation.

2. b. is the correct answer. (p. 264; video lesson, segment 1; objective 1)

a. is incorrect. Egocentrism is thinking that is self-centered.

c. is incorrect. This is not a concept in Piaget's theory.

d. is incorrect. Mental representation is an example of symbolic thought.

3. a. is the correct answer. (p. 265; objective 6)

4. c. is the correct answer. (p. 276; video lesson, segment 2; objective 8)

a. is incorrect. Egocentrism is self-centered thinking.

b. is incorrect. Although deception provides evidence of a theory of mind, the child in this example is not deceiving anyone.

d. is incorrect. Conservation is the understanding that the amount of a substance is unchanged by changes in its shape or placement.

5. d. is the correct answer. (pp. 285–286; objective 11)

a., b., & c. are incorrect. Chinese preschools place more emphasis on these attitudes and behaviors than do U.S. preschools.

6. c. is the correct answer. In Vygotsky's view, learning is a social activity more than a matter of individual discovery. Thus, social interaction that provides motivation and focuses attention facilitates learning. (p. 267; video lesson, segment 1; objective 2)

a., b., & d. are incorrect. These situations either provide no opportunity for social interaction (b & d) or do not challenge the children (a).

7. b. is the correct answer. (p. 274; objective 7)

a. is incorrect. Egocentrism is thinking that is self-focused.

c. is incorrect. Preschoolers do form memories of specific events; their retrieval, however, is often a composite of similar experiences.

d. is incorrect. This refers to preschoolers' emerging social understanding of others' perspectives.

8. a. is the correct answer. (p. 282; video lesson, segment 2; objective 9)

b. & d. are incorrect. The textbook does not discuss these aspects of language.

c. is incorrect. Pragmatics, which is not mentioned in the text, refers to the practical use of language in varying social contexts.

9. b. is the correct answer. (p. 282; video lesson, segment 2; objective 9)

10. a. is the correct answer. (pp. 265–266; video lesson, segment 1; objective 1)

11. d. is the correct answer. (pp. 268–269; objective 4)

a. is incorrect. Piaget believed that cognitive growth precedes language development.

b. & c. are incorrect. Chomsky focused on the acquisition of language, and Flavell emphasizes cognition.

12. c. is the correct answer. (p. 283; objective 9)

13. d. is the correct answer. (pp. 264–265; objective 5)

14. c. is the correct answer. (pp. 267–268; objective 3)

15. b. is the correct answer. (pp. 268–269; objective 4)

Lesson Review

Lesson 12

The Play Years
Cognitive Development

Please Note: Use this matrix to guide your study and achieve the learning objectives of this lesson. It will also help you to view the video, which defines and demonstrates important concepts and skills as they relate to everyday life.

Learning Objective	Textbook	Telecourse Student Guide	Video Lesson
1. Describe the major characteristics of preoperational thought, according to Piaget.	pp. 264–267	Key Terms: 1, 2, 3, 4, 5, 6, 7, 9; Practice Questions I: 1, 2, 9, 16, 20; Practice Questions II: 2, 3, 4, 7, 22, 23, 24; Applying Your Knowledge: 1, 2, 10.	Segment 1: *How Preschoolers Think*
2. Contrast Vygotsky's views on cognitive development with those of Piaget, focusing on the concept of guided participation.	pp. 267–268	Key Terms: 10; Practice Questions I: 24; Practice Questions II: 10, 26; Applying Your Knowledge: 6.	Segment 1: *How Preschoolers Think*
3. Explain the significance of the zone of proximal development and scaffolding in promoting cognitive growth.	p. 268	Key Terms: 11, 12; Practice Questions II: 5, 9, 17, 19; Applying Your Knowledge: 14.	Segment 1: *How Preschoolers Think*
4. Describe Vygotsky's view of the role of language in cognitive growth.	pp. 268–269	Key Terms: 13, 14; Practice Questions I: 17; Practice Questions II: 6, 25; Applying Your Knowledge: 11, 15.	
5. Discuss more recent research on conservation, and explain why findings have led to qualification or revision of Piaget's description of cognition during the play years.	pp. 264–266	Practice Questions I: 13, 15, 18; Practice Questions II: 8; Applying Your Knowledge: 13.	Segment 1: *How Preschoolers Think*

Learning Objective	Textbook	Telecourse Student Guide	Video Lesson
6. Discuss preschoolers' understanding of number concepts.	pp. 265–271	Practice Questions I: 19; Applying Your Knowledge: 3.	
7. Discuss young children's memory abilities and limitations, noting the role of personal meaning in their ability to recall events.	pp. 272–275	Key Terms: 15, 16; Practice Questions I: 4, 7, 8; Practice Questions II: 1, 12, 16; Applying Your Knowledge: 7.	Segment 2: *Words and Memories*
8. Explain the typical young child's theory of mind, noting how it is affected by culture and context, and relate it to the child's developing ability to understand pretense.	pp. 266, 276–278	Key Terms: 8, 17, 18; Practice Questions II: 18; Applying Your Knowledge: 4.	Segment 2: *Words and Memories*
9. Outline the sequence by which vocabulary and grammar develop during the play years, and discuss limitations in the young child's language abilities.	pp. 279–283	Key Terms: 19, 20, 22; Practice Questions I: 5, 6, 12, 21, 22; Practice Questions II: 11, 13, 14, 20; Applying Your Knowledge: 8, 9, 12.	Segment 2: *Words and Memories*
10. Explain the role of fast mapping in children's acquisition of language.	pp. 279–280	Key Terms: 19, 20, 21; Practice Questions I: 3, 14; Practice Questions II: 21.	Segment 2: *Words and Memories*
11. Identify the characteristics of a high-quality preschool program, and discuss the long-term benefits of preschool education for the child and his or her family.	pp. 285–286, 289–291	Key Terms: 23; Practice Questions I: 3, 10, 11, 23; Practice Questions II: 15; Applying Your Knowledge: 5.	Segment 3: *Early Childhood Education*

Playing and Socializing

Lesson 13

The Play Years:
Psychosocial Development

Preview

Lesson 13 explores the ways in which young children begin to relate to others in an ever-widening social environment. The lesson begins with emotional development and the continuing emergence of the sense of self. With their increasing social awareness, children become more concerned with how others evaluate them and better able to regulate their emotions.

Next, the lesson explores the origins of helpful, cooperative behaviors in young children, as well as aggression and other hurtful behaviors. These social skills reflect many influences, including the quality of early attachments and learning from playmates through various types of play, as well as from television.

The lesson also describes the increasing complexity of children's interactions with others, paying special attention to the different styles of parenting and how factors such as the cultural, ethnic, and community contexts influence parenting.

The lesson concludes with a description of children's emerging awareness of male-female differences and gender identity. Five major theories of gender-role development are considered.

As you complete this lesson, consider the psychosocial development of one or more preschoolers you know. Consider their self-understanding—what do they think and feel about themselves? How do they interact with adults and other children? What sort of play activities do they engage in, and how might this affect their development? How good are they at controlling their own emotions and behavior? Finally, consider the relationship these children have with their parents. How do the parents support and guide their kids, and how to they handle discipline and punishment?

Prior Telecourse Knowledge that Will Be Used in this Lesson

*   This lesson will return to Erik Erikson's theory (introduced in Lesson 1) that specifies eight stages of psychosocial development, each of which is characterized by a particular challenge, or developmental crisis, which is central to that stage of life and must be resolved:

    1. Trust vs. Mistrust (birth to 1 year)
    2. Autonomy vs. Shame and Doubt (1 to 3 years)
    3. **Initiative vs. Guilt (3 to 6 years)** ← **The Play Years**
    4. Industry vs. Inferiority (7 to 11 years)
    5. Identity vs. Role Confusion (adolescence)

6. Intimacy vs. Isolation (adulthood)

7. Generativity vs. Stagnation (adulthood)

8. Integrity vs. Despair (adulthood)

- This lesson will use the concept of theory of mind in its discussion of social awareness and the role of play during this period of development. Recall that theory of mind refers to a person's understanding of human mental processes, including the thoughts, feelings, and motivations of others.

- Five major developmental theories (from Lesson 1) will be used to help explain gender-role development during the play years. Recall that:

  1. Freud's theory specifies stages of psychosexual development, during which the child battles unconscious, biological impulses.

  2. Learning theory emphasizes the effect of conditioning, as the child responds to stimuli, reinforcement and modeling in his or her immediate environment.

  4. Cognitive theory emphasizes how the child's intellectual processes and thinking affect his or her beliefs and actions.

  5. Sociocultural theory reminds us that development is embedded in a rich cultural context, and is often influenced by the guidance of parents and mentors.

  6. Epigenetic systems theory emphasizes the interaction of biological and environmental forces that affect each person.

Learning Objectives

Use this information to guide your reading, viewing, thinking, and studying. After successfully completing this lesson, you should be able to:

1. Discuss emotional development during early childhood, focusing on emotional regulation.

2. Discuss the importance of positive self-evaluation during this period, noting the child's developing self-concept and self-esteem.

3. Describe prosocial and antisocial behaviors, offer examples of each, and discuss the preschooler's developing sense of empathy.

4. Describe the different forms of aggression demonstrated by young children, and discuss the role of television and video games in encouraging these and other antisocial behaviors.

5. Discuss the role of play in the development of social skills, focusing on the benefits of rough-and-tumble and sociodramatic play.

6. Compare the three classic styles of parenting, and discuss the factors that might account for variations in parenting style.

7. Discuss the pros and cons of physical punishment, and describe the most effective methods for disciplining a child.

8. Distinguish between sex differences and gender differences, and describe the developmental progression of gender awareness in young children.

9. Summarize five theories of gender-role development during the play years, noting important contributions of each.

   📖 **Read Chapter 10, "The Play Years: Psychosocial Development," pages 295–324.**

View the video for Lesson 13, "Playing and Socializing."

Segment 1: *Social Awareness*

Segment 2: *Emotional Regulation*

Segment 3: *Parenting Styles*

Summary

During the preschool years a child's self-confidence, social skills, and social roles become more fully developed. This growth coincides with the child's increased capacity for communication, imagination, and understanding of his or her social context. Much of this development occurs through play activities.

Play provides crucial experiences not only for motor and cognitive development but also for self-understanding and social interaction. Apparent in important types of play include **rough-and-tumble play**, in which children mimic aggression but actually have no intent to harm, and **sociodramatic play**, in which children act out various roles and themes in stories of their own creation. This exploration through play enables children to test their ability to convince others of their ideas and examine personal concerns in a nonthreatening manner.

In Erik Erikson's theory, the crisis of the play years is **initiative versus guilt**. The child is turning away from an exclusive attachment to parents and moving toward membership in the larger culture. A key factor in this developmental progression is learning **emotional regulation**—key aspect of the child's developing **emotional intelligence**. Because of brain maturation, children gain a much greater ability to direct or modify their feelings, particularly feelings of fear, frustration, and anger.

Some of the emotions that mature during the preschool years lead to **prosocial behaviors** such as sharing and cooperating, which are performed to benefit other people; for some children, however, **antisocial behaviors** such as hitting or insulting may also emerge. Antisocial behaviors are those that are intended to hurt someone else. Developmental psychologists differentiate among three types of aggression: **instrumental aggression**, **reactive aggression**, **relational aggression**, and **bullying aggression**.

The three classic styles of parenting include **authoritarian** parents, whose word is law and who often show little affection or nurturance; **permissive** parents, who make few demands on their children; and **authoritative** parents, who set limits and enforce rules but do so more democratically by listening to their children's ideas and being willing to make compromises. Among the reasons for parenting variations are culture, religion, ethnicity, and the family's economic well-being. Family size also affects parenting patterns, with large families easier to manage via authoritarian parenting.

Even at age 2, children know whether they are boys or girls and apply gender labels consistently. Each of the major developmental theories has a somewhat different explanation for gender differences. Psychoanalytic theorists focus on fears and fantasies that motivate children to initially adore their opposite-sex parent and then later identify with their same-sex parent. Learning theorists maintain that gender roles are instilled because parents and society provide models and reinforcement for appropriate gender-role behavior and punishment for inappropriate behavior. In explaining gender identify and gender-role development, cognitive theorists focus on children's growing understanding of male-female differences. For example, gender-schema theory argues that children develop gender schemas that help organize their knowledge about gender and direct their behavior. Sociocultural theorists emphasize the influence of cultural differences, and epigenetic systems theorists point out the biological tendencies that influence the child's brain patterns and behavior.

Special Note: We will cover the effects of television and video games (pp. 307–309) in more detail in telecourse Lesson 15, "Hazards Along the Way."

📖 **Review all reading assignments for this lesson.**

💻 **As assigned by your instructor, complete the optional online component for this lesson.**

Key Terms

Using your own words, write a brief definition or explanation of each of the following terms on a separate piece of paper.

1.	emotional regulation	18.	rough-and-tumble play
2.	externalizing problems	19.	sociodramatic play
3.	internalizing problems	20.	authoritarian parenting
4.	phobia	21.	permissive parenting
5.	self-concept	22.	authoritative parenting
6.	self-esteem	23.	neglectful parenting
7.	initiative versus guilt	24.	indulgent parenting
8.	emotional intelligence	25.	time-out
9.	peers	26.	sex differences
10.	prosocial	27.	gender differences
11.	antisocial	28.	phallic stage
12.	empathy	29.	Oedipus complex
13.	aggression	30.	identification
14.	instrumental aggression	31.	superego
15.	reactive aggression	32.	Electra complex
16.	relational aggression	33.	androgyny
17.	bullying aggression		

Practice Questions I

Multiple-Choice Questions

1. Preschool children have a clear (but not necessarily accurate) concept of self. Typically, the preschooler believes that she or he

   a. owns all objects in sight.

   b. is great at almost everything.

   c. is much less competent than peers and older children.

   d. is more powerful than her or his parents.

2. According to Freud, the third stage of psychosexual development, during which the penis is the focus of psychological concern and pleasure, is the

   a. oral stage.
   b. anal stage.
   c. phallic stage.
   d. latency period.

3. Because it helps children rehearse social roles, work out fears and fantasies, and learn cooperation, an important form of social play is

   a. sociodramatic play.
   b. mastery play.
   c. rough-and-tumble play.
   d. sensorimotor play.

4. The three basic patterns of parenting described by Diana Baumrind are

   a. hostile, loving, and harsh.
   b. authoritarian, permissive, and authoritative.
   c. positive, negative, and punishing.
   d. indulgent, neglecting, and traditional.

5. Authoritative parents are receptive and loving, but they also normally

   a. set limits and enforce rules.
   b. have difficulty communicating.
   c. withhold praise and affection.
   d. encourage aggressive behavior.

6. Children who watch a lot of violent television

   a. are more likely to be aggressive.
   b. become desensitized to violence.
   c. are less likely to attempt to mediate a quarrel between other children.
   d. have all of the above characteristics.

7. During the play years, a child's self-concept is defined largely by his or her

   a. expanding range of skills and competencies.
   b. physical appearance.
   c. gender.
   d. relationship with family members.

8. Learning theorists emphasize the importance of _____ in the development of the preschool child.

   a. identification
   b. praise and blame
   c. initiative
   d. a theory of mind

9. Children apply gender labels, and have definite ideas about how boys and girls behave, as early as age

   a. 3.

   b. 4.

   c. 5.

   d. 7.

10. In chaotic and dangerous environments, _____ parenting may be most beneficial to children.

    a. authoritative

    b. authoritarian

    c. traditional

    d. permissive

11. Six-year-old Elijah has superior verbal ability rivaling that of most girls his age. Dr. Laurent believes that although his sex is predisposed to slower language development, Elijah's upbringing in a linguistically rich home enhanced his biological capabilities. Dr. Laurent is evidently a proponent of

    a. cognitive theory.

    b. gender-schema theory.

    c. sociocultural theory.

    d. epigenetic systems theory.

12. Three-year-old Jake, who lashes out at the family pet in anger, is displaying signs of _____ problems and that he is emotionally _____.

    a. internalizing; overcontrolled

    b. internalizing; undercontrolled

    c. externalizing; overcontrolled

    d. externalizing; undercontrolled

13. When her friend hurts her feelings, Lauren shouts that she is a "mean old stinker!" Lauren's behavior is an example of

    a. instrumental aggression.

    b. reactive aggression.

    c. bullying aggression.

    d. relational aggression.

True or False Items

Write T (for true) or F (for false) on the line in front of each statement.

14. _____ According to Diana Baumrind, only authoritarian parents make maturity demands on their children.

15. _____ Children of authoritative parents tend to be successful, happy with themselves, and generous with others.

16. _____ True sex differences are more apparent in childhood than in adulthood.

17. _____ Spanking is associated with higher rates of aggression toward peers.

18. _____ Many gender differences are genetically based.

19. _____ Children from feminist or nontraditional homes seldom have stereotypic ideas about feminine and masculine roles.

20. _____ Developmentalists do not agree about how children acquire gender roles.

21. _____ Identification was defined by Freud as a defense mechanism in which people identify with others who may be stronger and more powerful than they.

Practice Questions II

Multiple-Choice Questions

1. Children of permissive parents are most likely to lack
   a. social skills.
   b. self-control.
   c. initiative and guilt.
   d. care and concern.

2. Children learn reciprocity, nurturance, and cooperation most readily from their interaction with
   a. their mothers.
   b. their fathers.
   c. friends.
   d. others of the same sex.

3. The initial advantages of parenting style
   a. do not persist past middle childhood.
   b. remain apparent through adolescence.
   c. are likely to be even stronger over time.
   d. have an unpredictable impact later in children's lives.

4. Which of the following best summarizes the current view of developmentalists regarding gender differences?
   a. Some gender differences are biological in origin.
   b. Most gender differences are biological in origin.
   c. Nearly all gender differences are cultural in origin.
   d. There is no consensus among developmentalists regarding the origin of gender differences.

5. According to Freud, a young boy's jealousy of his father's relationship with his mother, and the guilt feelings that result, are part of the
   a. Electra complex.
   b. Oedipus complex.
   c. phallic complex.
   d. penis envy complex.

6. The style of parenting in which the parents make few demands on children, the discipline is lax, and the parents are nurturant and accepting is
   a. authoritarian.
   b. authoritative.
   c. permissive.
   d. rejecting-neglecting.

7. Cooperating with a playmate is to _____ as insulting a playmate is to _____.
   a. antisocial behavior; prosocial behavior
   b. prosocial behavior; antisocial behavior
   c. emotional regulation; antisocial behavior
   d. prosocial behavior; emotional regulation

8. Which of the following children would probably be said to have a phobia?
   a. Noriko, who has an exaggerated and irrational fear of furry animals
   b. Nicky, who is frightened by loud thunder
   c. Nairobi, who doesn't like getting shots
   d. All of the above have phobias.

9. Which of the following theories advocates the development of gender identification as a means of avoiding guilt over feelings for the opposite-sex parent?
   a. learning
   b. sociocultural
   c. psychoanalytic
   d. social learning

10. A parent who wishes to use a time-out to discipline her son for behaving aggressively on the playground would be advised to
    a. have the child sit quietly indoors for a few minutes.
    b. tell her son that he will be punished later at home.
    c. tell the child that he will not be allowed to play outdoors for the rest of the week.
    d. choose a different disciplinary technique since time-outs are ineffective.

11. The preschooler's readiness to learn new tasks and play activities reflects his or her
    a. emerging competency and self-awareness.
    b. theory of mind.
    c. relationship with parents.
    d. growing identification with others.

12. Emotional regulation is in part related to maturation of a specific portion of the brain in the
    a. frontal cortex.
    b. parietal cortex.
    c. temporal lobe.
    d. occipital lobe.

13. In which style of parenting is the parents' word law and misbehavior strictly punished?

    a. permissive

    b. authoritative

    c. authoritarian

    d. traditional

14. Erikson noted that preschoolers eagerly begin many new activities but are vulnerable to criticism and feelings of failure; in other words, they experience the crisis of

    a. identity versus role confusion.

    b. initiative versus guilt.

    c. basic trust versus mistrust.

    d. efficacy versus helplessness.

Matching Items

Match each theorist, term, or concept with its corresponding description or definition.

Theorists, Terms, and Concepts

15. _____ rough-and-tumble play

16. _____ androgyny

17. _____ sociodramatic play

18. _____ prosocial behavior

19. _____ antisocial behavior

20. _____ Electra complex

21. _____ Oedipus complex

22. _____ authoritative

23. _____ authoritarian

24. _____ identification

25. _____ instrumental aggression

Descriptions or Definitions

    a. aggressive behavior whose purpose is to obtain an object desired by another

    b. Freudian theory that every daughter secretly wishes to replace her mother

    c. parenting style associated with high maturity demands and low parent-child communication

    d. an action performed for the benefit of another person without the expectation of reward

    e. Freudian theory that every son secretly wishes to replace his father

    f. parenting style associated with high maturity demands and high parent-child communication

    g. two children wrestle without serious hostility

    h. an action that is intended to harm someone else

    i. two children act out roles in a story of their own creation

    j. a defense mechanism through which children cope with their feelings of guilt during the phallic stage

    k. a balance of traditional male and female characteristics in an individual

Applying Your Knowledge

1. According to Freud, Jana eventually copes with the fear and anger she feels over her hatred of her mother and love of her father by
   a. identifying with her mother.
   b. copying her brother's behavior.
   c. adopting her father's moral code.
   d. competing with her brother for her father's attention.

2. A little girl who says she wants her mother to go on vacation so that she can marry her father is voicing a fantasy consistent with the _____ described by Freud.
   a. Oedipus complex
   b. Electra complex
   c. theory of mind
   d. crisis of initiative versus guilt

3. According to Erikson, *before* the preschool years children are incapable of feeling guilt because
   a. guilt depends on a sense of self, which is not sufficiently established in toddlerhood.
   b. they do not yet understand that they are male or female for life.
   c. this emotion is unlikely to have been reinforced at such an early age.
   d. guilt is associated with the resolution of the Oedipus complex, which occurs later in life.

4. Parents who are strict and aloof are most likely to make their children
   a. cooperative and trusting.
   b. obedient but unhappy.
   c. violent.
   d. withdrawn and anxious.

5. When four-year-old Bonita grabs for Aldo's beanie baby, Aldo slaps her hand away, displaying an example of
   a. bullying aggression.
   b. reactive aggression.
   c. instrumental aggression.
   d. relational aggression.

6. The belief that almost all sexual patterns are learned rather than inborn would find its strongest adherents among _____ theorists.
   a. cognitive
   b. learning
   c. psychoanalytic
   d. epigenetic systems

7. In explaining the origins of gender distinctions, Dr. Christie notes that every society teaches its children its values and attitudes regarding preferred behavior for men and women. Dr. Christie is evidently a proponent of

   a. gender-schema theory.
   b. sociocultural theory.
   c. epigenetic systems theory.
   d. psychoanalytic theory.

8. Five-year-old Keshawn has a better-developed sense of self and is more confident than Mark. According to the textbook, it is likely that Keshawn will also be more skilled at

   a. tasks involving verbal reasoning.
   b. social interaction.
   c. deception.
   d. all of the above.

9. Summarizing her report on neurological aspects of emotional regulation, Seema notes that young children who have internalizing problems tend to have greater activity in the

   a. right temporal lobe.
   b. left temporal lobe.
   c. right prefrontal cortex.
   d. left prefrontal cortex.

10. Concerning children's concept of gender, which of the following statements is true?

    a. Before the age of 3 or so, children think that boys and girls can change gender as they get older.
    b. Children as young as age 1 have a clear understanding of the physical differences between girls and boys and can consistently apply gender labels.
    c. Not until age 5 or 6 do children show a clear preference for gender-typed toys.
    d. All of the above are true.

11. Which of the following is **NOT** one of the features of parenting used by Diana Baumrind to differentiate authoritarian, permissive, and authoritative parents?

    a. maturity demands for the child's conduct
    b. efforts to control the child's actions
    c. nurturance
    d. adherence to stereotypic gender roles

12. Which of the following is true regarding the effects of spanking?

    a. Spanking seems to reduce reactive aggression.
    b. When administered appropriately, spanking promotes psychosocial development.
    c. Spanking is associated with increased aggression toward peers.
    d. None of the above is true.

13. Rodney and Jack are wrestling and hitting each other without intent to hurt. Although this rough-and-tumble play mimics negative, aggressive behavior, it serves a useful purpose, which is to

    a. rehearse social roles.

    b. develop interactive skills.

    c. improve fine motor skills.

    d. do both b and c.

Answer Key

Key Terms

1. Emotional regulation is the ability to manage and modify one's feelings, particularly feelings of fear, frustration, and anger. (p. 296; video lesson, segment 2; objective 1).

2. Young children who have externalizing problems tend to experience emotions outside themselves and lash out at other people or things. (p. 296; objective 1)

3. Children who have internalizing problems tend to be fearful and withdrawn as a consequence of their tendencies to keep their emotions bottled up inside themselves. (p. 296; objective 1)

4. A phobia is an exaggerated and irrational fear of an object or experience. (p. 298; objective 1)

5. Self-concept refers to what a child *thinks* about him- or herself; it is the child's answer to the question, "who am I?" (p. 299; video lesson, segment 2; objective 2)

6. Self-esteem refers to how a child *feels* about himself or herself; it has to do with how lovable the child feels. (p. 299; video lesson, segment 2; objective 2)

7. According to Erikson, the crisis of the preschool years is initiative versus guilt. In this crisis, young children eagerly take on new tasks and play activities and feel guilty when their efforts result in failure or criticism. (p. 301; objective 1)

8. Emotional intelligence refers to a person's understanding of how to interpret and express emotions. (p. 301; objective 1)

9. Peers are people of about the same age and status as oneself. (p. 302; objective 3)

10. Prosocial describes an action or behavior, such as cooperating or sharing, which is performed to benefit another person without the expectation of reward. (p. 302; video lesson, segment 2; objective 3)

11. Antisocial describes an action or action, such as hitting or insulting, which is intended to hurt another person. (p. 302; video lesson, segment 2; objective 3)

12. Empathy is a person's ability to understand the emotions of another person. (p. 303; objective 3)

13. Aggression is a form of antisocial behavior characterized by hostile attitudes and hurtful actions stemming from anger or frustration. (p. 303; objective 4)

14. Instrumental aggression is an action whose purpose is to obtain or retain an object desired by another. (p. 304; objective 4)

15. Reactive aggression is aggressive behavior that is an angry retaliation for some intentional or incidental act by another person. (p. 304; objective 4)

    Memory aid: Instrumental aggression is behavior that is instrumental in allowing a child to retain a favorite toy. Reactive aggression is a reaction to another child's behavior.

16. Aggressive behavior that takes the form of verbal insults or social rejection is called relational aggression. (p. 304; objective 4)

17. An unprovoked attack on another child is an example of bullying aggression. (p. 304; objective 4)

18. Rough-and-tumble play is physical play that often mimics aggression, but involves no intent to harm. (p. 305; video lesson, segment 1; objective 5)

19. In sociodramatic play, children act out roles and themes in stories of their own creation, allowing them to examine personal concerns in a nonthreatening manner. (p. 306; video lesson, segment 1; objective 5)

20. Authoritarian parenting is a style of child rearing in which the parents show little affection or nurturance for their children; maturity demands are high and parent-child communication is low. (p. 310; video lesson, segment 3; objective 6)

    Memory aid: Someone who is an authoritarian demands unquestioning obedience and acts in a dictatorial way.

21. Permissive parenting is a style of parenting in which the parents make few demands on their children, yet are nurturant and accepting, and communicate well with their children. (p. 310; video lesson, segment 3; objective 6)

22. Authoritative parenting is a style of parenting in which the parents set limits and enforce rules but do so more democratically than do authoritarian parents. (p. 310; video lesson, segment 3; objective 6)

    Memory aid: Authoritative parents act as authorities do on a subject—by discussing and explaining why certain family rules are in place.

23. Neglectful parenting is an abusive style of parenting in which the parents do not seem to care about their child at all. (p. 311; objective 6)

24. Indulgent parenting is an abusive style of parenting in which parents give in to their child's every whim. (p. 311; objective 6)

25. A time-out is a form of discipline in which a child is required to stop all activity and sit quietly for a few minutes. (p. 313; objective 7)

26. Sex differences are biological differences between females and males. (p. 315; objective 8)

27. Gender differences are cultural differences in the roles and behavior of males and females. (p. 315; objective 8)

28. In psychoanalytic theory, the phallic stage is the third stage of psychosexual development, in which the penis becomes the focus of psychological concerns and physiological pleasure. (p. 317; objective 9)

29. According to Freud, boys in the phallic stage of psychosexual development develop a collection of feelings, known as the Oedipus complex, that center on sexual attraction to the mother and resentment of the father. (p. 317; objective 9)

30. In Freud's theory, identification is the defense mechanism through which a person takes on the role and attitudes of a person more powerful than himself or herself. (p. 317; objective 9)

31. In psychoanalytic theory, the superego is the self-critical and judgmental part of personality that internalizes the moral standards set by parents and society. (p. 317; objective 9)

32. According to Freud, girls in the phallic stage may develop a collection of feelings, known as the Electra complex, that center on sexual attraction to the father and resentment of the mother. (p. 318; objective 9)

33. Androgyny is a balance of traditionally female and male gender characteristics in a person. (p. 321; objective 9)

Practice Questions I

Multiple-Choice Questions

1. b. is the correct answer. (pp. 299–300; video lesson, segment 2; objective 2)

2. c. is the correct answer. (p. 317; objective 9)

   a. & b. are incorrect. In Freud's theory, the oral and anal stages are associated with infant and early childhood development, respectively.

   d. is incorrect. In Freud's theory, the latency period is associated with development during the school years.

3. a. is the correct answer. (p. 306; video lesson, segment 1; objective 5)

   b. is incorrect. Mastery play is play that helps children develop new physical and intellectual skills.

   c. is incorrect. Rough-and-tumble play is physical play that mimics aggression.

   d. is incorrect. Sensorimotor play captures the pleasures of using the senses and motor skills.

4. b. is the correct answer. (p. 310; video lesson, segment 3; objective 6)

   d. is incorrect. Traditional is a variation of the basic styles uncovered by later research. Indulgent and neglecting are not discussed in the textbook.

5. a. is the correct answer. (p. 310; video lesson, segment 3; objective 6)

   b. & c. are incorrect. Authoritative parents communicate very well and are quite affectionate.

   d. is incorrect. This is not typical of authoritative parents.

6. d. is the correct answer. (pp. 308–309; objective 4)

7. a. is the correct answer. (pp. 299–300; objective 2)

8. b. is the correct answer. (p. 319; objective 9)

   a. is incorrect. This is the focus of Freud's phallic stage.

   c. is incorrect. This is the focus of Erikson's psychosocial theory.

   d. is incorrect. This is the focus of cognitive theorists.

9. a. is the correct answer. (p. 316; objective 8)

10. b. is the correct answer. (p. 311; objective 6)

11. d. is the correct answer. In accounting for Elijah's verbal ability, Dr. Laurent alludes to both genetic and environmental factors, a dead-giveaway for epigenetic systems theory. (p. 321; objective 9)

    a., b., & c. are incorrect. These theories do not address biological or genetic influences on development.

12. d. is the correct answer. (p. 296; objective 1)

13. d. is the correct answer. (p. 304; objective 4)

    a., b., & c. are incorrect. Each of these is an example of physical rather than verbal aggression.

True or False Items

14. F   All parents make some maturity demands on their children; maturity demands are high in both the authoritarian and authoritative parenting styles. (p. 310; video lesson, segment 3; objective 6)

15. T   (p. 311; video lesson, segment 3; objective 6)

16. F   Just the opposite is true. (p. 315; objective 8)

17. T   (pp. 313–315; objective 7)

18. T   (p. 321; objectives 8 & 9)

19. F   Children raised in feminist or nontraditional homes often surprise their parents by expressing stereotypic ideas about feminine and masculine roles. (p. 321; objective 9)

20. T   (pp. 317–321; objective 9)

21. T   (p. 317; objective 9)

Practice Questions II

Multiple-Choice Questions

1. b. is the correct answer. (p. 311; objective 6)

2. c. is the correct answer. (p. 307; video lesson, segment 1; objective 5)

   a. & b. are incorrect. Friends often provide better instruction than adults because they are likely to guide, challenge, and encourage a child's social interactions more frequently and intimately.

   d. is incorrect. The textbook does not indicate that same-sex friends are more important in learning these than friends of the other sex.

3. c. is the correct answer. (p. 311; objective 6)

4. a. is the correct answer. Recent research has found that the sexes are different in part because of subtle differences in brain development. (p. 322; objective 9)

5. b. is the correct answer. (p. 317; objective 9)

   a. & d. are incorrect. These are Freud's versions of phallic-stage development in little girls.

   c. is incorrect. There is no such thing as the "phallic complex."

6. c. is the correct answer. (p. 310; video lesson, segment 3; objective 6)

   a. & b. are incorrect. Both authoritarian and authoritative parents make high demands on their children.

   d. is incorrect. Rejecting-neglecting parents are quite cold and unengaged.

7. b. is the correct answer. (p. 302; video lesson, segment 2; objective 3)

8. a. is the correct answer. Exaggeration and irrationality are two hallmarks of phobias. (pp. 298–299; objective 1)

   b. & c. are incorrect. Neither of these fears seems exaggerated or irrational.

9. c. is the correct answer. (p. 317; objective 9)

   a. & d. are incorrect. Learning and social learning theories emphasize that children learn about gender by rewards and punishments and by observing others.

   b. is incorrect. Sociocultural theory focuses on the impact of the environment on gender identification.

10. a. is the correct answer. (p. 313; objective 7)

   b. & c. are incorrect. Time-outs involve removing a child from a situation in which misbehavior has occurred. Moreover, these threats of future punishment would likely be less effective because of the delay between the behavior and the consequence.

   d. is incorrect. Although developments stress the need to prevent misdeeds instead of punishing them, and warn that time-outs may have unintended consequences, they nevertheless can be an effective form of discipline.

11. a. is the correct answer. (pp. 299–300; video lesson, segment 1; objective 2)

    b. is incorrect. This viewpoint is associated only with cognitive theory.

    c. is incorrect. Although parent-child relationships are important to social development, they do not determine readiness.

    d. is incorrect. Identification is a Freudian defense mechanism.

12. a. is the correct answer. (p. 296; objective 1)

13. c. is the correct answer. (p. 310; video lesson, segment 3; objective 6)

14. b. is the correct answer. (p. 301; objective 1)

    a. & c. are incorrect. According to Erikson, these are the crises of adolescence and infancy, respectively.

    d. is incorrect. This is not a crisis described by Erikson.

Matching Items

15. g (p. 305; video lesson, segment 1; objective 5)

16. k (p. 321; objective 9)

17. i (p. 306; video lesson, segment 1; objective 5)

18. d (p. 302; video lesson, segment 2; objective 3)

19. h (p. 302; video lesson, segment 2; objective 3)

20. b (p. 318; objective 9)

21. e (p. 317; objective 9)

22. f (p. 310; video lesson, segment 3; objective 6)

23. c (p. 310; video lesson, segment 3; objective 6)

24. j (p. 317; objective 9)

25. a (p. 304; objective 4)

Applying Your Knowledge

1. a. is the correct answer. (pp. 317–318; objective 9)

2. b. is the correct answer. (p. 318; objective 9)

    a. is incorrect. According to Freud, the Oedipus complex refers to the male's sexual feelings toward his mother and resentment toward his father.

    c. & d. are incorrect. These are concepts introduced by cognitive theorists and Erik Erikson, respectively.

3. a. is the correct answer. (p. 301; objective 1)

    b. is incorrect. Erikson did not equate gender constancy with the emergence of guilt.

    c. & d. are incorrect. These reflect the viewpoints of learning theory and Freud, respectively.

4. b. is the correct answer. (p. 311; objective 6)

5. c. is the correct answer. The purpose of Aldo's action is clearly to retain the beanie baby, rather than to retaliate (b, which is incorrect), or bully Bonita (a, which is incorrect). (p. 304; objective 4)

    d. is incorrect. Relational aggression takes the form of a verbal insult.

6. b. is the correct answer. (p. 319; objective 9)

7. b. is the correct answer. (pp. 320–321; objective 9)

8. b. is the correct answer. (p. 299; objective 2)

   a. & c. are incorrect. The textbook does not link self-understanding with verbal reasoning or deception.

9. c. is the correct answer. (pp. 296–297; objective 1)

   a. & b. are incorrect. The temporal lobes are involved in speech and hearing, rather than emotional regulation.

   d. is incorrect. Children who have externalizing problems tend to have greater activity in this area.

10. a. is the correct answer. (p. 316; objective 8)

    b. is incorrect. Not until about age 3 can children consistently apply gender labels.

    c. is incorrect. By age 2, children prefer gender-typed toys.

11. d. is the correct answer. (p. 310; video lesson, segment 3; objective 6)

12. c. is the correct answer. (p. 314; objective 7)

13. b. is the correct answer. (pp. 305–306; objective 5)

Lesson Review

Lesson 13

The Play Years
Psychosocial Development

Please Note: Use this matrix to guide your study and achieve the learning objectives of this lesson. It will also help you to view the video, which defines and demonstrates important concepts and skills as they relate to everyday life.

Learning Objective	Textbook	Telecourse Student Guide	Video Lesson
1. Discuss emotional development during early childhood, focusing on emotional regulation.	pp. 296–301	Key Terms: 1, 2, 3, 4, 7, 8, 9; Practice Questions II: 8, 12; Applying Your Knowledge: 9.	Segment 2: *Emotional Regulation*
2. Discuss the importance of positive self-evaluation during this period, noting the child's developing self-concept and self-esteem.	pp. 299–301	Key Terms: 5, 6; Practice Questions I: 1, 7; Practice Questions II: 11, 14; Applying Your Knowledge: 3, 8.	Segment 2: *Emotional Regulation*
3. Describe prosocial and antisocial behaviors, offer examples of each, and discuss the preschooler's developing sense of empathy.	pp. 302–307	Key Terms: 10, 12; Practice Questions II: 7, 19; Applying Your Knowledge: 15.	Segment 1: *Social Awareness;* Segment 2: *Emotional Regulation*
4. Describe the different forms of aggression demonstrated by young children, and discuss the role of television and video games in encouraging these and other antisocial behaviors.	pp. 302–309	Key Terms: 11, 13, 14, 15, 16, 17; Practice Questions I: 6, 13; Practice Questions II: 25; Applying Your Knowledge: 5.	Segment 2: *Emotional Regulation*
5. Discuss the role of play in the development of social skills, focusing on the benefits of rough-and-tumble and sociodramatic play.	pp. 302–307	Key Terms: 18, 19; Practice Questions I: 3; Practice Questions II: 2, 15, 17, 18; Applying Your Knowledge: 13.	Segment 1: *Social Awareness*

Learning Objective	Textbook	Telecourse Student Guide	Video Lesson
6. Compare the three classic styles of parenting, and discuss the factors that might account variations in parenting style.	pp. 310–311, 320–324	Key Terms: 20, 21, 22, 23, 24; Practice Questions I: 4, 5, 10, 12, 14, 15; Practice Questions II: 1, 3, 6, 13, 22, 23; Applying Your Knowledge: 4, 11	Segment 3: *Parenting Styles*
7. Discuss the pros and cons of physical punishment, and describe the most effective methods for disciplining a child.	pp. 313–314, 321	Key Terms: 25; Practice Questions I: 17; Practice Questions II: 10; Applying Your Knowledge: 12.	
8. Distinguish between sex differences and gender differences, and describe the developmental progression of gender awareness in young children.	pp. 311–316, 321	Key Terms: 26, 27; Practice Questions I: 9, 16, 18, 19; Applying Your Knowledge: 10.	
9. Summarize five theories of gender-role development during the play years, noting important contributions of each.	pp. 317–322	Key Terms: 28, 29, 30, 31, 32, 33; Practice Questions I: 2, 9, 12, 20, 22, 23; Practice Questions II: 4, 5, 6, 10, 17, 21, 22, 25; Applying Your Knowledge: 1, 2, 6, 7.	

Developing Through Play

Lesson 14
The Play Years:
Summary

Preview

Lesson 14, which is the second of the unit summary lessons, reviews biosocial, cognitive, and psychosocial development during the play years between ages 2 and 6.

The overall theme of this lesson is that as preschoolers grow, their physical, cognitive, and psychosocial development makes possible new types of play activities. These new types of play activities create more opportunities for growth in each domain of development. During early childhood, play is a catalyst for development.

In the program, this interwoven nature of play and development is revealed in the stories of four children: three-year-old Jordan, who is flourishing in the care offered by an extended family; four-year-olds Maddy and Alex, fraternal twins who are following their own unique developmental paths; and four-and-a-half-year-old C.C., who was badly burned as an infant and then spent a year in **foster care** before being adopted by a loving family.

Prior Telecourse Knowledge that Will Be Used in this Lesson

- This lesson will return to the dual influences of heredity and environment (from Lesson 3). Recall that all human development is a product of the interaction between nature (our genes) and nurture (our environment).

- Biosocial development during early childhood (from Lesson 11) will be referred to as we review brain and motor skill development and the subject of child maltreatment.

- This lesson will also review cognitive development during early childhood (from Lesson 12) as we discuss language development, theory of mind, and the theories of Lev Vygotsky (guided participation, scaffolding).

- Psychosocial development during early childhood (from Lesson 13) will be referred to as we return to the concepts of self-concept, self-esteem, emotional regulation, and the different types of types of play that children engage in.

Learning Objectives

Use this information to guide your reading, viewing, thinking, and studying. After successfully completing this lesson, you should be able to:

1. Summarize biosocial development in early childhood, giving examples of brain and motor-skill development and childhood maltreatment.

2. Discuss the general pattern of cognitive development during early childhood, focusing on language development, theory of mind, and the role of caregivers.

3. Summarize psychosocial development during early childhood, focusing on self-concept, emotional regulation, and the various types of play and their influence.

4. Offer examples of how a child's development in any one domain (biosocial, cognitive, or psychosocial) can affect development in a different domain.

5. Discuss some things that parents can do to encourage the healthy development of their preschooler.

📖 **Read "Summary: The Play Years: Biosocial Development," pages 260–261; "Summary: The Play Years: Cognitive Development,") page 292; "Summary: The Play Years: Psychosocial Development," pages 323–324; and "The Developing Person So Far: The Play Years, Ages 2 Through 6," page 325. In addition, reread page 241, and review Chapters 8, 9, and 10.**

Video Viewing Tips

The video for Lesson 14 will feature four preschool children who offer living examples of some concepts you've learned in the previous three lessons. As you view the video, watch for the following issues and situations.

This video will clearly demonstrate the importance of *play* in early childhood. Note differences in the types of play these children engage in, and consider the range of effects on their biosocial, cognitive, and psychosocial development. Also, consider the level of gross and fine motor skills in these children and how that might affect their preference for certain play activities.

Pay close attention to the role of parents and other caregivers in this video, and try to guess their parenting style (authoritarian, permissive, authoritative). Also, look for examples of how these caregivers structure or scaffold individual learning situations for their children through a process of guided participation.

As you watch, consider how the heredity of these children and environmental factors interact to influence their development. For example, Maddy and Alex in segment two of the video are fraternal twins. Remember that fraternal (dizygotic) twins come from two different ova fertilized by two separate sperm. So, they have different genes just like any other siblings. While Maddy and Alex live in very similar environments, you'll see how their genetic differences have produced two very different young girls.

As always in these "Summary" videos, keep an eye out for any interaction between domains—how development in one domain can effect changes in a different domain. Before you watch this lesson, it may help you to review the vocabulary in the Key Terms section.

View the video for Lesson 14, "Developing Through Play."
Segment 1: *Jordan*
Segment 2: *Maddy and Alex*
Segment 3: *C.C.*

Summary

Children grow steadily taller and slimmer during the preschool years, and genetic background and nutrition are responsible for most of the variation seen in children throughout the world. The most significant aspect of growth is the continued maturation of the nervous system and the refinement of the visual, muscular, and cognitive skills that will be necessary for the child to function in school. Gross motor skills—such as running, jumping, and other key elements of play—improve dramatically during these years while fine motor skills, such as writing and drawing, develop more slowly.

Child maltreatment, including the abuse and neglect revealed in the poignant story of C.C., may cast a long shadow on the developing child. These problems are likely to occur in homes with immature parents, many children, and few personal and community resources.

Cognitive skills flourish during early childhood, especially in homes such as Jordan's, where the guided participation offered by loving family members stimulates memory, problem solving, and reasoning about number and theory of mind. In countless everyday instances, preschoolers reveal themselves to be remarkably thoughtful, insightful, and perceptive thinkers whose grasp of the causes of everyday events, memory of the past, and mastery of language is sometimes astounding. Still, you may recall Jordan's reaction when his father tried to get him to spell "house," which may be beyond his zone of proximal development. It's important for caregivers to provide age-appropriate activities that encourage development without demanding too much.

During the preschool years a child's self-confidence, social skills, and social roles become more fully developed. This growth coincides with the child's increased capacity for communication, imagination, and understanding of his or her social context. Self-concept emerges, as does the child's ability to regulate his or her emotions. As their social and cognitive skills develop, preschoolers engage in ever more imaginative types of play, which further stimulates development in each domain.

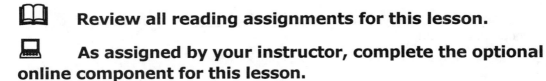 **Review all reading assignments for this lesson.**

As assigned by your instructor, complete the optional online component for this lesson.

Key Terms

Using your own words, write a brief definition or explanation of each of the following terms on a separate piece of paper.

1. injury control/harm reduction
2. child maltreatment
3. abuse
4. foster care
5. neglect
6. preoperational thought
7. egocentrism
8. irreversibility
9. conservation
10. guided participation
11. scaffold
12. theory of mind
13. fast mapping
14. overregularization
15. self-concept
16. initiative versus guilt
17. emotional regulation
18. prosocial behavior
19. antisocial behavior
20. rough-and-tumble play
21. sociodramatic play
22. authoritarian parenting
23. permissive parenting
24. authoritative parenting
25. self-esteem

Practice Questions

Multiple-Choice Questions

1. _____ refers to the tendency of young children to view the world exclusively from their own perspective.
   a. Egocenticism
   b. Centration
   c. Symbolic thought
   d. Theory of mind

2. In chaotic and dangerous environments, _____ parenting may be most beneficial to children.
   a. authoritative
   b. authoritarian
   c. traditional
   d. permissive

3. Skills that involve large body movements, such as running and jumping, are called
   a. activity-level skills.
   b. fine motor skills.
   c. gross motor skills.
   d. left-brain skills.

4. The brain's ongoing myelination during childhood helps children
   a. control their actions more precisely.
   b. react more quickly to stimuli.
   c. focus more easily on printed letters.
   d. do all of the above.

5. The leading cause of death in childhood is
   a. accidents.
   b. untreated diabetes.
   c. malnutrition.
   d. iron deficiency anemia.

6. When parents or caregivers do not provide adequate food, shelter, attention, or supervision, it is referred to as
   a. abuse.
   b. neglect.
   c. endangering.
   d. maltreatment.

7. Which of the following activities would probably be the most difficult for a five-year-old child?
   a. climbing a ladder
   b. catching a ball
   c. throwing a ball
   d. pouring juice from a pitcher without spilling it

8. The Russian psychologist Lev Vygotsky emphasized that
   a. language helps children form ideas.
   b. children form concepts first, then find words to express them.
   c. language and other cognitive developments are unrelated at this stage.
   d. preschoolers learn language only for egocentric purposes.

9. Compared with their rate of speech development, children's understanding of language develops
   a. more slowly.
   b. at about the same pace.
   c. more rapidly.
   d. more rapidly in some cultures than in others.

10. Relatively recent experiments have demonstrated that preschoolers can succeed at tests of conservation when
    a. they are allowed to work cooperatively with other children.
    b. the test is presented as a competition.
    c. the children are informed that their parents are observing them.
    d. the test is presented in a simple, gamelike way.

11. A preschooler who focuses his or her attention on only one feature of a situation is demonstrating a characteristic of preoperational thought called

   a. centration.
   b. overregularization.
   c. reversibility.
   d. egocentrism.

12. One characteristic of preoperational thought is

   a. the ability to categorize objects.
   b. the ability to count in multiples of 5.
   c. the inability to perform logical operations.
   d. difficulty adjusting to changes in routine.

13. In order to scaffold a child's cognitive skills, parents

   a. simplify tasks.
   b. interpret the activity.
   c. help children find answers, while anticipating mistakes.
   d. do all of the above.

14. Regarding the value of preschool education, most developmentalists believe that

   a. most disadvantaged children will not benefit from an early preschool education.
   b. most disadvantaged children will benefit from an early preschool education.
   c. because of sleeper effects, the early benefits of preschool education are likely to disappear by grade 3.
   d. the relatively small benefits of antipoverty measures such as Head Start do not justify their huge costs.

15. A preschooler fails to put together a difficult puzzle on her own, so her mother encourages her to try again, this time guiding her by asking questions such as, "For this space do we need a big piece or a little piece?" With Mom's help, the child successfully completes the puzzle. Lev Vygotsky would attribute the child's success to

   a. additional practice with the puzzle pieces.
   b. imitation of her mother's behavior.
   c. the social interaction with her mother that restructured the task to make its solution more attainable.
   d. modeling and reinforcement.

16. Preschool children have a clear (but not necessarily accurate) concept of self. Typically, the preschooler believes that she or he

   a. owns all objects in sight.
   b. is great at almost everything.
   c. is much less competent than peers and older children.
   d. is more powerful than her or his parents.

17. Because it helps children rehearse social roles, work out fears and fantasies, and learn cooperation, an important form of social play is

    a. sociodramatic play.
    b. mastery play.
    c. rough-and-tumble play.
    d. sensorimotor play.

18. The three basic patterns of parenting described by Diana Baumrind are

    a. hostile, loving, and harsh.
    b. authoritarian, permissive, and authoritative.
    c. positive, negative, and punishing.
    d. indulgent, neglecting, and traditional.

19. Authoritative parents are receptive and loving, but they also normally

    a. set limits and enforce rules.
    b. have difficulty communicating.
    c. withhold praise and affection.
    d. encourage aggressive behavior.

20. Summarizing her report on neurological aspects of emotional regulation, Seema notes that young children who have internalizing problems tend to have greater activity in the

    a. right temporal lobe.
    b. left temporal lobe.
    c. right prefrontal cortex.
    d. left prefrontal cortex.

21. The initial advantages of parenting style

    a. do not persist past middle childhood.
    b. remain apparent through adolescence.
    c. are likely to be even stronger over time.
    d. have an unpredictable impact later in children's lives.

22. The preschooler's readiness to learn new tasks and play activities reflects his or her

    a. emerging competency and self-awareness.
    b. theory of mind.
    c. relationship with parents.
    d. growing identification with others.

23. Erikson noted that preschoolers eagerly begin many new activities but are vulnerable to criticism and feelings of failure; in other words, they experience the crisis of

    a. identity versus role confusion.
    b. initiative versus guilt.
    c. basic trust versus mistrust.
    d. efficacy versus helplessness.

24. Rodney and Jack are wrestling and hitting each other without intent to hurt. Although this rough-and-tumble play mimics negative, aggressive behavior, it serves a useful purpose, which is to

    a. rehearse social roles.

    b. develop interactive skills.

    c. improve fine motor skills.

    d. do both b and c.

True or False Items

Write T (for true) or F (for false) on the line in front of each statement.

25. _____ Growth between ages 2 and 6 is more rapid than at any other period in the life span.

26. _____ The health care, genetic background, and nutrition of the preschool child are major influences on growth.

27. _____ Fine motor skills are usually easier for preschoolers to master than are gross motor skills.

28. _____ Most child maltreatment does not involve serious physical abuse.

29. _____ With the beginning of preoperational thought, most preschoolers can understand abstract words.

30. _____ A preschooler who says "You comed up and hurted me" is demonstrating a lack of understanding of English grammar.

31. _____ Vygotsky believed that cognitive growth is largely a social activity.

32. _____ Children of authoritative parents tend to be successful, happy with themselves, and generous with others.

Questions for Reflection

1. Considering the physical, cognitive, linguistic, and social development of children during early childhood, describe the type of toy that would be suitable for a three- or four-year-old child. In your description of the toy, be sure to include its design and construction, the play value of the toy, and the domain(s) of development the toy is intended to stimulate.

2. According to the lesson, the United States is one of the most violent nations in the world. In what ways does this context of violence promote child maltreatment? If it were in your power to completely shape the social context in which a child grew up, what steps would you take to help ensure that he or she would be protected from maltreatment?

3. Visit the children's section of your local library or bookstore. Ask the librarian or salesperson to guide you to a book that is a "classic" or well-loved storybook for children from 3 to 6 years of age. Examine the book carefully. If possible, read it aloud to a child or someone else. Then complete the following items.

    a. Give the title, name of the author and illustrator, and date of publication of the book.

    b. Summarize what the librarian or salesperson told you about why this book is a "classic" for this age group.

c. Give examples of any of the following story elements that appear in the book: rhyme and repetition; egocentrism (for example, animals that dress and talk like a child); centration (for example stories about characters who have only one prominent feature); story elements that reassure the child about the strong ties of family and friendship.

4. Give examples of how a child's development in any one domain (biosocial, cognitive, or psychosocial) can affect development in a different domain.

Answer Key

Key Terms

1. Injury control (also called harm reduction) is the practice of limiting the extent of injuries by planning ahead, controlling the circumstances, preventing certain dangerous activities, and adding safety features to others. (p. 249; objective 1)

2. Child maltreatment is intentional harm to, or avoidable endangerment of, anyone under age 18. (p. 252; video lesson, segment 3; objective 1)

3. Abuse refers to deliberate actions that are harmful to a child's well-being. (p. 252; objective 1)

4. Foster care is a legally sanctioned, publicly supported arrangement in which children are removed from their biological parents and temporarily given to another adult to nurture. (p. 258; video lesson, segment 3; objective 1)

5. Neglect refers to failure to appropriately meet a child's basic needs. (p. 252; objective 1)

6. According to Piaget, thinking between ages 2 and 6 is characterized by preoperational thought, meaning that children cannot yet perform logical operations; that is, they cannot use logical principles. (p. 264; objective 2)

7. Egocentrism refers to the tendency of young children to view the world exclusively from their own perspective. (p. 264; objective 2)

8. Irreversibility is the inability to recognize that reversing a transformation brings about the same conditions that existed prior to the transformation. (p. 265; objective 2)

9. Conservation is the understanding that the amount or quantity of a substance or object is unaffected by changes in its shape or configuration. (p. 265; objective 2)

10. According to Vygotsky, intellectual growth in young children is stimulated and directed by their guided participation in learning experiences. As guides, parents, teachers, and older children offer assistance with challenging tasks, model problem-solving approaches, provide explicit instructions as needed, and support the child's interest and motivation. (p. 267; video lesson, segment 1; objective 2)

11. Tutors who scaffold, structure children's learning experiences by simplifying tasks, maintaining children's interest, and solving problems, anticipating mistakes, among other things. (p. 268; video lesson, segment 1; objective 2)

12. A theory of mind is an understanding of mental processes, that is, of one's own or another's emotions, perceptions, intentions, and thoughts. (p. 276; video lesson, segments 1 & 2; objective 2)

13. Fast mapping is the process by which children rapidly learn new words by quickly connecting them to words and categories that are already understood. (p. 280; video lesson, segment 1; objective 2)

14. Overregularization occurs when children apply rules of grammar when they should not. It is seen in English, for example, when children add "s" to form the plural even in irregular cases that form the plural in a different way. (p. 282; objective 2)

15. Self-concept refers to what a child thinks about him- or herself; it is the child's answer to the question, "who am I?" (p. 299; video lesson, segment 1; objective 3)

16. According to Erikson, the crisis of the preschool years is initiative versus guilt. In this crisis, young children eagerly take on new tasks and play activities and feel guilty when their efforts result in failure or criticism. (p. 301; objective 3)

17. Emotional regulation is the ability to manage and modify one's feelings, particularly feelings of fear, frustration, and anger. (p. 296; objective 3)

18. Prosocial behavior is an action, such as cooperating or sharing, which is performed to benefit another person without the expectation of reward. (p. 302; video lesson, segment 3; objective 3)

19. Antisocial behavior is an action, such as hitting or insulting, which is intended to hurt another person. (p. 302; objective 3)

20. Rough-and-tumble play is physical play that often mimics aggression, but involves no intent to harm. (p. 305; objective 3)

21. In sociodramatic play, children act out roles and themes in stories of their own creation, allowing them to examine personal concerns in a nonthreatening manner. (p. 306; objective 3)

22. Authoritarian parenting is a style of child rearing in which the parents show little affection or nurturance for their children; maturity demands are high and parent-child communication is low. (p. 310; objective 3)

23. Permissive parenting is a style of parenting in which the parents make few demands on their children, yet are nurturant and accepting, and communicate well with their children. (p. 310; objective 3)

24. Authoritative parenting is a style of parenting in which the parents set limits and enforce rules but do so more democratically than do authoritarian parents. (p. 310; objective 3)

25. Self-esteem refers to how a child feels about himself or herself; it has to do with how lovable the child feels. (p. 299; video lesson, segment 1; objective 3)

Practice Questions

Multiple-Choice Questions

1. a. is the correct answer. (p. 264; objective 2)

2. b. is the correct answer. (p. 311; objective 3)

3. c. is the correct answer. (p. 245; video lesson, segments 1, 2, & 3; objective 1)

4. d. is the correct answer. (pp. 240, 243; objective 1)

5. a. is the correct answer. (p. 248; objective 1)

6. b. is the correct answer. (p. 252; video lesson, segment 3; objectives 1 & 5)

   a. is incorrect. Abuse is deliberate, harsh injury to the body.

   c. is incorrect. Endangerment was not discussed.

   d. is incorrect. Maltreatment is too broad a term.

7. d. is the correct answer. (p. 246; objective 1)

   a., b., & c. are incorrect. Preschoolers find these gross motor skills easier to perform than fine motor skills such as that described in d.

8. a. is the correct answer. (p. 282; objective 2)

b. is incorrect. This expresses the views of Piaget.

c. is incorrect. Because he believed that language facilitates thinking, Vygotsky obviously felt that language and other cognitive developments are intimately related.

d. is incorrect. Vygotsky did not hold this view.

9. c. is the correct answer. (p. 283; objective 2)

10. d. is the correct answer. (p. 266; objective 2)

11. a. is the correct answer. (p. 264; objective 2)

b. is incorrect. Overregularization is the child's tendency to apply grammatical rules even when he or she shouldn't.

c. is incorrect. Reversibility is the concept that reversing an operation, such as addition, will restore the original conditions.

d. is incorrect. This term is used to refer to the young child's belief that people think as he or she does.

12. c. is the correct answer. This is why the stage is called preoperational. (p. 264; objective 2)

13. d. is the correct answer. (p. 268; video lesson, segment 1; objective 3)

14. b. is the correct answer. (p. 290; objectives 2 & 5)

15. c. is the correct answer. (pp. 267–268; objectives 2 & 5)

16. b. is the correct answer. (pp. 299–300; objective 3)

17. a. is the correct answer. (p. 306; objective 3)

b. is incorrect. Mastery play is play that helps children develop new physical and intellectual skills.

c. is incorrect. Rough-and-tumble play is physical play that mimics aggression.

d. is incorrect. Sensorimotor play captures the pleasures of using the senses and motor skills.

18. b. is the correct answer. (p. 310; objective 3)

d. is incorrect. Traditional is a variation of the basic styles uncovered by later research. Indulgent and neglecting are not discussed in the textbook.

19. a. is the correct answer. (p. 310; objective 3)

b. & c. are incorrect. Authoritative parents communicate very well and are quite affectionate.

d. is incorrect. This is not typical of authoritative parents.

20. c. is the correct answer. (pp. 296–297; objective 3)

a. & b. are incorrect. The temporal lobes are involved in speech and hearing, rather than emotional regulation.

d. is incorrect. Children who have externalizing problems tend to have greater activity in this area.

21. c. is the correct answer. (p. 311; objectives 3 & 5)

22. a. is the correct answer. (pp. 299–300; objective 3)

b. is incorrect. This viewpoint is associated only with cognitive theory.

c. is incorrect. Although parent-child relationships are important to social development, they do not determine readiness.

d. is incorrect. Identification is a Freudian defense mechanism.

23. b. is the correct answer. (p. 301; objective 3)

a. & c. are incorrect. According to Erikson, these are the crises of adolescence and infancy, respectively.

d. is incorrect. This is not a crisis described by Erikson.

24. b. is the correct answer. (pp. 305–306; objective 3)

True or False Items

25. F   Growth actually slows down during the play years. (p. 237; objective 1)

26. T   (p. 238; objectives 1 & 5)

27. F   Fine motor skills are more difficult for preschoolers to master than are gross motor skills. (p. 246; video lesson, segments 1, 2, & 3; objective 1)

28. T   (p. 252; objective 1)

29. F   Preschoolers have difficulty understanding abstract words; their vocabulary consists mainly of concrete nouns and verbs. (p. 281; objective 2)

30. F   In adding "ed" to form a past tense, the child has indicated an understanding of the grammatical rule for making past tenses in English, even though the construction in these two cases is incorrect. (pp. 282–283; objective 2)

31. T   (p. 267; video lesson, segment 1; objective 2)

32. T   (p. 311; objectives 3 & 5)

Lesson Review

Lesson 14

The Play Years
Summary

Please Note: Use this matrix to guide your study and achieve the learning objectives of this lesson. It will also help you to view the video, which defines and demonstrates important concepts and skills as they relate to everyday life.

Learning Objective	Textbook	Telecourse Student Guide	Video Lesson
1. Summarize biosocial development in early childhood, giving examples of brain and motor-skill development and childhood maltreatment.	pp. 237–260	Key Terms: 1, 2, 3, 4, 5; Practice Questions: 3, 4, 5, 6, 7, 25, 26, 27, 28.	all segments
2. Discuss the general pattern of cognitive development during early childhood, focusing on language development, theory of mind, and the role of caregivers.	pp. 263–291	Key Terms: 6, 7, 8, 9, 10, 11, 12, 13, 14; Practice Questions: 1, 3, 8, 9, 10, 11, 12, 13, 14, 15, 29, 30, 31.	all segments
3. Summarize psychosocial development during early childhood, focusing on self-concept, emotional regulation, and the various types of play and their influence.	pp. 295–323	Key Terms: 15, 16, 17, 18, 19, 20, 21, 22, 23, 24, 25; Practice Questions: 2, 3, 16, 17, 18, 19, 20, 21, 22, 23, 24, 32.	all segments
4. Offer examples of how a child's development in any one domain (biosocial, cognitive, or psychosocial) can affect development in a different domain.			all segments
5. Discuss some things that parents can do to encourage the healthy development of their preschooler.		Practice Questions: 6, 13, 14, 15, 21, 26, 32.	all segments

Hazards Along the Way

Lesson 15

The Play Years:
Special Topic

Preview

This lesson explores two hazards along a child's development path: media and maltreatment. Although television and video games provide ready "babysitters," they also put children at risk. Research has linked media overexposure to a variety of negative effects. Although all children may not be adversely affected, electronic media can be hazardous to a child's biological, cognitive, and psychosocial well being.

This lesson will also focus on the disturbing subject of child maltreatment, including an in-depth exploration of its prevalence, contributing factors, consequences for future development, treatment, and prevention. In this context, appropriate discipline for children is also discussed.

As you complete this lesson, consider the relevant experiences of any child you know. About how many hours of television does this child watch per week? About how many hours does he or she spend playing video games? What is the nature of these programs and games? How much violence is presented and in what context? Has anyone you know experienced maltreatment as a child? What were the circumstances? What type of treatment (if any) did the child receive? What could have been done to prevent this maltreatment? How was this child disciplined in the home? Was physical punishment ever used?

Prior Telecourse Knowledge that Will Be Used in this Lesson

*   This lesson returns to the topic of child maltreatment, which was introduced in Lesson 11. Recall that maltreatment includes both *abuse* (deliberate action that causes harm) and *neglect* (inaction, inattention, or general failure to meet a child's basic needs).

*   This lesson will also discuss different strategies for disciplining a child (from Lesson 13), which can include explanation, criticism, persuasion, and/or physical punishment.

Learning Objectives

Use this information to guide your reading, viewing, thinking, and studying. After successfully completing this lesson, you should be able to

1. Discuss the effects of television and the media on a child's development.
2. Identify the various categories of child maltreatment, and discuss several factors that contribute to its occurrence.
3. Discuss the consequences, prevention and treatment of child abuse and neglect, including the concept of differential response.
4. Discuss permanency planning including foster care, kinship care, and adoption as long-term intervention options in cases of child maltreatment.
5. Discuss the impact of punishment on a child's development and describe alternative methods for disciplining a child.

📖 **Review Chapter 8, "Child Maltreatment," pages 252–260; and Chapter 10, "The Influence of Television and Video Games," pages 307–309, and "Punishment," pages 312–315.**

📼 **View the video for Lesson 15, "Hazards Along the Way."**

Segment 1: *Media Influences*

Segment 2: *Child Maltreatment: Causes and Consequences*

Segment 3: *Child Maltreatment: Treatment and Prevention*

Summary

A typical child in the United States watches more than three hours of television per day, more than any other age group. Among the criticisms of video watching are that it takes time from active and imaginative play; sends faulty messages about nutrition; provides sexist, racist, and ageist stereotypes; undermines sympathy for emotional pain; and undercuts attributes, skills, and values that lead to prosocial activity.

One longitudinal study found that teenagers who had watched educational television as young children earned higher grades and did more reading than others, especially if they were boys. On the other hand, teenagers who watched violent television programs as young children had lower grades than others, especially if they were girls. For these reasons, allowing a child unlimited and unsupervised media exposure could be seen as a form of **child maltreatment**.

Child maltreatment includes all intentional harm to, or avoidable endangerment of someone under age 18. Maltreatment falls into one of two broad categories: **abuse** and **neglect**. **Child abuse** includes all deliberate actions that are harmful to a child's well-being, including all physical, sexual, and emotional abuse. **Child neglect** refers to failures to act appropriately to meet a child's basic needs. One sign of neglect is **failure to thrive**, in which an infant or young child gains little or no weight, despite apparently normal health. Another sign is hypervigilance, in which an older child seems too nervous to concentrate on anything.

Although it is difficult to estimate the prevalence of maltreatment (reporting sources often are biased), the number of substantiated cases of child maltreatment in the United States is estimated to be about 1 million. Before a particular practice can be considered abusive, customs and community standards must be taken into account.

Communities vary in customs and goals regarding child-rearing, which means that what may be considered maltreatment in one place may not be in another. Two aspects of the overall context that seem conducive to maltreatment are poverty and social isolation.

Maltreated children often have difficulties in several areas. They may have trouble learning, in part because they may develop abnormal brain patterns that make learning difficult. The most serious of these is **shaken baby syndrome**, which can cause the child's neck to break and damage blood vessels and neural connections in the brain.

Children who are chronically maltreated tend to be slower to talk, underweight, less able to concentrate, and delayed in academic growth. They also tend to regard others as hostile and exploitive, and hence they are less friendly, more aggressive, and more isolated than other children. As adolescents and adults, they are more likely to engage in self-destructive and/or other destructive behaviors.

New laws requiring teachers, social workers, and other professionals to report possible maltreatment have resulted in increased reporting. Out of their concern that reporting does not create enough protection for a maltreated child, some experts advocate a policy of **differential response** that separates high-risk cases that may require complete investigation and removal of the child from low-risk cases that may only require some sort of supportive measure.

Permanency planning refers to the process of finding a long-term solution to the care of a child who has been abused. One option is **foster care**, a legal plan which transfers care of the child from the family to someone else. In one type of foster care, called **kinship care**, a relative of the maltreated child becomes the approved caregiver. A final option is **adoption**, which may be best when families are inadequate and children are young.

Public policy measures and other efforts designed to prevent maltreatment from ever occurring are called **primary prevention**. **Secondary prevention** focuses on spotting and treating the first symptoms of maltreatment. Last-ditch measures such as removing a child from an abusive home, jailing the perpetrator, and so forth constitute **tertiary prevention**.

For some, the difference between physical punishment and child abuse may be hard to distinguish. How a parent disciplines a child is an integral aspect of parenting style. To be effective, discipline should be more proactive than punitive. And, although most parents continue to believe that physical discipline is necessary at times, research suggests that children who are physically punished may learn to be more aggressive.

📖   **Review all reading assignments for this lesson.**

💻   **As assigned by your instructor, complete the optional online component for this lesson.**

Key Terms

Using your own words, write a brief definition or explanation of each of the following terms on a separate piece of paper.

1. child maltreatment
2. child abuse
3. child neglect
4. failure to thrive
5. reported maltreatment
6. substantiated maltreatment
7. differential response
8. shaken baby syndrome
9. post-traumatic stress disorder
10. permanency planning
11. foster care
12. kinship care
13. adoption
14. primary prevention
15. secondary prevention
16. tertiary prevention
17. time-out

Practice Questions

Multiple-Choice Questions

1. Children who watch a lot of violent television
    a. are more likely to be aggressive.
    b. become desensitized to violence.
    c. are less likely to attempt to mediate a quarrel between other children.
    d. have all of the above characteristics.

2. Which of the following is true regarding the effects of spanking?
    a. Spanking seems to reduce reactive aggression.
    b. When administered appropriately, spanking promotes psychosocial development.
    c. Spanking is associated with increased aggression toward peers.
    d. None of the above is true.

3. Which of the following is an example of tertiary prevention of child maltreatment?
    a. removing a child from an abusive home
    b. home visitation of families with infants by health professionals
    c. new laws establishing stiff penalties for child maltreatment
    d. public-policy measures aimed at creating stable neighborhoods

4. Which of the following is an example of secondary prevention of child maltreatment?
    a. removing a child from an abusive home
    b. jailing a maltreating parent
    c. home visitation of families with infants by health professionals
    d. public-policy measures aimed at creating stable neighborhoods

5. When parents or caregivers do not provide adequate food, shelter, attention, or supervision, it is referred to as
   a. abuse.
   b. neglect.
   c. endangering.
   d. maltreatment.

6. Which of the following is **NOT** true regarding foster care?
   a. Foster children often have behavioral problems.
   b. The number of foster children in the United States is increasing.
   c. Most foster children become maltreating caregivers.
   d. The average stay in foster care has decreased.

7. Children who have been maltreated often
   a. regard other children and adults as hostile and exploitative.
   b. are less friendly and more aggressive.
   c. are more isolated than other children.
   d. are all of the above.

8. Most child maltreatment
   a. does not involve serious physical abuse.
   b. involves a rare outburst from the perpetrator.
   c. involves a mentally ill perpetrator.
   d. can be predicted from the victim's personality characteristics.

9. A mayoral candidate is calling for sweeping policy changes to help ensure the well-being of children by promoting home ownership, high-quality community centers, and more stable neighborhoods. If these measures are effective in reducing child maltreatment, they would be classified as
   a. primary prevention.
   b. secondary prevention.
   c. tertiary prevention.
   d. differential response.

10. Parents who were abused as children
    a. almost always abuse their children.
    b. are more likely to neglect, but not necessarily abuse, their children.
    c. are no more likely than anyone else to mistreat their children.
    d. do none of the above.

11. One sign of child _____, in which an infant or young child gains little or no weight despite apparently normal health, is called _____.
    a. abuse; failure to thrive
    b. neglect; failure to thrive
    c. abuse; hypervigilance
    d. neglect; hypervigilance

Matching Items

Match each definition or description with its corresponding term.

Terms

12. _____ kinship care
13. _____ foster care
14. _____ child abuse
15. _____ child neglect

16. _____ primary prevention
17. _____ secondary prevention
18. _____ tertiary prevention
19. _____ time-out

Definitions or Descriptions

a. legal placement of a child in the care of someone other than his or her biological parents

b. a form of care in which a relative of a maltreated child takes over from the biological parents

c. procedures to prevent child maltreatment from ever occurring

d. actions that are deliberately harmful to a child's well-being

e. procedures for spotting and treating the early warning signs of child maltreatment

f. failure to appropriately meet a child's basic needs

g. procedures to halt maltreatment that has already occurred

h. a disciplinary technique that does not require physical punishment

Answer Key

Key Terms

1. Child maltreatment is intentional harm to, or avoidable endangerment of, anyone under age 18. (p. 252; video lesson, segment 2; objective 2)

2. Child abuse refers to deliberate actions that are harmful to a child's well-being. (p. 252; video lesson, segment 2; objective 2)

3. Child neglect refers to failure to appropriately meet a child's basic needs. (p. 252; video lesson, segment 2; objective 2)

4. A sign of possible child neglect, failure to thrive occurs when an otherwise healthy child gains little or no weight. (p. 252; objective 2)

5. Child maltreatment that has been officially reported to the police, or other authority, is called reported maltreatment. (p. 252; objective 2)

6. Child maltreatment that has been officially reported to authorities, and verified, is called substantiated maltreatment. (p. 252; objective 2)

7. Differential response refers to separating child maltreatment reports into two categories: high-risk cases that require immediate investigation and possible removal of the child, and low-risk cases that require supportive measures to encourage better parental care. (p. 254; objective 3)

8. A serious condition caused by sharply shaking an infant to stop his or her crying, shaken baby syndrome is associated with severe brain damage that results from internal hemorrhaging. (p. 256; objective 3)

9. Post-traumatic stress disorder (PTSD) is a syndrome triggered by exposure to an extreme traumatic stressor. In maltreated children, symptoms of PTSD include hyperactivity and hypervigilance, sleeplessness, and confusion between fantasy and reality. (p. 257; objective 3)

10. Permanency planning is the process of finding a long-term solution to the care of a child who has been abused. (p. 258; objective 4)

11. Foster care is a legally sanctioned, publicly supported arrangement in which children are removed from their biological parents and temporarily given to another adult to nurture. (p. 258; objective 4)

12. Kinship care is a form of foster care in which a relative of a maltreated child becomes the child's legal caregiver. (p. 258; objective 4)

13. Adoption is the process whereby nonbiological parents are given legal custody of a child. (p. 259; objective 4)

14. Primary prevention refers to public policy measures designed to prevent child maltreatment (or other harm) from ever occurring. (p. 259; video lesson, segment 3; objective 3)

15. Secondary prevention involves home visitation and other efforts to spot and treat the early warning signs of maltreatment before problems become severe. (p. 259; video lesson, segment 3; objective 3)

16. Tertiary prevention involves efforts to stop child maltreatment after it occurs and to treat the victim. Removing a child from an abusive home, jailing the perpetrator, and providing health care to the victim are examples of tertiary prevention. (p. 260; video lesson, segment 3; objective 3)

17. A time-out is a disciplinary technique in which the child is required to stop all activity and sit in a corner or stay indoors for a few minutes. (p. 313; objective 5)

Practice Questions

Multiple-Choice Questions

1. d. is the correct answer. (pp. 308–309; video lesson, segment 1; objective 1)

2. c. is the correct answer. (pp. 314–315; video lesson, segment 3; objective 5)

3. a. is the correct answer. (p. 260; video lesson, segment 3; objective 3)

   b. is incorrect. This is an example of secondary prevention.

   c. & d. are incorrect. These are examples of primary prevention.

4. c. is the correct answer. (p. 259; video lesson, segment 3; objective 3)

   a. & b. are incorrect. These are examples of tertiary prevention.

   d. is incorrect. This is an example of primary prevention.

5. b. is the correct answer. (p. 252; video lesson, segment 2; objective 2)

   a. is incorrect. Abuse is deliberate, harsh injury to the body.

   c. is incorrect. Endangerment was not discussed.

   d. is incorrect. Maltreatment is too broad a term.

6. c. is the correct answer. Foster children often become good, nonmaltreating caregivers. (p. 258; objective 4)

7. d. is the correct answer. (p. 257; video lesson, segment 2; objective 3)

8. a. is the correct answer. (p. 252; video lesson, segment 2; objective 2)

9. a. is the correct answer. (p. 259; video lesson, segment 3; objective 3)

   b. is incorrect. Had the candidate called for measures to spot the early warning signs of maltreatment, this answer would be true.

   c. is incorrect. Had the candidate called for jailing those who maltreat children or providing greater counseling and health care for victims, this answer would be true.

   d. is incorrect. Differential response is not an approach to prevention of maltreatment; rather, it refers to separate reporting procedures for high- and low-risk families.

10. d. is the correct answer. Approximately 30 percent of adults who were abused as children themselves become abusive parents. (p. 258; objective 2)

11. b. is the correct answer. (p. 252; objective 2)

Matching

12. b. is the correct answer (p. 258; objective 4)

13. a. is the correct answer (p. 258; objective 4)

14. d. is the correct answer (p. 252; video lesson, segment 2; objective 2)

15. f. is the correct answer (p. 252; video lesson, segment 2; objective 2)

16. c. is the correct answer (p. 259; video lesson, segment 3; objective 3)

17. e. is the correct answer (p. 259; video lesson, segment 3; objective 3)

18. g is the correct answer (p. 260; video lesson, segment 3; objective 3)

19. h is the correct answer (p. 313; objective 5)

Lesson Review

Lesson 15

The Play Years
Special Topic

Please Note: Use this matrix to guide your study and achieve the learning objectives of this lesson. It will also help you to view the video, which defines and demonstrates important concepts and skills as they relate to everyday life.

Learning Objective	Textbook	Telecourse Student Guide	Video Lesson
1. Discuss the effects of television and the media on a child's development.	pp. 308–309	Practice Questions: 1	Segment 1: *Media Influences*
2. Identify the various categories of child maltreatment, and discuss several factors that contribute to its occurrence.	pp. 252, 257–258	Key Terms: 1, 2, 3, 4, 5, 6; Practice Questions: 5, 8, 10, 11, 14, 15.	Segment 2: *Child Maltreatment: Causes & Consequences*
3. Discuss the consequences, prevention and treatment of child abuse and neglect, including the concept of differential response.	pp. 254–260	Key Terms: 7, 8, 9, 14, 15, 16; Practice Questions: 3, 4, 7, 9, 16, 17, 18.	Segment 2: *Child Maltreatment: Causes & Consequences*; Segment 3: *Child Maltreatment: Treatment & Prevention*
4. Discuss permanency planning including foster care, kinship care, and adoption as long-term intervention options in cases of child maltreatment.	pp. 258–260	Key Terms: 10, 11, 12, 13; Practice Questions: 6, 12, 13.	
5. Discuss the impact of punishment on a child's development and describe alternative methods for disciplining a child.	pp. 313–315	Key Terms: 17; Practice Questions: 2, 19.	Segment 3: *Child Maltreatment: Treatment & Prevention*

The Golden Years of Childhood

Lesson 16

The School Years:
Biosocial Development

Preview

This lesson introduces **middle childhood**, the years from about 6 to 11. Changes in physical size and shape are described, and the problem of **obesity** is addressed. The discussion then turns to the continuing development of motor skills during the school years. A final section examines the experiences of **children with special needs**, such as those diagnosed with **attention-deficit hyperactivity disorder (AD/HD)**. The causes of and treatments for these problems are discussed, with emphasis placed on insights arising from the new **developmental psychopathology** perspective. This perspective makes it clear that the manifestations of any special childhood problem will change, as the child grows older and that treatment must often focus on all three domains of development.

As you complete this lesson, think about any children you know in this age range. Consider their height and weight relative to other children of the same age (and younger). Are any of these children overweight? If so, speculate on the possible causes. Also, observe the motor skills of these children—how does their coordination compare with younger and older children? Do any of these children have a special problem or disorder, such as a learning disability or AD/HD? If so, how are they being treated? What kind of special services or treatment do they receive at school?

Prior Telecourse Knowledge that Will Be Used in this Lesson

- Biosocial development during infancy and toddlerhood (Lesson 6), as well as that during early childhood (Lesson 11) will be referred to as we discuss variations in physique and the development of motor skills during middle childhood.

- This lesson will return to the concept of *self-esteem* (Lesson 13), how a child feels about him- or herself. A child's perception of his or her biological development (especially relative to peers) can affect self-evaluation in both positive and negative ways.

Learning Objectives

Use this information to guide your reading, viewing, thinking, and studying. After successfully completing this lesson, you should be able to:

1. Describe normal physical growth and development during middle childhood, and account for the usual variations among children.

2. Discuss the problem of childhood obesity and its potential effects on a child's physical and psychological health.

3. Identify the major causes of obesity, and outline the best approaches for treatment.

4. Discuss other common health and biological problems of the school years, focusing on their causes, treatment, and impact on development.

5. Describe motor-skill development during the school years, focusing on variations due to gender, culture, and genetics.

6. Outline the developmental psychopathology perspective, and discuss its value in treating children with special needs.

7. Discuss the characteristics and possible causes of learning disabilities.

8. Describe the symptoms and possible causes of attention-deficit hyperactivity disorder (AD/HD).

9. Discuss the types of treatment available for children with attention-deficit hyperactivity disorder.

10. Describe techniques that have been tried in efforts to educate children with special needs.

📖 **Read Chapter 11, "The School Years: Biosocial Development," pages 327–357.**

📼 **View the video for Lesson 16, "The Golden Years of Childhood."**

      Segment 1: *Physical Growth*

      Segment 2: *Motor-Skill Development*

      Segment 3: *Special Needs*

Summary

For most boys and girls, the years of middle childhood are a time when biosocial development is smooth and uneventful. Children become slimmer than in earlier years, their limbs lengthen, their body proportions change, their muscles become stronger, and their lung capacity increases. Body maturation coupled with sufficient practice enables school-age children to master many motor skills.

Although malnutrition limits the growth of children in some regions of the world, most of the variations in physical development in developed countries are the result of heredity. Diet does exert its influence, however, by interacting with heredity, activity level, and other factors. In some cases, the result is obesity—a growing problem in North American children during the school years. Obese children are at increased risk of serious orthopedic and respiratory problems. The best way to get children to lose weight is to increase their physical activity and change their eating patterns. In some cases, a family-based treatment program of exercise and nutrition education is necessary. It is better to treat obesity early in life before habits that contribute to weight gain become well established.

Another serious problem for many children is **asthma**—a disorder characterized by chronic inflammation of the airways. Asthma is becoming increasingly prevalent in developed nations, indicating that environmental factors are to blame. Several aspects of modern life contribute to asthma, including crowded living conditions, airtight windows, carpeted floors, more bedding, dogs and cats living inside the house, and so forth.

The fact that growth is relatively slow in middle childhood may be part of the reason children become so much more skilled at controlling their bodies. With few exceptions, boys and girls are just about equal in physical abilities during the school years. Boys have somewhat greater upper-arm strength, whereas girls have greater overall flexibility. Expertise in specific skills depends primarily on motivation, guidance, and many hours of practice.

Motor habits that rely on coordinating both sides of the body improve because the corpus callosum between the brain's hemispheres continues to mature. In addition, rough-and-tumble play may help boys overcome their tendencies toward hyperactivity and learning disabilities because it helps with regulation in the frontal lobes of the brain. Motor-skill development is also influenced by culture, national policies, and genetic endowment.

For children with special needs, development can be limited by the difficulties posed by physical or mental disabilities. The field of **developmental psychopathology** applies insights from studies of normal development to the origins and treatment of childhood disorders to help these children learn and reach their full potential.

Children are said to have a **learning disability** when their difficulty with a particular skill is in surprising contrast with their overall intelligence level. One of the most puzzling problems in childhood is **attention-deficit/hyperactivity disorder (AD/HD)**, a behavior problem characterized by excessive activity, an inability to concentrate, and impulsive, sometimes aggressive behavior. AD/HD may arise from several factors, including genetic differences, teratogens, and family and environmental influences.

Special Note: We will discuss the topics of developmental psychopathology and autism (pages 342–345) in more detail in telecourse Lesson 26, "Different Paths." We will cover the use of tests and multiple intelligences (pages 346–349) in Lesson 20, "School Days."

Review all reading assignments for this lesson.

As assigned by your instructor, complete the optional online component for this lesson.

Key Terms

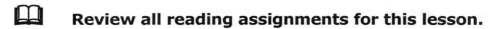

Using your own words, write a brief definition or explanation of each of the following terms on a separate piece of paper.

1. body mass index (BMI)
2. asthma
3. reaction time
4. child with special needs
5. developmental psychopathology
6. *Diagnostic and Statistical Manual of Mental Disorders* (DSM-IV-R)
7. mentally retarded
8. learning disabled
9. dyslexia
10. dyscalculia
11. AD/HD (attention-deficit/ hyperactivity disorder)
12. mainstreaming
13. resource room
14. inclusion
15. middle childhood
16. overweight
17. obesity
18. automatization
19. individual education plan
20. attention-deficit disorder (ADD)
21. least restrictive environment (LRE)

Practice Questions I

Multiple-Choice Questions

1. As children move into middle childhood,
   a. the rate of accidental death increases.
   b. sexual urges intensify.
   c. the rate of weight gain increases.
   d. biological growth slows and steadies.

2. During middle childhood,
   a. girls are usually stronger than boys.
   b. boys have greater physical flexibility than girls.
   c. boys have greater upper-arm strength than girls.
   d. the development of motor skills slows drastically.

3. To help obese children, nutritionists usually recommend
   a. strenuous dieting to counteract early overfeeding.
   b. the use of amphetamines and other drugs.
   c. more exercise, stabilization of weight, and time to "grow out" of the fat.
   d. no specific actions.

4. Dyslexia is a learning disability that affects the ability to
   a. do math.
   b. read.
   c. write.
   d. speak.

5. In relation to weight in later life, childhood obesity is
   a. not an accurate predictor of adolescent or adult weight.
   b. predictive of adolescent but not adult weight.
   c. predictive of adult but not adolescent weight.
   d. predictive of both adolescent and adult weight.

6. The developmental psychopathology perspective is characterized by its
   a. contextual approach.
   b. emphasis on individual therapy.
   c. emphasis on the cognitive domain of development.
   d. concern with all of the above.

7. The time—usually measured in fractions of a second—it takes for a person to respond to a particular stimulus is called
   a. the interstimulus interval.
   b. reaction time.
   c. the stimulus-response interval.
   d. response latency.

8. Researchers have suggested that excessive television watching is a possible cause of childhood obesity because
    a. television bombards children with persuasive junk food commercials.
    b. children often snack while watching television.
    c. body metabolism slows while watching television.
    d. of all the above reasons.

9. The underlying problem in attention-deficit hyperactivity disorder appears to be
    a. low overall intelligence.
    b. a neurological difficulty in paying attention.
    c. a learning disability in a specific academic skill.
    d. the existence of a conduct disorder.

10. Teacher behavior that seems to aggravate or increase problems in children with attention-deficit hyperactivity disorder tends to be
    a. too rigid.
    b. too permissive.
    c. too rigid or permissive.
    d. none of the above.

11. In developed countries, most of the variation in children's size and shape can be attributed to
    a. the amount of daily exercise.
    b. nutrition.
    c. genes.
    d. the interaction of the above factors.

12. Psychoactive drugs are most effective in treating attention-deficit hyperactivity disorder when they are administered
    a. before the diagnosis becomes certain.
    b. for several years after the basic problem has abated.
    c. as part of the labeling process.
    d. with psychological support or therapy.

True or False Items
Write T (for true) or F (for false) on the line in front of each statement.

13. _____ Physical variations in North American children are usually caused by diet rather than heredity.

14. _____ Childhood obesity usually does not correlate with adult obesity.

15. _____ Research shows a direct correlation between television watching and obesity.

16. _____ The quick reaction time that is crucial in some sports can be readily achieved with practice.

17. _____ Despite the efforts of teachers and parents, most children with learning disabilities can expect their disabilities to persist and even worsen as they enter adulthood.

18. _____ The best way for children to lose weight is through strenuous dieting.

19. _____ Most learning disabilities are caused by a difficult birth or other early trauma to the child.

20. _____ AD/HD is diagnosed more often in Great Britain than in the United States.

21. _____ The drugs sometimes given to children to reduce hyperactive behaviors have a reverse effect on adults.

Practice Questions II

Multiple-Choice Questions

1. During the years from age 7 to 11, the average child
   a. becomes slimmer.
   b. gains about 12 pounds a year.
   c. has decreased lung capacity.
   d. is more likely to become obese than at any other period in the life span.

2. Among the factors that are known to contribute to obesity are activity level, quantity of food eaten, and
   a. quality of food.
   b. television-watching.
   c. attitudes toward food.
   d. all of the above.

3. A specific learning disability that becomes apparent when a child experiences unusual difficulty in learning to read is
   a. dyslexia.
   b. dyscalcula (or dyscalculia).
   c. AD/HD.
   d. ADHDA.

4. Problems in learning to write, read, and do math are collectively referred to as
   a. learning disabilities.
   b. attention-deficit hyperactivity disorder.
   c. hyperactivity.
   d. dyscalcula (or dyscalculia).

5. A measure of obesity in which weight in kilograms is divided by the square of height in meters is the
   a. basal metabolic rate (BMR).
   b. body mass index (BMI).
   c. body fat index (BFI).
   d. basal fat ratio (BFR).

6. The most effective form of help for children with AD/HD is
   a. medication.
   b. psychological therapy.
   c. environmental change.
   d. a combination of some or all of the above.

7. A key factor in reaction time is
   a. whether the child is male or female.
   b. brain maturation.
   c. whether the stimulus to be reacted to is an auditory or visual one.
   d. all of the above.

8. Which of the following is true of children with a diagnosed learning disability?
   a. They are, in most cases, average or above average in intelligence.
   b. They often have a specific physical handicap, such as hearing loss.
   c. They often lack basic educational experiences.
   d. All of the above are true.

9. During the school years
   a. boys are, on average, at least a year ahead of girls in the development of physical abilities.
   b. girls are, on average, at least a year ahead of boys in the development of physical abilities.
   c. boys and girls are about equal in physical abilities.
   d. motor-skill development proceeds at a slower pace, since children grow more rapidly at this age than at any other time.

10. Whether a particular child is considered obese depends on
    a. the child's body type.
    b. his or her height.
    c. cultural standards.
    d. all of the above.

11. Which approach to education may best meet the needs of children with learning disabilities in terms of both skill remediation and social interaction with other children?
    a. mainstreaming
    b. special education
    c. inclusion
    d. resource rooms

12. Which of the following is **NOT** a contributing factor in most cases of AD/HD?
    a. genetic inheritance
    b. dietary sugar and caffeine
    c. prenatal damage
    d. postnatal damage

Matching Items

Match each term or concept with its corresponding description or definition.

Terms or Concepts

13. _____ mental retardation
14. _____ dyslexia
15. _____ dyscalculia
16. _____ learning disability
17. _____ attention-deficit hyperactivity disorder (AD/HD)

18. _____ asthma
19. _____ developmental psychopathology
20. _____ *Diagnostic and Statistical Manual of Mental Disorders* (DSM-IV)
21. _____ mainstreaming

Descriptions or Definitions

a. an unexpected difficulty with one or more academic skills

b. the diagnostic guide of the American Psychiatric Association

c. a pervasive delay in cognitive development

d. system in which learning-disabled children are taught in general education classrooms

e. difficulty in reading

f. chronic inflammation of the airways

g. behavior problem involving difficulty in concentrating, as well as excitability and impulsivity

h. difficulty in math

i. applies insights from studies of normal development to the study of childhood disorders

Applying Your Knowledge

1. According to developmentalists, the best game for a typical group of eight-year-olds would be

   a. football or baseball.

   b. basketball.

   c. one in which reaction time is not crucial.

   d. a game involving one-on-one competition.

2. Dr. Rutter, who believes that "we can learn more about an organism's normal functioning by studying its pathology and, likewise, more about its pathology by studying its normal condition," evidently is working from which of the following perspectives?

   a. clinical psychology

   b. developmental psychopathology

   c. behaviorism

   d. psychoanalysis

3. Nine-year-old Paul has difficulty concentrating on his class work for more than a few moments, repeatedly asks his teacher irrelevant questions, and is constantly disrupting the class with loud noises. If his difficulties persist, Paul is likely to be diagnosed as suffering from

   a. dyslexia.

   b. dyscalcula (or dyscalculia).

   c. autism.

   d. attention-deficit hyperactivity disorder.

4. Britta is an average-sized child from an average-height family. During middle childhood, she would be expected to grow _____ inches and gain _____ pounds per year.

   a. 1; 3

   b. 1; 10

   c. 2.5; 5

   d. 6.5; 15

5. Ten-year-old Clarence is inattentive, easily frustrated, and highly impulsive. Clarence may be suffering from

   a. dyslexia.

   b. dyscalcula (or dyscalculia).

   c. conduct disorder.

   d. attention-deficit hyperactivity disorder.

6. Of the following individuals, who is likely to have the fastest reaction time?

   a. a seven-year-old

   b. a nine-year-old

   c. an eleven-year-old

   d. an adult

7. Harold weighs about 20 pounds more than his friend Jay. During school recess, Jay can usually be found playing soccer with his classmates, while Harold sits on the sidelines by himself. Harold's rejection is likely the result of his

   a. being physically different.

   b. being dyslexic.

   c. intimidation of his schoolmates.

   d. being hyperactive.

8. In determining whether an eight-year-old has a learning disability, a teacher looks primarily for

   a. exceptional performance in a subject area.

   b. the exclusion of other explanations.

   c. both a and b.

   d. none of the above.

9. When she moved her practice to England, Dr. Williams was struck by the fact that British doctors seemingly used the same criteria she used to diagnose AD/HD to diagnose

    a. dyslexia.

    b. dyscalcula (or dyscalculia).

    c. conduct disorder.

    d. antisocial personality.

10. Danny has been diagnosed as having attention-deficit hyperactivity disorder. Every day his parents make sure that he takes the proper dose of Ritalin. His parents should

    a. continue this behavior until Danny is an adult.

    b. try different medications when Danny seems to be reverting to his normal overactive behavior.

    c. make sure that Danny also has psychotherapy.

    d. not worry about Danny's condition; he will outgrow it.

11. In concluding her presentation entitled "Facts and falsehoods regarding childhood obesity," Cheryl states that, contrary to popular belief, _____ is not a common cause of childhood obesity.

    a. television-watching

    b. lack of exercise

    c. overeating of high-fat foods

    d. a prenatal teratogen

12. Curtis is 8 years old, 48 inches (1.22 meters) tall, and weighs 58 pounds (26.4 kilograms). His BMI equals _____, making him statistically _____.

    a. 20; obese

    b. 20; overweight

    c. 17.7; normal body weight

    d. 17.7; obese

Answer Key

Key Terms

1. Body mass index (BMI) is a measure of obesity in which a person's weight in kilograms is divided by his or her height squared in meters (video lesson, segment 1; objective 2)

2. Asthma is a disorder in which the airways are chronically inflamed. (p. 335; objective 4)

3. Reaction time is the length of time it takes a person to respond to a particular stimulus. (p. 336; objective 5)

4. A child with special needs requires particular physical, intellectual, or social accommodations in order to learn. (p. 340; video lesson, segment 3; objective 6)

5. Developmental psychopathology is a new field that applies the insights from studies of normal development to the study and treatment of childhood disorders, and vice versa. (p. 342; video lesson, segment 3; objective 6)

6. Developed by the American Psychiatric Association, the *Diagnostic and Statistical Manual of Mental Disorders* (DSM-IV-R) is the leading means of distinguishing various emotional and behavioral disorders. (p. 343; objective 6)

7. Mental retardation is a pervasive delay in cognitive development. (p. 355; objective 7)

8. A learning disability is a difficulty in a particular cognitive skill that is not attributable to an overall intellectual slowness, a physical handicap, a severely stressful living condition, or a lack of basic education. (p. 346; video lesson, segment 3; objective 7)

9. Dyslexia is a learning disability in reading. (p. 349; video lesson, segment 3; objective 7)

10. Dyscalculia is a learning disability in math. (p. 349; video lesson, segment 3; objective 7)

11. The attention-deficit hyperactivity disorder (AD/HD) is a behavior problem in which the individual has great difficulty concentrating, is often excessively excitable and impulsive, and is sometimes aggressive. (p. 351; video lesson, segment 3; objective 8)

12. Mainstreaming is an educational approach in which children with special needs are included in regular classrooms. (p. 353; video lesson, segment 3; objective 10)

13. A resource room is a classroom in which children with special needs spend part of their day working with a trained specialist in order to learn basic skills. (p. 354; objective 10)

14. Inclusion is an educational approach in which children with special needs receive individualized instruction within a regular classroom setting. (p. 354; objective 10)

15. Middle childhood is the period from about age 7 to age 11.

16. A person is overweight if they weigh 20–29 percent above the ideal for a person of the same age and height.

17. A person is obese if they weigh 30 percent or more above the ideal for a person of the same age and height.

18. Automatization is the process by which thoughts and actions are repeated so often that they become almost automatic, requiring little or no conscious thought.

19. An individual education plan is a legal document that specifies the educational goals for a child with special needs.

20. A child with attention-deficit disorder (ADD) has great difficulty concentrating and may be prone to depression. Unlike the hyperactive child with ADHD, the child with ADD is not impulsive and overactive.

21. The least restrictive environment (LRE) is a legally required school setting that allows children with special needs to benefit from the instruction available to most children (often in traditional classrooms).

Practice Questions I

Multiple-Choice Questions

1. d. is the correct answer. (p. 331; video lesson, segment 1; objective 1)

2. c. is the correct answer. (p. 337; objective 1)

    a. is incorrect. Especially in forearm strength, boys are usually stronger than girls during middle childhood.

    b. is incorrect. During middle childhood, girls usually have greater overall flexibility than boys.

d. is incorrect. Motor-skill development improves greatly during middle childhood.

3. c. is the correct answer. (p. 334; video lesson, segment 1; objective 3)

a. is incorrect. Strenuous dieting can be physically harmful and often makes children irritable, listless, and even sick—adding to the psychological problems of the obese child.

b. is incorrect. The use of amphetamines to control weight is not recommended at any age.

4. b. is the correct answer. (p. 349; video lesson, segment 3; objective 7)

a. is incorrect. This is dyscalcula (or dyscalculia).

c. & d. are incorrect. The textbook does not give labels for learning disabilities in writing or speaking.

5. d. is the correct answer. (p. 334; video lesson, segment 1; objective 2)

6. a. is the correct answer. (p. 342; video lesson, segment 3; objective 6)

b. & c. are incorrect. Because of its contextual approach, developmental psychopathology emphasizes group therapy and all domains of development.

7. b. is the correct answer. (p. 336; objective 5)

8. d. is the correct answer. (p. 333; objective 3)

9. b. is the correct answer. (p. 351; video lesson, segment 3; objective 8)

10. c. is the correct answer. (p. 352; objective 9)

11. c. is the correct answer. (pp. 332–333; objective 1)

a. is incorrect. The amount of daily exercise a child receives is an important factor in his or her tendency toward obesity; exercise does not, however, explain most of the variation in childhood physique.

b. is incorrect. In some parts of the world, malnutrition accounts for most of the variation in physique; this is not true of developed countries, where most children get enough food to grow as tall as their genes allow.

12. d. is the correct answer. (pp. 352–353; objective 9)

True or False Items

13. F   Physical variations in children from developed countries are caused primarily by heredity. (p. 332; objective 1)

14. F   If obesity is established in middle childhood, it tends to continue into adulthood. (p. 334; video lesson, segment 1; objective 2)

15. T   (p. 333; objective 3)

16. F   In childhood, reaction time depends primarily on brain maturation, which is related to age. (p. 336; objective 5)

17. F   With the proper assistance, many children with learning disabilities develop into adults who are virtually indistinguishable from other adults in their educational and occupational achievements. (p. 343; video lesson, segment 3; objective 7)

18. F   Strenuous dieting during childhood can be dangerous. The best way to get children to lose weight is by increasing their activity level. (p. 333; video lesson, segment 1; objective 3)

19. F   The causes of learning disabilities are difficult to pinpoint and cannot be specified with certainty. (p. 351; video lesson, segment 3; objective 7)

20. F   AD/HD is more often diagnosed in the United States than in Great Britain. (p. 352; objective 8)

21. T   (p. 352; objective 9)

Practice Questions II

Multiple-Choice Questions

1. a. is the correct answer. (p. 332; video lesson, segment 1; objective 1)

   b. & c. are incorrect. During this period children gain about 5 pounds per year and experience increased lung capacity.

   d. is incorrect. Although childhood obesity is a common problem, the textbook does not indicate that a person is more likely to become obese at this age than at any other.

2. d. is the correct answer. (p. 333; objective 3)

3. a. is the correct answer. (p. 349; video lesson, segment 3; objective 7)

   b. is incorrect. This learning disability involves math rather than reading.

   c. & d. are incorrect. These disorders do not manifest themselves in a particular academic skill but instead appear in psychological processes that affect learning in general.

4. a. is the correct answer. (p. 346; video lesson, segment 3; objective 7)

   b. & c. are incorrect. AD/HD is a general learning disability that usually does not manifest itself in specific subject areas. Hyperactivity is a facet of this disorder.

   d. is incorrect. Dyscalcula (or dyscalculia) is a learning disability in math only.

5. b. is the correct answer. (video lesson, segment 1; objective 2)

6. d. is the correct answer. (p. 352; video lesson, segment 3; objective 9)

7. b. is the correct answer. (p. 336; objective 5)

8. a. is the correct answer. (p. 346; video lesson, segment 3; objective 7)

9. c. is the correct answer. (p. 337; objective 1)

10. d. is the correct answer. (pp. 331–332; video lesson, segment 1; objective 2)

11. c. is the correct answer. (p. 354; objective 10)

    a. is incorrect. Many general education teachers are unable to cope with the special needs of some children.

    b. & d. are incorrect. These approaches undermined the social integration of children with special needs.

12. b. is the correct answer. (p. 351; objective 8)

Matching Items

13. c (p. 346; objective 4)
14. e (p. 349; video lesson, segment 3; objective 7)
15. h (p. 349; video lesson, segment 3; objective 7)
16. a (p. 346; video lesson, segment 3; objective 7)
17. g (p. 351; video lesson, segment 3; objective 8)
18. f (p. 335; objective 4)
19. i (p. 342; video lesson, segment 3; objective 6)
20. b (p. 343; objective 6)
21. d (p. 353; video lesson, segment 3; objective 10)

Applying Your Knowledge

1. c. is the correct answer. (p. 336; objective 5)

    a. & b. are incorrect. Each of these games involves skills that are hardest for schoolchildren to master.

    d. is incorrect. Because one-on-one sports are likely to accentuate individual differences in ability, they may be especially discouraging to some children.

2. b. is the correct answer. (p. 342; video lesson, segment 3; objective 6)

3. d. is the correct answer. (p. 351; video lesson, segment 3; objective 8)

    a. & b. are incorrect. Paul's difficulty is in concentrating, not in reading (dyslexia) or math (dyscalcula or dyscalculia).

    c. is incorrect. Autism is characterized by a lack of communication skills.

4. c. is the correct answer. (p. 332; objective 1)

5. d. is the correct answer. (p. 351; video lesson, segment 3; objective 8)

6. d. is the correct answer. (p. 336; objective 5)

7. a. is the correct answer. (p. 334; objective 2)

    b., c., & d. are incorrect. Obese children are no more likely to be dyslexic, physically intimidating, or hyperactive than other children.

8. c. is the correct answer. (p. 346; video lesson, segment 3; objective 7)

9. c. is the correct answer. (p. 352; objective 8)

10. c. is the correct answer. Medication alone cannot ameliorate all the problems of AD/HD. (pp. 352–353; video lesson, segment 3; objective 9)

11. d. is the correct answer. There is no evidence that teratogens have anything to do with obesity. (p. 333; objective 3)

12. c. is the correct answer. BMI = weight/height squared. Therefore, BMI for Curtis = 26.4/1.49, or 17.7. For children at age 8, obesity begins at about 18 BMI. (video lesson, segment 1; objective 2)

Lesson Review

Lesson 16

The School Years
Biosocial Development

Please Note: Use this matrix to guide your study and achieve the learning objectives of this lesson. It will also help you to view the video, which defines and demonstrates important concepts and skills as they relate to everyday life.

Learning Objective	Textbook	Telecourse Student Guide	Video Lesson
1. Describe normal physical growth and development during middle childhood, and account for the usual variations among children.	pp. 331–332, 337, 341	Practice Questions I: 1, 2, 11, 13; Practice Questions II: 1, 9, 10; Applying Your Knowledge: 4.	Segment 1: *Physical Growth*
2. Discuss the problem of childhood obesity and its potential effects on a child's physical and psychological health.	pp. 332–335, 342	Key Terms: 1; Practice Questions I: 5, 14; Practice Questions II: 5, 10; Applying Your Knowledge: 7, 12.	Segment 1: *Physical Growth*
3. Identify the major causes of obesity, and outline the best approaches for treatment.	pp. 333–334	Practice Questions I: 3, 8, 15, 17, 18; Practice Questions II: 2; Applying Your Knowledge: 11.	Segment 1: *Physical Growth*
4. Discuss other common health and biological problems of the school years, focusing on their causes, treatment, and impact on development.	pp. 335, 346	Key Terms: 2; Practice Questions II: 13, 18.	
5. Describe motor-skill development during the school years, focusing on variations due to gender, culture, and genetics.	p. 336	Key Terms: 3; Practice Questions I: 7, 16; Practice Questions II: 7; Applying Your Knowledge: 1, 6.	Segment 2: *Motor-Skill Development*

Learning Objective	Textbook	Telecourse Student Guide	Video Lesson
6. Outline the developmental psychopathology perspective, and discuss its value in treating children with special needs.	pp. 340–343	Key Terms: 4, 5, 6; Practice Questions I: 6; Practice Questions II: 19, 20; Applying Your Knowledge: 2.	Segment 3: *Special Needs*
7. Discuss the characteristics and possible causes of learning disabilities.	pp. 346–351, 355	Key Terms: 7, 8, 9, 10; Practice Questions I: 4, 19; Practice Questions II: 3, 4, 8, 14, 15, 16; Applying Your Knowledge: 8.	Segment 3: *Special Needs*
8. Describe the symptoms and possible causes of attention-deficit hyperactivity disorder (AD/HD).	pp. 351–352	Key Terms: 11; Practice Questions I: 9, 20; Practice Questions II: 12, 17; Applying Your Knowledge: 3, 5, 9.	Segment 3: *Special Needs*
9. Discuss the types of treatment available for children with attention-deficit hyperactivity disorder.	pp. 352–353, 359–361	Practice Questions I: 10, 12, 21; Practice Questions II: 6; Applying Your Knowledge: 10.	Segment 3: *Special Needs*
10. Describe techniques that have been tried in efforts to educate children with special needs.	pp. 352–353	Key Terms: 12, 13, 14; Practice Questions II: 13, 21. Applying Your Knowledge: 7.	Segment 3: *Special Needs*

The Age of Reason

Lesson 17

The School Years:
Cognitive Development

Preview

Lesson 17 looks at the development of cognitive abilities in children from age 7 to 11. The first part of the lesson focuses on Jean Piaget's view of the child's cognitive development in this period, which involves a growing ability to use logic and reasoning. Next, we discuss changes in the child's **selective attention**, processing speed and capacity, memory strategies, **knowledge base**, and problem-solving strategies.

The lesson also looks at moral reasoning and language learning in the school years. During this time, children develop a more analytic understanding of words and show a marked improvement in pragmatic skills, such as changing from one form of speech to another when the situation so demands. The linguistic and cognitive advantages of bilingualism are discussed, as are educational and environmental conditions that are conducive to fluency in a second language.

The final part of the lesson describes innovative teaching methods, which emphasize active rather than passive learning and are derived from the developmental theories of Piaget, Vygotsky, and others. Studies that contrast these methods with more traditional approaches have shown their effectiveness in reading and math education. Comparing education in the United States, Japan, and the Republic of China illuminates several possible reasons for the disparities. The lesson concludes by examining measures of cognitive growth, such as tests, and variations in cultural standards.

As you complete this lesson, consider the cognitive development of a child you know and/or interview the parent of a child in this age range (about age 6 to 11). Describe the cognitive skills of this child. In other words, how well can he or she focus attention, solve problems, and apply logical principles to the world. How well can this child recall facts, events and other memories? Describe the language skills of this child relative to younger and older children, including vocabulary and grammar. Does he or she speak a second language? Now, consider this child's moral development. Describe his or her moral code and how it applies to everyday decisions? Finally, how well does this child perform in school? Speculate on why. What techniques are used in the classroom to teach subjects such as reading and math.

Prior Telecourse Knowledge that Will Be Used in this Lesson

- This lesson will introduce "**concrete operational thought,**" the third stage in Jean Piaget's theory of cognitive development (from Lesson 1). Recall that Piaget's theory specifies four major periods of cognitive development:

  1. Sensorimotor (birth to 2 years)
  2. Preoperational (2 to 6 years)
  3. **Concrete Operational (7 to 11 years)** ← **The School Years**
  4. Formal Operational (12 years through adulthood)

- During its exploration of school learning, this lesson will return to Lev Vygotsky's theory of development (from Chapter 2/Lesson 1). Recall that Vygotsky emphasized the importance of *guided participation,* a learning process in which an individual learns through social interaction with a mentor.

Learning Objectives

Use this information to guide your reading, viewing, thinking, and studying. After successfully completing this lesson, you should be able to:

1. Identify and describe the characteristics of concrete operational thought and give examples of how this type of thinking is demonstrated by schoolchildren.
2. Describe the components of the information-processing system, noting how they interact.
3. Discuss advances in the knowledge base, processing speed and capacity, and memory skills during middle childhood.
4. Discuss advances in selective attention and other cognitive control processes during the school years.
5. Describe language development during the school years, noting changing abilities in vocabulary, grammar, and code-switching.
6. Outline Kohlberg's stage theory of moral development and describe several criticisms of the theory.
7. Compare the academic performance of children in countries around the world, and identify differences in culture, school, and home life that may account for differences in academic performance.
8. Identify several conditions that foster the learning of a second language, and describe different strategies for teaching another language to school-age children.
9. Differentiate several approaches to teaching reading and math and discuss evidence regarding the effectiveness of these methods.

📖 **Read Chapter 12, "The School Years: Cognitive Development," pages 359–391.**

📼 **View the video for Lesson 17, "The Age of Reason."**

Segment 1: *How School-Age Children Think*

Segment 2: *Language Development*

Summary

Cognitive development between the ages of 7 and 11 is impressive, replaced by children's improved reasoning strategies, mastery of school-related skills, and use of language. For children around the world, the transition into middle childhood marks a passage into a new phase of cognitive development some call the "age of reason." For Piaget, the age of reason begins with the shift from preoperational to **concrete operational thought**. When this transition is complete, children are much better able to understand logical principles, as long as they are applied to tangible, concrete examples.

Among the logical operations schoolchildren acquire are the principle that an entity remains the same despite changes in its appearance (**conservation**), that certain characteristics of an object remain the same when other characteristics are changed (**identity**), that something that has been changed can be returned to its original state by reversing the process (**reversibility**), and that a change in one object can be compensated for by a corresponding change in another (**reciprocity**).

The information-processing view of cognitive development places more emphasis than Piaget does on the ways in which children process their experiences. The ability to selectively attend to, rehearse, store, organize, and retrieve information improves steadily during middle childhood. Schoolchildren also have a larger processing capacity and knowledge base than they did earlier. The ability to evaluate a cognitive task and to monitor one's performance, called **metacognition**, also improves during the school years. The information-processing approach emphasizes that the most effective way to teach is to adapt teaching materials and sequence of instruction to fit the needs of the individual child.

Logical thought processes also foster moral development, as school-age children become better able to grasp moral laws and ethical principles. Lawrence Kohlberg identified three levels of moral reasoning (each level including two stages):

- Preconventional: Emphasis on avoiding punishment and obtaining rewards. *Stage 1:* Might makes right. *Stage 2:* Look out for number one.

- Conventional: Emphasis on social rules. *Stage 3:* "good girl" and "nice boy." *Stage 4:* "law and order."

- Postconventional: Emphasis on moral principles. *Stage 5:* social contract. *Stage 6:* universal ethical principles.

Language development during these years is also extensive, with children showing improvement in vocabulary, grammar, and pragmatic use of language. This is clearly indicated by their newly found delight in words and their growing sophistication in telling jokes. School-age children can also easily engage in **code-switching**, from the **formal code** used with teachers to the **informal code** used with friends.

Special Note: We will cover the topic of school learning in more detail in telecourse Lesson 20, "School Days."

📖   **Review all reading assignments for this lesson.**

💻   **As assigned by your instructor, complete the optional online component for this lesson.**

Key Terms

Using your own words, write a brief definition or explanation of each of the following terms on a separate piece of paper.

1. concrete operational thought
2. classification
3. identity
4. reversibility
5. sensory register
6. working memory
7. long-term memory
8. knowledge base
9. control processes
10. selective attention
11. metacognition
12. code-switching
13. formal code
14. informal code
15. preconventional moral reasoning
16. conventional moral reasoning
17. postconventional moral reasoning
18. Defining Issues Test (DIT)
19. morality of care
20. morality of justice
21. phonics approach
22. whole-language approach
23. total immersion
24. conservation
25. reciprocity
26. information processing theory
27. bilingual education
28. English as a Second Language (ESL)

Practice Questions I

Multiple-Choice Questions

1. According to Piaget, the stage of cognitive development in which a person understands specific logical ideas and can apply them to concrete problems is called

   a. preoperational thought.
   b. operational thought.
   c. concrete operational thought.
   d. formal operational thought.

2. Which of the following is the most direct reason thinking speed continues to increase throughout adolescence?

   a. the increasing myelination of neural axons
   b. the continuing development of the frontal cortex
   c. learning from experience
   d. neurological maturation

3. The idea that an object that has been transformed in some way can be restored to its original form by undoing the process is

   a. identity.
   b. reversibility.
   c. total immersion.
   d. automatization.

4. Information-processing theorists contend that major advances in cognitive development occur during the school years because

   a. the child's mind becomes more like a computer as he or she matures.

   b. children become better able to process and analyze information.

   c. most mental activities become automatic by the time a child is about 13 years old.

   d. the major improvements in reasoning that occur during the school years involve increased long-term memory capacity.

5. The ability to filter out distractions and concentrate on relevant details is called

   a. metacognition.

   b. information processing.

   c. selective attention.

   d. decentering.

6. Concrete operational thought is Piaget's term for the school-age child's ability to

   a. reason logically about things and events he or she perceives.

   b. think about thinking.

   c. understand that certain characteristics of an object remain the same when other characteristics are changed.

   d. understand that moral principles may supercede the standards of society.

7. The term for the ability to monitor one's cognitive performance—to think about thinking—is

   a. pragmatics.

   b. information processing.

   c. selective attention.

   d. metacognition.

8. Long-term memory is _____ permanent and _____ limited than working memory.

   a. more; less

   b. less; more

   c. more; more

   d. less; less

9. In making moral choices, according to Gilligan, females are more likely than males to

   a. score at a higher level in Kohlberg's system.

   b. emphasize the needs of others.

   c. judge right and wrong in absolute terms.

   d. formulate abstract principles.

10. Compared to language development among more advantaged children, children from low-income families show deficits in

   a. vocabulary.

   b. syntax.

   c. sentence length.

   d. all of the above.

11. The formal code that children use in the classroom is characterized by

    a. limited use of vocabulary and syntax.

    b. context-bound grammar.

    c. extensive use of gestures and intonation to convey meaning.

    d. extensive vocabulary, complex syntax, and lengthy sentences.

12. Which of the following is **NOT** an approach used in the United States to avoid the shock of complete immersion in the teaching of English?

    a. reverse immersion

    b. English as a second language

    c. bilingual education

    d. bilingual-bicultural education

13. Code-switching occurs most often among

    a. low-income children.

    b. affluent children.

    c. ethnic minority children.

    d. all of the above; children of all backgrounds and ethnicities code-switch.

14. Between 9 and 11 years of age, children are most likely to demonstrate moral reasoning at which of Kohlberg's stages?

    a. preconventional

    b. conventional

    c. postconventional

    d. It is impossible to predict based only on a child's age.

15. Of the following, which was **NOT** identified as an important factor in the difference between success and failure in second-language learning?

    a. the age of the child

    b. the attitudes of the parents

    c. community values regarding second-language learning

    d. the difficulty of the language

True or False Items

Write T (for true) or F (for false) on the line in front of each statement.

16. _____ One major objection to Piaget's theory is that it describes the schoolchild as an active learner, a term appropriate only for preschoolers.

17. _____ Learning a second language fosters children's overall linguistic and cognitive development.

18. _____ During middle childhood, children are passionately concerned with issues of right and wrong.

19. _____ As a group, children from Japan, China, and Korea outscore children from the United States and Canada in math and science.

20. _____ The process of telling a joke involves pragmatic language skills usually not mastered before age 7.

21. _____ Code-switching, especially the occasional use of slang, is a behavior characteristic primarily of children in the lower social strata.

22. _____ The best time to learn a second language by listening and talking is during middle childhood.

23. _____ Most information that comes into the sensory register is lost or discarded.

24. _____ Information-processing theorists believe that advances in the thinking of school-age children occur primarily because of changes in long-term memory.

25. _____ New standards of math education in many nations emphasize problem-solving skills rather than simple memorization of formulas.

Practice Questions II

Multiple-Choice Questions

1. According to Piaget, eight- and nine-year-olds can reason only about concrete things in their lives. "Concrete" means

   a. logical.
   b. abstract.
   c. tangible or specific.
   d. mathematical or classifiable.

2. Recent research regarding Piaget's theory has found that

   a. cognitive development seems to be considerably more affected by sociocultural factors than Piaget's descriptions imply.
   b. the movement to a new level of thinking is much less erratic than Piaget predicted.
   c. there is no "5-to-7 shift."
   d. all of the above are true.

3. The increase in processing speed that occurs during middle childhood is partly the result of

   a. ongoing myelination of axons.
   b. neurological development in the limbic system.
   c. the streamlining of the knowledge base.
   d. all of the above.

4. When psychologists look at the ability of children to receive, store, and organize information, they are examining cognitive development from a view based on

   a. the observations of Piaget.
   b. information processing.
   c. learning theory.
   d. the idea that the key to thinking is the sensory register.

5. Kohlberg's stage theory of moral development is based on his research on a group of boys and on
   a. psychoanalytic ideas.
   b. Piaget's theory of cognitive development.
   c. Carol Gilligan's research on moral dilemmas.
   d. questionnaires distributed to a nationwide sample of high school seniors.

6. The logical operations of concrete operational thought are particularly important to an understanding of the elementary-school subject(s) of
   a. spelling.
   b. reading.
   c. math and science.
   d. social studies.

7. Although older school-age children are generally at the conventional level of moral reasoning, when they reach a particular level depends on
   a. the specific context and the child's opportunity to discuss moral issues.
   b. the level of moral reasoning reached by their parents.
   c. how strongly their peers influence their thinking.
   d. whether they are male or female.

8. Which of the following Piagetian ideas is **NOT** widely accepted by developmentalists today?
   a. The thinking of school-age children is characterized by a more comprehensive logic than that of preschoolers.
   b. Children are active learners.
   c. How children think is as important as what they know.
   d. Once a certain type of reasoning ability emerges in children, it is evenly apparent in all domains of thinking.

9. Processing capacity refers to
   a. the ability to selectively attend to more than one thought.
   b. the amount of information that a person is able to hold in working memory.
   c. the size of the child's knowledge base.
   d. all of the above.

10. The retention of new information is called
    a. retrieval.
    b. storage.
    c. automatization.
    d. metacognition.

11. According to Kohlberg, a person who is a dutiful citizen and obeys the laws set down by society would be at which level of moral reasoning?
    a. preconventional stage one
    b. preconventional stage two
    c. conventional
    d. postconventional

12. Which aspect of the information-processing system assumes an executive role in regulating the analysis and transfer of information?

    a. sensory register

    b. working memory

    c. long-term memory

    d. control processes

13. An example of schoolchildren's growth in metacognition is their understanding that

    a. transformed objects can be returned to their original state.

    b. rehearsal is a good strategy for memorizing, but outlining is better for understanding.

    c. objects may belong to more than one class.

    d. they can use different language styles in different situations.

14. Which of the following most accurately states the relative merits of the phonics approach and the whole-language approach to teaching reading?

    a. The phonics approach is more effective.

    b. The whole-language approach is more effective.

    c. Both approaches have merit.

    d. Both approaches have been discarded in favor of newer, more interactive methods of instruction.

15. Regarding bilingual education, many contemporary developmentalists believe that

    a. the attempted learning of two languages is confusing to children and delays proficiency in either one or both languages.

    b. bilingual education is linguistically, culturally, and cognitively advantageous to children.

    c. second-language education is most effective when the child has not yet mastered the native language.

    d. bilingual education programs are too expensive to justify the few developmental advantages they confer.

Matching Items

Match each term or concept with its corresponding description or definition.

Terms or Concepts

16. _____ automatization   22. _____ retrieval

17. _____ reversibility   23. _____ storage

18. _____ conventional   24. _____ metacognition

19. _____ identity   25. _____ immersion

20. _____ information processing   26. _____ postconventional

21. _____ selective attention   27. _____ preconventional

Descriptions or Definitions

    a. the ability to screen out distractions and concentrate on relevant information

    b. the idea that a transformation process can be undone to restore the original conditions

    c. the idea that certain characteristics of an object remain the same even when other characteristics change

d. developmental perspective that conceives of cognitive development as the result of changes in the processing and analysis of information

e. moral reasoning in which the individual focuses on his or her own welfare

f. moral reasoning in which the individual follows principles that supersede the standards of society

g. an educational technique in which instruction occurs entirely in the second language

h. accessing previously learned information

i. holding information in memory

j. moral reasoning in which the individual considers social standards and laws to be primary

k. process by which familiar mental activities become routine

l. the ability to evaluate a cognitive task and to monitor one's performance on it

Applying Your Knowledge

1. Of the following statements made by children, which best exemplifies the logical principle of identity?

   a. "You can't leave first base until the ball is hit!"

   b. "See how the jello springs back into shape after I poke my finger into it?"

   c. "I know it's still a banana, even though it's mashed down in my sandwich."

   d. "You're my friend, so I don't have to use polite speech like I do with adults."

2. Which of the following statements is the clearest indication that the child has grasped the principle of reversibility?

   a. "See, the lemonade is the same in both our glasses; even though your glass is taller than mine, it's narrower."

   b. "Even though your dog looks funny, I know it's still a dog."

   c. "I have one sister and no brothers. My parents have two children."

   d. "I don't cheat because I don't want to be punished."

3. Compared to her four-year-old sister, nine-year-old Andrea is more likely to seek explanations that are

   a. intuitive.

   b. generalizable.

   c. subjective.

   d. all of the above.

4. Dr. Larsen believes that the cognitive advances of middle childhood occur because of basic changes in children's thinking speed, knowledge base, and memory retrieval skills. Dr. Larsen evidently is working from the _____ perspective.

   a. Piagetian

   b. Vygotskian

   c. information-processing

   d. psychoanalytic

5. Some researchers believe that cognitive processing speed and capacity increase during middle childhood because of
   a. the myelination of nerve pathways.
   b. the maturation of the frontal cortex.
   c. better use of cognitive resources.
   d. all of the above.

6. A child's ability to tell a joke that will amuse his or her audience always depends on
   a. the child's mastery of reciprocity and reversibility.
   b. code switching.
   c. the child's ability to consider another's perspective.
   d. an expansion of the child's processing capacity.

7. For a ten-year-old, some mental activities have become so familiar or routine as to require little mental work. This development is called
   a. selective attention.
   b. identity.
   c. metacognition.
   d. automatization.

8. Lana is age 4 and her brother Roger is 7. The fact that Roger remembers what their mother just told them about playing in the street while Lana is more interested in the children playing across the street is the result of improvements in Roger's
   a. control processes.
   b. automatization.
   c. selective attention.
   d. long-term memory.

9. Which of the following statements is the best example of Kohlberg's concept of stage 1 preconventional moral reasoning?
   a. "Might makes right."
   b. "Law and order."
   c. "Nice boys do what is expected of them."
   d. "Look out for number one."

10. According to Carol Gilligan, a girl responding to the hypothetical question of whether an impoverished child should steal food to feed her starving dog is most likely to
    a. respond according to a depersonalized standard of right and wrong.
    b. hesitate to take a definitive position based on the abstract moral premise of "right and wrong."
    c. immediately respond that the child was justified in stealing the food.
    d. respond unpredictably, based on her own personal experiences.

11. Four-year-old Tasha, who is learning to read by sounding out the letters of words, evidently is being taught using which approach?

    a. phonics

    b. whole-word

    c. immersion

    d. reverse immersion

12. As compared with her five-year-old brother, seven-year-old Althea has learned to adjust her vocabulary to her audience. This is known as

    a. selective attention.

    b. a retrieval strategy.

    c. code-switching.

    d. classification.

13. Critics of Kohlberg's theory of moral development argue that it

    a. places too much emphasis on sociocultural factors.

    b. places too much emphasis on traditional, religious beliefs.

    c. is biased toward liberal, Western cultural beliefs.

    d. can't be tested.

Answer Key

Key Terms

1. During Piaget's stage of concrete operational thought, lasting from ages 7 to 11, children can think logically about concrete events and objects but are not able to reason abstractly. (p. 359; video lesson, segment 1; objective 1)

2. Classification is the concept that objects can be organized into categories or classes according to some common property. (p. 360; objective 1)

3. In Piaget's theory, identity is the logical principle that certain characteristics of an object remain the same even when other characteristics change. (p. 361; video lesson, segment 1; objective 1)

4. Reversibility is the logical principle that a transformation process can be reversed to restore the original conditions. (p. 361; video lesson, segment 1; objective 1)

5. Sensory register is the memory system that stores incoming stimuli for a fraction of a second, after which it is passed into working memory, or discarded as unimportant; also called short-term memory. (p. 363; video lesson, segment 1; objective 2)

6. Working memory is the part of memory that handles current, conscious mental activity. (p. 363; video lesson, segment 1; objective 2)

7. Long-term memory is the part of memory that stores unlimited amounts of information for days, months, or years. (p. 364; video lesson, segment 1; objective 2)

8. The knowledge base is a body of knowledge in a particular area that has been learned and on which additional learning can be based. (p. 364; objective 3)

9. Control processes (such as selective attention and retrieval strategies) regulate the analysis and flow of information in memory. (p. 365; objective 4)

10. Selective attention is the ability to screen out distractions and concentrate on relevant information. (p. 366; objective 4)

11. Metacognition is the ability to evaluate a cognitive task to determine what to do and to monitor one's performance on that task. (p. 366; objective 4)

12. Code switching is a pragmatic communication skill involving changing from one form of speech to another. (p. 371; video lesson, segment 2; objective 5)

13. The formal code is a form of speech used by children in school and other formal situations, characterized by extensive vocabulary, complex syntax, and lengthy sentences. (p. 371; video lesson, segment 2; objective 5)

14. The informal code is a form of speech used by children in casual situations, characterized by limited vocabulary and syntax. (p. 372; video lesson, segment 2; objective 5)

15. Kohlberg's first level of moral reasoning, preconventional moral reasoning, emphasizes obedience to authority in order to avoid punishment (stage 1) and being nice to other people so they will be nice to you (stage 2). (pp. 373–374; objective 6)

16. Kohlberg's second level of moral reasoning, conventional moral reasoning, emphasizes winning the approval of others (stage 3) and obeying the laws set down by those in power (stage 4). (pp. 373–374; objective 6)

17. Kohlberg's third level, postconventional moral reasoning, emphasizes the social and contractual nature of moral principles (stage 5) and the existence of universal ethical principles (stage 6). (pp. 373–374; objective 6)

18. The Defining Issues Test (DIT) is a questionnaire that measures moral reasoning by asking people to rank various possible resolutions to moral dilemmas. (p. 375; objective 6)

19. Compared with boys and men, girls and women are more likely to develop a morality of care that is based on comparison, nurturance, and concern for the well-being of others. (p. 375; objective 6)

20. Compared with girls and women, boys and men are more likely to develop a morality of justice based on depersonalized standards of right and wrong. (p. 375; objective 6)

21. The phonics approach is a method of teaching reading by having children learn the sounds of letters before they begin to learn words. (p. 381 ; objective 9)

22. The whole-language approach is a method of teaching reading by encouraging children to develop all their language skills simultaneously. (p. 381; objective 9)

23. Total immersion is an approach to bilingual education in which the child's instruction occurs entirely in the new language. (p. 384; video lesson, segment 2; objective 8)

24. Conservation is the principle that the amount of a substance is unaffected by changes in its appearance. (p. 265; video lesson, segment 1; objective 1)

25. Reciprocity is the logical principle that two objects, quantities, or actions can be mutually related, such that a change in one can be compensated for by a corresponding or opposite change in another. (video lesson, segment 1; objective 1)

26. Information processing theory is a perspective that compares human thinking processes, by analogy, to computer analysis of data—from sensory input through brain reactions, connections, and stored memories, to output. (p. 176; video lesson, segment 1; objective 2)

27. Bilingual education is an approach to teaching a second language that also advances knowledge in the first language. Instruction occurs, side by side, in two languages. (video lesson, segment 2; objective 8)

Lesson 17/The School Years: Cognitive Development   **269**

28. English as a second language (ESL) instruction is an approach to teaching English in which English is the only language of instruction for students who speak many other native languages. (video lesson, segment 2; objective 8)

Practice Questions I

Multiple-Choice Questions

1. c. is the correct answer. (p. 359; video lesson, segment 1; objective 1)

   a. is incorrect. Preoperational thought is "pre-logical" thinking.

   b. is incorrect. There is no such stage in Piaget's theory.

   d. is incorrect. Formal operational thought extends logical reasoning to abstract problems.

2. c. is the correct answer. (p. 364; objective 3)

   a., b., & d. are incorrect. Although myelination and the development of the frontal cortex, which are both examples of neurological maturation, partly account for increasing speed of processing, learning is a more direct cause.

3. b. is the correct answer. (p. 361; video lesson, segment 1; objective 1)

   a. is incorrect. This is the concept that certain characteristics of an object remain the same even when other characteristics change.

   c. is incorrect. This is the concept that a change in one dimension of an object can be compensated for by a change in another dimension.

   d. is incorrect. This is the process by which familiar mental activities become routine and automatic.

4. b. is the correct answer. (p. 363; video lesson, segment 1; objectives 2, 3, & 4)

   a. is incorrect. Information-processing theorists use the mind-computer metaphor at every age.

   c. is incorrect. Although increasing automatization is an important aspect of development, the information-processing perspective does not suggest that most mental activities become automatic by age 13.

   d. is incorrect. Most of the important changes in reasoning that occur during the school years are the result of the improved processing capacity of the person's working memory.

5. c. is the correct answer. (pp. 365–366; objective 4)

   a. is incorrect. This is the ability to evaluate a cognitive task and to monitor one's performance on it.

   b. is incorrect. Information processing is a perspective on cognitive development that focuses on how the mind analyzes, stores, retrieves, and reasons about information.

   d. is incorrect. Decentering, which refers to the school-age child's ability to consider more than one aspect of a problem simultaneously, is not discussed in this chapter.

6. a. is the correct answer. (p. 359; video lesson, segment 1; objective 1)

   b. is incorrect. This refers to metacognition.

   c. is incorrect. This refers to Piaget's concept of identity.

   d. is incorrect. This is characteristic of Kohlberg's postconventional moral reasoning.

7. d. is the correct answer. (p. 366; objective 4)

   a. is incorrect. Pragmatics refers to the practical use of language to communicate with others.

b. is incorrect. The information-processing perspective views the mind as being like a computer.

c. is incorrect. This is the ability to screen out distractions in order to focus on important information.

8. a. is the correct answer. (pp. 363–364; video lesson, segment 1; objective 2)

9. b. is the correct answer. (pp. 375–376; objective 6)

10. d. is the correct answer. (p. 367; objective 5)

11. d. is the correct answer. (pp. 371–372; video lesson, segment 2; objective 5)

12. a. is the correct answer. (p. 384; objective 8)

13. d. is the correct answer. (p. 372; video lesson, segment 2; objective 1)

14. b. is the correct answer. (p. 374; objective 6)

15. d. is the correct answer. (p. 385; objective 8)

True or False Items

16. F Most educators agree that the school-age child, like the preschooler, is an active learner. (p. 363; objective 2)

17. T (p. 383; video lesson, segment 2; objective 8)

18. T (pp. 373, 377; objective 6)

19. T (p. 380; objective 7)

20. T (p. 370; video lesson, segment 2; objective 5)

21. F Code-switching (including occasional use of slang) is a behavior demonstrated by all children. (p. 372; video lesson, segment 2; objective 5)

22. F The best time to learn a second language by listening and talking is during early childhood. (p. 383; objective 8)

23. T (p. 363; video lesson, segment 1; objective 2)

24. F They believe that the changes are the result of basic changes in control processes. (p. 365; video lesson, segment 1; objective 4)

25. T (p. 383; objectives 7 & 9)

Practice Questions II

Multiple-Choice Questions

1. c. is the correct answer. (pp. 359–360; video lesson, segment 1; objective 1)

2. a. is the correct answer. (p. 363; objective 1)

3. a. is the correct answer. (p. 364; video lesson, segment 1; objective 3)

b. is incorrect. Neurological development in the frontal cortex facilitates processing speed during middle childhood. The limbic system, which was not discussed in this chapter, is concerned with emotions.

c. is incorrect. Processing speed is facilitated by growth, rather than streamlining, of the knowledge base.

4. b. is the correct answer. (p. 363; video lesson, segment 1; objective 2)

5. b. is the correct answer. (p. 373; objective 6)

6. c. is the correct answer. (p. 361; video lesson, segment 1; objective 1)

7. a. is the correct answer. (p. 377; objective 6)

b., c., & d. are incorrect. Although these may be factors, they don't necessarily determine the child's level of moral reasoning.

8. d. is the correct answer. (p. 363; video lesson, segment 1; objective 1)

9. b. is the correct answer. (p. 364; video lesson, segment 1; objective 2)

10. b. is the correct answer. (p. 364; video lesson, segment 1; objective 3)

   a. is incorrect. This is the accessing of already learned information.

   c. is incorrect. Automatization is the process by which well-learned activities become routine and automatic.

   d. is incorrect. This is the ability to evaluate a task and to monitor one's performance of it.

11. c. is the correct answer. (p. 374; objective 6)

12. d. is the correct answer. (p. 365; video lesson, segment 1; objective 2)

   a. is incorrect. The sensory register stores incoming information for a split second.

   b. is incorrect. Working memory is the part of memory that handles current, conscious mental activity.

   c. is incorrect. Long-term memory stores information for days, months, or years.

13. b. is the correct answer. (pp. 366–367; objective 4)

14. c. is the correct answer. (p. 381; objective 9)

15. b. is the correct answer. (pp. 384–385; objective 8)

Matching Items

16. k (p. 364; objective 4)

17. b (p. 361; video lesson, segment 1; objective 1)

18. j (p. 373; objective 6)

19. c (p. 361; video lesson, segment 1; objective 1)

20. d (p. 363; video lesson, segment 1; objective 2)

21. a (p. 366; objective 4)

22. h (p. 364; video lesson, segment 1; objective 3)

23. i (p. 364; video lesson, segment 1; objective 3)

24. l (p. 366; objective 4)

25. g (p. 384; video lesson, segment 2; objective 8)

26. f (p. 373; objective 6)

27. e (p. 373; objective 6)

Applying Your Knowledge

1. c. is the correct answer. (p. 361; video lesson; objective 1)

   a., b., & d. are incorrect. Identity is the logical principle that certain characteristics of an object (such as the shape of a banana) remain the same even when other characteristics change.

2. a. is the correct answer. (p. 361; video lesson; objective 1)

   b., c., & d. are incorrect. Reversibility is the logical principle that something that has been changed (such as the height of lemonade poured from one glass into another) can be returned to its original shape by reversing the process of change (pouring the liquid back into the other glass).

3. b. is the correct answer. (p. 361; objective 1)

4. c. is the correct answer. (p. 363; objective 2)

   a. is incorrect. This perspective emphasizes the logical, active nature of thinking during middle childhood.

b. is incorrect. This perspective emphasizes the importance of social interaction in learning.

d. is incorrect. This perspective does not address the development of cognitive skills.

5. d. is the correct answer. (p. 364; objective 3)

6. c. is the correct answer. Joke-telling is one of the clearest demonstrations of schoolchildren's improved pragmatic skills, including the ability to know what someone else will think is funny. (p. 370; video lesson, segment 2; objective 5)

7. d. is the correct answer. (p. 364; objective 4)

a. is incorrect. Selective attention is the ability to focus on important information and screen out distractions.

b. is incorrect. Identity is the logical principle that certain characteristics of an object remain the same even when other characteristics change.

c. is incorrect. Metacognition is the ability to evaluate a task and to monitor one's performance of it.

8. c. is the correct answer. (p. 365; objective 4)

a. is incorrect. Control processes regulate the analysis and flow of information.

b. is incorrect. Automatization refers to the tendency of well-rehearsed mental activities to become routine and automatic.

d. is incorrect. Long-term memory is the part of memory that stores information for days, months, or years.

9. a. is the correct answer. (p. 374; objective 6)

b. & c. are incorrect. These exemplify conventional moral reasoning.

d. is incorrect. This exemplifies stage 2 preconventional moral reasoning.

10. b. is the correct answer. Gilligan contends that females' morality of care makes them reluctant to judge right and wrong in absolute terms because they are socialized to be nurturing and caring. (p. 375; objective 6)

11. a. is the correct answer. (p. 381; objective 5)

b. is incorrect. This approach encourages children to develop all their language skills at the same time.

c. & d. are incorrect. These are approaches to bilingual instruction, not reading instruction.

12. c. is the correct answer. (p. 371; video lesson; objective 5)

13. c. is the correct answer. (p. 375; objective 6)

Lesson Review

Lesson 17

The School Years
Cognitive Development

Please Note: Use this matrix to guide your study and achieve the learning objectives of this lesson. It will also help you to view the video, which defines and demonstrates important concepts and skills as they relate to everyday life.

Learning Objective	Textbook	Telecourse Student Guide	Video Lesson
1. Identify and describe the characteristics of concrete operational thought and give examples of how this type of thinking is demonstrated by schoolchildren.	pp. 359–363, 372	Key Terms: 1, 2, 3, 4, 24, 25; Practice Questions I: 1, 2, 6, 8, 17, 19; Practice Questions II: 1, 2, 6, 8, 17, 19; Applying Your Knowledge: 1, 2, 3.	Segment 1: *How School-Age Children Think;* Segment 2: *Language Development*
2. Describe the components of the information-processing system, noting how they interact.	pp. 363–365	Key Terms: 5, 6, 7, 26; Practice Questions I: 4, 8, 16, 23; Practice Questions II: 4, 9, 12, 20; Applying Your Knowledge: 4.	Segment 1: *How School-Age Children Think*
3. Discuss advances in the knowledge base, processing speed and capacity, and memory skills during middle childhood.	pp. 363–364	Key Terms: 8; Practice Questions I: 2, 4; Practice Questions II: 3, 10, 22, 23; Applying Your Knowledge: 5.	Segment 1: *How School-Age Children Think*
4. Discuss advances in selective attention and cognitive control processes during the school years.	pp. 363–367	Key Terms: 9, 10, 11; Practice Questions I: 4, 5, 7, 24; Practice Questions II: 13, 16, 21, 24; Applying Your Knowledge: 7, 8.	Segment 1: *How School-Age Children Think*
5. Describe language development during the school years, noting changing abilities in vocabulary, grammar, and code-switching.	pp. 367–374, 386	Key Terms: 12, 13, 14; Practice Questions I: 10, 11, 20, 21; Applying Your Knowledge: 11, 12.	Segment 2: *Language Development*

Learning Objective	Textbook	Telecourse Student Guide	Video Lesson
6. Outline Kohlberg's stage theory of moral development and describe several criticisms of the theory.	pp. 365, 373–377	Key Terms: 15, 16, 17, 18, 19, 20; Practice Questions I: 9, 14, 18; Practice Questions II: 5, 7, 11, 18, 26, 27; Applying Your Knowledge: 9, 13.	
7. Compare the academic performance of children in countries around the world, and identify differences in school and home life that may account for differences in academic performance.	pp. 374, 380–383	Practice Questions I: 19, 25.	
8. Identify several conditions that foster the learning of a second language, and describe different strategies for teaching another language to school-age children.	pp. 383–385	Key Terms: 23, 27, 28; Practice Questions I: 12, 15, 17, 22; Practice Questions II: 15, 25.	Segment 2: *Language Development*
9. Differentiate several approaches to teaching reading and math and discuss evidence regarding the effectiveness of these methods.	pp. 381–383	Key Terms: 21, 22; Practice Questions I: 25; Practice Questions II: 14.	

A Society of Children

Lesson 18

The School Years:
Psychosocial Development

Preview

We have seen that from about ages 7 to 11, the child becomes stronger and more competent, mastering the biosocial and cognitive abilities that are important in his or her culture. Psychosocial accomplishments are equally impressive.

This lesson begins by exploring the growing social competence of school-age children. Starting with the theories of Freud and Erikson, it moves on to discuss the perspectives of learning, cognitive, sociocultural, and epigenetic systems theorists. The lesson continues with a discussion of the school-age child's growing social awareness and self-understanding.

Children's interaction with peers and others in their ever-widening social world is the next subject of this lesson. In addition to the changing nature of friendships, the problem of bullies and their victims is discussed.

The lesson also explores the structure and function of families in middle childhood, including the experience of parental divorce and remarriage. The lesson closes with a discussion of the ways in which children cope with stressful situations.

As you complete this lesson, recall some of your own social experiences during this age range (7 to 11). How did you spend a typical day? Were you a "social animal" or more of a loner? Who were the friends you spent time with? How do you think your peers at school would have described you during this period? Did you have a school or neighborhood bully? Did you grow up in a family with both of your biological parents or in some other **family structure**? What challenges did you face during this period of life and how did you handle them?

Prior Telecourse Knowledge that Will Be Used in this Lesson

*   The developmental theories of Erik Erikson (from Lesson 1) will be used to help explain psychosocial development during the school years. Recall that Erikson's theory specifies eight stages of psychosocial development, each of which is characterized by a particular challenge, or developmental crisis, which is central to

that stage of life and must be resolved. This lesson will highlight Erikson's fourth stage, "Industry vs. Inferiority":

1. Trust vs. Mistrust (birth to 1 year)
2. Autonomy vs. Shame and Doubt (1 to 3 years)
3. Initiative vs. Guilt (3 to 6 years)
4. **Industry vs. Inferiority (7 to 11 years)** ← **The School Years**
5. Identity vs. Role Confusion (adolescence)
6. Intimacy vs. Isolation (adulthood)
7. Generativity vs. Stagnation (adulthood)
8. Integrity vs. Despair (adulthood)

- This lesson will revisit the concept of "theory of mind" (from Lesson 12), an understanding of human mental processes. During the school years, children gain an increasingly better understanding of the thoughts, emotions, needs, and motivations of others—which allows them to interact more effectively in their social world.

Learning Objectives

Use this information to guide your reading, viewing, thinking, and studying. After successfully completing this lesson, you should be able to:

1. Describe the rising competence and independence of middle childhood from different theoretical perspectives, including Erikson's crisis of "industry vs. inferiority."
2. Define social cognition, and explain how children's theory of mind and emotional understanding evolve during middle childhood.
3. Describe the development of self-understanding during middle childhood and its implications for children's self-esteem.
4. Discuss the importance of peer groups, providing examples of how school-age children develop their own subculture and explaining the importance of this development.
5. Discuss how friendship circles change during the school years.
6. Describe the special problems of rejected children, including bullies and their victims, and discuss possible ways of helping such children.
7. Identify five essential ways in which families nurture school-age children.
8. Differentiate among various family structures, describe how family structures have changed in recent decades, and discuss their impact on the development of school-age children.
9. Summarize the benefits of children living with both biological parents, identify situations in which this may not be the best situation for children, and discuss the potential impact of divorce.
10. Identify the variables that influence the impact of stresses on schoolchildren, and discuss those factors that seem especially important in helping children to cope with problems.

📖 **Read Chapter 13, "The School Years: Psychosocial Development," pages 393–426.**

📺 **View the video for Lesson 18, "A Society of Children."**
Segment 1: *Peers*
Segment 2: *Family*
Segment 3: *Coping*

Summary

The major theories of development emphasize similar characteristics in describing the school-age child. They portray an individual who is much more independent, capable, and open to the challenges of the world. Erikson, for example, refers to these years as the time of industry, while Freud says that sexual concerns are latent. Erikson's "industry" refers to children being busy learning all the skills that will make them productive adults. This means that children in the school years should be learning how to read, write, calculate, socialize with others, and trying things like sports or dance or skill-building hobbies. Learning new skills is the "work" of the school-age child.

As school-age children develop their theory of mind and powers of **social cognition**, they are increasingly aware of the motives, emotions, and personality traits that are the foundation of others' behavior. As their social skills improve, school age children also become better able to adjust their own behavior to interact appropriately with others.

The expanded social world of children in the school years is full of opportunities for growth, as children create their own subculture or "society"—complete with its own language, values, and codes of behavior—and friendships become more selective and exclusive. This expanded world also presents challenges and special problems. This lesson discusses the impact of low self-esteem, divorce, **single-parent families**, **blended families**, and other arrangements on children's psychosocial development. Most children, however, are sufficiently resilient and resourceful to cope with the stresses they may face during middle childhood. The emotional stability of parents and the amount of attention each child receives are significant factors in their healthy adjustment to environmental stress. How well a family nurtures and supports a child depends on how well it meets the child's basic needs, encourages learning, nurtures peer relationships, provides harmony and stability, and develops the child's self-esteem. While children can thrive in almost any structure, children living with both biological parents (either in nuclear or extended families) tend to fare the best.

Special Note: We will discuss how children and adolescents react to stress and cope with problems (pages 419–425) in more detail in telecourse Lesson 25, "Crashing Hard into Adulthood."

📖 **Review all reading assignments for this lesson.**

💻 **As assigned by your instructor, complete the optional online component for this lesson.**

Key Terms

Using your own words, write a brief definition or explanation of each of the following terms on a separate piece of paper.

1. latency
2. industry versus inferiority
3. social cognitive theory
4. social cognition
5. peer group
6. social comparison
7. society of children
8. aggressive-rejected children
9. withdrawn-rejected children
10. bullying
11. family function
12. family structure
13. nuclear family
14. extended family
15. single-parent family
16. blended family
17. grandparent family
18. adoptive family
19. foster family

Practice Questions I

Multiple-Choice Questions

1. Social cognition is defined as
   a. a person's awareness and understanding of human personality, motives, emotions, and interactions.
   b. the ability to form friendships easily.
   c. a person's skill in persuading others to go along with his or her wishes.
   d. the ability to learn by watching another person.

2. A common thread running through the five major developmental theories is that cultures throughout history have selected age 6 as the time for
   a. a period of latency.
   b. the emergence of a theory of mind.
   c. more independence and responsibility.
   d. intellectual curiosity.

3. The best strategy for helping children who are at risk of developing serious psychological problems because of multiple stresses would be to
   a. obtain assistance from a psychiatrist.
   b. change the household situation.
   c. increase the child's competencies or social supports.
   d. reduce the peer group's influence.

4. Compared with preschoolers, older children are more likely to blame
   a. failure on bad luck.
   b. teachers and other authority figures.
   c. their parents for their problems.
   d. themselves for their shortcomings.

5. As rejected children get older,
   a. their problems often get worse.
   b. their problems usually decrease.
   c. their friendship circles typically become larger.
   d. the importance of the peer group to their self-esteem grows weaker.

6. Compared with average or popular children, rejected children tend to be
   a. brighter and more competitive.
   b. affluent and "stuck-up."
   c. economically disadvantaged.
   d. socially immature.

7. A family that consists of two parents, at least one of whom has children from another union, is called a(n) _____ family.
   a. nuclear
   b. extended
   c. blended
   d. single-parent

8. Single parenthood can be beneficial to children when
   a. grandparents are actively helpful.
   b. the child has numerous siblings.
   c. the parent has a live-in boyfriend or girlfriend.
   d. stepchildren are included as siblings.

9. Older schoolchildren tend to be _____ vulnerable to the stresses of life than children who are just beginning middle childhood because they _____.
   a. more; tend to overpersonalize their problems
   b. less; have better developed skills for coping with problems
   c. more; are more likely to compare their well-being with that of their peers
   d. less; are less egocentric

10. Between the ages of 7 and 11, the overall frequency of various psychological problems
   a. increases in both boys and girls.
   b. decreases in both boys and girls.
   c. increases in boys and decreases in girls.
   d. decreases in boys and increases in girls.

11. Studies of single-parent homes demonstrate that when compared with others of the same ethnicity and socioeconomic status, children
    a. fare better in mother-only homes.
    b. fare better in father-only homes, especially if the children are girls.
    c. develop quite similarly in both mother-only and father-only homes.
    d. fare better than children in two-parent homes.

12. During the school years, children become _____ selective about their friends, and their friendship groups become _____.
    a. less; larger
    c. more; larger
    b. less; smaller
    d. more; smaller

13. Erikson sees the crisis of the school years as that of
    a. industry versus inferiority.
    b. acceptance versus rejection.
    c. initiative versus guilt.
    d. male versus female.

True or False Items

Write T (for true) or F (for false) on the line in front of each statement.

14. _____ As they evaluate themselves according to increasingly complex self-theories, school-age children typically experience a rise in self-esteem.

15. _____ During middle childhood, acceptance by the peer group is valued more than having a close friend.

16. _____ Divorce almost always adversely affects the children for at least a year or two.

17. _____ The quality of family interaction seems to be a more powerful predictor of children's development than the actual structure of the family.

18. _____ The income of single-parent households is about the same as that of two-parent households in which only one parent works.

19. _____ School-age children are less able than younger children to cope with the chronic stresses that are troublesome at any age.

20. _____ Unpopular children don't change in popularity status over time.

21. _____ Friendships become more selective and exclusive as children grow older.

Practice Questions II

Multiple-Choice Questions

1. Children who are categorized as _____ are particularly vulnerable to bullying.
   a. aggressive-rejected
   b. passive-aggressive
   c. withdrawn-rejected
   d. passive-rejected

2. The main reason for the special vocabulary, dress codes, and behaviors that flourish within the society of children is that they
   a. lead to clubs and gang behavior.
   b. are unknown to or unapproved by adults.
   c. imitate adult-organized society.
   d. provide an alternative to useful work in society.

3. In the area of social cognition, developmentalists are impressed by the school-age child's increasing ability to
   a. identify and take into account other people's viewpoints.
   b. develop an increasingly wide network of friends.
   c. relate to the opposite sex.
   d. resist social models.

4. The school-age child's greater understanding of emotions is best illustrated by
   a. an increased tendency to take everything personally.
   b. more widespread generosity and sharing.
   c. enhanced understanding of the motivation, origin, and potential future consequences of the actions of others.
   d. a refusal to express unfelt emotions.

5. Typically, children in middle childhood experience a decrease in self-esteem as a result of
   a. a wavering self-theory.
   b. increased awareness of personal shortcomings and failures.
   c. rejection by peers.
   d. difficulties with members of the opposite sex.

6. A ten-year-old's sense of self-esteem is most strongly influenced by his or her
   a. peers.
   b. siblings.
   c. mother.
   d. father.

7. Which of the following most accurately describes how friendships change during the school years?

    a. Friendships become more casual and less intense.

    b. Older children demand less of their friends.

    c. Older children change friends more often.

    d. Close friendships increasingly involve members of the same sex, ethnicity, and socioeconomic status.

8. Which of the following is an accurate statement about school-age bullies?

    a. They are unapologetic about their aggressive behavior.

    b. They usually have friends who abet, fear, and admire them.

    c. Their popularity fades over the years.

    d. All of the above are accurate statements.

9. Which of the following is true of children who live with both biological parents?

    a. They tend to have fewer physical and emotional problems.

    b. They tend to have fewer learning difficulties.

    c. They spend more time with their fathers in their homes.

    d. All of the above are true.

10. Two factors that most often help the child cope well with multiple stresses are social support and

    a. social comparison.

    b. competence in a specific area.

    c. remedial education.

    d. referral to mental health professionals.

11. Some developmentalists believe that the advantage that traditional families confer on the psychosocial development of children is overstated because

    a. many studies do not take sufficient account of other factors that affect child development, such as income.

    b. very little reliable research has been conducted on this issue.

    c. parents often are not honest in reporting their children's problems.

    d. of all of the above reasons.

12. Family _____ is more crucial to children's well-being than family _____ is.

    a. structure; socioeconomic status

    b. socioeconomic status; stability

    c. stability; socioeconomic status

    d. functioning; structure

13. According to Freud, the period between ages 7 and 11 when a child's sexual drives are relatively quiet is the

    a. phallic stage.

    b. genital stage.

    c. period of latency.

    d. period of industry versus inferiority.

14. Research studies have found that children who are forced to cope with one serious ongoing stress (for example, poverty or large family size) are

    a. more likely to develop serious psychiatric problems than children with none of these stresses.

    b. no more likely to develop problems than other children.

    c. more likely to develop intense, destructive friendships than other children.

    d. less likely to be accepted by their peer group.

Matching Items

Match each term or concept with its corresponding description or definition.

Terms or Concepts

15. _____ learning theory

16. _____ social cognition

17. _____ social comparison

18. _____ cognitive theory

19. _____ society of children

20. _____ aggressive-rejected

21. _____ withdrawn-rejected

22. _____ sociocultural theory

23. _____ epigenetic systems theory

24. _____ blended family

25. _____ extended family

Descriptions or Definitions

    a. focused on the acquisition of new skills

    b. adults living with their children from previous marriages as well as their own biological children

    c. an awareness and understanding of others' motives and emotions

    d. one parent, usually the father, sets strict guidelines and rules

    e. focused on the development of social awareness

    f. children who are disliked because of their confrontational nature

    g. evaluating one's abilities by measuring them against those of other children

    h. three or more generations of biologically related individuals living together

    i. contributions from every family member are valued

    j. children who are disliked because of timid, anxious behavior

    k. views middle schoolers' independence as the result of a species need

    l. the games, vocabulary, dress codes, and culture of children

    m. focused on the development of self-understanding

Applying Your Knowledge

1. As an advocate of the epigenetic systems perspective, Dr. Wayans is most likely to explain a ten-year-old child's new independence as the result of
   a. the repression of psychosexual needs.
   b. the acquisition of new skills.
   c. greater self-understanding.
   d. the child's need to join the wider community and the parents' need to focus on younger children.

2. Dr. Ferris believes that skill mastery is particularly important because children develop views of themselves as either competent or incompetent in skills valued by their culture. Dr. Ferris is evidently working from the perspective of
   a. behaviorism.
   b. social learning theory.
   c. Erik Erikson's theory of development.
   d. Freud's theory of development.

3. Cheryl, who is low achieving, shy, and withdrawn, is rejected by most of her peers. Her teacher, who wants to help Cheryl increase her self-esteem and social acceptance, encourages her parents to
   a. transfer Cheryl to a different school.
   b. help their daughter improve her motor skills.
   c. help their daughter learn to accept more responsibility for her academic failures.
   d. help their daughter improve her skills in relating to peers.

4. Miguel, who has no children of his own, is worried about his twelve-year-old niece because she wears unusual clothes and uses vocabulary unknown to him. What should Miguel do?
   a. Tell his niece's parents that they need to discipline their daughter more strictly.
   b. Convince his niece to find a new group of friends.
   c. Recommend that his niece's parents seek professional counseling for their daughter, because such behaviors often are the first signs of a lifelong pattern of antisocial behavior.
   d. Miguel need not necessarily be worried because children typically develop their own subculture of speech, dress, and behavior.

5. Compared with her seven-year-old brother Tommy, ten-year-old Peggy is more likely to describe their cousin
   a. in terms of physical attributes.
   b. as feeling exactly the same way she does when they are in the same social situation.
   c. in terms of personality traits.
   d. in terms of their cousin's outward behavior.

6. Seven-year-old Camille fumes after a friend compliments her new dress, thinking that the comment was intended to be sarcastic. Camille's reaction is an example of
   a. egocentrism.
   b. feelings of inferiority.
   c. the distorted thought processes of an emotionally disturbed child.
   d. immature social cognition.

7. In contrast to younger children, 10-year-old children will often
   a. deny that friendships are important.
   b. state that they prefer same-sex playmates.
   c. have one "best" friend to whom they are quite loyal.
   d. be less choosy about whom they call a friend.

8. Children who are bullies during elementary school
   a. usually remain antisocial.
   b. usually change without encouragement.
   c. later are more likely to form an intense friendship with one person who did not have bully difficulties earlier on.
   d. often become victims of bullying at later ages.

9. After years of an unhappy marriage, Roger and Sheila file for divorce and move 500 miles apart. In ruling on custody for their seven-year-old daughter, the wise judge decides
   a. joint custody should be awarded, because this arrangement is nearly always the most beneficial for children.
   b. the mother should have custody, because this arrangement is nearly always the most beneficial for children in single-parent homes.
   c. the father should have custody, because this arrangement is nearly always the most beneficial for children in single-parent homes.
   d. to investigate the competency of each parent, because whoever was the more competent and more involved parent before the divorce should continue to be the primary caregiver.

10. Of the following children, who is likely to have the lowest overall self-esteem?
    a. Maggie, age 5
    b. Taylor, age 7
    c. Christopher, age 9
    d. Jasmine, age 10

11. Ten-year-old Troy is less optimistic and self-confident than his five-year-old sister. This may be explained in part by the tendency of older children to

    a. evaluate their abilities by comparing them with their own competencies a year or two earlier.
    b. evaluate their competencies by comparing them with those of others.
    c. be less realistic about their own abilities.
    d. do both b and c.

12. Based on research on the norms for childhood aggression, which of the following schoolchildren is likely to be viewed most favorably by his or her peers?

    a. Mike, the class bully
    b. Gwendolyn, who is not arrogant but doesn't shy away from defending herself whenever necessary
    c. Evan, who often suffers attacks from his peers yet refuses to retaliate
    d. Megan, who often suffers attacks from her peers yet refuses to retaliate

13. Of the following children, who is most likely to become a bully?

    a. Callie, who is taller than average
    b. Ricky, who is above average in verbal assertiveness
    c. Matthew, who is insecure and lonely
    d. Amy, who is frequently subjected to physical punishment and verbal criticism at home

14. Which of the following was **NOT** listed as a reason that children living with both biological parents tend to fare best?

    a. Two adults can provide more complete caregiving than one.
    b. Married, biological parents are usually better able to provide financially for their children.
    c. Biological parents are generally more emotionally mature than other parents.
    d. All mammals, including humans, have a genetic impulse to protect and nurture their own children.

Answer Key

Key Terms

1. In Freud's theory, middle childhood is a period of latency, during which emotional drives are quieter and psychosexual needs are repressed. (p. 393; objective 1)

2. According to Erikson, the crisis of middle childhood is that of industry versus inferiority, in which children try to master many skills and develop views of themselves as either competent or incompetent and inferior. (p. 393; video lesson, introduction; objective 1)

3. Social cognitive theory stresses the importance of maturation and experience in stimulating learning, cognition, and cultural advances in children. (p. 394; objective 1)

4. Social cognition refers to a person's awareness and understanding of the personalities, motives, emotions, intentions, and interactions of other people and groups. (p. 396; objective 2)

5. A peer group is a group of individuals of roughly the same age and social status who play, work, or learn together. (p. 397; video lesson, segment 1; objective 4)

6. Social comparison is the tendency to assess one's abilities, achievements, and social status by measuring them against those of others, especially those of one's peers. (p. 397; objective 3)

7. Children in middle childhood develop and transmit their own subculture, called the society of children, which has its own games, vocabulary, dress codes, and rules of behavior. (p. 398; objective 4)

8. The peer group shuns aggressive-rejected children because they are overly confrontational. (p. 400; objective 6)

9. Withdrawn-rejected children are shunned by the peer group because of their withdrawn and anxious behavior. (p. 400; video lesson, segment 1; objective 6)

10. Bullying is the repeated, systematic effort to inflict harm on a child through physical, verbal, or social attack. (p. 402; video lesson, segment 1; objective 6)

11. Family function refers to the ways families work to foster the development of children by meeting their physical needs, encouraging them to learn, and by providing harmony and stability. (p. 408; objective 7)

12 Family structure refers to the legal and genetic relationships that exist between members of a particular family. (p. 408; video lesson, segment 2; objective 8)

13. A nuclear family consists of two parents and their mutual biological offspring. (p. 410; video lesson, segment 2; objective 8)

14. An extended family is one that includes grandparents, aunts, cousins, or other relatives in addition to parents and their children. (p. 410; objective 8)

15. A single-parent family consists of one parent and his or her (usually biological) children. (p. 410; video lesson, segment 2; objective 8)

16. A blended family consists of two parents, at least one with biological children from another union. (p. 410; objective 8)

17. A grandparent family consists of children living with their grandparents instead of with their parents. (p. 410; objective 8)

18. An adoptive family consists of one or more nonbiological children who adults have legally taken as their own. (p. 410; objective 8)

19. A foster family consists of one or more orphaned, neglected, or delinquent children who are temporarily being cared for by an unrelated adult. (p. 410; objective 8)

Practice Questions I

Multiple-Choice Questions

1. a. is the correct answer. (p. 396; objective 2)
2. c. is the correct answer. (p. 395; objective 2)
3. c. is the correct answer. (pp. 422–423; video lesson, segment 3; objective 10)

4. d. is the correct answer. (pp. 396–397; video lesson; objective 3)

   a., b., & c. are incorrect. Compared with preschool children, schoolchildren are more self-critical, and their self-esteem dips, so they blame themselves.

5. a. is the correct answer. (pp. 400–402; objective 6)

6. d. is the correct answer. (p. 401; video lesson, segment 1; objective 6)

7. c. is the correct answer. (pp. 410; objective 8)

8. a. is the correct answer. (p. 414; video lesson, segment 2; objective 9)

   b., c., & d. are incorrect. These factors are likely to increase, rather than decrease, stress, and therefore to have an adverse effect on children.

9. b. is the correct answer. (p. 420; objective 10)

10. b. is the correct answer. (p. 420; objective 10)

11. c. is the correct answer. (pp. 413–414; objective 8)

12. d. is the correct answer. (pp. 399–400; objective 5)

13. a. is the correct answer. (p. 393; video lesson, introduction; objective 1)

True or False Items

14. F   In fact, just the opposite is true. (p. 397; objective 3)

15. F   In fact, just the opposite is true. (p. 399; video lesson, segment 1; objectives 4 & 5)

16. T   (p. 415; video lesson, segment 2; objective 9)

17. T   (p. 414; video lesson, segment 2; objectives 7 & 8)

18. F   The income of single-parent households is substantially lower than that of two-parent households in which only one parent works. (p. 413; objective 8)

19. F   Because of the coping strategies that school-age children develop, they are better able than younger children to cope with stress. (p. 420; objective 10)

20. F   (p. 400; objective 6)

21. T   (pp. 399–400; video lesson, segment 1; objective 5)

Practice Questions II

Multiple-Choice Questions

1. c. is the correct answer. (p. 402; video lesson, segment 1; objective 6)

   a. is incorrect. These are usually bullies.

   b. & d. are incorrect. These are not subcategories of rejected children.

2. b. is the correct answer. (p. 398; objective 4)

3. a. is the correct answer. (p. 396; objective 2)

   b. is incorrect. Friendship circles typically become smaller during middle childhood, as children become more choosy about their friends.

   c. & d. are incorrect. These issues are not discussed in the textbook.

4. c. is the correct answer. (p. 396; objective 2)

5. b. is the correct answer. (p. 397; objective 3)

   a. is incorrect. This tends to promote, rather than reduce, self-esteem.

   c. is incorrect. Only 10 percent of schoolchildren experience this.

   d. is incorrect. This issue becomes more important during adolescence.

6. a. is the correct answer. (pp. 397–398; video lesson, segment 1; objectives 3 & 4)

7. d. is the correct answer. (p. 399; objective 5)

   a., b., & c. are incorrect. In fact, just the opposite is true of friendship during the school years.

8. d. is the correct answer. (p. 404; objective 6)

9. d. is the correct answer. (pp. 412–413; objectives 8 & 9)

10. b. is the correct answer. (p. 422; video lesson, segment 3; objective 10)

11. a. is the correct answer. (p. 413; objectives 8 & 9)

    b. is incorrect. In fact, a great deal of research has been conducted on this issue.

    c. is incorrect. There is no evidence that this is so.

12. d. is the correct answer. (p. 410; video lesson, segment 2; objectives 7 & 8)

13. c. is the correct answer. (p. 393; objective 1)

14. b. is the correct answer. (p. 420; objective 10)

    c. & d. are incorrect. The textbook did not discuss how stress influences friendship or peer acceptance.

Matching Items

15. a (p. 394; objective 1)

16. c (p. 396; objective 2)

17. g (p. 397; objective 3)

18. m (p. 394; objective 1)

19. l (p. 398; objective 4)

20. f (p. 400; objective 6)

21. j (p. 400; objective 6)

22. e (p. 394; objective 1)

23. k (p. 394; objective 1)

24. b (p. 410; objective 8)

25. h (p. 410; objective 8)

Applying Your Knowledge

1. d. is the correct answer. (p. 394; objective 1)

   a. is incorrect. This describes an advocate of Freud's theory of development.

   b. is incorrect. This is the viewpoint of a learning theorist.

   c. is incorrect. This is the viewpoint of a cognitive theorist.

2. c. is the correct answer. The question describes what is, for Erikson, the crisis of middle childhood: industry versus inferiority. (p. 393; objective 1)

3. d. is the correct answer. (pp. 401–402; video lesson, introduction; objective 6)

   a. is incorrect. Because it would seem to involve "running away" from her problems, this approach would likely be more harmful than helpful.

   b. is incorrect. Improving motor skills is not a factor considered in the textbook and probably has little value in raising self-esteem in such situations.

   c. is incorrect. If Cheryl is like most school-age children, she is quite self-critical and already accepts responsibility for her failures.

4. d. is the correct answer. (p. 398; video lesson, segment 1; objective 4)

5. c. is the correct answer. (p. 396; objective 2)

   a., b., & d. are incorrect. These are more typical of preschoolers.

6. d. is the correct answer. (p. 396; objective 2)

   a. is incorrect. Egocentrism is self-centered thinking. In this example, Camille is misinterpreting her friend's comment.

   b. & c. are incorrect. There is no reason to believe that Camille is suffering from an emotional disturbance or that she is feeling inferior.

7. c. is the correct answer. (pp. 399–400; video lesson, segment 1; objective 5)

8. a. is the correct answer. (p. 402; objective 6)

9. d. is the correct answer. (p. 415; objective 9)

10. d. is the correct answer. Self-esteem decreases throughout middle childhood. (p. 397; objective 3)

11. b. is the correct answer. (p. 397; objective 3)

    a. & c. are incorrect. These are more typical of preschoolers than school-age children.

12. b. is the correct answer. (p. 402; video lesson, segment 1; objective 6)

    a. is incorrect. Although a certain amount of aggression is the norm during childhood, children who are perceived as overly arrogant or aggressive are not viewed very favorably.

    c. & d. are incorrect. Both girls and boys are expected to defend themselves when appropriate and are viewed as weak if they do not.

13. d. is the correct answer. (p. 404; objective 6)

    a. & b. are incorrect. It is taller-than-average boys and verbally assertive girls who are more likely to bully others.

    c. is incorrect. This is a common myth.

14. c. is the correct answer. Although emotional maturity is an important factor in family functioning, the textbook does not suggest that biological parents are more mature than other parents. (p. 412; objectives 8 & 9)

Lesson Review

Lesson 18

The School Years
Psychosocial Development

Please Note: Use this matrix to guide your study and achieve the learning objectives of this lesson. It will also help you to view the video, which defines and demonstrates important concepts and skills as they relate to everyday life.

Learning Objective	Textbook	Telecourse Student Guide	Video Lesson
1. Describe the rising competence and independence of middle childhood from different theoretical perspectives, including Erikson's crisis of "industry vs. inferiority."	pp. 393–397	Key Terms: 1, 2, 3, 6; Practice Questions I: 13, 14; Practice Questions II: 13, 15, 18, 22, 23; Applying Your Knowledge: 1, 2.	
2. Define social cognition, and explain how children's theory of mind and emotional understanding evolve during middle childhood.	pp. 395–397	Key Terms: 4; Practice Questions I: 1, 2; Practice Questions II: 3, 4, 16, 17; Applying Your Knowledge: 5, 6.	Segment 1: *Peers*
3. Describe the development of self-understanding during middle childhood and its implications for children's self-esteem.	pp. 396–398	Practice Questions I: 4; Practice Questions II: 5, 6; Applying Your Knowledge: 10, 11.	Segment 1: *Peers*
4. Discuss the importance of peer groups, providing examples of how school-age children develop their own subculture and explaining the importance of this development.	pp. 397–399	Key Terms: 5, 7; Practice Questions I: 15; Practice Questions II: 2, 6, 17, 19; Applying Your Knowledge: 4.	Segment 1: *Peers*
5. Discuss how friendship circles change during the school years.	pp. 397–400	Practice Questions I: 12, 15, 21; Practice Questions II: 7; Applying Your Knowledge: 7.	Segment 1: *Peers*

Learning Objective	Textbook	Telecourse Student Guide	Video Lesson
6. Describe the special problems of unpopular children, bullies and their victims, and discuss possible ways of helping such children.	pp. 400–404	Key Terms: 8, 9, 10; Practice Questions I: 5, 6, 20; Practice Questions II: 1, 8, 20, 21; Applying Your Knowledge: 8, 12, 13.	Segment 1: *Peers*
7. Identify five essential ways in which families nurture school-age children.	pp. 408–414	Key Terms: 11; Practice Questions I: 17; Practice Questions II: 12.	Segment 2: *Family*
8. Differentiate among various basic family structures, describe how family structures have changed in recent decades, and discuss their impact on the development of school-age children.	pp. 408–410	Key Terms: 12, 13, 14, 15, 16, 17, 18, 19; Practice Questions I: 7, 11, 17, 18; Practice Questions II: 9, 11, 12, 24, 25; Applying Your Knowledge: 14	Segment 2: *Family*
9. Summarize the benefits of children living with both biological parents, identify situations in which this may not be the best situation for children, and discuss the potential impact of divorce.	pp. 412–413, 420	Practice Questions I: 8, 16; Practice Questions II: 9, 11; Applying Your Knowledge: 9, 14.	
10. Identify the variables that influence the impact of stresses on schoolchildren, and discuss those factors that seem especially important in helping children to cope with problems.	pp. 401–402, 410, 420–423	Practice Questions I: 3, 9, 10, 19; Practice Questions II: 10, 14; Applying Your Knowledge: 3.	Segment 3: *Coping*

On the Road of Accomplishment

Lesson 19

The School Years:
Summary

Preview

This lesson summarizes biosocial, cognitive, and psychosocial development during the school years (ages 6 to 11).

Middle childhood is a time of achievement, when children rapidly rise from one new accomplishment to another. Erik Erikson captured this idea in his psychosocial crisis for this age period: *industry vs. inferiority*. School-age children are busy trying to master whatever their culture values. Depending on how successful they are, they judge themselves as either competent or incompetent. In the video for this lesson, the developmental issues and accomplishments of middle childhood are revealed in the stories of four individual children.

Although children grow more slowly during this period, they learn to use their bodies in new, more complex ways. Cognitive development between the ages of 6 and 11 is equally impressive, as revealed in children's reasoning strategies, mastery of school-related skills, and use of language. Psychosocial development during middle childhood is characterized by an expanding social world of peer relationships and friendships, along with children's growing awareness of their own personalities, motives, and emotions, as well as those of others.

Prior Telecourse Knowledge that Will Be used in this Lesson

- Biosocial development during middle childhood (from Lesson 16) will be referred to as we discuss the development of motor skills and children with special needs.

- Cognitive development during middle childhood (from Lesson 17) will be referred to as language development is discussed, including the development of a second language.

- Psychosocial development during middle childhood (from Lesson 18) will be referred to as we discuss the child's expanding social world and different family structures (nuclear, single-parent, and blended).

- In the last video segment, you'll see the process of "conditioning" used to treat Sean, a boy with AD/HD (attention-deficit/hyperactivity disorder). Recall from the discussion of behaviorism (in Lesson 1) that *operant conditioning* occurs when a response is gradually learned via *reinforcement*, such as offering a child rewards for positive behavior.

Learning Objectives

Use this information to guide your reading, viewing, thinking, and studying. After successfully completing this lesson, you should be able to:

1. Give examples of the basic pattern of motor-skill development, and discuss variations in biosocial development during middle childhood.

2. Describe cognitive development during middle childhood, focusing on language development and the advantages and challenges of learning English as a second language during this time.

3. Discuss psychosocial development during middle childhood, giving examples of the main developments in the child's social life and self-understanding.

4. Describe the symptoms of AD/HD (attention-deficit/hyperactivity disorder), and discuss the types of treatment available for children with this disorder.

📖 **Read "Summary: The School Years: Biosocial Development," pages 356–357; "Summary: The School Years: Cognitive Development," pages 390–391; "Summary: The School Years: Psychosocial Development," pages 425–426, and "The Developing Person So Far: The School Years, Ages 6 Through 11," page 427.**

Video Viewing Tips

The video for this lesson will feature four school-age children—Jazzmyn (9), Nikki (9), Truong (7), and Sean (11). Each has individual talents, interests, and backgrounds that make his or her journey unique. As you watch each segment, look for these key issues and themes:

Consider how the biosocial development of these four children may have affected their social interactions and self-concept. For example, a child's physical accomplishments can often influence his or her social status and self-esteem (something you're likely to remember if you've ever stood in line to "choose up sides" for a ballgame). Note any significant challenges these children face in their biological development and how these challenges may affect other domains.

Listen to how these children use language, and consider how this might affect their development in other domains. Improved language skills combined with a developing "theory of mind" and social cognition can allow the school-age child to see another person's point of view. This can lead to more sophisticated social interactions and negotiations—crucial skills in the development of relations within the peer group.

Also, note the influence of the school experience on these children. Teachers, the classroom, and the playground provide contexts for development outside the secure and accepting home environment. Watch for evidence of social comparison within the "society of children." How the child handles these often-unforgiving environments can influence his or her self-concept for years to come.

Finally, consider each child's family structure and function. A family that delivers all the basic needs provides a child with the security and confidence to explore the greater physical and social world. Also, note the parenting style in each family and speculate on how this may have affected each child's development. Relationships with parents often provide the prototype for relations with authority figures outside the home.

📟 **View the video for Lesson 19, "On the Road of Accomplishment."**

      Segment 1: *Jazzmyn*

      Segment 2: *Nikki*

      Segment 3: *Truong*

      Segment 4: *Sean*

Summary

Many children, including Nikki in the video lesson, benefit from their parents' authoritative style that encourages communication and independent thinking. For this and other reasons, Nikki is growing up to be a very independent young lady. For children such as Truong, growing up in a family of recent immigrants to the United States poses special challenges in learning to speak a new language and adjust to a new culture. Yet, Truong is meeting these challenges well. A new language is generally learned more easily prior to adolescence, which is why Truong can pick up English more easily than his parents can. Children who have AD/HD (attention-deficit/hyperactivity disorder), such as Sean, find that development in each of the three domains is much more difficult for them than for children without the disorder. With the help of a special form of behavioral conditioning, however, Sean is regaining his developmental stride. It should be noted that not all children with attention deficit exhibit hyperactive behavior like Sean; children who display significant inattention and impulsivity without the hyperactivity are diagnosed with attention-deficit disorder (ADD).

Although most children follow a similar path of growth in each of the three domains of development, their individual achievements depend on their own unique combination of interests, genetics, and talents, as well as the environmental influences exerted by their family, friends, school, and culture. For most boys and girls, the years of middle childhood are a time when biosocial development is smooth and uneventful. Body maturation coupled with sufficient practice enables school-age children to master many motor skills.

Cognitive development between the ages of 6 and 11 is impressive, as reflected by children's reasoning strategies, mastery of school-related skills, and use of language. For children around the world, the transition into middle childhood marks a passage into a new phase of cognitive development some call the "age of reason." For Piaget, the age of reason begins with the shift from preoperational to concrete operational thought. When this transition is complete, children are much better able to understand logical principles, as long as they are applied to concrete examples.

As school-age children develop a more complex view of social interactions, their social awareness and theory of mind begin to mature, and they become increasingly aware of the motives, emotions, and personality traits that are the foundation of others' behavior. As their social skills improve, school-age children also become better able to adjust their own behavior to interact appropriately with others. As they do so, children further develop their self-concept and self-esteem through social comparison—especially with peers.

📖   **Review all reading assignments for this lesson.**

💻   **As assigned by your instructor, complete the optional online component for this lesson.**

Key Terms

Using your own words, write a brief definition or explanation of each of the following terms on a separate piece of paper.

1. learning disability
2. attention-deficit/hyperactivity disorder (AD/HD)
3. mainstreaming
4. middle childhood
5. developmental psychopathology
6. *Diagnostic and Statistical Manual of Mental Disorders* (DSM-IV)
7. attention-deficit disorder (ADD)
8. least restrictive environment
9. concrete operational thought
10. total immersion
11. Industry versus inferiority
12. social cognition
13. social comparison
14. society of children
15. nuclear family
16. single-parent family
17. blended family
18. extended family
19. code switching

Practice Questions

Multiple-Choice Questions

1. As children move into middle childhood,
   a. the rate of accidental death increases.
   b. sexual urges intensify.
   c. the rate of weight gain increases.
   d. biological growth slows and steadies.

2. The increase in processing speed that occurs during middle childhood is partly the result of
   a. ongoing myelination of axons.
   b. neurological development in the limbic system.
   c. the streamlining of the knowledge base.
   d. all of the above.

3. The underlying problem in attention-deficit hyperactivity disorder appears to be
   a. low overall intelligence.
   b. a neurological difficulty in paying attention.
   c. a learning disability in a specific academic skill.
   d. the existence of a conduct disorder.

4. According to the textbook, the most effective form of help for children with AD/HD is
   a. medication.
   b. psychological therapy.
   c. environmental change.
   d. a combination of some or all of the above.

5. Which of the following is true of children with a diagnosed learning disability?
   a. They are, in most cases, average in intelligence.
   b. They often have a specific physical handicap, such as hearing loss.
   c. They often lack basic educational experiences.
   d. All of the above are true.

6. During the school years
   a. boys are, on average, at least a year ahead of girls in the development of physical abilities.
   b. girls are, on average, at least a year ahead of boys in the development of physical abilities.
   c. boys and girls are about equal in physical abilities.
   d. motor-skill development proceeds at a slower pace, since children grow more rapidly at this age than at any other time.

7. Which approach to education may best meet the needs of children with learning disabilities in terms of both skill remediation and social interaction with other children?
   a. mainstreaming
   b. special education
   c. inclusion
   d. resource rooms

8. In determining whether an eight-year-old has a learning disability, a teacher looks primarily for
   a. exceptional performance in a subject area.
   b. the exclusion of other explanations.
   c. both a and b.
   d. none of the above.

9. According to Carol Gilligan, a girl responding to the hypothetical question of whether an impoverished child should steal food to feed her starving dog is most likely to
   a. respond according to a depersonalized standard of right and wrong.
   b. hesitate to take a definitive position based on the abstract moral premise of "right and wrong."
   c. immediately respond that the child was justified in stealing the food.
   d. respond unpredictably, based on her own personal experiences.

10. According to developmentalists, the best game for a typical group of eight-year-olds would be
    a. football or baseball.
    b. basketball.
    c. one in which reaction time is not crucial.
    d. a game involving one-on-one competition.

11. According to Piaget, eight- and nine-year-olds can reason only about concrete things in their lives. "Concrete" means

  a. logical.

  b. abstract.

  c. tangible or specific.

  d. mathematical or classifiable.

12. The logical operations of concrete operational thought are particularly important to an understanding of the elementary-school subject(s) of

  a. spelling.

  b. reading.

  c. math and science.

  d. social studies.

13. Which of the following Piagetian ideas is **NOT** widely accepted by developmentalists today?

  a. The thinking of school-age children is characterized by a more comprehensive logic than that of preschoolers.

  b. Children are active learners.

  c. How children think is as important as what they know.

  d. Once a certain type of reasoning ability emerges in children, it is evenly apparent in all domains of thinking.

14. An example of schoolchildren's growth in metacognition is their understanding that

  a. transformed objects can be returned to their original state.

  b. they can study more efficiently if they discriminate between challenging tasks and information that they already know.

  c. objects may belong to more than one class.

  d. they can use different language styles in different situations.

15. Social cognition is defined as

  a. a person's awareness and understanding of human personality, motives, emotions, and interactions.

  b. the ability to form friendships easily.

  c. a person's skill in persuading others to go along with his or her wishes.

  d. the ability to learn by watching another person.

16. A common thread running through the five major developmental theories is that cultures throughout history have selected ages 7 to 11 as the time for

  a. a period of latency.

  b. the emergence of a theory of mind.

  c. more independence and responsibility.

  d. intellectual curiosity.

17. The best strategy for helping children who are at risk of developing serious psychological problems because of multiple stresses would be to

    a. obtain assistance from a psychiatrist.

    b. change the household situation.

    c. increase the child's competencies or social supports.

    d. reduce the peer group's influence.

18. Compared with average or popular children, rejected children tend to be

    a. brighter and more competitive.

    b. affluent and "stuck-up."

    c. economically disadvantaged.

    d. socially immature.

19. Between the ages of 7 and 11, the overall frequency of various psychological problems

    a. increases in both boys and girls.

    b. decreases in both boys and girls.

    c. increases in boys and decreases in girls.

    d. decreases in boys and increases in girls.

20. Erikson sees the crisis of the school years as that of

    a. industry versus inferiority.

    b. acceptance versus rejection.

    c. initiative versus guilt.

    d. male versus female.

21. In the area of social cognition, developmentalists are impressed by the school-age child's increasing ability to

    a. identify and take into account other people's viewpoints.

    b. develop an increasingly wide network of friends.

    c. relate to the opposite sex.

    d. resist social models.

22. The school-age child's greater understanding of emotions is best illustrated by

    a. an increased tendency to take everything personally.

    b. more widespread generosity and sharing.

    c. enhanced understanding of the motivation, origin, and potential future consequences of the actions of others.

    d. a refusal to express unfelt emotions.

23. Two factors that most often help the child cope well with multiple stresses are social support and

    a. social comparison.

    b. competence in a specific area.

    c. remedial education.

    d. referral to mental health professionals.

24. Which of the following was **NOT** listed as a reason that children living with both biological parents tend to fare best?

    a. Two adults can provide more complete caregiving than one.

    b. Married, biological parents are usually better able to provide financially for their children.

    c. Biological parents are generally more emotionally mature than other parents.

    d. All mammals, including humans, have a genetic impulse to protect and nurture their own children.

True or False Items

Write T (for true) or F (for false) on the line in front of each statement.

25. _____ As they evaluate themselves according to increasingly complex self-theories, school-age children typically experience a rise in self-esteem.

26. _____ During middle childhood, acceptance by the peer group is valued more than having a close friend.

27. _____ The quality of family interaction seems to be a more powerful predictor of children's development than the actual structure of the family.

28. _____ School-age children are adept at tasks important in second-language acquisition.

29. _____ Code-switching, especially the occasional use of slang, is a behavior characteristic primarily of children in the lower social strata.

30. _____ Physical variations in North American children are usually caused by diet rather than heredity.

31. _____ Childhood obesity usually does not correlate with adult obesity.

32. _____ Despite the efforts of teachers and parents, most children with learning disabilities can expect their disabilities to persist and even worsen as they enter adulthood.

Questions for Reflection

1. Did any of the children's stories in the video lesson provide insight into your own childhood or (for those who are parents) that of your children? What did you learn about yourself or your children?

2. Which qualities and experiences of the children in the program would you hope to see in any children you might have? Why? Which qualities and experiences would you prefer not to see?

3. What experiences of middle childhood were *not* portrayed in the program? Which of these should have been included?

4. What are some of the losses that occur during middle childhood? What new potentials emerge during this stage of life? In what ways do these losses and gains relate to developmental events specific to childhood?

Answer Key

Key Terms

1. A learning disability is a difficulty in a particular cognitive skill that is not attributable to an overall intellectual slowness, a physical handicap, a severely stressful living condition, or a lack of basic education. (p. 346; objective 1)

2. The attention-deficit/hyperactivity disorder (AD/HD) is a neurological disorder in which the individual has great difficulty concentrating, is often excessively excitable and impulsive, and is sometimes aggressive. (p. 351; video lesson, segment 4; objective 4)

3. Mainstreaming is an educational approach in which children with special needs are included in regular classrooms. (p. 353; objective 1)

4. Middle childhood is generally defined as the period from age 6 or 7 to 11. (p. 331; objectives 1, 2, & 3)

5. Developmental psychopathology is a new field that applies the insights from studies of normal development to the study and treatment of childhood disorders, and vice versa. (p. 342; objective 1)

6. Developed by the American Psychiatric Association, the *Diagnostic and Statistical Manual of Mental Disorders* (DSM-IV) is the leading means of distinguishing various emotional and behavioral disorders. (p. 343; objective 1)

7. Attention-deficit disorder (ADD) is a condition in which a child has great difficulty concentrating, but, unlike a hyperactive child, is not impulsive and overactive. (p. 351; objective 1)

8. A school setting known as the least restrictive environment is a legally required setting in which children with special needs are offered as much freedom as possible to benefit from the instruction available to other children. (p. 353; objective 2)

9. During Piaget's stage of concrete operational thought, lasting from ages 7 to 11, children can think logically about concrete events and objects but are not able to reason abstractly. (p. 359; objective 2)

10. Total immersion is an approach to bilingual education in which the child's instruction occurs entirely in the new language. (p. 384; objective 2)

11. According to Erikson, the crisis of middle childhood is that of industry versus inferiority, in which children try to master many skills and develop views of themselves as either competent or incompetent and inferior. (p. 393; objective 3)

12. Social cognition refers to a person's awareness and understanding of the personalities, motives, emotions, intentions, and interactions of other people and groups. (p. 396; objective 3)

13. Social comparison is the tendency to assess one's abilities, achievements, and social status by measuring them against those of others, especially those of one's peers. (p. 397; video lesson, segment 1; objective 3)

14. Children in middle childhood develop and transmit their own subculture, called the society of children, which has its own games, vocabulary, dress codes, and rules of behavior. (p. 398; video lesson, segment 3; objective 3)

15. A nuclear family consists of two parents and their mutual biological offspring. (p. 410; video lesson, segments 3 & 4; objective 3)

16. A single-parent family consists of one parent and his or her (usually biological) children. (p. 410; video lesson, segment 1; objective 3)

17. A blended family consists of two parents, at least one with biological children from another union. (p. 410; video lesson, segment 2; objective 3)

18. An extended family is one that includes grandparents, aunts, cousins, or other relatives in addition to parents and their children. (p. 410; objective 3)

19. Code-switching is a pragmatic communication skill involving changing from one form of speech to another. (p. 371; objective 2)

Practice Questions

Multiple-Choice Questions

1. d. is the correct answer. (pp. 331–332; video lesson, segment 1; objective 1)

2. a. is the correct answer. (p. 364; objective 2)

    b. is incorrect. Neurological development in the frontal cortex facilitates processing speed during middle childhood. The limbic system, which was not discussed in this lesson, is concerned with emotions.

    c. is incorrect. Processing speed is facilitated by growth, rather than streamlining, of the knowledge base.

3. b. is the correct answer. (p. 351; video lesson, segment 4; objective 4)

4. d. is the correct answer. (p. 352; video lesson, segment 4; objective 4)

5. a. is the correct answer. (p. 346; objective 1)

6. c. is the correct answer. (p. 337; video lesson, segment 1; objective 1)

7. c. is the correct answer. (p. 354; objective 1)

    a. is incorrect. Many general education teachers are unable to cope with the special needs of some children.

    b. & d. are incorrect. These approaches undermined the social integration of children with special needs.

8. c. is the correct answer. (p. 346; objective 1)

9. b. is the correct answer. Gilligan contends that females' morality of care makes them reluctant to judge right and wrong in absolute terms because they are socialized to be nurturing and caring. (pp. 375–376; objective 2)

10. c. is the correct answer. (p. 336; objective 1)

    a. & b. are incorrect. Each of these games involves skills that are hardest for schoolchildren to master.

    d. is incorrect. Because one-on-one sports are likely to accentuate individual differences in ability, they may be especially discouraging to some children.

11. c. is the correct answer. (pp. 359–360; video lesson, segment 2; objective 2)

12. c. is the correct answer. (p. 361; objective 2)

13. d. is the correct answer. (pp. 359–363; objective 2)

14. b. is the correct answer. (pp. 366–367; objective 2)

15. a. is the correct answer. (p. 396; objective 3)

16. c. is the correct answer. (p. 395; objective 3)

17. c. is the correct answer. (pp. 422–423; objective 3)

18. d. is the correct answer. (p. 401; objective 3)

19. b. is the correct answer. (p. 420; objective 3)

20. a. is the correct answer. (p. 393; objective 3)

21. a. is the correct answer. (p. 396; video lesson, segment 2; objective 3)

    b. is incorrect. Friendship circles typically become smaller during middle childhood, as children become choosier about their friends.

    c. & d. are incorrect. These issues are not discussed in the lesson.

22. c. is the correct answer. (p. 396; objective 3)

23. b. is the correct answer. (p. 422; objective 3)

24. c. is the correct answer. Although emotional maturity is an important factor in family functioning, the textbook does not suggest that biological parents are more mature than other parents. (pp. 412–413; objective 3)

True or False Items

25. F   In fact, just the opposite is true. (p. 397; objective 3)

26. F   In fact, just the opposite is true. (p. 399; objective 3)

27. T   (p. 410; objective 3)

28. T   (p. 385; video lesson, segment 3; objective 2)

29. F   Code switching (including occasional use of slang) is a behavior demonstrated by all children. (p. 371; objective 2)

30. F   Physical variations in children from developed countries are caused primarily by heredity. (p. 332; objective 1)

31. F   If obesity is established in middle childhood, it tends to continue into adulthood. (p. 334; objective 1)

32. F   With the proper assistance, many children with learning disabilities develop into adults who are virtually indistinguishable from other adults in their educational and occupational achievements. (p. 355; objective 1)

Lesson Review

Lesson 19

The School Years
Summary

Please Note: Use this matrix to guide your study and achieve the learning objectives of this lesson. It will also help you to view the video, which defines and demonstrates important concepts and skills as they relate to everyday life.

Learning Objective	Textbook	Telecourse Student Guide	Video Lesson
1. Give examples of the basic pattern of motor-skill development, and discuss variations in biosocial development during middle childhood.	pp. 331, 337, 341–346, 351–354	Key Terms: 1, 3, 4, 5, 6, 7; Practice Questions: 1, 5, 6, 7, 8, 10, 30, 31, 32.	all segments
2. Describe cognitive development during middle childhood, focusing on language development and the advantages and challenges of learning English as a second language during this time.	pp. 331, 336, 353, 359–367, 375–376	Key Terms: 4, 8, 9, 10, 19; Practice Questions: 2, 9, 11, 12, 13, 14, 28, 29.	all segments
3. Discuss psychosocial development during middle childhood, giving examples of the main developments in the child's emotional life.	pp. 393–401, 410–420	Key Terms: 4, 11, 13, 14, 15, 16, 17, 18; Practice Questions: 15, 16, 17, 18, 19, 20, 21, 22, 23, 24, 25, 26, 27.	all segments
4. Describe the symptoms of AD/HD (attention-deficit/hyperactivity disorder), and discuss the types of treatment available for children with this disorder.	pp. 351–352	Key Terms: 2; Practice Questions: 3, 4.	Segment 4: *Sean*

School Days

Lesson 20
The School Years:
Special Topic

Preview

This lesson follows the story of Mario, a fifth grade student, who struggled socially and academically until he met a devoted teacher, Erik Rossman, who found a way to motivate and encourage the boy. Mario's transformation poignantly illustrates the powerful influence that teachers and schools can have on children. It also raises a number of questions that are addressed in this lesson: What should we teach our children and who should decide? What is "good teaching"? Is there too much emphasis on testing today? How do the major developmental theories inform and guide teachers?

While you're studying this lesson, talk to a schoolteacher and/or a child you know who attends a public or private elementary school. How is the school day organized, what's the typical schedule each day? How many children are in each class? What subjects are taught? How does the instructor teach each subject, what techniques are used? How does the teacher assess and evaluate student learning? What type of tests are given and how often? How does the teacher motivate students to study? In what other ways can the school experience shape a child's development, both inside and outside the classroom?

Prior Telecourse Knowledge that Will Be Used in this Lesson
*   The theories of Jean Piaget, Lev Vygotsky, and B. F. Skinner (from Lesson 1) will be discussed as we explore the various methods used by skilled teachers.

Learning Objectives

Use this information to guide your reading, viewing, thinking, and studying. After successfully completing this lesson, you should be able to:

1. Summarize how curriculum and academic standards are typically selected in formal school systems, and how these choices can ultimately affect a child's development.

2. Outline the constructivist philosophy, describe emergent curriculum, and discuss the potential advantages and disadvantages of this approach to education.

3. Discuss the socializing influence of school and identify the social skills that children learn at school both inside and outside the classroom.

4. Explain how the theories of Jean Piaget, Lev Vygotsky, and B. F. Skinner have shaped how children are taught in the classroom.

5. Define the concept of multiple intelligences, identify different types of intelligence, and discuss the possible benefits and challenges of applying this theory in classroom situations.

6. Summarize what parents can do to support the learning experience of their school-age children.

7. Differentiate between achievement and aptitude tests and discuss the pros and cons of using tests to evaluate student knowledge and performance.

📖 **Review textbook pages 346–349 ("Aptitude and Achievement," "IQ Tests," and "Changing Policy: One Intelligence Score or Many?"), and 380–389 ("Schools, Values, and Research," "Deciding How Children Should Learn," and "Educational Structures and Policies")**

📼 **View the video for Lesson 20, "School Days."**

Segment 1: *What Do We Teach?*

Segment 2: *How Do We Teach?*

Segment 3: *How Do We Measure Success?*

Summary

While schooling of some sort is required by law in most communities worldwide, who receives instruction, in what subjects, and how they receive this instruction varies enormously. In addition to teaching academic subjects, school is a major socializing force that helps children find their places in society.

Although the specific styles of education will vary, depending on teacher personality and cultural assumptions, any developmental approach to education attempts to engage every student in the learning process. In the United States, the content of K–12 (kindergarten through 12th grade) instruction—what we call **curriculum**—is mandated separately by each state's Board of Education, which also establishes levels of competency—or standards—in reading, math, social studies, and all other academic subjects. These competency levels form a **standards-based curriculum** that guides instruction in the classroom.

An alternative approach is **emergent curriculum**, which attempts to more directly address the needs and abilities of each individual student. This approach has its roots in **constructivist philosophy,** which proposes that knowledge is constructed and not transmitted. Those who follow this philosophy believe that children learn best through active interactions with their environment. A new emergent approach in math—for example—replaces rote learning with hands-on materials and active discussion that relates directly to the students interests and prior experience. Such an approach promotes problem solving and a deeper level of understanding. Although standards-based and emergent curricula each have their strengths and weaknesses, both depend on the child's motivation for learning.

Each of the major theories of development has had an impact on contemporary education. For instance, the use of goals and rewards or **reinforcement** in the classroom stems from B. F. Skinner's principles of **operant conditioning**, and the emphasis on learning through active participation and exploration of the environment derives from the ideas of Jean Piaget. As a third example, teachers who pay particular attention to the role of social interaction in learning are following the ideas of Lev Vygotsky. Finally, most teachers recognize that each child has a unique style of learning and demonstrates what Howard Gardner and Robert Sternberg have called "multiple intelligences." Sternberg believes that there are three distinct types of intelligence: academic, creative, and practical. Similarly, Howard Gardner describes seven distinct intelligences: linguistic, logical-mathematical, musical, spatial, body-kinesthetic, interpersonal, and intrapersonal.

The issue of testing in education remains controversial because a child's test performance can be affected by nonacademic factors, such as the capacity to pay attention and concentrate, emotional stress, health, language difficulties, and test-taking anxiety. **Achievement tests** are designed to measure what a child has learned, while **aptitude tests** are designed to measure learning potential. Achievement tests take one of two forms. A **norm-referenced** test compares student performance to an average set by other students who have taken the same test. Instead of comparing to others, a **standards-based** or **criterion-referenced** test compares each student's performance to predetermined standards or competencies.

The most commonly used aptitude tests are intelligence tests or **IQ tests**. In some versions of these tests, a person's score is translated into a mental age, which is divided by the person's chronological age and multiplied by 100 to determine his or her IQ. IQ scores may seriously underestimate the intellectual potential of a disadvantaged child or overestimate that of a child from an advantaged background.

📖 **Review all reading assignments for this lesson.**

💻 **As assigned by your instructor, complete the optional online component for this lesson.**

Key Terms

Using your own words, write a brief definition or explanation of each of the following terms on a separate piece of paper.

1. curriculum
2. hidden curriculum
3. standards-based curriculum
4. emergent curriculum
5. constructivist philosophy
6. operant conditioning
7. multiple intelligences
8. IQ tests
9. aptitude
10. achievement tests
11. norm-referenced
12. standards-based or criterion-referenced

Practice Questions

Multiple-Choice Questions

1. Tests that measure a child's potential to learn a new subject are called _____ tests.
   a. aptitude
   b. achievement
   c. norm-referenced
   d. criterion-referenced

2. In the earliest IQ tests, a child's score was calculated by dividing the child's _____ age by his or her _____age to find the _____ quotient.

   a. mental; chronological; intelligence

   b. chronological; mental; intelligence

   c. intelligence; chronological; mental

   d. intelligence; mental; chronological

3. Aptitude and achievement testing are controversial because

   a. they don't provide valid and reliable results.

   b. test performance can be affected by many factors other than the child's intellectual potential or academic achievement.

   c. they often fail to identify serious learning problems.

   d. of all of the above reasons.

4. Tests that measure what a child has already learned are called _____ tests.

   a. aptitude

   b. vocational

   c. achievement

   d. intelligence

5. Which of the following is **NOT** a type of intelligence identified in Robert Sternberg's theory?

   a. academic

   b. practical

   c. achievement

   d. creative

6. Angela was born in 1984. In 1992, she scored 125 on an intelligence test. Using the original formula, what was Angela's mental age when she took the test?

   a. 6

   b. 8

   c. 10

   d. 12

7. Raymond's score on a test indicated that his ability equals that of a typical fifth-grade student. The test Raymond took evidently was

   a. criterion-referenced.

   b. norm-referenced.

   c. an aptitude test.

   d. all of the above.

8. Howard Gardner and Robert Sternberg would probably be most critical of traditional aptitude and achievement tests because they

   a. inadvertently reflect certain nonacademic competencies.

   b. do not reflect knowledge of cultural ideas.

   c. measure only a limited set of intellectual abilities.

   d. underestimate the intellectual potential of disadvantaged children.

9. During the school board meeting, a knowledgeable parent proclaimed that the board's position on achievement testing and class size was an example of the district's "hidden curriculum." The parent was referring to

   a. unofficial and unstated educational priorities of the school district.

   b. political agendas of individual members of the school board.

   c. legal mandates for testing and class size established by the state board of education.

   d. none of the above.

10. Judy's mother has some questions about the curriculum in her daughter's school. The principal informs her that the curriculum is set by

   a. each teacher.

   b. each school

   c. the State Board of Education.

   d. the National Education Association.

11. Today, most public schools primarily teach

   a. standards-based curriculum.

   b. an emergent curriculum.

   c. constructivist curriculum.

   d. none of the above.

12. The idea that reinforcing a desired classroom behavior makes that behavior more likely to happen again stems most directly from the ideas of

   a. Lev Vygotsky.

   b. Jean Piaget.

   c. Howard Gardner.

   d. B. F. Skinner.

13. The idea that children learn best through active participation and exploration based on their natural curiosity stems most directly from the ideas of

   a. Lev Vygotsky.

   b. Jean Piaget.

   c. Howard Gardner.

   d. B. F. Skinner.

14. A middle school science teacher who mentors students and structures her lessons to emphasize social interaction and cooperative learning is apparently an advocate of the ideas of

    a. Lev Vygotsky.

    b. Jean Piaget.

    c. Howard Gardner.

    d. B. F. Skinner.

True or False Items

Write T (for true) or F (for false) on the line in front of each statement.

15. _____ In the United States, children are required by law to attend school.

16. _____ Emergent curriculum has its roots in behaviorism.

17. _____ Today, most educators have discarded emergent curriculum because it is ineffective.

18. _____ Sadly, there is little connection between educational curriculum in the United States and the ideas of developmental theorists.

19. _____ Jean Piaget emphasized the role of social interaction in the learning process.

20. _____ Most teachers believe that "good teaching is good teaching," and that all children should be taught the same way.

21. _____ Most school districts use aptitude tests to measure how much and how well a child has learned in a specific subject area.

22. _____ A test that is graded "on a curve" is an example of a norm-referenced test.

23. _____ Research shows that standardized testing tends to expand the curriculum to subjects such as art and music that might otherwise be excluded.

24. _____ Research shows clearly that children learn better when there are fewer children in each class.

Answer Key

Key Terms

1. The subjects and topics that children are taught in a particular grade consitutes the curriculum for that grade. (video lesson, segment 1; objective 1)

2. Each school has a hidden curriculum consisting of an unofficial set of rules and priorities that influence the actual curriculum and every aspect of the school's environment. (p. 386; objective 1)

3. A standards-based curriculum is one that is based on a level of competency for each subject, typically set by the state and local school boards. (video lesson, segment 1; objective 1)

4. An emergent curriculum is one that derives more from the needs, abilities, and interests of each individual student than from a standard set of competencies deemed important for all students. (video lesson, segment 1; objective 2)

5. The constructivist philosophy is based on the idea that knowledge is "constructed" in the mind of each individual. It suggests that children learn best from direct interactions and first-hand experiences, which take into account their previous knowledge and personal interests. (video lesson, segment 1; objective 2)

6. As described by B. F. Skinner, operant conditioning is a form of learning in which desired behaviors are made more likely to occur through reinforcement or punishment. (p. 41; video lesson, segment 2; objective 4)

7. Howard Gardner and Robert Sternberg propose that humans have different types of intellectual aptitudes and abilities called multiple intelligences, rather than a single, underlying ability (as emphasized in standard IQ tests). (p. 348; video lesson, segment 2; objective 5)

8. IQ tests are aptitude tests, which were originally designed to yield a measure of intelligence, calculated as mental age divided by chronological age, multiplied by 100. (p. 346; objective 7)

9. Aptitude tests are tests designed to measure potential, rather than actual, accomplishment. (p. 346; objective 7)

10. Achievement tests are tests that measure what a child has already learned about a particular subject. (p. 346; video lesson, segment 3; objective 7)

11. An achievement test that is norm-referenced is based on a certain level of achievement that is usual, such as grade level. A student's performance is compared to the performance of other students. (p. 346; video lesson, segment 3; objective 7)

12. An achievement test that is standards-based (also called criterion-referenced) is based on a specific standard of performance, such as how well a child reads. A child's performance is compared to the standard rather than the performance of other students.(p. 346; video lesson, segment 3; objective 7)

Practice Questions

Multiple-Choice Questions

1. a. is the correct answer. (p. 346; video lesson, segment 3; objective 7)

    b. is incorrect. Achievement tests measure what has already been learned.

    c. is incorrect. Vocational tests, which, as their name implies, measure what a person has learned about a particular trade, are achievement tests.

    d. is incorrect. Intelligence tests measure general aptitude, rather than aptitude for a specific subject.

2. a. is the correct answer. (pp. 346; objective 7)

3. b. is the correct answer. (pp. 346–347; video lesson, segment 3; objective 7)

4. c. is the correct answer. (p. 346; video lesson, segment 3; objective 7)

5. c. is the correct answer. (p. 348; video lesson, segment 2; objective 5)

6. c. is the correct answer. (p. 346; objective 7)

7. b. is the correct answer. (p. 346; video lesson, segment 3; objective 7)

    a. is incorrect. Criterion-referenced tests specify a certain standard of performance rather than comparing performance to that of others.

    c. is incorrect. Aptitude tests measure the potential to learn rather than how much material has already been mastered.

8. c. is the correct answer. Both Sternberg and Gardner believe that there are multiple intelligences rather than the narrowly defined abilities measured by traditional aptitude and achievement tests. (pp. 348; video lesson, segment 2; objective 5)

a., b., & d. are incorrect. Although these criticisms are certainly valid, they are not specifically associated with Sternberg or Gardner.

9. a. is the correct answer. (p. 386; objective 1)

10. c. is the correct answer. (video lesson, segment 1; objective 1)

11. a. is the correct answer. (video lesson, segment 1; objective 1)

12. d. is the correct answer. (video lesson, segment 2; objective 4)

a. is incorrect. Lev Vygotsky emphasized the role of social interaction in learning.

b. is incorrect. Jean Piaget emphasized the importance of active participation and exploration in learning.

c. is incorrect. Howard Gardner is known for his theory that there are multiple intelligences.

13. b. is the correct answer. (video lesson, segment 2; objective 4)

a. is incorrect. Lev Vygotsky emphasized the role of social interaction in learning.

c. is incorrect. Howard Gardner is known for his theory that there are multiple intelligences.

d. is incorrect. B. F. Skinner is known for his theory of operant conditioning, which emphasizes the influence of reinforcement on classroom behaviors.

14. a. is the correct answer. (video lesson, segment 2; objective 4)

True-False Items

15. T (video lesson, introduction; objective 1)

16. F Emergent curriculum has its roots in constructivist philosophy. (video lesson, segment 1; objective 2)

17. F Emergent curriculum is increasingly being used with positive results, often in conjunction with standards-based curriculum. (video lesson, segment 1; objective 2)

18. F The major theories of development are highly evident in contemporary education. (video lesson, segment 2; objective 4)

19. F Lev Vygotsky emphasized the role of social interaction in learning; Piaget emphasized active exploration and experimentation. (video lesson, segment 2; objective 4)

20. F Most teachers agree that children differ in their intelligences and learning styles. (video lesson, segment 2; objective 5)

21. F Most school districts use achievement tests for this purpose; aptitude tests measure a student's *potential* to learn. (p. 346; video lesson, segment 3; objective 7)

22. T (video lesson, segment 3; objective 7)

23. F Testing generally *narrows* the curriculum to exclude subjects such as these, which tend not to be covered on standardized achievement tests. (video lesson, segment 3; objective 7)

24. F Despite this widespread belief, research support is mixed, at best. (p. 386; objective 1)

Lesson Review

Lesson 20

The School Years
Special Topic

Please Note: Use this matrix to guide your study and achieve the learning objectives of this lesson. It will also help you to view the video, which defines and demonstrates important concepts and skills as they relate to everyday life.

Learning Objective	Textbook	Telecourse Student Guide	Video Lesson
1. Summarize how curriculum and academic standards are typically selected in formal school systems, and how these choices can ultimately affect a child's development.	p. 386	Key Terms: 1, 2, 3; Practice Questions: 9, 10, 11, 15, 24.	Segment 1: *What Do We Teach?*
2. Outline the constructivist philosophy, describe emergent curriculum, and discuss the potential advantages and disadvantages of this approach to education.		Key Terms: 4, 5; Practice Questions: 16, 17.	Introduction
3. Discuss the socializing influence of school and identify the social skills that children learn at school both inside and outside the classroom.			Segment 2: *How Do We Teach?*
4. Explain how the theories of Jean Piaget, Lev Vygotsky, and B. F. Skinner have shaped how children are taught in the classroom.		Key Terms: 6; Practice Questions: 12, 13, 14, 18, 19.	Segment 1: *What Do We Teach?*
5. Define the concept of multiple intelligences, identify different types of intelligence, and discuss the possible benefits and challenges of applying this theory in classroom situations.	p. 348	Key Terms: 7; Practice Questions: 5, 8, 20.	Segment 2: *How Do We Teach?*
6. Summarize what parents can do to support the learning experience of their school-age children.			Segment 2: *How Do We Teach?*
7. Differentiate between achievement and aptitude tests and discuss the pros and cons of using tests to evaluate student knowledge and performance.	pp. 346–347	Key Terms: 8, 9, 10, 11, 12; Practice Questions: 1, 2, 3, 4, 6, 7, 21, 22, 23.	Segment 3: *How Do We Measure Success?*

Explosions

Lesson 21

Adolescence:
Biosocial Development

Preview

Between the ages of 11 and 20, young people cross the great divide between childhood and adulthood that we call **adolescence**. This crossing encompasses all three domains of development—biosocial, cognitive, and psychosocial. Lesson 21 focuses on the dramatic changes that occur in the biosocial domain, beginning with **puberty** and the **growth spurt**. The biosocial metamorphosis of the adolescent is discussed in detail, with emphasis on sexual maturation, nutrition, and the effects of the timing of puberty, including possible problems arising from early or late maturation.

Although adolescence is, in many ways, a healthy time of life, this lesson addresses three health hazards that too often affect children of this age: sexual abuse, poor nutrition, and use of alcohol, tobacco, and other drugs.

As you begin this lesson, reflect on your own experience in adolescence. Recall your physical growth and development during this period (i.e., height, weight, voice changes, hair growth, developing curves/shoulders). Did you develop any earlier or later than your peers? How did these changes make you feel? How well did you eat and take care of yourself physically? What pressures did you feel regarding sex and the use of drugs and alcohol?

Prior Telecourse Knowledge that Will Be used in this Lesson
*   Biosocial development during infancy (Lesson 6), early childhood (Lesson 11), and middle childhood (Lesson 16) will be referred to as we discuss physical developments during adolescence. As you'll learn, the rate of growth in adolescence is second only to the rapid growth experienced prenatally (in the womb) and postnatally (during the first year of life).
*   Five theories of development introduced in Lesson 1 (psychoanalytic, learning, cognitive, sociocultural, and epigenetic) will be used to offer alternative explanations for eating disorders in adolescence.

Learning Objectives

Use this information to guide your reading, viewing, thinking, and studying. After successfully completing this lesson, you should be able to:

1. Identify and describe the biological events of puberty.
2. Identify several factors that influence the onset of puberty.

Lesson 21/Adolescence: Biosocial Development   **315**

3. Discuss the consequences for boys and girls who experience early or late onset of puberty.

4. Describe the growth spurt experienced during adolescence by both boys and girls, including changes in weight, height, and the body's internal organ system.

5. Describe the development of sexual characteristics in males and females during puberty, and distinguish between primary and secondary sex characteristics.

6. Discuss the emotional and psychological impact of pubertal hormones and how this impact is influenced by social context.

7. Describe factors that have an impact on the adolescent's development of a positive body image.

8. Define childhood sexual abuse, discuss its prevalence, and describe its consequences for development.

9. Discuss the nutritional needs and problems of adolescents.

10. Define the major types of eating disorders, and discuss how different theories of development might explain them.

11. Discuss the use and abuse of alcohol, tobacco, and other drugs among adolescents today, including prevalence, significance for development, and the best methods of prevention.

📖 **Read Chapter 14, "Adolescence: Biosocial Development," pages 429–463.**

🎦 **View the video for Lesson 21, "Explosions."**

     Segment 1: *Puberty*

     Segment 2: *Body Image*

     Segment 3: *Health*

Summary

Puberty begins when a hormonal signal from the hypothalamus stimulates hormone production in the pituitary gland, which, in turn, triggers hormone production by the adrenal glands and by the **gonads** (sex glands). The major physical changes of puberty generally occur in the same sequence for everyone and are usually complete three or four years after they have begun. Variation in growth is related to sex, genetic inheritance, nutrition, and other factors.

The sequence of growth during puberty is from the extremities inward, making many adolescents temporarily big-footed, long-legged, and short-waisted. Internal organs also grow, including the lungs (which triple in weight) and the heart (which doubles in size and slows in rate). These changes give the adolescent increased physical endurance. The lymphoid system—including the tonsils and adenoids—decreases in size at adolescence, making teenagers less susceptible than children to respiratory ailments. The growth and maturation of the sex organs, called **primary sex characteristics**, that result in the development of reproductive potential are signaled by the first menstrual period (**menarche**) in girls and by the first ejaculation (**spermarche**) in boys.

Attitudes toward menarche, and spermarche have changed over the past two decades, and—for the most part—fewer young people face these events with anxiety, embarrassment, or guilt. Young people who experience puberty at the same time as their friends tend to view the experience more positively than those who do not. The effects of early and late maturation differ for boys and girls. Girls find *early* maturation more difficult because of the added pressures that accompany sexual maturation. Boys find *late* maturation more difficult because of the correlation between peer status and a mature build.

Parents who are in conflict with each other, immature, socially isolated, alcoholic, or drug-abusing are more likely to be sexually abusive or so neglectful that their children are vulnerable to abuse from others. The psychological effects of **sexual abuse** depend on the extent and duration of the abuse, the age of the child, and the reactions of family members and authorities once the abuse is known. Unlike younger victims of abuse, adolescents are prone to becoming self-destructive through substance abuse or eating disorders, running away from home, risking AIDS through unsafe sex, or even attempting suicide.

The two main eating disorders, **anorexia nervosa** and **bulimia nervosa**, emerge any time from about age 10 to age 30, but the most hazardous periods are at the beginning of adolescence (about age 13) and just after high school (age 18). Learning theory sees destructive eating as part of a stimulus-response chain in which low self-esteem and depression trigger extreme dieting, and fasting, bingeing, and purging serve as powerful reinforcers. Sociocultural explanations focus on cultural pressures to be "slim and trim." Psychoanalytic explanations focus on unresolved conflicts with mothers, while cognitive explanations highlight the desire of women to project a strong, self-controlled image. Epigenetic explanations suggest that anorexics and bulimics discover that self-starvation blocks the hormonal events of puberty, thereby removing the sexual pressures of normal maturation.

Drug abuse always harms physical and psychological development. **Drug use** may or may not be harmful, depending in part on how mature the drug user is and his or her reason for using the drug. Drug use is also increasing among younger adolescents. This is cause for particular concern because research has shown that, when used by young adolescents, tobacco, alcohol, and marijuana act as **gateway drugs**, opening the door to regular use of multiple and more dangerous drugs such as cocaine, heroin, and drugs such as Ecstasy, Crystal Meth, and so on.

Special Note: We will cover the topics of unwanted pregnancy and sexual abuse (pp. 446–449) in more detail in Lesson 25, "Crashing Hard into Adulthood."

📖 **Review all reading assignments for this lesson.**

💻 **As assigned by your instructor, complete the optional online component for this lesson.**

Key Terms

Using your own words, write a brief definition or explanation of each of the following terms on a separate piece of paper.

1. adolescence
2. puberty
3. hypothalamus
4. pituitary gland
5. adrenal glands
6. HPA axis
7. gonads
8. estrogen
9. testosterone
10. menarche
11. spermarche
12. growth spurt
13. primary sex characteristics
14. secondary sex characteristics
15. body image
16. sexually transmitted diseases (STDs)
17. sexual abuse
18. childhood sexual abuse
19. body mass index (BMI)
20. anorexia nervosa
21. bulimia nervosa
22. drug use
23. drug abuse
24. drug addiction
25. gateway drugs
26. generational forgetting

Practice Questions I

Multiple-Choice Questions

1. Which of the following most accurately describes the sequence of pubertal development in girls?

   a. breast buds and pubic hair; growth spurt in which fat is deposited on hips and buttocks; first menstrual period; ovulation

   b. growth spurt; breast buds and pubic hair; first menstrual period; ovulation

   c. first menstrual period; breast buds and pubic hair; growth spurt; ovulation

   d. breast buds and pubic hair; growth spurt; ovulation; first menstrual period

2. Although both sexes grow rapidly during adolescence, boys typically begin their accelerated growth about

   a. a year or two later than girls.

   b. a year earlier than girls.

   c. the time they reach sexual maturity.

   d. the time facial hair appears.

3. The first readily observable sign of the onset of puberty is

   a. the voice lowers.

   b. the appearance of facial, body, and pubic hair.

   c. a change in the shape of the eyes.

   d. a lengthening of the torso.

4. More than any other group in the population, adolescent girls are likely to have
   a. asthma.
   b. acne.
   c. iron-deficiency anemia.
   d. testosterone deficiency.

5. The HPA axis is the
   a. route followed by many hormones to regulate stress, growth, sleep, and appetite.
   b. pair of sex glands in humans.
   c. cascade of sex hormones in females and males.
   d. area of the brain that regulates the pituitary gland.

6. For males, the secondary sex characteristic that usually occurs last is
   a. breast enlargement.
   b. the appearance of facial hair.
   c. growth of the testes.
   d. the appearance of pubic hair.

7. For girls, the specific event that is taken to indicate sexual maturity is
   _____. For boys, it is _____.
   a. the growth of breast buds; voice deepening
   b. menarche; spermarche
   c. an ovulation; the testosterone surge
   d. the growth spurt; pubic hair

8. The most significant hormonal changes of puberty include a marked increase
   of _____ in _____ and a marked increase of
   _____ in _____.
   a. progesterone; boys; estrogen; girls
   b. estrogen; boys; testosterone; girls
   c. progesterone; girls; estrogen; boys
   d. estrogen; girls; testosterone; boys

9. In general, most adolescents are
   a. overweight.
   b. satisfied with their appearance.
   c. dissatisfied with their appearance.
   d. unaffected by cultural attitudes about beauty.

10. Of the following, who is most likely to suffer from anorexia nervosa?
    a. Bill, a 23-year-old professional football player
    b. Florence, a 30-year-old account executive
    c. Lynn, an 18-year-old college student
    d. Carl, a professional dancer

11. The damage caused by sexual abuse depends on all of the following factors **EXCEPT**

    a. repeated incidence.

    b. the gender of the perpetrator.

    c. distorted adult-child relationships.

    d. impairment of the child's ability to develop normally.

12. Early physical growth and sexual maturation

    a. tend to be equally difficult for girls and boys.

    b. tend to be more difficult for boys than for girls.

    c. tend to be more difficult for girls than for boys.

    d. are easier for both girls and boys than late maturation.

13. Epinephrine and norepinephrine are _____ that are released by the _____ gland.

    a. neurotransmitters; pituitary

    b. hormones; pituitary

    c. neurotransmitters; adrenal

    d. hormones; adrenal

14. Body mass index (BMI) is calculated by dividing

    a. height in meters by weight in kilograms.

    b. weight in kilograms by height in meters.

    c. height in meters squared by weight in kilograms.

    d. weight in kilograms by height in meters squared.

15. Professor Wilson, who believes that the roots of eating disorders are in the gene pool of our species and the evolutionary mandate to reproduce, is evidently a proponent of which theory?

    a. psychoanalytic

    b. behaviorism

    c. epigenetic systems

    d. sociocultural

True or False Items

Write T (for true) or F (for false) on the line in front of each statement.

16. ____ More calories are necessary during adolescence than at any other period during the life span.

17. ____ Anorexia is suspected if a person's BMI is 18 or lower.

18. ____ The first indicator of reproductive potential in males is menarche.

19. ____ Lung capacity, heart size, and total volume of blood increase significantly during adolescence.

20. ____ Puberty generally begins sometime between ages 8 and 14.

21. ____ Girls who mature late and are thinner than average tend to be satisfied with their weight.

22. ____ The strong emphasis on physical appearance is unique to adolescents and finds little support from teachers, parents, and the larger culture.

23. ____ Childhood habits of overeating and underexercising usually lessen during adolescence.

24. ____ The problems of the early-maturing girl tend to be temporary.

25. ____ Both the sequence and timing of pubertal events vary greatly from one young person to another.

Practice Questions II

Multiple-Choice Questions

1. Which of the following is the correct sequence of pubertal events in boys?
   a. growth spurt; pubic hair; first ejaculation; lowering of voice
   b. pubic hair; first ejaculation; growth spurt; lowering of voice
   c. lowering of voice; pubic hair; growth spurt; first ejaculation
   d. growth spurt; lowering of voice; pubic hair; first ejaculation

2. Which of the following statements about adolescent physical development is **NOT** true?
   a. Hands and feet generally lengthen before arms and legs.
   b. Facial features usually grow before the head itself reaches adult size and shape.
   c. Oil, sweat, and odor glands become more active.
   d. The lymphoid system increases slightly in size, and the heart increases by nearly half.

3. In puberty, a hormone that increases markedly in girls (and only somewhat in boys) is
   a. estrogen.
   b. testosterone.
   c. androgen.
   d. menarche.

4. Nutritional deficiencies in adolescence are frequently the result of
   a. eating red meat.
   b. exotic diets or food fads.
   c. an ovulatory menstruation.
   d. excessive exercise.

5. In females, puberty is typically marked by a(n)
   a. significant widening of the shoulders.
   b. significant widening of the hips.
   c. enlargement of the torso and upper chest.
   d. decrease in the size of the eyes and nose.

6. Nonreproductive sexual characteristics, such as the deepening of the voice and the development of breasts, are called

   a. gender-typed traits.

   b. primary sex characteristics.

   c. secondary sex characteristics.

   d. pubertal prototypes.

7. Puberty is initiated when hormones are released from the _____, then from the _____, and then from the adrenal glands and the _____.

   a. hypothalamus; pituitary; gonads

   b. pituitary; gonads; hypothalamus

   c. gonads; pituitary; hypothalamus

   d. pituitary; hypothalamus; gonads

8. The typical bulimic patient is a

   a. college-age woman.

   b. teenage girl who starves herself to the point of emaciation.

   c. woman in her late forties.

   d. teenager who suffers from life-threatening obesity.

9. With regard to appearance, adolescent girls are most commonly dissatisfied with

   a. timing of maturation.

   b. eyes and other facial features.

   c. weight.

   d. legs.

10. Statistically speaking, to predict the age at which a girl first has sexual intercourse, it would be most useful to know her

   a. socioeconomic level.

   b. race or ethnic group.

   c. religion.

   d. age at menarche.

11. Individuals who experiment with drugs early are

   a. typically affluent teenagers who are experiencing an identity crisis.

   b. more likely to have multiple drug-abuse problems later on.

   c. less likely to have alcohol-abuse problems later on.

   d. usually able to resist later peer pressure leading to long-term addiction.

12. Compounding the problem of sexual abuse of boys, abused boys

   a. feel shame at the idea of being weak.

   b. have fewer sources of emotional support.

   c. are more likely to be abused by fathers.

   d. have all of the above problems.

13. Puberty is most accurately defined as the period
    a. of rapid physical growth that occurs during adolescence.
    b. during which sexual maturation is attained.
    c. of rapid physical growth and sexual maturation that ends childhood.
    d. during which adolescents establish identities separate from their parents.

14. Which of the following does **NOT** typically occur during puberty?
    a. The lungs increase in size and capacity.
    b. The heart's size and rate of beating increase.
    c. Blood volume increases.
    d. The lymphoid system decreases in size.

15. Teenagers' susceptibility to respiratory ailments typically _____ during adolescence, due to a(n) _____ in the size of the lymphoid system.
    a. increases; increase
    b. increases; decrease
    c. decreases; increase
    d. decreases; decrease

Matching Items

Match each definition or description with its corresponding term.

Terms

16. _____ puberty

17. _____ GH (growth hormone)

18. _____ testosterone

19. _____ estrogen

20. _____ growth spurt

21. _____ primary sex characteristics

22. _____ menarche

23. _____ spermarche

24. _____ secondary sex characteristics

25. _____ body image

26. _____ anorexia nervosa

27. _____ bulimia nervosa

Definitions or Descriptions

a. onset of menstruation

b. period of rapid physical growth and sexual maturation that ends childhood

c. hormone that increases dramatically in boys during puberty

d. hormone that increases steadily during puberty in both sexes

e. an affliction characterized by binge-purge eating

f. hormone that increases dramatically in girls during puberty

g. first sign is increased bone length and density

h. attitude toward one's physical appearance

i. an affliction characterized by self-starvation

j. physical characteristics not involved in reproduction

k. the sex organs involved in reproduction

l. first ejaculation containing sperm

Applying Your Knowledge

1. Fifteen-year-old Latoya is preoccupied with her "disgusting appearance" and seems depressed most of the time. The best thing her parents could do to help her through this difficult time would be to

   a. ignore her self-preoccupation since their attention would only reinforce it.

   b. encourage her to "shape up" and not give in to self-pity.

   c. kid her about her appearance in the hope that she will see how silly she is acting.

   d. offer practical advice, such as clothing suggestions, to improve her body image.

2. Thirteen-year-old Rosa, an avid runner and dancer, is worried because most of her friends have begun to menstruate regularly. Her doctor tells her

   a. that she should have a complete physical exam, because female athletes usually menstruate earlier than average.

   b. not to worry, since female athletes usually menstruate later than average.

   c. that she must stop running immediately, because the absence of menstruation is a sign of a serious health problem.

   d. that the likely cause of her delayed menarche is an inadequate diet.

3. Twelve-year-old Kwan is worried because his twin sister has suddenly grown taller and more physically mature than he. His parents should

   a. reassure him that the average boy is one or two years behind the average girl in the onset of the growth spurt.

   b. tell him that within a year or less he will grow taller than his sister.

   c. tell him that one member of each fraternal twin pair is always shorter.

   d. encourage him to exercise more to accelerate the onset of his growth spurt.

4. Calvin, the class braggart, boasts that because his beard has begun to grow, he is more virile than his male classmates. Jacob informs him that

   a. the tendency to grow facial and body hair has nothing to do with virility.

   b. beard growth is determined by heredity.

   c. girls also develop some facial hair and more noticeable hair on their arms and legs, so it is clearly not a sign of masculinity.

   d. all of the above are true.

5. The most likely source of status for a late-maturing, middle-socioeconomic status boy would be

   a. academic achievement or vocational goal.

   b. physical build.

   c. athletic prowess.

   d. success with the opposite sex.

6. Which of the following students is likely to be the most popular in a sixth-grade class?

   a. Vicki, the most sexually mature girl in the class

   b. Sandra, the tallest girl in the class

   c. Brad, who is at the top of the class scholastically

   d. Dan, the tallest boy in the class

7. Regarding the effects of early and late maturation on boys and girls, which of the following is **NOT** true?

   a. Early maturation is usually easier for boys to manage than it is for girls.

   b. Late maturation is usually easier for girls to manage than it is for boys.

   c. Late-maturing girls may be drawn into older peer groups and may exhibit problem behaviors such as early sexual activity.

   d. Late-maturing boys may not "catch up" physically, or in terms of their self-images, for many years.

8. As a psychoanalyst, Dr. Mendoza is most likely to believe that eating disorders are caused by

   a. contemporary pressure to be "slim and trim."

   b. low self-esteem and depression, which act as a stimulus for destructive patterns of eating.

   c. unresolved conflicts with parents.

   d. the desire of working women to project a strong, self-controlled image.

9. Which of the following adolescents is likely to begin puberty at the earliest age?

   a. Aretha, an African-American teenager who hates exercise

   b. Todd, a football player of European ancestry

   c. Kyu, an Asian-American honors student

   d. There is too little information to make a prediction.

10. Of the following teenagers, those most likely to be distressed about their physical development are

    a. late-maturing girls.

    b. late-maturing boys.

    c. early-maturing boys.

    d. girls or boys who masturbate.

11. Thirteen-year-old Kristin seems apathetic and lazy to her parents. You tell them

    a. that Kristin is showing signs of chronic depression.

    b. that Kristin may be experiencing psychosocial difficulties.

    c. that Kristin has a poor attitude and needs more discipline.

    d. to have Kristin's iron level checked.

12. I am a hormone that rises steadily during puberty in both males and females. What am I?

    a. estrogen

    b. testosterone

    c. GH (growth hormone)

    d. menarche

13. Eleven-year-old Linda, who has just begun to experience the first signs of puberty, laments, "When will the agony of puberty be over?" You tell her that the major events of puberty typically end about _____ after the first visible signs appear.

    a. 6 years
    b. 3 or 4 years
    c. 2 years
    d. 1 year

Answer Key

Key Terms
1. Adolescence is the period of biological, cognitive, and psychosocial transition from childhood to adulthood. (p. 431; video lesson, segment 1; objective 1)

2. Puberty is the period of rapid physical growth and sexual maturation that ends childhood and brings the young person to adult size, shape, and sexual potential. (p. 432; video lesson, segment 1; objective 1)

3. The hypothalamus is the part of the brain that regulates eating, drinking, body temperature, and the production of hormones by the pituitary gland. (p. 432; objectives 1 & 2)

4. The pituitary gland, under the influence of the hypothalamus, produces hormones that regulate growth and control other glands. (p. 432; objectives 1 & 2)

5. The adrenal glands secrete epinephrine and norephinephrine, hormones that prepare the body to deal with emergencies or stress. (p. 432; objectives 1 & 2)

6. The HPA axis (hypothalamus/pituitary/adrenal axis) is the route followed by many hormones to trigger puberty, regulate stress, growth, and other bodily changes. (p. 433; objectives 1 & 2)

7. The gonads are the pair of sex glands in humans—the ovaries in girls and the testes or testicles in boys. (p. 433; video lesson, segment 1; objectives 2 & 5)

8. Estrogen is a sex hormone that is secreted in greater amounts by females than males. (p. 433; objectives 2 & 5)

9. Testosterone is a sex hormone that is secreted more by males than by females. (p. 433; objectives 2 & 5)

10. Menarche, which refers to the first menstrual period, is the specific event that is taken to indicate fertility in adolescent girls. (p. 434; video lesson, segment 1; objectives 1 & 5)

11. Spermarche, which refers to the first ejaculation of seminal fluid containing sperm, is the specific event that is taken to indicate fertility in adolescent boys. (p. 434; video lesson, segment 1; segment 1; objectives 1 & 5)

12. The growth spurt, which begins with an increase in bone length and density and includes rapid weight gain and organ growth, is one of the many observable signs of puberty. (p. 436; video lesson, segment 1; objective 4)

13. During puberty, changes in the primary sex characteristics involve those sex organs that are directly involved in reproduction. (p. 439; video lesson, segment 1; objective 5)

14. During puberty, changes in the secondary sex characteristics involve parts of the body that are not directly involved in reproduction but that signify sexual development. (p. 439; video lesson, segment 1; objective 5)

15. Body image refers to adolescents' mental conception of, and attitude toward, their physical appearance. (p. 443; video lesson, segment 2; objective 7)

16. Sexually transmitted diseases (STDs) such as syphilis, gonorrhea, herpes, and AIDS, are those that are spread by sexual contact. (p. 445; objective 8)

17. Sexual abuse is the use of an unconsenting person for one's own sexual pleasure. (p. 448; objective 8)

18. Childhood sexual abuse is any activity in which an adult uses a child for his or her own sexual stimulation or pleasure—even if the use does not involve physical contact. (p. 448; objective 8)

19. A measure of obesity, body mass index (BMI) is calculated by dividing a person's weight in kilograms by his or her height in meters squared. (p. 450; objective 9)

20. Anorexia nervosa is a serious eating disorder in which a person restricts eating to the point of emaciation and possible starvation. (p. 452; objective 10)

21. Bulimia nervosa is an eating disorder in which the person engages repeatedly in episodes of binge eating followed by purging through induced vomiting or the abuse of laxatives. (p. 454; objective 10)

22. Drug use is the ingestion of a drug, regardless of the amount or affect of ingestion. (p. 456; video lesson, segment 3; objective 11)

23. Drug abuse is the ingestion of a drug to the extent that it impairs the user's well-being. (p. 456; video lesson, segment 3; objective 11)

24. Drug addiction is a person's dependence on a drug or a behavior in order to feel physically or psychologically at ease. (p. 456; video lesson, segment 3; objective 11)

25. Gateway drugs are drugs—usually tobacco, alcohol, and marijuana—whose use increases the risk that a person will later use harder drugs. (p. 456; objective 11)

26. Generational forgetting is the tendency of each new generation to ignore lessons (such as the hazards of drug use) learned by the previous cohort. (p. 458; objective 11)

Practice Questions I

Multiple-Choice Questions

1. a. is the correct answer. (p. 436; video lesson, segment 1; objective 1)

2. a. is the correct answer. (p. 437; video lesson, segment 1; objectives 1 & 2)

3. b. is the correct answer. (p. 436; video lesson, segment 1; objective 1)

4. c. is the correct answer. This is because each menstrual period depletes some iron from the body. (p. 451; objective 9)

5. a. is the correct answer. (p. 433; objectives 1 & 3)

    b. is incorrect. This describes the gonads.

    c. is incorrect. These include estrogen and testosterone.

    d. is incorrect. This is the hypothalamus.

6. b. is the correct answer. (p. 436; video lesson, segment 1; objective 5)

7. b. is the correct answer. (p. 439; video lesson, segment 1; objectives 1 & 5)

8. d. is the correct answer. (p. 433; objective 1)

9. c. is the correct answer. (pp. 434–444; video lesson, segment 2; objective 7)

   a. is incorrect. Although some adolescents become overweight, many diet and lose weight in an effort to attain a desired body image.

   d. is incorrect. On the contrary, cultural attitudes about beauty are an extremely influential factor in the formation of a teenager's body image.

10. c. is the correct answer. (pp. 452–453; objective 10)

    a. & d. are incorrect. Eating disorders are more common in women than in men.

    b. is incorrect. Eating disorders are more common in younger women.

11. b. is the correct answer. (pp. 448–449; objective 8)

12. c. is the correct answer. (p. 444; objective 3)

13. d. is the correct answer. Also known as adrenaline and noradrenaline, epinephrine and norepinephrine are hormones released by the adrenal glands. (p. 432; video lesson, segment 2; objective 3)

14. d. is the correct answer. (p. 450; objective 9)

15. c. is the correct answer. (p. 455; objective 10)

True or False Items

16. T (p. 450; objective 9)

17. T (p. 452; objective 10)

18. F The first indicator of reproductive potential in males is ejaculation of seminal fluid containing sperm (spermarche). Menarche (the first menstrual period) is the first indication of reproductive potential in females. (p. 434; video lesson, segment 1; objectives 1 & 5)

19. T (p. 438; objective 4)

20. T (p. 433; video lesson, segment 1; objectives 1 & 2)

21. F Studies show that the majority of adolescent girls, even those in the thinnest group, want to lose weight. (p. 432; objectives 3 & 7)

22. F The strong emphasis on appearance is reflected in the culture as a whole; for example, teachers (and, no doubt, prospective employers) tend to judge people who are physically attractive as being more competent than those who are less attractive. (p. 452; video lesson, segment 2; objective 7)

23. F These habits generally worsen during adolescence. (pp. 450–451; objectives 9 & 10)

24. F (p. 445; objective 3)

25. F Although there is great variation in the timing of pubertal events, the sequence is very similar for all young people. (p. 436; video lesson, segment 1; objective 2)

Practice Questions II

Multiple-Choice Questions

1. b. is the correct answer. (p. 436; objective 1)

2. d. is the correct answer. During adolescence, the lymphoid system decreases in size and the heart doubles in size. (p. 438; objective 4)

3. a. is the correct answer. (p. 433; video lesson, segment 1; objective 1)

   b. is incorrect. Testosterone increases markedly in boys.

   c. is incorrect. Androgen is another name for testosterone.

   d. is incorrect. Menarche is the first menstrual period.

4. b. is the correct answer. (p. 451; objective 9)

5. b. is the correct answer. (p. 437; video lesson, segment 1; objective 1)

   a. is incorrect. The shoulders of males tend to widen during puberty.

   c. is incorrect. The torso typically lengthens during puberty.

   d. is incorrect. The eyes and nose increase in size during puberty.

6. c. is the correct answer. (p. 439; video lesson, segment 1; objective 5)

   a. is incorrect. Although not a term used in the textbook, a gender-typed trait is one that is typical of one sex but not of the other.

   b. is incorrect. Primary sex characteristics are those involving the reproductive organs.

   d. is incorrect. This is not a term used by developmental psychologists.

7. a. is the correct answer. (p. 432; video lesson, segment 1; objectives 1 & 2)

8. a. is the correct answer. (pp. 454; objective 10)

   b. is incorrect. This describes an individual suffering from anorexia nervosa.

   c. is incorrect. Eating disorders are much more common in younger women.

   d. is incorrect. Most individuals with bulimia nervosa are usually close to normal in weight.

9. c. is the correct answer. (p. 443; video lesson, segment 2; objective 7)

   a. is incorrect. If the timing of maturation differs substantially from that of the peer group, dissatisfaction is likely; however, this is not the most common source of dissatisfaction in teenage girls.

   b. & d. are incorrect. Although teenage girls are more likely than boys to be dissatisfied with certain features, which body parts are troubling varies from girl to girl.

10. d. is the correct answer. (p. 444; objectives 3 & 7)

11. b. is the correct answer. (p. 456; objective 11)

12. a. is the correct answer. (p. 449; objective 8)

   b. is incorrect. This was not discussed in the lesson.

   c. is incorrect. This is true of girls.

13. c. is the correct answer. (p. 432; video lesson, segment 1; objective 1)

14. b. is the correct answer. Although the size of the heart increases during puberty, heart rate decreases. (p. 438; objective 4)

15. d. is the correct answer. (p. 438; objective 4)

Matching Items

16. b (p. 432; video lesson, segment 1; objective 1)

17. d (p. 433; video lesson, segment 1; objective 1)

18. c (p. 433; video lesson, segment 1; objective 1)

19. f (p. 433; video lesson, segment 1; objective 1)

20. g (p. 436; video lesson, segment 1; objective 4)

21. k (p. 439; video lesson, segment 1; objective 5)

22. a (p. 434; video lesson, segment 1; objectives 1 and 5)

23. l (p. 434; video lesson, segment 1; objectives 1 & 5)

24. j (p. 439; video lesson, segment 1; objective 5)

25. h (p. 443; video lesson, segment 2; objective 7)

26. i (p. 452; objective 10)

27. e (p. 454; objective 10)

Applying Your Knowledge

1. d. is the correct answer. (p. 443; video lesson, segment 2; objective 7)

   a., b., & c. are incorrect. These would likely make matters worse.

2. b. is the correct answer. (p. 435; objective 2)

   a. is incorrect. Because they typically have little body fat, female dancers and athletes menstruate later than average.

   c. is incorrect. Delayed maturation in a young dancer or athlete is usually quite normal.

   d. is incorrect. The text does not indicate that the age of menarche varies with diet.

3. a. is the correct answer. (p. 434; objective 2)

   b. is incorrect. It usually takes longer than one year for a prepubescent male to catch up with a female who has begun puberty.

   c. is incorrect. This is not true.

   d. is incorrect. The text does not suggest that exercise has an effect on the timing of the growth spurt.

4. d. is the correct answer. (p. 440; objective 5)

5. a. is the correct answer. (p. 445; video lesson, segment 2; objective 3)

   b., c., & d. are incorrect. These are more typically sources of status for early-maturing boys.

6. d. is the correct answer. (pp. 444–445; video lesson, segment 2; objective 3)

   a. & b. are incorrect. Early-maturing girls are often teased and criticized by their friends.

   c. is incorrect. During adolescence, physical stature is typically a more prized attribute among peers than is scholastic achievement.

7. c. is the correct answer. It is early-maturing girls who are often drawn into older peer groups. (p. 444; objective 3)

8. c. is the correct answer. (p. 455; objective 10)

   a. is incorrect. Those who emphasize sociocultural theory would more likely offer this explanation.

   b. is incorrect. Those who emphasize learning theory would more likely offer this explanation.

   d. is incorrect. Those who emphasize cognitive theory would more likely offer this explanation.

9. a. is the correct answer. African-Americans often begin puberty earlier than Asian-Americans or Americans of European ancestry. Furthermore, females who are inactive menstruate earlier than those who are more active. (p. 435; objective 2)

10. b. is the correct answer. (p. 444; video lesson, segment 2; objective 3)

    a. is incorrect. Late maturation is typically more difficult for boys than for girls.

    c. is incorrect. Early maturation is generally a positive experience for boys.

    d. is incorrect. Adolescent masturbation is no longer the source of guilt or shame that it once was.

11. d. Kristin's symptoms are typical of iron-deficiency anemia, which is more common in teenage girls than in any other age group. (p. 451; objective 9)

12. c. is the correct answer. (p. 433; objective 1)

    a. is incorrect. Only in girls do estrogen levels rise markedly during puberty.

    b. is incorrect. Only in boys do testosterone levels rise markedly during puberty.

    d. is incorrect. Menarche is the first menstrual period.

13. b. is the correct answer. (p. 432; video lesson, segment 1; objective 1)

Lesson Review

Lesson 21

Adolescence
Biosocial Development

Please Note: Use this matrix to guide your study and achieve the learning objectives of this lesson. It will also help you to view the video, which defines and demonstrates important concepts and skills as they relate to everyday life.

Learning Objective	Textbook	Telecourse Student Guide	Video Lesson
1. Identify and describe the biological events of puberty.	pp. 431–439	Key Terms: 1, 2, 3, 4, 5, 6, 10, 11; Practice Questions I: 1, 2, 3, 5, 7, 8, 18, 20; Practice Questions II: 1, 3, 5, 7, 13, 16, 17, 18, 19, 22, 23; Applying Your Knowledge: 12, 13.	Segment 1: *Puberty*
2. Identify several factors that influence the onset of puberty.	pp. 432–437	Key Terms: 3, 4, 5, 6, 7, 8, 9; Practice Questions I: 2, 5, 20, 25; Practice Questions II: 7; Applying Your Knowledge: 2, 3, 9.	
3. Discuss the consequences for boys and girls who experience early or late onset of puberty.	pp. 432–433, 444–445	Practice Questions I: 12, 13, 21, 24; Practice Questions II: 10; Applying Your Knowledge: 5, 6, 7, 10.	Segment 2: *Body Image*
4. Describe the growth spurt experienced during adolescence by both boys and girls, including changes in weight, height, and the body's internal organ system.	pp. 436–438	Key Terms: 12; Practice Questions I: 19; Practice Questions II: 2, 14, 15, 20.	Segment 1: *Puberty*
5. Describe the development of sexual characteristics in males and females during puberty, and distinguish between primary and secondary sex characteristics.	pp. 433–440, 452	Key Terms: 7, 8, 9, 10, 11, 13, 14; Practice Questions I: 6, 7, 18; Practice Questions II: 6, 21, 22, 23, 24; Applying Your Knowledge: 4.	Segment 1: *Puberty*

Learning Objective	Textbook	Telecourse Student Guide	Video Lesson
6. Discuss the emotional and psychological impact of pubertal hormones and how this impact is influenced by social context.	pp. 440–443	Practice Questions I: 22; Practice Questions II: 9; Applying Your Knowledge: 1.	Segment 1: *Puberty* Segment 2: *Body Image*
7. Describe factors that have an impact on the adolescent's development of a positive body image.	pp. 432, 443–444, 452	Key Terms: 15; Practice Questions I: 9, 21, 22; Practice Questions II: 9, 10, 25; Applying Your Knowledge: 1.	Segment 2: *Body Image*
8. Define childhood sexual abuse, discuss its prevalence, and describe its consequences for development.	pp. 445–449	Key Terms: 16, 17, 18; Practice Questions I: 11; Practice Questions II: 12.	Segment 1: *Puberty*
9. Discuss the nutritional needs and problems of adolescents.	pp. 450–451	Practice Questions I: 4, 14, 16, 23; Practice Questions II: 4; Applying Your Knowledge: 11.	Segment 3: *Health*
10. Define the major types of eating disorders, and discuss how different theories of development might explain them.	pp. 450–456	Key Terms: 19, 20, 21; Practice Questions I: 14, 15, 17; Practice Questions II: 8, 26, 27; Applying Your Knowledge: 8.	
11. Discuss the use and abuse of alcohol, tobacco, and other drugs among adolescents today, including prevalence, significance for development, and the best methods of prevention.	pp. 455–458	Key Terms: 22, 23, 24, 25, 26; Practice Questions II: 11.	Segment 3: *Health*

What If?

Lesson 22

Adolescence:
Cognitive Development

Preview

Lesson 22 begins by describing the cognitive advances of adolescence, especially the emerging ability to think in an adult way, that is, to be logical, to think in terms of possibilities, to reason scientifically and abstractly.

Not all adolescents attain this level of reasoning ability, however, and even those who do spend much of their time thinking at less advanced levels. For instance, adolescents may have difficulty thinking rationally about themselves and their immediate experiences, often seeing themselves as psychologically unique and more socially significant than they really are.

The lesson also addresses the question, "What kind of school best fosters adolescent intellectual growth?" Many adolescents enter secondary school feeling less motivated and more vulnerable to self-doubt than they did in elementary school. The rigid behavioral demands and intensified competition of most secondary schools do not, unfortunately, provide a supportive learning environment for adolescents.

The lesson concludes with an example of adolescent thinking at work: decision making in the area of sexual behavior. The discussion relates choices made by adolescents to their cognitive abilities and typical shortcomings, and it suggests ways in which adolescents may be helped to make healthy choices.

Throughout this lesson, recall your own cognitive development during adolescence. In what ways was your thinking more like an adult's, and in what ways was it still "youthful?" Did you think about yourself, about your interests, and your future? Reflect on your experiences in middle and secondary school. Did you get what you consider to be a good education? Why or why not? Were you motivated to learn? What did you think about sex at this age? How did you make decisions regarding sex, drugs, and so forth? Did you have any formal sex education in school or elsewhere?

Prior Telecourse Knowledge that Will Be Used in this Lesson
- This lesson will return to Piaget's theory of cognitive development (from Lesson 1). Recall that Piaget's theory specifies four major periods of development, the fourth and final stage being *formal operational thought*:
  1. Sensorimotor (Birth to 2 years)
  2. Preoperational (2 to 6 years)
  3. Concrete Operational (7 to 11 years)
  4. **Formal Operational (12 years through adolescence)** ← **Adolescence**

Learning Objectives

Use this information to guide your reading, viewing, thinking, and studying. After successfully completing this lesson, you should be able to:

1. Describe changes in the thinking of adolescents.
2. Describe Piaget's concept of formal operational thinking and provide examples of adolescents' emerging ability to reason deductively and inductively.
3. Discuss adolescent egocentrism and give three examples of egocentric fantasies or fables.
4. Describe the concept of person–environment fit and explain how schools can be organized to more effectively meet adolescents' cognitive needs.
5. Describe the major ethnic and cultural factors that can affect adolescent schooling, and discuss the potential impact of employment on academic performance.
6. Briefly discuss the adolescent's decision-making process.
7. Identify the cognitive and social factors affecting adolescent decision making regarding sex.
8. Discuss the relative effectiveness of sex education, both at home and in the classroom.

📖 **Read Chapter 15, "Adolescence: Cognitive Development," pages 465–495.**

📹 **View the video for Lesson 22, "What If?"**

Segment 1: *Formal Operational Thought*

Segment 2: *Educating Adolescents*

Segment 3: *Adolescent Decision-Making*

Summary

The basic skills of thinking, learning, and remembering continue to be refined during the adolescent years. According to most developmentalists, the distinguishing feature of adolescent thought is the capacity to think in terms of possibility rather than only in terms of reality.

Piaget described the reasoning that characterizes adolescence as **formal operational thought**, which arises from maturation and experience. On the whole, adolescents are able to fantasize, speculate, and hypothesize much more readily and on a much grander scale than younger children are. With this capacity for **hypothetical thought**, the adolescent is able to consider the here and now as one among many alternative possibilities. In addition, the capacities for **deductive reasoning** (deriving conclusions from premises), and **inductive reasoning** (reasoning from one or more specific experiences or facts to a general conclusion) become refined.

Developmental psychologists have described **adolescent egocentrism** as a stage of development in which young people typically consider their own psychological experiences (love and anger, for example) to be unique. The **invincibility fable** that they are somehow immune to common dangers and the **personal fable** that their lives are unique or heroic are further examples of adolescents' egocentrism. As another part of their egocentrism, adolescents often create for themselves an **imaginary audience** that allows them to fantasize about how others will react to their appearance and behavior.

With regard to education, the optimum **person–environment fit** depends not only on the individual's developmental stage, cognitive abilities, and learning style, but also on the society's traditions, educational objectives, and future needs, which vary substantially from place to place and time to time. As students move from primary to secondary school, their motivation and grades usually fall. One reason is that secondary schools are more competitive than cooperative. For adolescents, smaller schools with engaging instruction that invites logical as well as personal reflections seem best.

Because they often think about possibilities rather than practicalities, and because egocentrism makes it difficult to plan ahead, adolescents tend not to make major decisions about their future plans on their own. On matters of personal lifestyle, however, they do make decisions, sometimes ones that involve considerable risk. Because of their sense of personal invincibility, many teens underestimate the chances of getting pregnant or of contracting a sexually transmitted disease (STD). In addition, teens often fail to think through all the possible consequences of their behavior, focusing instead only on immediate concerns. Sex education that encourages thinking, role playing, and discussion about sexuality is more effective than traditional programs that focus only on biological facts. School programs designed to address these issues have resulted in decreased sexual activity, teenage pregnancies, and increased condom use.

📖 **Review all reading assignments for this lesson.**

💻 **As assigned by your instructor, complete the optional online component for this lesson.**

Key Terms

Using your own words, write a brief definition or explanation of each of the following terms on a separate piece of paper.

1. hypothetical thought
2. inductive reasoning
3. deductive reasoning
4. formal operational thought
5. postformal thought
6. adolescent egocentrism
7. invincibility fable
8. personal fable
9. imaginary audience
10. person–environment fit
11. volatile mismatch
12. high-stakes tests
13. self-handicapping
14. sexually active

Practice Questions I

Multiple-Choice Questions

1. Many psychologists consider the distinguishing feature of adolescent thought to be the ability to think in terms of
   a. moral issues.
   b. concrete operations.
   c. possibility, not just reality.
   d. logical principles.

2. Piaget's last stage of cognitive development is
   a. formal operational thought.
   b. concrete operational thought.
   c. universal ethical principles.
   d. symbolic thought.

3. Advances in metamemory and metacognition deepen adolescents' abilities in
   a. studying.
   b. the invincibility fable.
   c. the personal fable.
   d. adolescent egocentrism.

4. The adolescent who takes risks and feels immune to the laws of mortality is showing evidence of the
   a. invincibility fable.
   b. personal fable.
   c. imaginary audience.
   d. death instinct.

5. Imaginary audiences, invincibility fables, and personal fables are expressions of adolescent
   a. morality.
   b. thinking games.
   c. decision making.
   d. egocentrism.

6. The typical adolescent is
   a. tough-minded.
   b. indifferent to public opinion.
   c. self-absorbed and hypersensitive to criticism.
   d. all of the above.

7. When adolescents enter secondary school, many
   a. experience a drop in their academic self-confidence.
   b. are less motivated than they were in elementary school.
   c. are less conscientious than they were in elementary school.
   d. experience all of the above.

8. During adolescence, which area of the brain becomes more densely packed and efficient, enabling adolescents to analyze possibilities and to pursue goals more effectively?
   a. hypothalamus
   b. brain stem
   c. adrenal glands
   d. prefrontal cortex

9. Thinking that begins with a general premise and then draws logical conclusions from it is called

   a. inductive reasoning.
   b. deductive reasoning.
   c. "the game of thinking."
   d. hypothetical reasoning.

10. Serious reflection on important issues is a wrenching process for many adolescents because of their newfound ability to reason

    a. inductively.
    b. deductively.
    c. hypothetically.
    d. symbolically.

11. Hypothetical-deductive thinking is to heuristic thinking as

    a. rational analysis is to intuitive thought.
    b. intuitive thought is to rational analysis.
    c. experiential thinking is to intuitive reasoning.
    d. intuitive thinking is to analytical reasoning.

12. Many adolescents seem to believe that their own sexual behaviors will not lead to pregnancy. This belief is an expression of the

    a. personal fable.
    b. invincibility fable.
    c. imaginary audience.
    d. "game of thinking."

13. A parent in which of the following countries is least likely to approve of her daughter's request to take a part-time job after school?

    a. the United States
    b. Germany
    c. Great Britain
    d. Japan

14. In a new method of sex education, adolescents

    a. develop reasoning skills to resist sexual pressures.
    b. are exposed to scare tactics designed to discourage sexual activity.
    c. are taught by teenagers who have contracted a sexually transmitted disease.
    d. experience all of the above.

15. To estimate the risk of a behavior, such as unprotected sexual intercourse, it is most important that the adolescent be able to think clearly about

    a. universal ethical principles.
    b. personal beliefs and self-interest.
    c. probability.
    d. peer pressure.

True or False Items

Write true or false on the line in front of each statement.

16. _____ Statistically, adolescents are safer in schools than in their neighborhoods.

17. _____ Adolescents are generally better able than eight-year-olds at recognizing the validity of arguments that clash with their own beliefs.

18. _____ Everyone attains the stage of formal operational thought by adulthood.

19. _____ Most adolescents who engage in risky behavior are unaware of the consequences, and potential costs, of their actions.

20. _____ Adolescents often create an imaginary audience as they envision how others will react to their appearance and behavior.

21. _____ Many states are banning high-stakes tests because of their negative influence on adolescents.

22. _____ The teen birth rate continues to rise throughout the world.

23. _____ Inductive reasoning is a hallmark of formal operational thought.

24. _____ Adolescents are the group with the highest rates of drug abuse.

25. _____ Tertiary education is the informal learning that occurs outside the school system.

Practice Questions II

Multiple-Choice Questions

1. Adolescents who fall prey to the invincibility fable may be more likely to
   a. engage in risky behaviors.
   b. suffer from depression.
   c. have low self-esteem.
   d. drop out of school.

2. Thinking that extrapolates from a specific experience to form a general premise is called
   a. inductive reasoning.
   b. deductive reasoning.
   c. "the game of thinking."
   d. hypothetical reasoning.

3. Recent research regarding Piaget's theory has found that
   a. many adolescents arrive at formal operational thinking later than Piaget predicted.
   b. formal operational thinking is more likely to be demonstrated in certain domains than in others.
   c. whether formal operational thinking is demonstrated depends in part on an individual's experiences, talents, and interests.
   d. all of the above are true.

4. When young people overestimate their significance to others, they are displaying
   a. concrete operational thought.
   b. adolescent egocentrism.
   c. a lack of cognitive growth.
   d. immoral development.

5. The personal fable refers to adolescents imagining that
   a. they are immune to the dangers of risky behaviors.
   b. they are always being scrutinized by others.
   c. their own lives are unique, heroic, or even mythical.
   d. the world revolves around their actions.

6. The typical secondary school environment
   a. has more rigid behavioral demands than the average elementary school.
   b. does not meet the cognitive needs of the typical adolescent.
   c. emphasizes ego-involvement learning.
   d. is described by all of the above.

7. As compared to elementary schools, most secondary schools exhibit all of the following **EXCEPT**
   a. a more flexible approach to education.
   b. intensified competition.
   c. more punitive grading practices.
   d. less individualized attention.

8. A study of 13- to 15-year-old French schoolchildren found that
   a. the proportion of children testing at the formal operational level remained constant over a 10-year period.
   b. the proportion of children testing at the formal operational level changed substantially over a 10-year period.
   c. adolescent girls were more likely than boys to have achieved formal operational thinking.
   d. adolescent boys were more likely than girls to have achieved formal operational thinking.

9. Research has shown that adolescents who work at after-school jobs more than 20 hours per week
   a. are more likely to use drugs as adults.
   b. have lower grades.
   c. tend to feel less connected to their families.
   d. have all of the above characteristics.

10. One of the hallmarks of formal operational thought is
    a. egocentrism.
    b. deductive thinking.
    c. symbolic thinking.
    d. all of the above.

11. In explaining adolescent advances in thinking, sociocultural theorists emphasize
    a. the accumulated improvement in specific skills.
    b. mental advances resulting from the transition from primary school to secondary school.
    c. the completion of the myelination process in cortical neurons.
    d. advances in metacognition.

12. After failing his first chemistry test, fifteen-year-old Louis begins studying less and says he "never wanted to be a doctor anyway." Louis' behavior is an example of
    a. the personal fable.
    b. the invincibility fable.
    c. self-handicapping.
    d. postformal thinking.

13. Evidence that revised sex education programs are working comes from the fact that _____ (are) declining.
    a. the birth rate among teenagers
    b. the percentage of sexually active teenagers
    c. the use of condoms among teenagers
    d. all of the above

14. The most important characteristic of effective schools is
    a. self-paced instruction.
    b. dividing classes into students with similar abilities.
    c. a standardized procedure for teaching each subject.
    d. high, clearly stated, and attainable goals.

Matching Items
Match each definition or description with its corresponding term.

Terms
15. _____ invincibility fable
16. _____ imaginary audience
17. _____ person–environment fit
18. _____ hypothetical thought
19. _____ deductive reasoning
20. _____ inductive reasoning
21. _____ formal operational thought
22. _____ volatile mismatch
23. _____ adolescent egocentrism

Definitions or Descriptions
a. the tendency of adolescents to focus on themselves to the exclusion of others
b. adolescents feel immune to the consequences of dangerous behavior
c. a creation of adolescents, who are preoccupied with how others react to their appearance and behavior
d. the match or mismatch between an adolescent's needs and the educational setting
e. reasoning about propositions that may or may not reflect reality
f. the last stage of cognitive development, according to Piaget
g. thinking that moves from premise to conclusion

h. thinking that moves from a specific experience to a general premise

i. a clash between a teenager's needs and the structure and functioning of his or her school

Applying Your Knowledge

1. A 13-year-old can create and solve logical problems on the computer but is not usually reasonable, mature, or consistent in his or her thinking when it comes to people and social relationships. This supports the finding that

    a. some children reach the stage of formal operational thought earlier than others.

    b. the stage of formal operational thought is not attained by age 13.

    c. formal operational thinking may be demonstrated in certain domains and not in other domains.

    d. older adolescents and adults often do poorly on standard tests of formal operational thought.

2. An experimenter hides a ball in her hand and says, "Either the ball in my hand is red or it is not red." Most preadolescent children say

    a. the statement is true.

    b. the statement is false.

    c. they cannot tell if the statement is true or false.

    d. they do not understand what the experimenter means.

3. Fourteen-year-old Monica is very idealistic and often develops crushes on people she doesn't even know. This reflects her newly developed cognitive ability to

    a. deal simultaneously with two sides of an issue.

    b. take another person's viewpoint.

    c. imagine possible worlds and people.

    d. see herself as others see her.

4. Which of the following is the best example of a personal fable?

    a. Adriana imagines that she is destined for a life of fame and fortune.

    b. Ben makes up stories about his experiences to impress his friends.

    c. Kalil questions his religious beliefs when they seem to offer little help for a problem he faces.

    d. Julio believes that every girl he meets is attracted to him.

5. Which of the following is the best example of the adolescent's ability to think hypothetically?

    a. Twelve-year-old Stanley feels that people are always watching him.

    b. Fourteen-year-old Mindy engages in many risky behaviors, reasoning that, "nothing bad will happen to me."

    c. Fifteen-year-old Philip feels that no one understands his problems.

    d. Thirteen-year-old Josh delights in finding logical flaws in virtually everything his teachers and parents say.

6. Frustrated because of the dating curfew her parents have set, Lucinda exclaims, "You just don't know how it feels to be in love!" Lucinda's thinking demonstrates

   a. the invincibility fable.

   b. the personal fable.

   c. the imaginary audience.

   d. adolescent egocentrism.

7. Compared to her 13-year-old brother, 17-year-old Yolanda is likely to

   a. be more critical about herself.

   b. be more egocentric.

   c. have less confidence in her abilities.

   d. be more capable of reasoning hypothetically.

8. Nathan's fear that his friends will ridicule him because of a pimple that has appeared on his nose reflects a preoccupation with

   a. his personal fable.

   b. the invincibility fable.

   c. an imaginary audience.

   d. preconventional reasoning.

9. Thirteen-year-old Malcolm, who lately is very sensitive to the criticism of others, feels significantly less motivated and capable than when he was in elementary school. Malcolm is probably

   a. experiencing a sense of vulnerability that is common in adolescents.

   b. a lower-track student.

   c. a student in a task-involvement classroom.

   d. all of the above.

10. A high school principal who wished to increase the interest level and achievement of minority and female students would be well advised to

    a. create classroom environments that are not based on competitive grading procedures.

    b. encourage greater use of standardized testing in the elementary schools that feed students to the high school.

    c. separate students into academic tracks based on achievement.

    d. do all of the above.

11. Seventy-year-old Mark can't understand why his daughter doesn't want her teenage son to work after school. "In my day," he says, "we learned responsibility and a useful trade by working throughout high school." You wisely point out that

    a. most after-school jobs for teens today are not very meaningful.

    b. after-school employment tends to have a more negative impact on boys than girls.

    c. attitudes are changing; today, most American parents see adolescent employment as a waste of time.

    d. teens in most European countries almost never work after school.

12. Who is the **LEAST** likely to display mature decision making?

    a. Brenda, an outgoing 17-year-old art student

    b. Fifteen-year-old Kenny, who has few adults in whom he confides

    c. Monique, a well-educated 15-year-old

    d. Damon, an 18-year-old high school graduate who lives alone

13. After hearing that an unusually aggressive child has been in full-time day care since he was age 1, 16-year-old Jerry concludes that nonparental care leads to behavior problems. Jerry's conclusion is an example of

    a. inductive reasoning.

    b. deductive reasoning.

    c. hypothetical thinking.

    d. adolescent egocentrism.

14. On a test of moral reasoning, sixteen-year-old Lyndsey decides that a person who steals an expensive medicine to save a friend's life is guilty of a crime, but should not be punished because of the circumstances. Lyndsey's reasoning is an example of

    a. inductive reasoning.

    b. preconventional moral reasoning.

    c. postformal thinking.

    d. self-handicapping.

15. Dr. Malone, who wants to improve the effectiveness of her adolescent sex-education class, would be well advised to

    a. focus on the biological facts of reproduction and disease, because teenage misinformation is largely responsible for the high rates of unwanted pregnancy and STDs.

    b. personalize the instruction, in order to make the possible consequences of sexual activity more immediate to students.

    c. teach boys and girls in separate classes, so that discussion can be more frank and open.

    d. use all of the above strategies.

Answer Key

Key Terms

1. Hypothetical thought involves reasoning about propositions and possibilities that may or may not reflect reality. (p. 466; video lesson, segment 1; objective 2)

2. Inductive reasoning is thinking that moves from one or more specific experiences to a general conclusion. (p. 467; video lesson, segment 1; objective 2)

3. Deductive reasoning is thinking that moves from the general to the specific, or from a premise to a logical conclusion. (p. 467; video lesson, segment 1; objective 2)

4. In Piaget's theory, the last stage of cognitive development, which arises from a combination of maturation and experience, is called formal operational thought. A hallmark of formal operational thinking is the capacity for hypothetical, logical, and abstract thought. (p. 468; video lesson, segment 1; objective 2)

5. Postformal thought is reasoning beyond formal thought that struggles to reconcile logic and experience, and is well suited to solving real-world problems. (p. 469; video lesson, segment 1; objective 2)

6. Adolescent egocentrism refers to the tendency of adolescents to see themselves as much more socially significant than they actually are. (p. 472; video lesson, segment 1; objective 3)

7. Adolescents who experience the invincibility fable feel that they are immune to the dangers of risky behaviors. (pp. 472–473; video lesson, segment 1; objective 3)

8. Another example of adolescent egocentrism is the personal fable, through which adolescents imagine their own lives as unique, heroic, or even mythical. (p. 473; video lesson, segment 1; objective 3)

   Memory aid: A fable is a mythical story.

9. Adolescents often create an imaginary audience for themselves, as they assume that others are as intensely interested in them as they themselves are. (p. 473; video lesson, segment 1; objective 3)

10. The term person–environment fit refers to the best setting for personal growth, as in the optimum educational setting. (p. 478; video lesson, segment 2; objective 4)

11. When teenagers' individual needs do not match the size, routine, and structure of their schools, a volatile mismatch may occur. (p. 479; video lesson, segment 2; objective 4)

12. Self-handicapping involves making deliberate choices that will impede a person's chances of success, often to preserve self-esteem. (p. 483; objectives 4 & 6)

13. High-stakes tests are tests that have serious consequences for those who take them, including determining whether they will be promoted to the next grade in school or allowed to graduate. (pp. 484–485; objective 4)

14. Traditionally, sexually active teenagers were those who have had intercourse. (p. 490; objectives 7 & 8)

Practice Questions I

Multiple-Choice Questions

1. c. is the correct answer. (p. 468; video lesson, segment 1; objective 1)

   a. is incorrect. Although moral reasoning becomes much deeper during adolescence, it is not limited to this stage of development.

   b. & d. are incorrect. Concrete operational thought, which is logical, is the distinguishing feature of childhood thinking.

2. a. is the correct answer. (pp. 467–468; video lesson, segment 1; objective 2)

   b. is incorrect. In Piaget's theory, this stage precedes formal operational thought.

   c. & d. are incorrect. These are not stages in Piaget's theory.

3. a. is the correct answer. (p. 465; objective 1)

   b., c., & d. are incorrect. These are examples of limited reasoning ability during adolescence.

4. a. is the correct answer. (pp. 472–473; video lesson, segment 1; objective 3)

   b. is incorrect. This refers to adolescents' tendency to imagine their own lives as unique, heroic, or even mythical.

   c. is incorrect. This refers to adolescents' tendency to fantasize about how others will react to their appearance and behavior.

   d. is incorrect. This is a concept in Freud's theory.

5. d. is the correct answer. These thought processes are manifestations of adolescents' tendency to see themselves as being much more central and important to the social scene than they really are. (p. 472; video lesson, segment 1; objective 3)

6. c. is the correct answer. (pp. 465, 472; video lesson, segment 1; objective 1)

7. d. is the correct answer. (pp. 482–483; objective 4)

8. d. is the correct answer. (p. 466; objective 1)

9. b. is the correct answer. (p. 467; video lesson, segment 1; objective 2)

   a. is incorrect. Inductive reasoning moves from specific facts to a general conclusion.

   b. & c. are incorrect. The "game of thinking," which is an example of hypothetical reasoning, involves the ability to think creatively about possibilities.

10. c. is the correct answer. (pp. 468–469; video lesson, segment 1; objective 1)

11. a. is the correct answer. (pp. 468–469, 472; objective 1 & 2)

   c. is incorrect. Heuristic thinking is both experiential *and* intuitive.

12. b. is the correct answer. (pp. 472–473; objectives 3 and 7)

   a. is incorrect. This refers to adolescents' tendency to imagine their own lives as unique, heroic, or even mythical.

   c. is incorrect. This refers to adolescents' tendency to fantasize about how others will react to their appearance and behavior.

   d. is incorrect. This is the adolescent ability to suspend knowledge of reality in order to think playfully about possibilities.

13. d. is the correct answer. Japanese adolescents almost never work after school. (p. 488; objective 5)

   a. is incorrect. American parents generally approve of adolescent employment.

   b. & c. are incorrect. Jobs are an important part of the school curriculum in many European countries.

14. a. is the correct answer. (p. 491; objective 8)

15. c. is the correct answer. (p. 487; objective 7)

True or False Items

16. T   (p. 485; objective 4)

17. T   (p. 469; video lesson, segment 1; objectives 1 & 2)

18. F   Some people never reach the stage of formal operational thought. (p. 471; video lesson, segment 1; objective 2)

19. F   Adolescent behavior is guided by assumptions about risks and benefits. (pp. 486–487; objective 7)

20. T   (p. 473; video lesson, segment 1; objective 3)

21. F   High-stakes testing is mandated by virtually every state legislature in the United States. (p. 484; objectives 4 & 5)

22. F   The teen birth rate worldwide has dropped significantly since 1990. (p. 490; objectives 6 & 7)

23. F   Deductive reasoning is a hallmark of formal operational thought, although adolescents continue to improve their inductive reasoning skills as well. (p. 467; video lesson, segment 1; objective 2)

24. F   Young adults are the most likely age group to abuse drugs. (p. 486; objective 6)

25. F   Also called higher education, tertiary education includes colleges and universities. (p. 479; objective 4)

Practice Questions II

Multiple-Choice Questions

1. a. is the correct answer. (pp. 472–473; video lesson, segment 1; objective 3)

   b., c., & d. are incorrect. The invincibility fable leads some teens to believe that they are immune to the dangers of risky behaviors; it is not necessarily linked to depression, low self-esteem, or the likelihood that an individual will drop out of school.

2. a. is the correct answer. (p. 467; video lesson, segment 1; objective 2)

   b. is incorrect. Deductive reasoning begins with a general premise and then draws logical conclusions from it.

   c. & d. are incorrect. The "game of thinking," which is an example of hypothetical reasoning, involves the ability to think creatively about possibilities.

3. d. is the correct answer. (pp. 471; video lesson, segment 1; objective 2)

4. b. is the correct answer. (p. 472; video lesson, segment 1; objective 3)

5. c. is the correct answer. (p. 473; video lesson, segment 1; objective 3)

   a. is incorrect. This describes the invincibility fable.

   b. is incorrect. This describes the imaginary audience.

   d. is incorrect. This describes adolescent egocentrism in general.

6. d. is the correct answer. (p. 481; objective 4)

7. a. is the correct answer. (p. 481; objective 4)

8. b. is the correct answer. (p. 471; objective 2)

   c. & d. are incorrect. This study did not report a gender difference in the proportion of children who attained formal thinking.

   d. is incorrect. This is not a type of classroom environment discussed in the textbook.

9. d. is the correct answer. (p. 489; objective 5)

10. b. is the correct answer. (p. 467; video lesson, segment 1; objective 2)

11. b. is the correct answer. (p. 468; objective 1)

    a. & d. are incorrect. These are more likely to be emphasized by information-processing theorists.

    c. is incorrect. This reflects the biological perspective on development.

12. c. is the correct answer. (p. 483; objective 4)

    a.   & b. are incorrect. These refer to the egocentric tendency of adolescents to believe their lives are heroic (personal fable) and immune to the laws of mortality (invincibility fable).

    d. is incorrect. Postformal thinking is a type of reasoning that is well-suited to solving practical problems because it moves beyond pure logic to benefit from the wisdom of experience.

13. a. is the correct answer. (pp. 490–491; objective 8)

    b. & c. are incorrect. These are on the rise.

14. d. is the correct answer. (pp. 482–484; objective 4)

Matching Items

15. b (pp. 472–473; video lesson, segment 1; objective 3)

16. c (p. 473; video lesson, segment 1; objective 3)

17. d (p. 478; video lesson, segment 2; objective 4)

18. e (p. 466; video lesson, segment 1; objective 1)

19. g (p. 467; video lesson, segment 1; objective 2)

20. h (p. 467; video lesson, segment 1; objective 2)

21. f (p. 468; video lesson, segment 1; objective 2)

22. i (p. 479; video lesson, segment 2; objective 4)

23. a (p. 472; video lesson, segment 1; objective 3)

Applying Your Knowledge

1. c. is the correct answer. (p. 471; video lesson, segment 1; objective 2)

2. c. is the correct answer. Although this statement is logically verifiable, preadolescents who lack formal operational thought cannot prove or disprove it. (pp. 467–468; objective 2)

3. c. is the correct answer. (p. 466; video lesson, segment 1; objective 1)

4. a. is the correct answer. (p. 473; video lesson, segment 1; objective 3)

    b. & d. are incorrect. These behaviors are more indicative of a preoccupation with the imaginary audience.

    c. is incorrect. Kalil's questioning attitude is a normal adolescent tendency that helps foster moral reasoning.

5. d. is the correct answer. (pp. 466–467; video lesson, segment 1; objective 1)

    a. is incorrect. This is an example of the imaginary audience.

    b. is incorrect. This is an example of the invincibility fable.

    c. is incorrect. This is an example of adolescent egocentrism.

6. d. is the correct answer. (p. 472; video lesson, segment 1; objective 3)

7. d. is the correct answer. (pp. 466–467; video lesson, segment 1; objective 1)

8. c. is the correct answer. (p. 473; video lesson, segment 1; objective 3)

    a. is incorrect. In this fable adolescents see themselves destined for fame and fortune.

    b. is incorrect. In this fable young people feel that they are somehow immune to the consequences of common dangers.

    d. is incorrect. This is a stage of moral reasoning in Kohlberg's theory.

9. a. is the correct answer. (pp. 481–483; objective 4)

10. a. is the correct answer. (p. 484; objective 4)

11. a. is the correct answer. (p. 489; objective 5)

    b. is incorrect. There is no evidence of a gender difference in the impact of employment on adolescents.

    c. & d. are incorrect. In fact, just the opposite is true.

12. b. is the correct answer. Mature decision making is least likely to be displayed by adolescents who are under age 16, who have less education, and who have few adults to talk with. (p. 487; objective 6)

13. a. is the answer. (p. 467; objective 2)

    b. is incorrect. Keenan is reasoning from the specific to the general, rather than vice versa.

    c. is incorrect. Keenan is thinking about an actual observation, rather than a hypothetical possibility.

    d. is incorrect. Keenan's reasoning is focused outside himself, rather than being self-centered.

14. c. is the correct answer. Postformal thinking is capable of combining contradictory elements (such as the possibility that someone who steals should not be punished) into a comprehensive whole. (p. 469; objective 2)

    a. is incorrect. Inductive reasoning is more typical of logical, formal operational thought.

    b. is incorrect. preconventional moral reasoning, which is not discussed in this chapter, is a morality based on avoiding punishment.

    d. is incorrect. Self-handicapping refers to choices people make to preserve their self-esteem, at the cost of impeding their chances for success.

15. b. is the correct answer. (pp. 466, 491; objective 8)

Lesson Review

Lesson 22

Adolescence
Cognitive Development

Please Note: Use this matrix to guide your study and achieve the learning objectives of this lesson. It will also help you to view the video, which defines and demonstrates important concepts and skills as they relate to everyday life.

Learning Objective	Textbook	Telecourse Student Guide	Video Lesson
1. Describe changes in the thinking of adolescents.	pp. 465–472, 483	Practice Questions I: 1, 3, 6, 8, 10, 11, 17, 18; Practice Questions II: 11; Applying Your Knowledge: 3, 5, 7, 13.	Segment 1: *Formal Operational Thought*
2. Describe Piaget's concept of formal operational thinking and provide examples of adolescents' emerging ability to reason deductively and inductively.	pp. 466–469, 471	Key Terms: 1, 2, 3, 4, 5; Practice Questions I: 2, 9, 11, 17, 23; Practice Questions II: 2, 3, 8, 10, 18, 19, 20, 21; Applying Your Knowledge: 1, 2, 13, 14.	Segment 1: *Formal Operational Thought*
3. Discuss adolescent egocentrism and give three examples of egocentric fantasies or fables.	pp. 472–473	Key Terms: 6, 7, 8, 9; Practice Questions I: 4, 5, 12, 20; Practice Questions II: 1, 4, 5, 15, 16, 23; Applying Your Knowledge: 4, 6, 8.	Segment 1: *Formal Operational Thought*
4. Describe the concept of person-environment fit and explain how schools can be organized to more effectively meet adolescents' cognitive needs.	pp. 478–484	Key Terms: 10, 11, 12, 13; Practice Questions I: 7, 16, 21, 25; Practice Questions II: 6, 7, 12, 14, 17, 22; Applying Your Knowledge: 9, 10.	Segment 2: *Educating Adolescents*
5. Describe the major ethnic and cultural factors that can affect adolescent schooling, and discuss the potential impact of employment on academic performance.	pp. 484–489	Practice Questions I: 13, 21; Practice Questions II: 9; Applying Your Knowledge: 11.	

Learning Objective	Textbook	Telecourse Student Guide	Video Lesson
6. Briefly discuss the adolescent's decision-making process.	pp. 486–491	Key Terms: 12 Practice Questions I: 22, 24; Applying Your Knowledge: 12.	Segment 3: *Adolescent Decision-Making*
7. Identify the cognitive and social factors affecting adolescent decision making regarding sex.	pp. 472–473, 486–490	Key Terms:14; Practice Questions I: 12, 14, 15, 19, 22.	Segment 3: *Adolescent Decision-Making*
8. Discuss the relative effectiveness of sex education, both at home and in the classroom.	pp. 466, 472–473, 490–491	Key Terms: 14; Practice Questions II: 13; Applying Your Knowledge: 15.	

Who Am I?

Lesson 23

Adolescence:
Psychosocial Development

Preview

Adolescence brings a heightened quest for self-understanding and **identity**, a crucial process in the transition from childhood to adulthood. Lesson 23 focuses on the psychosocial development, particularly the formation of identity, required for the attainment of adult status and maturity. Suicide—one of the most perplexing problems of adolescence—is also explored. The special problems posed by adolescent lawbreaking are discussed, and suggestions for alleviating or treating these problems are given.

The influences of family, peers and society on adolescent development are examined in some detail. During this period, the biological imperative of reproductive viability comes to fruition. In many cultures, the plan of life allows for an easy transition into adult life. In technologically advanced societies, another decade of preparation is needed before self-reliance becomes practical. The resulting tension can be difficult to manage.

The lesson concludes with the message that, while no other period of life except infancy is characterized by so many changes in the three domains of development, for most young people the teenage years are happy ones. Furthermore, serious problems in adolescence do not necessarily lead to lifelong problems.

As you complete this lesson, consider your own psychosocial development during adolescence. How would you define your identity at that time? What kind of person were you? What was your relationship with your parents like? Was there much friction or bickering? If so, over which kinds of issues? Describe your social circles, your peers and friends. Did these people have a positive or negative influence on your development? Did you have any romantic relationships? What were they like? Did you or someone you know ever think about suicide during this time? What were the circumstances? Did you know someone who broke the law or got arrested? What was the situation?

Prior Telecourse Knowledge that Will Be Used in this Lesson

- This lesson will return to Erik Erikson's theory from Lesson 1 that specifies eight stages of *psychosocial development,* each of which is characterized by a particular challenge, or *developmental crisis,* which is central to that stage of life and must be resolved. This lesson will focus on Erikson's fifth stage called "identity vs. role confusion":
    1. Trust vs. Mistrust (birth to 1 year)
    2. Autonomy vs. Shame and Doubt (1 to 3 years)
    3. Initiative vs. Guilt (3 to 6 years)

4. Industry vs. Inferiority (7 to 11 years)
   5. **Identity vs. Role Confusion** ← Adolescence
   6. Intimacy vs. Isolation (Adulthood)
   7. Generativity vs. Stagnation (Adulthood)
   8. Integrity vs. Despair (Adulthood)

- In a discussion of family influences during adolescence, this lesson will return to the concept of "parenting styles" introduced in Lesson 13. Recall that three basic styles include *authoritarian* (parents expect unquestioning obedience and offer little affection), *permissive* (affectionate but with few demands), and *authoritative* (parents expect obedience, set appropriate limits, and offer affection).

Learning Objectives

Use this information to guide your reading, viewing, thinking, and studying. After successfully completing this lesson, you should be able to:

1. Define the concept of identity and describe the development of identity during adolescence, incorporating Erikson's crisis of "identity versus role confusion."
2. Describe the concepts of "possible selves" and "false self."
3. Describe the five major identity statuses or conditions , and give an example of each one.
4. Discuss the influence of society and culture on identity formation, and describe the challenges encountered by minority adolescents in achieving their identity.
5. Discuss parent-child relationships during adolescence.
6. Discuss the role of peers, friends, and male-female relationships in adolescence.
7. Discuss adolescent suicide, noting its prevalence, contributing factors, warning signs, and gender and cultural variations.
8. Discuss delinquency among adolescents today, noting its incidence and prevalence, significance for later development, and best approaches for prevention and treatment.

📖 **Read Chapter 16, "Adolescence: Psychosocial Development," pages 497–531.**

📼 **View the video for Lesson 23, "Who Am I?"**
      Segment 1: *Identity*
      Segment 2: *Friends and Family*

Summary

Adolescence heightens the search for self-understanding because of the momentous changes that occur during the teenage years. Many adolescents experience the emergence of **possible selves**, or diverse perceptions of identity in different groups or settings.

According to Erik Erikson, the psychosocial challenge of adolescence is **identity versus role confusion**. The specific task of this challenge is the search for identity, both as an individual and as a member of the larger community. When the search for identify becomes overwhelming and confusing, adolescents may experience an identity crisis. The ultimate goal, **identity achievement**, occurs when adolescents establish their own goals and values by abandoning some of those set by parents and society while accepting others.

Some adolescents form an identity prematurely, a process called **foreclosure**. Other adolescents, unable to find alternative roles that are truly their own, simply rebel and become the opposite of what is expected of them, adopting a **negative identity**. Others experience **identity diffusion**, with few commitments to goals or values, whether those of parents, peers, or the larger society. Many adolescents declare an **identity moratorium**, often by using an institutionalized time-out such as college or voluntary military service as a means of postponing final decisions about career or marriage. While identity formation is a major task of adolescence, many people don't reach identity achievement until early adulthood (or later) and most continue to shape and refine their identities throughout the life span.

For immigrants and minority adolescents, identity formation is particularly complex because they must find the right balance between their ethnic background and the values of the society at large. This may cause them to embrace a negative identity or, as is more often the case, to foreclose on identity prematurely.

Research studies demonstrate that the **generation gap** is not as wide as it is popularly assumed to be. Indeed, studies have found substantial agreement between parents and adolescents on political, religious, educational, and vocational opinions and values. However, there is a **generational stake**, which refers to the particular needs and concerns of each generation in the parent-adolescent relationship, as well as the natural tendency to see the family in a certain way.

The adolescent's peer group is a social institution that eases the transition from childhood to adulthood by functioning in a variety of ways. Peer groups function as a source of information and social support, a group of contemporaries who are experiencing similar struggles. As adolescents associate themselves with a particular subgroup, peers help them define who they are by helping them define who they are not. Peer groups also serve as a sounding board for exploring and defining one's values and aspirations.

While the search for identity brings with it certain difficulties, most adolescents reach adulthood safe and secure. Others have special problems, including delinquent behavior and depression that may lead to suicide. Thinking about suicide (**suicide ideation**) is quite common among high school students. Fortunately, most suicide attempts in adolescence do not result in death. Deliberate acts of self-destruction that do not cause death are referred to as **parasuicide**. Whether or not suicidal ideation leads to suicide or parasuicide depends on the availability of lethal methods, **parental monitoring**, the use of alcohol and other drugs, and the attitudes about suicide that are held by the adolescent's family, friends, and culture.

📖 **Review all reading assignments for this lesson.**

💻 **As assigned by your instructor, complete the optional online component for this lesson.**

Key Terms

Using your own words, write a brief definition or explanation of each of the following terms on a separate piece of paper.

1. identity
2. possible selves
3. false self
4. identity versus role confusion
5. identity achievement
6. foreclosure
7. negative identity
8. identity diffusion
9. identity moratorium
10. gender identity
11. rite of passage
12. suicidal ideation
13. parasuicide
14. cluster suicide
15. internalizing problems
16. externalizing problems
17. incidence
18. prevalence
19. adolescence-limited offender
20. life-course persistent offender
21. generation gap
22. generational stake
23. bickering
24. parental monitoring
25 peer pressure

Practice Questions I

Multiple-Choice Questions

1. According to Erikson, the primary task of adolescence is that of establishing
   a. basic trust.
   b. an identity.
   c. intimacy.
   d. integrity.

2. According to developmentalists who study identity formation, foreclosure involves
   a. accepting an identity prematurely, without exploration.
   b. taking time off from school, work, and other commitments.
   c. opposing parental values.
   d. failing to commit oneself to a vocational goal.

3. When adolescents adopt an identity that is the opposite of the one they are expected to adopt, they are considered to be taking on a
   a. foreclosed identity.
   b. diffused identity.
   c. negative identity.
   d. reverse identity.

4. The main sources of emotional support for most young people who are establishing independence from their parents are
   a. older adolescents of the opposite sex.
   b. older siblings.
   c. teachers.
   d. peer groups.

5. For members of minority ethnic groups, identity achievement may be particularly complicated because
   a. their cultural ideal clashes with the Western emphasis on adolescent self-determination.
   b. democratic ideology espouses a color-blind, multiethnic society in which background is irrelevant.
   c. parents and other relatives tend to emphasize ethnicity and expect teens to honor their roots.
   d. of all of the above reasons.

6. In a crime-ridden neighborhood, parents can protect their adolescents by keeping close watch over activities, friends, and so on. This practice is called
   a. generational stake.
   b. foreclosure.
   c. peer screening.
   d. parental monitoring.

7. Which of the following is **NOT** a common manifestation of the adolescent tendency to take on a false self?
   a. trying to impress or please others
   b. nonconformity resulting from anger toward society
   c. feeling that parents and peers have rejected one's "true self"
   d. experimenting with different behaviors "just to see how it feels"

8. Fourteen-year-old Juan believes that his parents are hopelessly out of touch and old-fashioned. Juan's parents deal patiently with his acts of rebellion and believe that, at heart, Juan is a good boy. This is an example of
   a. moral judgment.
   b. emerging independence.
   c. generational stake.
   d. parental restructuring.

9. Because of the conflict between their ethnic background and the larger culture, minority adolescents will most often
   a. reject the traditional values of both their ethnic culture and the majority culture.
   b. foreclose on identity prematurely.
   c. declare a moratorium.
   d. experience identity diffusion.

10. Fifteen-year-old Cindy, who has strong self-esteem and is trying out a new, artistic identity "just to see how it feels," is apparently exploring
    a. an acceptable false self.
    b. a pleasing false self.
    c. an experimental false self.
    d. none of the above.

11. Chinese-American, Korean-American, and Mexican-American teens generally _____ conflict with parents _____ European-American teens.

   a. have; that begins at later ages than
   b. have less intense; that begins at the same age as
   c. have very frequent; that ends at an earlier age than
   d. rarely have; but are more distressed by that conflict than

12. Compared with other adolescents, suicidal adolescents are

   a. more concerned about the future.
   b. academically average students.
   c. likely to have few steady friends.
   d. less likely to have attempted suicide.

13. The early signs of life-course persistent offenders include all of the following EXCEPT

   a. signs of brain damage early in life.
   b. antisocial school behavior.
   c. delayed sexual intimacy.
   d. use of alcohol and tobacco at an early age.

15. Conflict between parents and adolescent offspring is

   a. most likely to involve fathers and their later-born offspring.
   b. more frequent in single-parent homes.
   c. more likely between early-maturing offspring and their mothers.
   d. not likely in any of the above situations.

15. Conflict between parents and adolescent offspring is

   a. most likely to involve fathers and their early-maturing offspring.
   b. more frequent in single-parent homes.
   c. more likely between firstborns and their parents than between later-borns and their parents.
   d. not likely in any of the above situations.

True or False Items

Write T (for true) or F (for false) on the line in front of each statement.

   16. _____ In cultures where everyone's values are similar and social change is slight, identity is relatively easy to achieve.

   17. _____ Most adolescents have political views and educational values that are markedly different from those of their parents.

   18. _____ Peer pressure is inherently destructive to the adolescent seeking an identity.

   19. _____ For most adolescents, group socializing and dating precede the establishment of true intimacy with one member of the opposite sex.

20. _____ Of the three distinct types of false selves (pleasing, acceptable, or experimental), the experimental is displayed most often by teens with the highest self-esteem.

21. _____ Most adolescent self-destructive acts are a response to an immediate and specific psychological blow.

22. _____ The majority of adolescents report that they have at some time engaged in law-breaking that might have led to arrest.

23. _____ In finding themselves, teens try to find an identity that is stable, consistent, and mature.

24. _____ Most parent-adolescent conflict centers around concerns about adolescent delinquency and sexual behavior.

25. _____ There are distinct ethnic and gender differences in adolescent suicide rates.

Practice Questions II

Multiple-Choice Questions

1. Recent studies of adolescents in European nations experiencing massive social change have generally found that
   a. their lives were seriously disrupted.
   b. a disproportionate number experienced severe identity crises.
   c. their search for identity was not adversely affected.
   d. boys experienced more difficulty forming their identities than did girls.

2. Which of the following was **NOT** identified as a factor influencing adolescent parasuicide or suicide rates?
   a. availability of lethal means (e.g., a gun)
   b. parental supervision
   c. alcohol and other drugs
   d. increased arguing with parents

3. Parent-child conflict among Chinese-, Korean-, and Mexican-American families often surfaces late in adolescence because these cultures
   a. emphasize family closeness.
   b. value authoritarian parenting.
   c. encourage autonomy in children.
   d. do all of the above.

4. Becoming a distinct self-determined individual is not always compatible with connections to one's heritage and peer group, causing some adolescents to experience a(n)
   a. generational stake.
   b. identity crisis.
   c. foreclosure of identity.
   d. rejecting-neglecting identity.

5. Fifteen-year-old Molly rarely eats. Her weight has dropped drastically over the past year. She spends much of her time in her bedroom and rarely socializes with friends. Her behavior indicates

   a. parent-adolescent conflict.

   b. parasuicide.

   c. externalizing problems.

   d. internalizing problems.

6. Which of the following is **NOT** true regarding peer relationships among gay and lesbian adolescents?

   a. Romantic attachments are usually slower to develop.

   b. In homophobic cultures, many gay teens try to conceal their homosexual feelings by becoming heterosexually involved.

   c. Many girls who will later identify themselves as lesbians are oblivious to these sexual urges as teens.

   d. In many cases, a lesbian girl's best friend is a boy, who is more at ease with her sexuality than another girl might be.

7. The adolescent experiencing identity diffusion is typically

   a. very apathetic.

   b. a risk-taker, anxious to experiment with alternative identities.

   c. willing to accept parental values wholesale, without exploring alternatives.

   d. one who rebels against all forms of authority.

8. Cross-sequential studies of individuals from ages 6 to 18 show that

   a. children feel less competent each year in most areas of their lives.

   b. feelings of competence become more similar in males and females as time goes on.

   c. boys self-esteem decreases more than girls' does.

   d. all of the above are true.

9. Crime statistics show that during adolescence

   a. males and females are equally likely to be arrested.

   b. males are more likely to be arrested than females.

   c. females are more likely to be arrested than males.

   d. males commit more crimes than females but are less likely to be arrested.

10. Which of the following is the most common problem among adolescents?

    a. pregnancy

    b. daily use of illegal drugs

    c. minor law-breaking

    d. attempts at suicide

11. A period during which a young person experiments with different identities, postponing important choices, is called a(n)

    a. identity foreclosure.

    b. negative identity.

    c. identity diffusion.

    d. identity moratorium.

12. When adolescents' political, religious, educational, and vocational opinions are compared with their parents', the so-called "generation gap" is
    a. much smaller than when the younger and older generations are compared overall.
    b. much wider than when the younger and older generations are compared overall.
    c. wider between parents and sons than between parents and daughters.
    d. wider between parents and daughters than between parents and sons.

13. Which of the following was **NOT** cited as a reason for teens with low self-esteem to take on a false self?
    a. feelings of worthlessness
    b. tendency to feel depressed
    c. inability to perform well in school
    d. feelings of hopelessness, that is, that life will not improve

14. Parent-teen conflict tends to center on issues related to
    a. politics and religion.
    b. education.
    c. vacations.
    d. daily details, such as musical tastes.

15. According to a review of studies from various nations, suicidal ideation is
    a. not as common among high school students as is popularly believed.
    b. more common among males than females.
    c. more common among females than among males.
    d. so common among high school students that it might be considered normal.

Matching Items
Match each definition or description with its corresponding term.

Terms
16. _____ identity achievement

17. _____ foreclosure

18. _____ negative identity

19. _____ identity diffusion

20. _____ identity moratorium

21. _____ generation gap

22. _____ generational stake

23. _____ parental monitoring

24. _____ cluster suicide

25. _____ parasuicide

Definitions or Descriptions
    a. premature identity formation
    b. a group of suicides that occur in the same community, school, or time period
    c. the adolescent has few commitments to goals or values
    d. differences between the younger and older generations
    e. self-destructive act that does not result in death
    f. awareness of where children are and what they are doing

Lesson 23/Adolescence: Psychosocial Development   **359**

g.　an individual's self-definition

h.　a time-out period during which adolescents experiment with alternative identities

i.　the adolescent establishes his or her own goals and values

j.　family members in different developmental stages see the family in different ways

k.　an identity opposite of the one an adolescent is expected to adopt

Applying Your Knowledge

1.　From childhood, Sharon thought she wanted to follow in her mother's footsteps and be a homemaker. Now, at age 40 with a home and family, she admits to herself that what she really wanted to be was a medical researcher. Erik Erikson would probably say that Sharon

   a.　adopted a negative identity when she was a child.

   b.　experienced identity foreclosure at an early age.

   c.　never progressed beyond the obvious identity diffusion she experienced as a child.

   d.　took a moratorium from identity formation.

2.　Fifteen-year-old David is rebelling against his devoutly religious parents by taking drugs, stealing, and engaging in other antisocial behaviors. Evidently, David has

   a.　foreclosed on his identity.

   b.　declared an identity moratorium.

   c.　adopted a negative identity.

   d.　experienced identity diffusion.

3.　Fourteen-year-old Sean, who is fiercely proud of his Irish heritage, is prejudiced against members of several other ethnic groups. It is likely that, in forming his identity, Sean

   a.　attained identity achievement.

   b.　foreclosed on his identity.

   c.　declared a lengthy moratorium.

   d.　experienced identity diffusion.

4.　In 1957, 6-year-old Raisel and her parents emigrated from Poland to the United States. Compared with her parents, who grew up in a culture in which virtually everyone held the same religious, moral, political, and sexual values, Raisel is likely to have

   a.　an easier time achieving her own unique identity.

   b.　a more difficult time forging her identity.

   c.　a greater span of time in which to forge her own identity.

   d.　a shorter span of time in which to forge her identity.

5.　An adolescent exaggerates the importance of differences in her values and those of her parents. Her parents see these differences as smaller and less important. This phenomenon is called the

   a.　generation gap.

   b.　generational stake.

   c.　family enigma.

   d.　parental imperative.

6. In our society, the most obvious examples of institutionalized moratoria on identity formation are

    a. the Boy Scouts and the Girl Scouts.

    b. college and the peacetime military.

    c. marriage and divorce.

    d. bar mitzvahs and baptisms.

7. First-time parents Norma and Norman are worried that, during adolescence, their healthy parental influence will be undone as their children are encouraged by peers to become sexually promiscuous, drug-addicted, or delinquent. Their wise neighbor, who is a developmental psychologist, tells them that

    a. during adolescence, peers are generally more likely to complement the influence of parents than they are to pull their friends in the opposite direction.

    b. research suggests that peers provide a negative influence in every major task of adolescence.

    c. only through authoritarian parenting can parents give children the skills they need to resist peer pressure.

    d. unless their children show early signs of learning difficulties or antisocial behavior, parental monitoring is unnecessary.

8. Thirteen-year-old Cassandra is constantly experimenting with different behaviors and possible identities. It is likely that she

    a. has low self-esteem.

    b. foreclosed prematurely on her identity.

    c. has great self-understanding.

    d. comes from a home environment in which there is considerable tension and conflict.

9. In forming an identity, the young person seeks to make meaningful connections with his or her past. This seeking is described by Erikson as an unconscious striving for

    a. individual uniqueness.

    b. peer-group membership.

    c. continuity of experience.

    d. vocational identity.

10. Statistically, the person least likely to commit a crime is a(n)

    a. African-American or Latino adolescent.

    b. middle-class white male.

    c. white adolescent of any socioeconomic background.

    d. Asian American.

11. Ray was among the first of his friends to have sex, drink alcohol, and smoke cigarettes. These attributes, together with his having been hyperactive and having poor emotional control, would suggest that Ray is at high risk of

    a. becoming an adolescent-limited offender.

    b. becoming a life-course persistent offender.

    c. developing an antisocial personality.

    d. foreclosing his identity prematurely.

12. Carl is a typical 16-year-old adolescent who has no special problems. It is likely that Carl has

    a. contemplated suicide.

    b. engaged in some minor illegal act.

    c. struggled with "who he is."

    d. done all of the above.

13. Statistically, who of the following is most likely to commit suicide?

    a. Micah, an African-American female

    b. Yan, an Asian-American male

    c. James, a Native American male

    d. Alison, a European-American female

14. Coming home from work, Malcolm hears a radio announcement warning parents to be alert for possible cluster suicide signs in their teenage children. What might have precipitated such an announcement?

    a. government statistics that suicide has been on the rise since the 1990s

    b. the highly publicized suicide of a local teen

    c. the recent crash of an airliner, killing all on board

    d. any of the above

Answer Key

Key Terms

1. Identity, as used by Erikson, refers to a person's self-definition as a separate individual in terms of roles, attitudes, beliefs, and aspirations. (p. 497; video lesson, segment 1; objective 1).

2. Many adolescents try out possible selves, or variations on who they are, and who they might like to become. (p. 497; video lesson, segment 1; objective 2)

3. Some adolescents display a false self, acting in ways that are contrary to who they really are in order to be accepted (the acceptable false self), to impress or please others (the pleasing false self), or "just to see how it feels" (the experimental false self). (p. 498; objective 2)

4. Erikson's term for the psychosocial crisis of adolescence, identity versus role confusion, refers to adolescents' need to combine their self-understanding and social roles into a coherent identity. (p. 498; video lesson, segment 1; objective 1)

5. In Erikson's theory, identity achievement occurs when adolescents attain their new identity by establishing their own goals and values and abandoning some of those set by their parents and culture and accepting others. (p. 498; video lesson, segment 1; objective 3)

6. In identity foreclosure, according to Erikson, the adolescent forms an identity prematurely, accepting earlier roles and parental values wholesale, without truly forging a unique personal identity. (p. 499; video lesson, segment 1; objective 3)

7. Adolescents who take on a negative identity, according to Erikson, adopt an identity that is the opposite of the one they are expected to adopt. (p. 499; video lesson, segment 1; objective 3)

8. Adolescents who experience identity diffusion, according to Erikson, have few commitments to goals or values and are often apathetic about trying to find an identity. (p. 499; video lesson, segment 1; objective 3)

9. According to Erikson, in the process of finding a mature identity, many young people seem to declare an identity moratorium, a kind of time-out during which they experiment with alternative identities without trying to settle on any one. (p. 499; video lesson, segment 1; objective 3)

10. Gender identity is a person's self-identification of being female or male, including the roles and behaviors that society assigns to that sex. (p. 501; objective 1)

11. A rite of passage is a dramatic ceremony marking the transition from childhood to adulthood. (p. 505; objective 1)

12. Suicidal ideation refers to thinking about committing suicide, usually with some serious emotional and intellectual overtones. (p. 508; objective 7)

13. Parasuicide is a deliberate act of self-destruction that does not result in death. (p. 510; objective 7)

14. A cluster suicide refers to a series of suicides or suicide attempts that are precipitated by one initial suicide, usually that of a famous person or a well-known peer. (p. 511; objective 7)

15. Internalizing problems are inwardly expressed emotional problems such as eating disorders, self-mutilation, and drug abuse. (p. 512; objective 8)

16. Externalizing problems are outwardly expressed emotional problems such as injuring others, destroying property, and defying authority. (p. 512; objective 8)

17. Incidence is how often a particular circumstance (such as lawbreaking) occurs. (p. 513; objective 8)

18. Prevalence is how widespread a particular behavior or circumstance is. (p. 513; objective 8)

19. Adolescence-limited offenders are juvenile delinquents, whose criminal activity stops by age 21. (p. 515; objective 8)

20. Life-course-persistent offenders are adolescent lawbreakers who later become career criminals. (p. 515; objective 8)

21. The generation gap refers to the alleged distance between generations in values, behaviors, and knowledge. (p. 516; video lesson; objective 5)

22. The generational stake refers to the tendency of each family member, because of that person's different developmental stage, to see the family in a certain way. (p. 517; video lesson, segment 2; objective 5)

23. Bickering refers to the repeated, petty arguing that typically occurs in early adolescence about common, daily life activities. (p. 517; video lesson, segment 2; objective 5)

24. Parental monitoring is parental watchfulness about where one's child is and what he or she is doing, and with whom. (p. 518; objective 5)

25. Peer pressure refers to the social pressure to conform to one's friends in behavior, dress, and attitude. It may be positive or negative in its effects. (p. 519; video lesson, segment 2; objective 6)

Practice Questions I

Multiple-Choice Questions

1. b. is the correct answer. (p. 498; video lesson, segment 1; objective 1)

   a. is incorrect. According to Erikson, this is the crisis of infancy.

   c. & d. are incorrect. In Erikson's theory, these crises occur later in life.

2. a. is the correct answer. (p. 499; video lesson, segment 1; objective 3)

   b. is incorrect. This describes an identity moratorium.

   c. is incorrect. This describes a negative identity.

   d. is incorrect. This describes identity diffusion.

3. c. is the correct answer. (p. 499; video lesson, segment 1; objective 3)

4. d. is the correct answer. (p. 519; video lesson, segment 2; objective 6)

5. d. is the correct answer. (pp. 502–503; video lesson, segments 1 & 2; objective 4)

6. d. is the correct answer. (p. 518; objective 5)

   a. is incorrect. The generational stake refers to differences in how family members from different generations view the family.

   b. is incorrect. Foreclosure refers to the premature establishment of identity.

   c. is incorrect. Peer screening is an aspect of parental monitoring, but it was not specifically discussed in the textbook.

7. b. is the correct answer. (p. 498; objective 2)

8. c. is the correct answer. (pp. 516–517; video lesson, segment 2; objective 5)

9. b. is the correct answer. (p. 503; objective 4)

   a. is incorrect. This occurs in some cases, but not in most cases.

   c. is incorrect. Moratorium is a time-out in identity formation in order to allow the adolescent to try out alternative identities. It is generally not a solution in such cases.

   d. is incorrect. Young people who experience identity diffusion are often apathetic, which is not the case here.

10. c. is the correct answer. (p. 498; objective 2)

    a. & b. are incorrect. Teenagers who try out these false selves tend to feel either worthless and depressed (acceptable false self), or experience the psychological consequences of living an identity just to impress or please others (pleasing false self).

11. a. is the correct answer. (p. 514; objectives 4 & 5)

12. c. is the correct answer. (p. 511; objective 7)

13. c. is the correct answer. Most life-course persistent offenders are among the earliest of their cohort to have sex. (p. 515–516; objective 8)

14. b. is the correct answer. (p. 511; objective 7)

15. c. is the correct answer. (p. 517; objective 5)

    a. is incorrect. In fact, parent-child conflict is more likely to involve mothers and their early-maturing offspring.

True or False Items

16. T   (p. 504; objective 4)

17. F   Numerous studies have shown substantial agreement between parents and their adolescent children on political opinions and educational values. (pp. 516–517; video lesson, segment 2; objective 5)

18. F   Just the opposite is true. (pp. 519–521; video lesson, segment 2; objective 6)

19. T   (p. 522; objective 6)

20. T   (p. 498; objective 2)

21. F   Most self-destructive acts reflect long-standing problems. (p. 528; objective 7)

22. T   (pp. 514–515; objective 8)

23. T   (p. 498; objective 1)

24. F   (p. 517; objective 5)

25. T   (p. 511; objective 7)

Practice Questions II

Multiple-Choice Questions

1. c. is the correct answer. (p. 508; objective 1)

2. d. is the correct answer. In fact, just the opposite is true: a sudden loss of interest in friends and family may be a warning sign of suicide. (p. 511; objective 7)

3. a. is the correct answer. For this reason, autonomy in their offspring tends to be delayed. (p. 518; objectives 4 & 5)

4. b. is the correct answer. (p. 503; objective 1)

5. d. is the correct answer. (p. 512; video lesson, segment 2; objective 5)

6. d. is the correct answer. Lesbian adolescents find it easier to establish strong friendships with same-sex heterosexual peers than homosexual teenage boys do. (pp. 523–524; objective 6)

7. a. is the correct answer. (p. 499; video lesson, segment 1; objective 3)

   b. is incorrect. This describes an adolescent undergoing an identity moratorium.

   c. is incorrect. This describes identity foreclosure.

   d. is incorrect. This describes an adolescent who is adopting a negative identity.

8. d. is the correct answer. (p. 507; objective 1)

9. b. is the correct answer. (p. 514; objective 8)

10. c. is the correct answer. (p. 514; objective 8)

11. d. is the correct answer. (p. 499; video lesson, segment 1; objective 3)

    a. is incorrect. Identity foreclosure occurs when the adolescent prematurely adopts an identity, without fully exploring alternatives.

    b. is incorrect. Adolescents who adopt an identity that is opposite to the one they are expected to develop have taken on a negative identity.

    c. is incorrect. Identity diffusion occurs when the adolescent is apathetic and has few commitments to goals or values.

12. a. is the correct answer. (p. 516; video lesson, segment 2; objective 5)

    c. & d. are incorrect. The textbook does not suggest that the size of the generation gap varies with the offspring's sex.

13. c. is the correct answer. (p. 498; objective 2)

Lesson 23/Adolescence: Psychosocial Development   **365**

14. d. is the correct answer. (p. 498; objective 5)

a., b., & c. are incorrect. In fact, on these issues parents and teenagers tend to show substantial agreement.

15. d. is the correct answer. (p. 508; objective 7)

Matching Items

16. i (p. 498; video lesson, segment 1; objective 1)
17. a (p. 499; video lesson, segment 1; objective 1)
18. k (p. 499; video lesson, segment 1; objective 3)
19. c (p. 499; video lesson, segment 1; objective 3)
20. h (p. 499; video lesson, segment 1; objective 3)
21. d (p. 516; video lesson, segment 2; objective 5)
22. j (p. 517; video lesson, segment 2; objective 5)
23. f (p. 518; objective 5)
24. b (p. 511; objective 7)
25. e (p. 510; objective 7)

Applying Your Knowledge

1. b. is the correct answer. Apparently, Sharon never explored alternatives or truly forged a unique personal identity. (p. 499; video lesson, segment 1; objective 3)

a. is incorrect. Individuals who rebel by adopting an identity that is the opposite of the one they are expected to adopt have taken on a negative identity.

c. is incorrect. Individuals who experience identity diffusion have few commitments to goals or values. This was not Sharon's problem.

d. is incorrect. Had she taken a moratorium on identity formation, Sharon would have experimented with alternative identities and perhaps would have chosen that of a medical researcher.

2. c. is the correct answer. (p. 499; video lesson, segment 1; objective 3)

3. b. is the correct answer. (p. 499; video lesson, segment 1; objective 3)

a. is incorrect. Identity achievers often have a strong sense of ethnic identification, but usually are low in prejudice.

c. & d. are incorrect. The textbook does not present research that links ethnic pride and prejudice with either identity diffusion or moratorium.

4. b. is the correct answer. Minority adolescents struggle with finding the right balance between transcending their background and becoming immersed in it. (pp. 502–503; objective 4)

c. & d. are incorrect. The textbook does not suggest that the amount of time adolescents have to forge their identities varies from one ethnic group to another or has changed over historical time.

5. b. is the correct answer. (p. 517; video lesson, segment 2; objective 5)

a. is incorrect. The generation gap refers to actual differences in attitudes and values between the younger and older generations. This example is concerned with how large these differences are perceived to be.

c. & d. are incorrect. These terms are not used in the textbook in discussing family conflict.

6. b. is the correct answer. (p. 499; objective 3)

7. a. is the correct answer. (p. 524; video lesson, segment 2; objective 6)

   b. is incorrect. In fact, just the opposite is true.

   c. is incorrect. Developmentalists recommend authoritative, rather than authoritarian, parenting.

   d. is incorrect. Parental monitoring is important for all adolescents.

8. c. is the correct answer. (pp. 498–500; video lesson; objective 2)

   a., b., & d. are incorrect. Experimenting with possible selves is a normal sign of adolescent identity formation.

9. c. is the correct answer. (p. 502; objective 1)

10. d. is the correct answer. (p. 514; objective 8)

11. b. is the correct answer. (p. 515; objective 8)

12. d. is the correct answer. (pp. 498, 508, 514; objectives 1, 7, & 8)

13. c. is the correct answer. (p. 511; objective 7)

14. b. is the correct answer. (p. 511; objective 7)

Lesson Review

Lesson 23

Adolescence
Psychosocial Development

Please Note: Use this matrix to guide your study and achieve the learning objectives of this lesson. It will also help you to view the video, which defines and demonstrates important concepts and skills as they relate to everyday life.

Learning Objective	Textbook	Telecourse Student Guide	Video Lesson
1. Define the concept of identity and describe the development of identity during adolescence, incorporating Erikson's crisis of "identity versus role confusion."	pp. 497–508	Key Terms: 1, 4, 10, 11; Practice Questions I: 1, 23; Practice Questions II: 1, 4, 8, 16, 17; Applying Your Knowledge: 9, 12.	Segment 1: *Identity*
2. Describe the concepts of "possible selves" and "false self."	pp. 497–498, 502	Key Terms: 2, 3; Practice Questions I: 7, 10, 20; Practice Questions II: 13; Applying Your Knowledge: 8.	Segment 1: *Identity*
3. Describe the five major identity statuses or conditions, and give an example of each one.	pp. 498–499	Key Terms: 5, 6, 7, 8, 9; Practice Questions I: 2, 3; Practice Questions II: 7, 11, 18, 19, 20; Applying Your Knowledge: 1, 2, 3, 6.	Segment 1: *Identity*
4. Discuss the influence of society and culture on identity formation, and describe the challenges encountered by minority adolescents in achieving their identity.	pp. 502–504, 518	Practice Questions I: 5, 9, 11, 16; Practice Questions II: 3; Applying Your Knowledge: 4.	Segment 1: *Identity*
5. Discuss parent-child relationships during adolescence.	pp. 516–519, 524–526	Key Terms: 21, 22, 23, 24; Practice Questions I: 6, 8, 15, 17, 24; Practice Questions II: 3, 5, 12, 14, 21, 22, 23; Applying Your Knowledge: 5.	Segment 2: *Friends and Family*

Learning Objective	Textbook	Telecourse Student Guide	Video Lesson
6. Discuss the role of peers, friends, and male-female relationships in adolescence.	pp. 519–524, 527	Key Terms: 25; Practice Questions I: 4, 18, 19; Practice Questions II: 6; Applying Your Knowledge: 7.	
7. Discuss adolescent suicide, noting its prevalence, contributing factors, warning signs, gender and cultural variations.	pp. 508–511, 528	Key Terms: 12, 13, 14; Practice Questions I: 12, 14, 21, 25; Practice Questions II: 2, 15, 24, 25; Applying Your Knowledge: 12, 13, 14.	
8. Discuss delinquency among adolescents today, noting its incidence and prevalence, significance for later development, and best approaches for prevention and treatment.	pp. 508–511	Key Terms: 15, 16, 17, 18, 19, 20; Practice Questions I: 13, 22; Practice Questions II: 9, 10; Applying Your Knowledge: 10, 11, 12.	

The Home Stretch

Lesson 24

Adolescence:
Summary

Preview

Lesson 24 summarizes biosocial, cognitive, and psychosocial development during adolescence. These years are an exciting time, when the talents, abilities, and values that have been unfolding over childhood blossom and reveal the directions a teenager's life is likely to take.

In the biosocial domain of development, the changes of adolescence have a memorable and lifelong impact on our bodies and self-images. In the cognitive domain, adolescents become increasingly able to speculate, hypothesize, and use logic. Perhaps most significantly, the logical and idealistic thinking of adolescence represents a significant step in the process of creating a life story and forming an identity.

As adolescents forge an identity and try to make wise choices about their futures, their social context encourages some paths and closes others. The result of this interaction, in the ideal case, will be young people who are sure of themselves and able to pass through the vulnerable years of adolescence successfully.

Prior Telecourse Knowledge that Will Be Used in this Lesson

- Biosocial development during adolescence (from Lesson 21) will be referred to as we discuss the impact of puberty, the growth spurt, and chronic illness on a teenager's development.

- Cognitive development during adolescence (from Lesson 22) will be referred to as we explore how advancing cognitive skills help teenagers make the many decisions they are faced with as they consider their futures.

- Psychosocial development during adolescence (from Lesson 23) will be referred to as we consider the formation of identity and the impact that parents, peers and mentors have on teenagers.

Learning Objectives

Use this information to guide your reading, viewing, thinking, and studying. After successfully completing this lesson, you should be able to:

1. Describe biosocial development during adolescence, focusing on the impact of puberty and sexual maturation on teenagers.

2. Explain how thinking changes during adolescence and discuss the impact of these changes on adolescent decision making.

3. Discuss psychosocial development during adolescence, focusing on the formation of identity and the influence of parents, mentors and the peer group.

📖 **Read Chapter 14, pages 462–463; ("Summary: Adolescence: Biosocial Development"); Chapter 15, pages 494–495 ("Summary: Adolescence: Cognitive Development"); Chapter 16, pages 529–530 ("Summary: Adolescence: Psychosocial Development"), and 531 ("The Developing Person So Far: Adolescence").**

Video Viewing Tips

The video for this lesson will feature three adolescent children—Ashley (16), Bayleigh (13) and Alejandro (17)—each from different backgrounds and circumstances. As you watch their stories unfold, look for these recurring issues and themes:

Note the biological development of these teens—their heredity, overall health, and the changes they are experiencing associated with puberty. Consider how this development compares with their peers, and how this might affect their body image.

Also, observe how the thinking of these adolescents compares with that of younger children, say, in The School Years. Watch how they apply their new abilities to reason and think hypothetically to the decisions they are making about their future. Look for any evidence of egocentric thinking, including personal or invincibility fables.

Consider how these children view themselves, their identity. Listen for their goals and aspirations—their dreams of quest and conquest. Note the similarities and differences between their personalities, and any evidence of possible selves or foreclosure.

Also, observe closely how these adolescents relate to their peers—the role of friendship in their lives, their place in the friendship group, and their strength of will when challenged by peers. Consider both the positive and negative influence of their friends, and the relative value they place on friendships as opposed to personal goals.

Finally, what role do parents and other adults play in the lives of these kids? Note the different family structures (e.g., single-parent, nuclear) and how the parents are meeting the needs of these children. Also, try to discern each adult's parenting style (i.e., authoritarian, permissive, authoritative), and consider the influence of counselors, mentors and other adults.

📼 **View the video for Lesson 24, "The Home Stretch."**
    Segment 1: *Ashley*
    Segment 2: *Bayleigh*
    Segment 3: *Alejandro*

Summary

For most people, adolescence is an eventful time of life that brings dramatic changes in each domain of development. Along with rapid physical growth, the changes associated with sexual maturation contribute a new dimension to the ways in which adolescents think about themselves and relate to others. Young people who experience puberty at the same time as their friends tend to view the experience more positively than those who experience it early or late.

Equally important changes occur in cognition as adolescents become increasingly able to think abstractly and logically. Unlike younger children, whose thinking is tied to concrete operations, adolescents (with their ability to use formal operations) are able to consider possibilities as well as reality. Adolescent thought has certain shortcomings, however, including difficulties in theoretical thinking and distortions associated with egocentrism. Because adolescent thought is egocentric, young people tend to overestimate their significance to others, a tendency that is often reflected in their belief in their own invincibility, their expectations of heroic lives, and their views about people's reactions to their appearance and behavior. As adolescents become more open to the opinions of others, their egocentrism puts them in an emotional bind—eager for lively intellectual interaction but vulnerable to self-doubt. Adolescents' cognitive immaturity makes it difficult for them to make rational decisions about many personal and emotionally charged issues, including sexuality.

In the psychosocial domain of development, adolescence brings the dawning of commitment to a personal identity and future, to other people, and to ideologies. The central psychosocial challenge of adolescence is the search for identity, both as an individual and as a member of the larger community. When the search for identity becomes overwhelming and confusing, adolescents may experience an identity crisis. Friends, family, community, and culture are powerful forces that act to help or hinder the adolescent's transition from childhood to adulthood. The peer group is a social institution that eases the transition from childhood to adulthood by functioning as a source of information and a self-help group of contemporaries who are experiencing similar struggles, and by serving as a sounding board for exploring and defining one's values and aspirations.

Review all reading assignments for this lesson.

As assigned by your instructor, complete the optional online component for this lesson.

Key Terms

Using your own words, write a brief definition or explanation of each of the following terms on a separate piece of paper.

1. puberty
2. menarche
3. growth spurt
4. spermarche
5. body image
6. formal operational thought
7. hypothetical thought
8. inductive reasoning
9. deductive reasoning
10. invincibility fable
11. personal fable

12. person–environment fit
13. identity
14. possible selves
15. identity versus role confusion
16. identity achievement
17. foreclosure
18. generational stake
19. parental monitoring
20. peer pressure
21. imaginary audience

Practice Questions

Multiple-Choice Questions

1. In general, most adolescents are
   a. overweight.
   b. satisfied with their appearance.
   c. dissatisfied with their appearance.
   d. unaffected by cultural attitudes about beauty.

2. Early physical growth and sexual maturation
   a. tend to be equally difficult for girls and boys.
   b. tend to be more difficult for boys than for girls.
   c. tend to be more difficult for girls than for boys.
   d. are easier for both girls and boys than late maturation.

3. Nutritional deficiencies in adolescence are frequently the result of
   a. eating red meat.
   b. exotic diets or food fads.
   c. anovulatory menstruation.
   d. excessive exercise.

4. Puberty is initiated when hormones are released from the _____, then from the _____, and then from the adrenal glands and the _____.
   a. hypothalamus; pituitary; gonads
   b. pituitary; gonads; hypothalamus
   c. gonads; pituitary; hypothalamus
   d. pituitary; hypothalamus; gonads

5. Individuals who experiment with drugs early are
   a. typically affluent teenagers who are experiencing an identity crisis.
   b. more likely to have multiple drug-abuse problems later on.
   c. less likely to have alcohol-abuse problems later on.
   d. usually able to resist later peer pressure leading to long-term addiction.

6. Many psychologists consider the distinguishing feature of adolescent thought to be the ability to think in terms of
   a. moral issues.
   b. concrete operations.
   c. possibility, not just reality.
   d. logical principles.

7. The adolescent who takes risks and feels immune to the laws of mortality is showing evidence of the

   a. invincibility fable.
   b. personal fable.
   c. imaginary audience.
   d. death instinct.

8. Imaginary audiences, invincibility fables, and personal fables are expressions of adolescent

   a. morality.
   b. thinking games.
   c. decision making.
   d. egocentrism.

9. The typical adolescent is

   a. tough-minded.
   b. indifferent to public opinion.
   c. self-absorbed and hypersensitive to criticism.
   d. all of the above.

10. Serious reflection on important issues is a wrenching process for many adolescents because of their newfound ability to reason

    a. inductively.
    b. deductively.
    c. hypothetically.
    d. symbolically.

11. The main sources of emotional support for most young people who are establishing independence from their parents are

    a. older adolescents of the opposite sex.
    b. older siblings.
    c. teachers.
    d. peer groups.

12. For members of minority ethnic groups, identity achievement may be particularly complicated because

    a. their cultural ideal may clash with the Western emphasis on adolescent self-determination.
    b. democratic ideology espouses a color-blind, multiethnic society in which background is irrelevant.
    c. parents and other relatives tend to emphasize ethnicity and expect teens to honor their roots.
    d. of all of the above reasons.

13. Adolescents help each other in many ways, including
    a. identity formation.
    b. independence.
    c. social skills.
    d. all of the above.

14. First-time parents Norma and Norman are worried that during adolescence, their healthy parental influence will be undone as their children are encouraged by peers to become sexually promiscuous, drug-addicted, or delinquent. Their wise neighbor, who is a developmental psychologist, tells them that
    a. during adolescence, peers are generally more likely to complement the influence of parents than they are to pull their friends in the opposite direction.
    b. research suggests that peers provide a negative influence in every major task of adolescence.
    c. only through authoritarian parenting can parents give children the skills they need to resist peer pressure.
    d. unless their children show early signs of learning difficulties or antisocial behavior, parental monitoring is unnecessary.

True or False Items
Write T (for true) or F (for false) on the line in front of each statement.

15. _____ More calories are necessary during adolescence than at any other period during the life span.

16. _____ Puberty generally begins sometime between ages 8 and 14.

17. _____ Childhood habits of overeating and underexercising usually lessen during adolescence.

18. _____ Everyone attains the stage of formal operational thought by adulthood.

19. _____ Inductive reasoning is a hallmark of formal operational thought.

20. _____ In cultures where everyone's values are similar and social change is slight, identity is relatively easy to achieve.

21. _____ Peer pressure is inherently destructive to the adolescent seeking an identity.

Questions for Reflection

1. Consider your body image (your opinion about your physical appearance) when you were in the eighth or ninth grade—when you were 13 or 14 years old.
   a. What did you consider your "best feature"?
   b. What did you consider your "worst feature"—the aspect of your appearance that you felt required the most care, upgrading or camouflage?
   c. Compared to your classmates and friends, were you an average-maturing, early-maturing, or late-maturing individual? What impact do you feel the timing of your puberty had on you at the time? What impact has it had on who you are today?

2. Did any of the stories depicted in the video lesson provide insight into your own adolescence (or that of your children)? What did you learn about yourself (or your children)?

3. A central theme of this five-lesson unit is that identity formation is a primary task of adolescence. Ideally, adolescents develop a clear picture of their unique standing in the larger social world to which they belong. But the development of identity doesn't end during adolescence; rather it continues to evolve over the life span. To help you apply this truth to your own life story, write five answers to the simple question, "Who am I?" You may respond in terms of your social roles, responsibilities, or commitments; the groups to which you belong; your beliefs and values; your personality traits and abilities; and your needs, feelings, and behavior patterns. List only things that are really important to you TODAY and that would, if lost, make a real difference in your sense of who you are.

	Rank Today	**Rank Five Years Ago**
1. I am	_____	_____
2. I am	_____	_____
3. I am	_____	_____
4. I am	_____	_____
5. I am	_____	_____

After you have completed your list, RANK the importance of each item to your identity today assigning a number from 1 (most important) to 5 (least important). Then do the same for your identity five years ago. What differences do you see? What do you feel accounts for any differences you observe?

Answer Key

Key Terms
1. Puberty is a period of rapid growth and sexual change that occurs in early adolescence and produces a person of adult size, shape, and sexual potential. (p. 432, video lesson, segment 2; objective 1)

2. Menarche is a female's first menstrual period. (p. 434, video lesson, segment 2; objective 1)

3. Growth spurt is the period of relatively sudden and rapid physical growth of every part of the body that occurs during puberty. (p. 436, video lesson, segment 2; objective 1)

4. Spermarche is a male's first ejaculation of live sperm. (p. 434, objective 1)

5. Body image is a person's mental concept of how his or her body appears. (p. 443; objective 1)

6. Formal operational thought in Piaget's theory, the fourth and final stage of cognitive development; arises from combination of maturation and experience. (p. 468; objective 2)

7. Hypothetical thought is thought that involves propositions and possibilities that may or may not reflect reality. (p. 466; objective 2)

8. Inductive reasoning is reasoning from one or more specific experiences or facts to a general conclusion. (p. 467; objective 2)

9. Deductive reasoning is reasoning from a general hypothesis, through logical steps, to a specific conclusion. (p. 467; objective 2)

10. Invincibility fable is the fiction, fostered by adolescent egocentrism, that one is immune to common dangers, such as those associated with unprotected sex, drug abuse, or high-speed driving. (p. 472; video lesson, segment 2; objective 2)

11. Personal fable is the egocentric idea, held by many adolescents, that one is destined for fame and fortune and/or great accomplishments. (p. 473; objective 2)

12. Person–environment fit is the degree to which a particular environment is conducive to the growth of a particular individual. (p. 478; video lesson, segment 1; objective 2)

13. Identity (as used by Erikson) is a consistent definition of oneself as a unique individual, in terms of roles, attitudes, beliefs, and aspirations. (p. 497; video lesson, segment 2; objective 3)

14. Possible selves are various intellectual fantasies about what the future might bring if one or another course of action is chosen. (p. 497; objective 3)

15. Identity versus role confusion is Erikson's term for the fifth stage of development, in which the person tries to figure out "Who am I?" but is confused as to which of many roles to adopt. (p. 498; objective 3)

16. Identity achievement is Erikson's term for a person's forming an identity and understanding who he or she is as a unique individual, in accord with past experiences and future plans. (p. 498; video lesson, segment 3; objective 3)

17. Foreclosure is Erikson's term for premature identity formation, in which the young person adopts the values of parents, or other significant people, wholesale, without questioning and analysis. (p. 499; objective 3)

18. Generational stake is the need of each generation to view family interactions from its own perspective, because each has a different investment in the family scenario. (p. 517; video lesson, segment 1; objective 3)

19. Parental monitoring is parental awareness of what one's children are doing, where, and with whom. (p. 518; objective 3)

20. Peer pressure is social pressure to conform with one's friends or contemporaries in behavior, dress, and attitude; usually considered negative, as when peers encourage each other to defy adult standards. (p. 519; video lesson, segments 1 & 3; objective 3)

21. Imaginary audience is a teenager's false belief, stemming from adolescent egocentrism, that others are intensely interested in his or her appearance and behavior. (p. 473; objective 2)

Practice Questions

Multiple-Choice Questions

1. c. is the correct answer. (pp. 443–444; objective 1)

   a. is incorrect. Although some adolescents become overweight, many diet and lose weight in an effort to attain a desired body image.

d. is incorrect. On the contrary, cultural attitudes about beauty are an extremely influential factor in the formation of a teenager's body image.

2. c. is the correct answer. (pp. 444–445; objective 1)

3. b. is the correct answer. (pp. 451–453; objective 1)

4. a. is the correct answer. (pp. 432–433; objective 1)

5. b. is the correct answer. (p. 456; objective 1)

6. c. is the correct answer. (p. 468; video lesson, segments 1 & 3; objective 2)

   a. is incorrect. Although moral reasoning becomes much deeper during adolescence, it is not limited to this stage of development.

   b. & d. are incorrect. Concrete operational thought, which is logical, is the distinguishing feature of childhood thinking.

7. a. is the correct answer. (pp. 472–473; video lesson, segment 2; objective 2)

   b. is incorrect. This refers to adolescents' tendency to imagine their own lives as unique, heroic, or even mythical.

   c. is incorrect. This refers to adolescents' tendency to fantasize about how others will react to their appearance and behavior.

   d. is incorrect. This is a concept in Freud's theory.

8. d. is the correct answer. These thought processes are manifestations of adolescents' tendency to see themselves as being much more central and important to the social scene than they really are. (p. 472; video lesson, segments 1, 2, & 3; objective 2)

9. c. is the correct answer. (p. 465, 472; objective 2)

10. c. is the correct answer. (p. 468–469; objective 2)

11. d. is the correct answer. (p. 519; video lesson, segment 1; objective 3)

12. d. is the correct answer. (pp. 502–504; video lesson, segments 1 & 3; objective 3)

13. d. is the correct answer. (pp. 522–524; video lesson, segments 1 & 2; objective 3)

14. a. is the correct answer. (pp. 524; video lesson, segment 1; objective 3)

    b. is incorrect. In fact, just the opposite is true.

    c. is incorrect. Developmentalists recommend authoritative, rather than authoritarian, parenting.

    d. is incorrect. Parental monitoring is important for all adolescents.

True or False Items

15. T   (p. 450; objective 1)

16. T   (p. 433; objective 1)

17. F   These habits generally worsen during adolescence. (pp. 450–451; objective 1)

18. F   Some people never reach the stage of formal operational thought. (p. 471; objective 2)

19. F   Deductive reasoning is a hallmark of formal operational thought. (p. 467; video lesson, segment 1; objective 2)

20. T   (p. 504; objective 3)

21. F   Just the opposite is true. (pp. 519–520; video lesson, segment 1; objective 3)

Lesson Review

Lesson 24
Adolescence
Summary

Please Note: Use this matrix to guide your study and achieve the learning objectives of this lesson. It will also help you to view the video, which defines and demonstrates important concepts and skills as they relate to everyday life.

Learning Objective	Textbook	Telecourse Student Guide	Video Lesson
1. Describe biosocial development during adolescence, focusing on the impact of puberty and sexual maturation on teenagers.	pp. 432–436, 443–450	Key Terms: 1, 2, 3, 4, 5; Practice Questions: 1, 2, 3, 4, 5, 15, 16, 17.	Segment 2 *Bayleigh*
2. Explain how thinking changes during adolescence and discuss the impact of these changes on adolescent decision making.	pp. 465–478	Key Terms: 6, 7, 8, 9, 10, 11, 21; Practice Questions: 6, 7, 8, 9, 10, 18, 19.	Segment 1: *Ashley* Segment 2: *Bayleigh* Segment 3: *Alejandro*
3. Discuss psychosocial development during adolescence, focusing on the formation of identity and the influence of parents, mentors and the peer group.	pp. 497–504, 516–527	Key Terms: 12, 13, 14, 15, 16, 17, 18, 19, 20; Practice Questions: 11, 12, 13, 14, 20, 21.	Segment 1: *Ashley* Segment 2: *Bayleigh* Segment 3: *Alejandro*

Crashing Hard Into Adulthood

Lesson 25

Adolescence:
Special Topic

Preview

Although the expanding world of the teen years is filled with opportunities for growth, it can also present challenges and potential problems. This lesson discusses a few of the more significant challenges that some children and adolescents face in our society, including poverty, abuse, and parental neglect. Kids who face problems like these are often called "at-risk" because they are more vulnerable to a range of negative outcomes such as unwanted pregnancy, drug abuse, and delinquency.

But, research reveals that many "at-risk" children are able to deal with their challenges and live happy and successful lives as adults. Experts call this **resilience**, the ability to adapt and succeed in the face of adversity. Particularly important to a teen's ability to cope with problems are his or her competencies and networks of social support. With the help of positive role models and community-based intervention programs, even teenagers who have grown up under the most adverse circumstances may be sufficiently resilient and resourceful to cope with the stresses they face in life.

As you complete this lesson, think of any child or teenager you know about who has faced considerable stress or hardship in his or her life. How old is the child? What were the challenges that he or she faced? What kind of support did this child find at home? What help did he or she find outside the home? Speculate on how situations like this might be prevented.

Prior Telecourse Knowledge that Will Be Used in this Lesson

*   This lesson will return to the concepts of hypothetical thought, adolescent egocentrism and the invincibility fable (from Lesson 22) as it explores the relationship between adolescent thinking and high-risk behaviors. Recall that people who believe the invincibility fable think that nothing bad will happen to them.

*   The concepts of false self, negative identity and peer pressure (from Lesson 23) will be discussed. A negative identity is taken on with rebellious defiance because it is the opposite of what parents or society expect.

Learning Objectives

Use this information to guide your reading, viewing, thinking, and studying. After successfully completing this lesson, you should be able to:

1. Identify the essential ways that functional families nurture children and teenagers.
2. Describe the impact of poverty, homelessness, and other adverse conditions on the development of children, and discuss ways adults can help them cope with these problems.
3. Describe the prevalence of sexual abuse in adolescence and its consequences for development.
4. Explain how adolescent thinking and decision making often promotes high-risk behaviors such as unprotected sex, drug use, and delinquency.
5. Discuss delinquency among adolescents today, noting its prevalence, significance for later development, and best approaches for prevention and treatment.

📖 **Review Chapter 13, "Family Function," pages 408–410, and "Coping with Problems," pages 419–425; Chapter 14, "Unwanted Pregnancies" and "Sexual Abuse," pages 446–449; Chapter 15, "Adolescent Decision Making," pages 486–493; and Chapter 16, "Rebellion and Destructiveness," pages 512–516.**

📼 **View the video for Lesson 25, "Crashing Hard Into Adulthood."**

> **Segment 1:** *Getting Off Track*
>
> **Segment 2:** *Getting Back On Track*

Summary

Healthy families provide for children's basic needs; they encourage and monitor peer relations, encourage and foster education, help to build the teen's self-esteem, and provide a stable context in which development can occur.

Teens who are faced with the adversity of **sexual abuse**, violence, poverty, or negligent parents are "at risk" and face special challenges as they move into adulthood. Fortunately, social programs directed toward at-risk teens can provide the support and context that may be missing in the individual's life.

Family structure refers to the legal and genetic relationships between members of a particular family. Traditional nuclear families are not the only structures in which healthy development of children can occur. However, when the family breaks up, as in divorce or separation, children lose the harmony and stability they need.

Girls who have been sexually abused at a young age, and especially those who have been abused by trusted caregivers, often experience a loss of self-esteem and do not see themselves as worthwhile individuals. Later, they may find intimate relationships difficult to establish.

Adolescent egocentrism, feelings of invincibility, inability to extend their newly found powers of hypothetical reasoning to all areas of their lives can explain why high-risk behaviors are particularly likely to occur during the teenage years.

The likelihood that a given stress will produce psychological fallout depends on the number of stresses the child is experiencing concurrently and on the degree to which these stresses affect the overall patterns of the child's daily life, and how many protective barriers and coping patterns are in place.

A child who is at risk because of poor parenting, difficult temperament, or poverty is likely to still be at risk as an adolescent. Particularly important to a teenager's **resilience** is his or her competencies—especially social, academic, and creative skills. Competencies boost self-esteem and often enable the child to employ various practical coping strategies. For this reason, older children are generally less vulnerable to the stresses of life than are children who are just beginning middle childhood.

Schools and teachers play a significant role in the development of competence. Another important element that helps children deal with problems is the social support they receive from friends, relatives, pets, or their religious faith and practice. Positive role models and mentors often play an important role in triggering children's native spark of resiliency. Teenagers who have grown up under adverse conditions since early childhood may need to learn new social skills to become healthy, productive adults.

Effective intervention programs often take a psychosocial approach in which the family, the school, the community, peers, and the individual him- or herself interact. Research studies show that high expectations are a hallmark of children who do well in school and in life.

📖   **Review all reading assignments for this lesson.**

💻   **As assigned by your instructor, complete the optional online component for this lesson.**

Key Terms

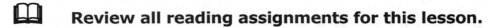

Using your own words, write a brief definition or explanation of each of the following terms on a separate piece of paper.

1. family function
2. family structure
3. resilience
4. sexual abuse
5. child sexual abuse
6. internalizing problems
7. externalizing problems
8. incidence
9. prevalence
10. adolescence-limited offender
11. life-course-persistent offender

Practice Questions

Multiple-Choice Questions

1. Which of the following is **NOT** identified as one of the basic elements that healthy families provide to a teenager's life?

    a. assistance in building the child's self-esteem

    b. a stable context in which to develop

    c. physical discipline

    d. monitoring peer relations

2. Teens are said to be "at risk" when
    a. one or more elements of healthy family function are missing in their lives.
    b. they experiment with "gateway" drugs.
    c. they join cliques or gangs.
    d. they establish their own "society of children."

3. The best strategy for helping children who are at risk of developing serious psychological problems because of multiple stresses would be to
    a. obtain assistance from a psychiatrist.
    b. increase the child's competencies or social supports.
    c. change the household situation.
    d. reduce the peer group's influence.

4. Older schoolchildren tend to be _____ vulnerable to the stresses of life than children who are just beginning middle childhood because they _____.
    a. more; tend to overpersonalize their problems
    b. less; have better developed coping skills
    c. more; are more likely to compare their well-being with that of their peers
    d. less; are less egocentric

5. Which of the following was **NOT** identified as a pivotal issue in determining whether divorce or some other problem will adversely affect a child during the school years?
    a. how many other stresses the child is already experiencing
    b. how many protective buffers are in place
    c. how much the stress affects the child's daily life
    d. the specific structure of the child's family

6. One factor that most often help the child cope well with multiple stresses is social support and
    a. social comparison.
    b. competence in a specific area.
    c. remedial education.
    d. referral to mental health professionals.

7. Research studies have found that, as compared to children without major stress, children who are forced to cope with one serious ongoing stress (for example, poverty or large family size) are
    a. more likely to develop serious psychiatric problems.
    b. no more likely to develop problems.
    c. more likely to develop intense, destructive friendships.
    d. less likely to be accepted by their peer group.

8. The adolescent who takes risks and feels immune to the laws of mortality is showing evidence of the
    a. invincibility fable.
    b. personal fable.
    c. imaginary audience.
    d. death instinct.

9. The tendency to focus only on the pleasant outcomes of risky behaviors is an expression of adolescent

   a. morality.

   b. thinking games.

   c. decision-making.

   d. egocentrism.

10. Many adolescents seem to believe that their lovemaking will not lead to pregnancy. This belief is an expression of the

    a. personal fable.

    b. invincibility fable.

    c. imaginary audience.

    d. "game of thinking."

11. Adolescents who grow up in poverty or other severely adverse conditions may be more likely to

    a. engage in risky behaviors.

    b. feel worthless.

    c. have low self-esteem.

    d. experience all of the above.

12. For many teenage girls who become pregnant, pregnancy is

    a. not planned.

    b. not avoided.

    c. based on their need to find somebody to give them universal love.

    d. characterized by all of the above.

Answer Key

Key Terms

1. Family function describes the ways in which a family nurtures and supports its children so they can reach the full potential of their physical, cognitive and psychosocial development. (p. 408; video lesson; objective 1)

2. Family structure is the legal and genetic relationship among members of a particular family. Children can thrive in almost any family structure. (p. 408; objective 1)

3. Resilience is a dynamic process including positive adaptation in the context of significant adversity. (p. 420; video lesson, segment 2; objective 2)

4. Sexual abuse is the use of an unconsenting person for one's own sexual pleasure. (p. 448; video lesson, segment 1; objective 3)

5. Child sexual abuse is any activity in which an adult uses a child for his or her sexual pleasure. (p. 448; video lesson, segment 1; objective 3)

6. Internalizing problems are turned inward, when troubled individuals do harm to themselves. (p. 512; objective 5)

7. Externalizing problems are turned outward, which people "act out," injure others, destroy property, or defy authority. (p. 512; objective 5)

8. Incidence means how often a particular event, behavior or circumstance occurs. (p. 513; objective 5)

9. Prevalence means how widespread within a population a particular behavior or circumstance is. (p. 513; objective 5)

10. Adolescence-limited offender is a person whose criminal activity stops by age 21. (p. 515; objective 5)

11. Life-course-persistent offender is a person whose criminal activity begins in adolescence and continues through life, a career criminal. (p. 515; objective 5)

Practice Questions

Multiple-Choice Questions

1. c. is the correct answer. (p. 408; video lesson, segment 1; objective 1)

2. a. is the correct answer. (video lesson, segment 1; objective 1)

3. b. is the correct answer. (pp. 422–423; video lesson, segment 1; objective 2)

4. b. is the correct answer. (pp. 424–425; objective 2)

5. d. is the correct answer. (pp. 420–421; objective 2)

6. b. is the correct answer. (p. 422; objective 2)

7. b. is the correct answer. (pp. 420–421; objective 2)

   c. & d. are incorrect. The lesson did not discuss how stress influences friendship or peer acceptance.

8. a. is the correct answer. (pp. 472–473; video lesson, segment 1; objective 4)

   b. is incorrect. This refers to adolescents' tendency to imagine their own lives as unique, heroic, or even mythical.

   c. is incorrect. This refers to adolescents' tendency to fantasize about how others will react to their appearance and behavior.

   d. is incorrect. This is a concept in Freud's theory.

9. d. is the correct answer. These thought processes are manifestations of adolescents' tendency to see themselves as being much more central and important to the social scene than they really are. (p. 472; video lesson, segment 1; objective 4)

10. b. is the correct answer. (pp. 472–473; video lesson, segment 1; objective 4)

    a. is incorrect. This refers to adolescents' tendency to imagine their own lives as unique, heroic, or even mythical.

    c. is incorrect. This refers to adolescents' tendency to fantasize about how others will react to their appearance and behavior.

    d. is incorrect. This is the adolescent ability to suspend knowledge of reality in order to think playfully about possibilities.

11. d. is the correct answer. (pp. 409, 421; video lesson, segment 1; objective 2)

12. d. is the correct answer. (video lesson, segment 1; objective 4)

Lesson Review

Lesson 25

Adolescence
Special Topic

Please Note: Use this matrix to guide your study and achieve the learning objectives of this lesson. It will also help you to view the video, which defines and demonstrates important concepts and skills as they relate to everyday life.

Learning Objective	Textbook	Telecourse Student Guide	Video Lesson
1. Identify the essential ways that functional families nurture children and teenagers.	p. 408	Key Terms: 1, 2; Practice Questions: 1, 2.	all segments
2. Describe the impact of poverty, homelessness, and other adverse conditions on the development of children, and discuss ways adults can help them cope with these problems.	pp. 409, 420–425	Key Terms: 3; Practice Questions: 3, 4, 5, 6, 7, 11.	all segments
3. Describe the prevalence of sexual abuse in adolescence and its consequences for development.	p. 448	Key Terms: 4, 5.	all segments
4. Explain how adolescent thinking and decision making often promotes high-risk behaviors such as unprotected sex, drug use, and delinquency.	pp. 472–473	Practice Questions: 8, 9, 10, 12.	all segments
5. Discuss delinquency among adolescents today, noting its prevalence, significance for later development, and best approaches for prevention and treatment.	pp. 512–516	Key Terms: 6, 7, 8, 9, 10, 11.	all segments

Different Paths

Lesson 26

Closing:
Developmental Psychopathologies

Preview

For most boys and girls, the years of infancy, childhood, and adolescence are a time when biosocial development is smooth and uneventful. Body maturation coupled with sufficient practice enables the mastery of many motor skills. Most children follow similar paths as they grow and mature. But what about children who are born with serious disorders and disabilities? How is their development affected and what can be done to assist them?

These and related questions are the focus of this lesson, which introduces Timmy, Jonathan, and Amelia—three children born with special needs. In this final telecourse lesson, we revisit several of the major developmental themes that have guided our investigation of the biosocial, cognitive, and psychosocial changes from conception through adolescence. As we learn more about normal child development, *all* children can benefit, especially those whose developmental journey follows a different path.

Prior Telecourse Knowledge that Will Be Used in this Lesson

- In its focus on children with special needs, this lesson will revisit the *developmental psychopathology* perspective (from Lesson 16). Recall that this approach uses what we know about typical development in the diagnosis and treatment of various disabilities and disorders.

- This lesson will also return to the process of *operant conditioning* (from Lesson 1). As you'll learn, this technique—sometimes called "behavior modification"—is used successfully with children who have certain disorders.

- The notions of *theory of mind* (Lesson 12) and *emotional regulation, self-concept, and self-esteem* (from Lesson 13) will be discussed as the lesson examines how different disabilities and disorders can affect a child's cognitive and psychosocial development.

Learning Objectives

Use this information to guide your reading, viewing, thinking, and studying. After successfully completing this lesson, you should be able to:

1. Explain the developmental psychopathology perspective, and discuss its value in treating children with special needs.

2. Identify the symptoms of tuberous sclerosis, autism, and epilepsy, and describe the most effective treatments for these disorders.

3. Summarize the characteristics of learning disabilities.

4. Outline the symptoms and possible causes of AD/HD (attention-deficit/hyperactivity disorder) and summarize various treatments available for children with this disorder.

5. Describe techniques that have been tried in efforts to educate children with special needs.

📖 **Review Chapter 11, "The School Years: Biosocial Development," pages 339–346, 349–355.**

📟 **View the video for Lesson 26, "Different Paths."**

   Segment 1: _Timmy_

   Segment 2: _Jonathan_

   Segment 3: _Amelia_

Summary

For the most part, childhood and adolescence are a time of relatively smooth development. For many children, however, the growth of new motor skills, social relationships, and ways of thinking is encumbered by a physical or mental disability. This lesson pays special attention to the causes, effects and treatments of disorders and disabilities such as **autism**, **epilepsy**, and blindness.

The new field of **developmental psychopathology** applies insights from studies of normal development to the origins and treatment of childhood disorders, and vice versa. The _Diagnostic and Statistical Manual of Mental Disorders_ (**DSM-IV-R**) recognizes that each child's cultural frame of reference needs to be understood before any disorder can be diagnosed.

Autism is known as a **pervasive developmental disorder** because it can produce a range of different effects across the biosocial, cognitive and psychosocial domains. Autism is also known as a _spectrum disorder_, because its effects can range from mild to severe. Autistic children are unable, unwilling, or uninterested in communicating with or understanding others; they are often mute; they do not engage in imaginative play; and they typically score in the mentally retarded range of intellectual performance. **Asperger syndrome** is a disorder in which a person has unusual difficulty with social perceptions and skills but has near normal communication skills.

Autism is typically detected very early in life, when deficiencies in communication abilities, social skills, and imaginative play first appear. Unaffected by the opinions of others, autistic children usually lack _emotional regulation_. The social disinterest of autistic children has caused some researchers to speculate that autistic children lack a _theory of mind_—that is, the awareness that psychological processes exist in other people. Twin studies make it clear that genetic factors play a role in autism. However, genes are not the whole story. In all likelihood, a genetic vulnerability in combination with either prenatal or early postnatal damage leads to autism. The most successful treatment for autism usually combines long-term behavior therapy with individual attention.

As you learned in Lesson 16, specific **learning disabilities** are said to exist when a child has no apparent physical problem, is not intellectually slow, does not live in severely stressful conditions, and does not lack basic education, but nevertheless has difficulty mastering academic skills such as reading (**dyslexia**), math (**dyscalculia**), spelling, or writing. The criteria for diagnosing a learning disability include disparity between expected performance on a given skill and actual performance and exclusion of other possible explanations, such as abuse, biological disability, or poor teaching.

One of the most puzzling childhood problems is **attention-deficit/hyperactivity disorder (AD/HD)** in which the child has great difficulty concentrating for more than a few moments at a time and is almost always in motion. A child with AD/HD is unusually impulsive, distractible, and sometimes aggressive. AD/HD children seem to have a neurological difficulty in paying attention. Estimates of the prevalence of AD/HD vary from 1 to 5 percent, in part because the diagnostic criteria vary from nation to nation. Four times as many boys as girls have this disorder.

📖   **Review all reading assignments for this lesson.**

💻   **As assigned by your instructor, complete the optional online component for this lesson.**

Key Terms

Using your own words, write a brief definition or explanation of each of the following terms on a separate piece of paper.

1. child with special needs
2. individual education plan (IEP)
3. developmental psychopathology
4. *Diagnostic and Statistical Manual of Mental Disorders* (DSM-IV-R)
5. pervasive developmental disorders
6. autism
7. Asperger syndrome
8. mentally retarded
9. learning-disabled
10. dyslexia
11. dyscalculia
12. comorbidity

13. AD/HD (attention-deficit/ hyperactivity disorder)
14. attention-deficit disorder (ADD)
15. mainstreaming
16. resource room
17. least restrictive environment (LRE)
18. inclusion
19. tuberous sclerosis
20. behavior modification
21. social story
22. Picture Exchange Communication System (PECS)
23. epilepsy
24. Braille

Practice Questions I

Multiple-Choice Questions

1. Dyslexia is a learning disability that primarily affects the ability to
   a. do math.
   b. read.
   c. focus attention.
   d. speak.

2. The developmental psychopathology perspective proposes
   a. a contextual approach to diagnosis.
   b. that disabilities may get better or worse over time.
   c. that abnormality is normal.
   d. all of the above.

3. The underlying problem in attention-deficit/hyperactivity disorder appears to be
   a. low overall intelligence.
   b. a neurological difficulty in paying attention.
   c. a learning disability in a specific academic skill.
   d. the existence of a conduct disorder.

4. Comorbidity refers to
   a. the presence of more than one disorder in one person at the same time
   b. the teaching of special needs children in a special classroom.
   c. the teaching of special needs children with other children in a regular classroom.
   d. the lifelong struggle in psychological development that special needs children often face.

5. Autistic children generally have severe deficiencies in all **EXCEPT**
   a. social skills.
   b. imaginative play.
   c. gross motor skills.
   d. communication ability.

6. Psychoactive drugs are most effective in treating attention-deficit/hyperactivity disorder when they are administered
   a. before the diagnosis becomes certain.
   b. for several years after the basic problem has abated.
   c. as part of the labeling process.
   d. with psychological support or therapy.

7. Tuberous sclerosis is a chronic illness that can affect the ability to
   a. do math and write.
   b. read.
   c. pick up social cues from others.
   d. do all of the above.

8. When developmentalists say that autism is a spectrum disorder, they mean that
   a. its effects can range from mild to severe.
   b. it is treated most effectively with medication.
   c. the prognosis for recovery is slim.
   d. the disorder advances very rapidly.

9. Four out of five children diagnosed with autism
   a. are boys.
   b. are girls.
   c. were undernourished.
   d. were born prematurely.

10. The neurological disorder in which a synchronized discharge of electricity occurs in one part or all of the brain is
    a. epilepsy.
    b. tuberous sclerosis.
    c. Tay-Sachs syndrome.
    d. fragile-X syndrome.

11. Autistic children are often taught scripts for how to behave in new, or difficult, situations. These scripts are called
    a. social stories.
    b. memes.
    c. discreet trials.
    d. zones of proximal development.

True or False Items

Write T (for true) or F (for false) on the line in front of each statement.

12. _____ Despite the efforts of teachers and parents, most children with learning disabilities can expect their disabilities to persist and even worsen as they enter adulthood.

13. _____ Stressful living conditions are an important consideration in diagnosing a learning disability.

14. _____ AD/HD is diagnosed more often in Great Britain than in the United States.

15. _____ The drugs sometimes given to children to reduce hyperactive behaviors have a reverse effect on adults.

16. _____ For serious disorders such as autism, parents typically play only a small role in their children's developmental progress.

Practice Questions II

Multiple-Choice Questions

1. A specific learning disability that becomes apparent when a child experiences unusual difficulty in learning to read is
   a. dyslexia.
   b. dyscalculia.
   c. AD/HD.
   d. ADHDA.

2. Problems in learning to write, read, and do math are collectively referred to as
   a. learning disabilities.
   b. attention-deficit/hyperactivity disorder.
   c. hyperactivity.
   d. dyscalculia.

3. The most effective form of help for children with AD/HD is
   a. medication.
   b. psychological therapy.
   c. environmental change.
   d. a combination of some or all of the above.

4. The earliest noticeable symptoms of autism usually include
   a. the lack of spoken language.
   b. abnormal social responsiveness.
   c. both a. and b.
   d. unpredictable.

5. Which of the following is true of children with a diagnosed learning disability?
   a. They are, in most cases, average in intelligence.
   b. They often have a specific physical handicap, such as hearing loss.
   c. They often lack basic educational experiences.
   d. All of the above are true.

6. Which approach to education may best meet the needs of children with learning disabilities in terms of both skill remediation and social interaction with other children?
   a. mainstreaming
   b. special education
   c. inclusion
   d. resource rooms

7. Asperger syndrome is a disorder in which
   a. body weight fluctuates dramatically over short periods of time.
   b. verbal skills seem normal, but social perceptions and skills are abnormal.
   c. an autistic child is extremely aggressive.
   d. a child of normal intelligence has difficulty in mastering a specific cognitive skill.

8. Which of the following is **NOT** cited as a contributing factor in most cases of AD/HD?

    a. genetic inheritance

    b. dietary sugar and caffeine

    c. prenatal damage

    d. postnatal damage

9. The disorder characterized by difficulties in social interaction and verbal and nonverbal communication is

    a. epilepsy.

    b. autism.

    c. tuberous sclerosis.

    d. fragile-X syndrome.

10. One of the most effective interventions for children with autism is

    a. traditional psychotherapy.

    b. antipsychotic medication.

    c. behavior modification.

    d. none of the above.

11. The Picture Exchange Communication System (PECS) is designed to help children who

    a. are blind learn to read Braille.

    b. are autistic learn to communicate more effectively.

    c. are epileptic learn to control the severity of their seizures.

    d. have all of the above conditions succeed in life.

Matching Items

Match each definition or description with its corresponding term.

Terms

12. _____ dyslexia

13. _____ dyscalculia

14. _____ mental retardation

15. _____ attention-deficit/hyperactivity disorder

16. _____ social story

17. _____ echolalia

18. _____ autism

19. _____ developmental psychopathology

20. _____ DSM-IV-R

21. _____ learning disability

22. _____ mainstreaming

Definitions or Descriptions

    a. speech that repeats, word for word, what has just been heard

    b. the diagnostic guide of the American Psychiatric Association

    c. a pervasive delay in cognitive development

    d. system in which children with learning disabilities are taught in general education classrooms

    e. disorder characterized by the absence of a theory of mind

f. a mental script to help children with special needs prepare for new events

g. behavior problem involving difficulty in concentrating, as well as excitability and impulsivity

h. difficulty in math

i. applies insights from studies of normal development to the study of childhood disorders

j. an unexpected difficulty with a particular area of learning

k. difficulty in reading

Applying Your Knowledge

1. Dr. Rutter, who believes that knowledge about normal development can be applied to the study and treatment of psychological disorders, evidently is working from which of the following perspectives?

   a. clinical psychology

   b. developmental psychopathology

   c. behaviorism

   d. psychoanalysis

2. Nine-year-old Jack has difficulty concentrating on his classwork for more than a few moments, repeatedly asks his teacher irrelevant questions, and is constantly disrupting the class with loud noises. If his difficulties persist, Jack is likely to be diagnosed as suffering from

   a. dyslexia.

   b. dyscalculia.

   c. autism.

   d. attention-deficit/hyperactivity disorder.

3. Ten-year-old Clarence is inattentive, easily frustrated, is highly impulsive and moves excessively even when sleeping. Clarence may be suffering from

   a. dyslexia.

   b. dyscalculia.

   c. attention-deficit disorder.

   d. attention-deficit/hyperactivity disorder.

4. In determining whether an eight-year-old has a learning disability, a teacher looks primarily for

   a. exceptional performance in a subject area.

   b. the exclusion of other explanations.

   c. absence of an obvious physical handicap.

   d. all of the above.

5. In the U.S., symptoms such as aggression and inattentiveness in school, commonly result in a diagnosis of AD/HD. In Great Britain, the same symptoms frequently result in which of the following diagnoses?

   a. dyslexia

   b. dyscalculalia

   c. conduct disorder

   d. antisocial personality

6. If you were to ask an autistic child with echolalia, "What's your name?" the child would probably respond by saying

    a. nothing.

    b. "What's your name?"

    c. "Your name what's?"

    d. something that was unintelligible.

7. In the video lesson, doctors removed a large portion of Jonathan's left hemisphere in order to prevent

    a. epileptic seizures.

    b. blindness.

    c. autism.

    d. self-destructive behaviors.

8. Danny has been diagnosed as having attention-deficit/hyperactivity disorder. Every day his parents make sure that he takes the proper dose of Ritalin. His parents should

    a. continue this behavior until Danny is an adult.

    b. try different medications when Danny seems to be reverting to his normal overactive behavior.

    c. make sure that Danny also has psychotherapy.

    d. not worry about Danny's condition; he will outgrow it.

9. Behavior modification for children with autism focuses on teaching them

    a. how to make eye contact.

    b. how to respond to speech.

    c. how to interact with other people.

    d. all of the above.

10. Discreet trial training is a form of

    a. biomedical therapy for autistic children.

    b. teaching Braille.

    c. prenatal genetic counseling.

    d. behavior modification that breaks things down into small steps that are individually taught.

Answer Key

Key Terms

1. A child with special needs requires particular physical, intellectual, or social accommodations in order to learn. (pp. 340–341; objective 1)

2. An individual education plan (IEP) is a legal document that specifies a set of educational goals for a child with special needs. (p. 342; objectives 1 & 5)

3. Developmental psychopathology is a new field that applies the insights from studies of normal development to the study and treatment of childhood disorders. (p. 342; video lesson, introduction; objective 1)

4. DSM-IV-R is the fourth edition of the *Diagnostic and Statistical Manual of Mental Disorders*, developed by the American Psychiatric Association, the leading means of distinguishing various emotional and behavioral disorders. (p. 343; objective 1)

5. A pervasive development disorder, such as autism, is one that affects numerous aspects of a child's psychological growth and can impair the development of critical life skills. (p. 343; objectives 1 & 2)

6. Autism is a severe disturbance of early childhood characterized by an inability or unwillingness to communicate with others, poor social skills, and diminished imagination. (p. 343; video lesson, segment 1; objective 2)

7. Asperger syndrome is a disorder in which a person has many symptoms of autism, despite having near normal communication skills. (p. 343; objective 2)

8. Mental retardation is a pervasive delay in cognitive development. (p. 346; objectives 1 & 3)

9. A learning disability is a difficulty in a particular cognitive skill that is not attributable to overall intellectual slowness, a physical handicap, a severely stressful living condition, or a lack of basic education. (p. 346; objective 3)

10. Dyslexia is a learning disability in reading. (p. 349; objective 3)

11. Dyscalculia is a learning disability in math. (p. 349; objective 3)

12. Comorbidity refers to the presence of more than one disorder in a person at the same time. (p. 351; objectives 1 & 3)

13. AD/HD (attention-deficit/hyperactivity disorder) is a behavior problem in which the individual has great difficulty concentrating, is often excessively excitable and impulsive, and is sometimes aggressive. (p. 351; objective 4)

14. ADD (attention-deficit disorder) is a condition in which a child has great difficulty concentrating but is not overactive. (p. 351; objective 4)

15. Mainstreaming is an educational approach in which children with special needs are included in regular classrooms. (p. 353; objective 5)

16. A resource room is a classroom equipped with special material, in which children with special needs spend part of their day working with a trained specialist in order to learn basic skills. (p. 354; objective 5)

17. A least restrictive environment (LRE) is a school setting that offers special needs children as much freedom as possible to benefit from the instruction available to other children, often in a mainstreamed classroom. (p. 353; objective 5)

18. Inclusion is an educational approach in which children with special needs receive individualized instruction within a regular classroom setting. (p. 354; objective 5)

19. Tuberous sclerosis is a genetic disorder in which lesions develop on the brain, often triggering seizures and autistic behaviors. (video lesson, segment 1; objective 2)

20. Behavior modification is the goal of operant conditioning that focuses on eliminating undesirable behaviors and establishing new, desirable ones, through the use of reinforcement, time outs, and other environmental consequences. (video lesson, segment 1; objective 2)

21. A social story is a mental script that children with special needs can practice to prepare for and deal with new and difficult events and situations. (video lesson, segment 1; objectives 2 & 5)

22. The Picture Exchange Communication System (PECS) is a visual tool that helps autistic children develop speech and language. (video lesson, segment 1; objectives 2 & 5)

23. Epilepsy is a neurological disorder in which a synchronized discharge of electricity in one part or all of the brain makes it malfunction for the duration of the seizure. (video lesson, segment 2; objective 2)

24. Braille is a system of tactile or touch reading for people who are blind which used a series of embossed dots arranged in quadrangular letter spaces or cells. (video lesson, segment 3; objective 5)

Practice Questions I

Multiple-Choice Questions

1. b. is the correct answer. (p. 349; objective 3)

   a. is incorrect. This is dyscalculia.

   c. & d. are incorrect. The textbook does not give labels for learning disabilities in writing or speaking.

2. d. is the correct answer. (pp. 342–343; video lesson, introduction; objective 1)

3. b. is the correct answer. (pp. 351; objective 4)

4. a. is the correct answer. (p. 351; objectives 1 & 3)

5. c. is the correct answer. (p. 344; video lesson, segment 1; objective 2)

6. d. is the correct answer. (pp. 352; objective 4)

7. d. is the correct answer. (video lesson, segment 1; objective 2)

8. a. is the correct answer. (video lesson, segment 1; objectives 1 & 2)

9. a. is the correct answer. (video lesson, segment 1; objective 2)

   c. & d. are incorrect. These risk factors were not linked to autism in the lesson.

10. a. is the correct answer. (video lesson, segment 2; objective 2)

    b. is incorrect. Although this disorder is linked to developmental deficits in every domain, it is not characterized by electrical discharges in the brain.

11. a. is the correct answer (video lesson, segment 1; objectives 2 & 5)

    b. & d. are incorrect. These terms not used in the lesson.

    c. is incorrect. Discrete trial training is a technique for systematically teaching children with special needs.

True or False Items

12. F   With the proper assistance, many children with learning disabilities develop into adults who are virtually indistinguishable from other adults in their educational and occupational achievements. (pp. 350, 355; objectives 3 & 5)

13. F   Stressful living conditions must be excluded before diagnosing a learning disability. (p. 346; objective 3)

14. F   AD/HD is more often diagnosed in the United States than in Britain. (p. 352; objective 4)

15. T   (p. 352; objective 5)

16. F   Parents and other caregivers play a major role in the developmental progress of children with special needs. (video lesson, segments 1, 2 & 3; objectives 1, 2 & 5)

Practice Questions II

Multiple-Choice Questions

1. a. is the correct answer. (p. 349; objective 3)

   b. is incorrect. This learning disability involves math rather than reading.

   c. & d. are incorrect. These disorders do not manifest themselves in a particular academic skill but instead appear in psychological processes that affect learning in general.

2. a. is the correct answer. (pp. 346, 349; objective 3)

   b. & c. are incorrect. AD/HD is a general learning disability that usually does not manifest itself in specific subject areas. Hyperactivity is a facet of this disorder.

   d. is incorrect. Dyscalculia is a learning disability in math only.

3. d. is the correct answer. (p. 352; objective 4)

4. c. is the correct answer. (p. 344; video lesson, segment 1; objective 2)

5. a. is the correct answer. (p. 346; objective 3)

6. c. is the correct answer. (p. 354; objective 5)

   a. is incorrect. Many general education teachers are unable to cope with the special needs of some children.

   b. & d. are incorrect. These approaches undermine the social integration of children with special needs.

7. b. is the correct answer. (p. 343; objective 2)

8. b. is the correct answer. (p. 351; objective 4)

9. b. is the correct answer. (p. 343; video lesson, segment 1; objective 2)

   a. is incorrect. Epilepsy is characterized by seizures.

   c. is incorrect. Although many children with tuberous sclerosis become autistic, some do not, and therefore do not develop these symptoms of autism.

   d. is incorrect. This disorder was not discussed.

10. c. is the correct answer. (video lesson, segment 1; objectives 2 & 5)

11. b. is the correct answer. (video lesson, segment 1; objectives 2 & 5)

Matching Items

12. k (p. 349; objective 3)

13. h (p. 349; objective 3)

14. c (p. 346; objective 3)

15. g (p. 351; objective 4)

16. f (video lesson, segment 1; objective 5)

17. a (p. 344; objective 2)

18. e (pp. 276, 343; video lesson, segment 1; objective 2)

19. i (p. 342; video lesson, introduction; objective 1)

20. b (p. 343; objective 1)

21. j (p. 346; objective 3)

22. d (p. 353; objective 5)

Applying Your Knowledge

1. b. is the correct answer. (p. 342; video lesson, introduction; objective 1)

2. d. is the correct answer. (p. 351; objective 4)

   a. & b. are incorrect. Jack's difficulty is in concentrating, not in reading (dyslexia) or math (dyscalculia).

   c. is incorrect. Autism is characterized by a lack of communication skills.

3. d. is the correct answer. (p. 351; objective 4)

4. d. is the correct answer. (p. 346; objective 3)

5. c. is the correct answer. (p. 352; objective 4)

6. b. is the correct answer. (p. 344; objective 2)

7. a. is the correct answer. (video lesson, segment 2; objective 2)

8. c. is the correct answer. Medication alone cannot ameliorate all the problems of AD/HD. (p. 352; objective 4)

9. d. is the correct answer. (video lesson, segment 1; objectives 2 & 5)

10. d. is the correct answer. (video lesson, segment 1; objective 5)

    a. is incorrect. Discreet trial training is a form of behavior therapy.

Lesson Review

Lesson 26

Closing
Developmental Psychopathologies

Please Note: Use this matrix to guide your study and achieve the learning objectives of this lesson. It will also help you to view the video, which defines and demonstrates important concepts and skills as they relate to everyday life.

Learning Objective	Textbook	Telecourse Student Guide	Video Lesson
1. Explain the new developmental psychopathology perspective, and discuss its value in treating children with special needs.	pp. 342–346, 351	Key Terms: 1, 2, 3, 4, 5, 8, 12; Practice Questions I: 2, 4, 8, 16; Practice Questions II: 19, 20; Applying Your Knowledge: 1.	Introduction
2. Identify the symptoms of tuberous sclerosis, autism, and epilepsy, and describe the most effective treatment for these disorders.	pp. 343–344	Key Terms: 5, 6, 7, 19, 20, 21, 22, 23; Practice Questions I: 5, 7, 8, 9, 10, 11, 16; Practice Questions II: 4, 7, 9, 10, 17, 18; Applying Your Knowledge: 6, 7, 9.	Segment 1: *Timmy* Segment 2: *Jonathan*
3. Discuss the characteristics of learning disabilities.	pp. 351–353	Key Terms: 8, 9, 10, 11, 12; Practice Questions I: 1, 4, 12, 13; Practice Questions II: 1, 2, 5, 12, 13, 14, 21; Applying Your Knowledge: 4.	
4. Describe the symptoms and possible causes of AD/HD (attention-deficit/hyperactivity disorder) and ADHDA (attention-deficit/hyperactivity disorder with aggression).	pp. 351–352	Key Terms: 13, 14; Practice Questions I: 3, 6, 14; Practice Questions II: 3, 8, 15; Applying Your Knowledge: 2, 3, 5, 8.	

Learning Objective	Textbook	Telecourse Student Guide	Video Lesson
5. Describe techniques that have been tried in efforts to educate children with special needs.	pp. 350–355	Key Terms: 2, 15, 16, 17, 18, 21, 22, 24; Practice Questions I: 11, 12, 15, 16; Practice Questions II: 6, 10, 11, 16, 22; Applying Your Knowledge: 9, 10.	Segment 1: *Timmy* Segment 2: *Jonathan* Segment 3: *Amelia*